Critical Multicultural Analysis of Children's Literat~~~~

Mirrors, Windows, and Door~

D0103512

Maria José Botelho
University of Massachusetts Amherst
and
Ontario Institute for Studies in Education/
University of Toronto

and

Masha Kabakow Rudman
University of Massachusetts Amherst

Routledge
Taylor & Francis Group
NEW YORK AND LONDON

First published 2009
by Routledge
270 Madison Ave, New York, NY 10016

Simultaneously published in the UK
by Routledge
2 Park Square, Milton Park, Abingdon, Oxon OX14 4RN

Routledge is an imprint of the Taylor & Francis Group, an informa business

Typeset in Minion by
RefineCatch Limited, Bungay, Suffolk
Printed and bound in the United States of America on acid-free paper by
Edwards Brothers, Inc.

Library of Congress Cataloging-in-Publication Data
Botelho, Maria José, 1961–
    Critical multicultural analysis of children's literature : mirrors, windows
and doors / by Maria José Botelho and Masha Kabakow Rudman.
        p. cm.—(Language, culture, and teaching)
    1. Children's literature—History and criticism.   2. Young adult
literature—History and criticism.   3. Multiculturalism in literature.
I. Rudman, Masha Kabakow.   II. Title.
    PN1009.5.M84B68 2009
    809′.89282—dc22

                                                            2008043368

ISBN: 0–415–99666–X (hbk)
ISBN: 0–805–83711–6 (pbk)
ISBN: 0–203–88520–1 (ebk)

ISBN: 978–0–415–99666–2 (hbk)
ISBN: 978–0–805–83711–7 (pbk)
ISBN: 978–0–203–88520–8 (ebk)

For Jim and our children, Emma June and Elihu Bellamy, with all my love
MJB

With heartfelt thanks to Maria, the perfect writing partner, colleague,
and friend
MKR

Contents

Foreword

SONIA NIETO
Professor Emerita
University of Massachusetts Amherst

Nancy Larrick's 1965 groundbreaking article, "The All-White World of Children's Literature" pointed out what many already knew but were reluctant to voice, that is, that children's literature was a racist domain. In the context of children's literature, the emperor had no clothes, and the fiction of a representative children's literature was laid to rest.

It has been over 40 years since that historic article was first published. The field of multicultural children's literature was born partly as a result of the awareness inspired by that article as well as by demands from within and outside the discipline of children's literature. It has been a robust and exciting area of study and practice for at least three decades. Because of advocacy on the part of various communities, as well as the nation's changing demographics, and the publishing industry's recognition that their bottom line could improve if they were more inclusive, children's books today reflect a much broader racial and ethnic representation than ever before. But is that all there should be to making children's literature more inclusive, more socially just, more democratic?

Maria José Botelho and Masha Kabakow Rudman's *Critical Multicultural Analysis of Children's Literature: Mirrors, Windows, and Doors* represents the next step in the evolution of the field. In their insistence that an analysis of power relations must play a decisive role in how we read children's literature, they invite readers to think about the interplay of race, class, and gender in books (and, indeed, in life in general). They ask us to think about the context in which children's books are published, written, disseminated, read, and used in the curriculum. That is, they want us to recognize that the school and library are not islands unto themselves but rather that they exist within a sociopolitical context that is global, national, and local. This context currently includes, on the national and world levels, globalization policies that are leading to increased poverty and deprivation, particularly in developing countries. In those countries, it is a context that is resulting in decreasing opportunities and increasing oppression, and consequently, in greater immigration and, at the same time, in harsher immigration policies, particularly in Western Europe and the United States. It is also a context that includes an undeclared war in which thousands of Americans and hundreds of thousands of Iraqis have been killed; and a "war on terror" leading to a growing fear of the "Other" in our own nation, a chipping away of our civil rights, and, on an international level, to a greater mistrust of the United States among many other nations in the world. In schools, and, increasingly, in colleges and universities, the context includes rigid accountability structures, the scripting of the curriculum and erosion of faculty rights, and even the imposition of particular teaching methods (for example, at the school level, the exclusive use of phonics) or approaches to research (in schools of education, inflexible conceptions of "scientifically based research") that make teaching, and especially the teaching of literature to children, almost an impossibility in many schools. This is the context that Botelho and Rudman think about as they ask us to consider using a critical multicultural analysis of children's literature in our work as teachers and teacher educators.

The critical multicultural analysis of children's literature presupposes an understanding of this sociopolitical context. In these pages, you will find, for instance, a history of the publishing industry in terms of children's literature, as well as a history of the representation of people of color in the literature. You will find theoretical discussions of the social constructions of race, class, and gender, and a deconstruction of multiculturalism. You will learn to use various lenses to develop multiple analyses of the same texts, and you will read descriptions and analyses of many children's books. While theorizing about gender, you will read about the Cinderella story in numerous global contexts; while learning about the controversies and conflicts inherent in the topic of hair, you will find cogent and helpful analyses of children's books that treat this topic in many different ways. And, at the end of the book, you will find yourself engaged in conversation not just with the authors but also with Junko Yokota, Mingshui Cai, and Patrick Shannon, some of the most significant scholars in the field, as they reflect on the critical teaching of children's literature. Throughout, you will discover that it is the weaving together of theory and practice that makes this book especially unique and timely.

Children's literature is a contested terrain, as is multicultural education.

Taken together, they pose a formidable challenge to both classroom teachers and academics. As such, they are of fundamental significance for the Language, Culture, and Teaching Series and a welcome addition to our understanding of children's literature. Rather than deny the inherent conflicts and tensions in the field, in *Critical Multicultural Analysis of Children's Literature: Mirrors, Windows, and Doors*, Maria José Botelho and Masha Kabakow Rudman confront, deconstruct, and reconstruct these terrains by proposing a reframing of the field. In the process, they invite readers to, in the words of Paulo Freire, read both "the word and the world" (Freire, 1970), that is, to reflect on the words in the text and on their meaning in their lives and in the world so that they can become active agents in the world. Surely all of us—children, teachers, and academics—can benefit from this more expansive understanding of what it means to read books.

Works Cited

Freire, Paul (1970). *Pedagogy of the oppressed.* New York: Seabury Press.
Larrick, Nancy (1965, September). The all-white world of children's books, *Saturday Review*, 48 (11), 63–65.

Preface

The metaphors of mirrors, windows, and doors permeate the scholarly dialogue of "multicultural children's literature" as using literature to provide ways to affirm and gain entry into one's own culture and the culture of others. These are powerful metaphors because they presuppose that literature can authentically mirror or reflect one's life; look through a window to view someone else's world; and open doors offering access both into and out of one's everyday condition. The mirror invites self-contemplation and affirmation of identity. The window permits a view of other people's lives. The door invites interaction.

George Lakoff and Mark Johnson (1980) argue that metaphors govern both our thought and action, that is, these conceptual systems influence "how we perceive the world, how we get around the world, and how we relate to other people" (Lakoff & Johnson, 1980: 3). Metaphors are often implicit; we are not aware of them. But if we examine our language use, Lakoff and Johnson maintain, we will find evidence of how they define and shape everyday experiences.

By examining the metaphors of mirrors, windows, and doors, we can identify how they structure our perceptions (how we perceive), thoughts (how we think), and actions (what we do). In our book, we reclaim these metaphors and take children beyond text to self connections and link them to social practice. We expand how children perceive multiculturalism and children's literature, and create a space for reading power through critical multicultural analysis.

The prevailing pedagogies for studying multiculturalism in children's literature have emerged from the black-white oversimplification of race relations in the United States. While the racialized context of the United States contributes to this paradigm it distracts us from the more complex intragroup and intergroup cultural dynamics and social relations, rendering many cultural experiences invisible and making the complexities of power relations an abstraction. Further, it supports the erroneous assumption that in naming literature "multicultural," it represents diverse experiences other than White, European American.

In this book, we argue for a critical multicultural analysis of children's literature, an orientation towards reading, learning, teaching, and the world. This kind of analysis can help readers deconstruct taken-for-granted assumptions about language, meaning, reading, and literature, and leads to "resocialization" (Shor, 1992) for and construction of a society that is socially just.

When we untangle multiculturalism from "multicultural children's literature," we can ask: Who is represented, underrepresented, misrepresented, and/or invisible? How is power exercised? We can challenge all texts. We can argue with the author, question assumptions, unmask ideologies, and examine how the author uses language. We can speculate on ways to acknowledge alternative perspectives. And we can re-imagine and transform the world in which we live (Botelho, 1998, 2004).

We advocate for reading that goes beyond stretching children's cultural imagination, to reading that fosters historical and sociopolitical imagination. Bringing a critical lens to the study of multiculturalism in children's literature invites the reader to deconstruct dominant ideologies of U.S. society (e.g., race, class, gender, and individualism) which privilege those whose interests, values, and beliefs are represented by these worldviews. It is reading power, the complex web of sociopolitical relations.

Race, class, and gender matter. Critical multicultural analysis brings socioeconomic class into the conversations about race and gender, so we can better understand how these systems of oppression intersect (hooks, 2000). A critical multicultural analysis of children's literature interrupts the social myth that we live in a classless, equitable, and just society, and that everyone has access to the "American Dream" as long as they demonstrate initiative, effort, and ability (Sleeter, 1998). This dominant ideology circulates in children's books.

Our past and present social locations and aspirations for the future have implications for where and how we might take action in challenging existing power relations. Bronwyn Davies (1999) argues that feminist poststructuralist theory requires a "recognition of oneself as historically and discursively located, that is, as located in a context (or contexts) where that which is taken as given (both in the everyday world and in the world of theorists and researchers) forms a background that necessarily shapes any question. What is understood as askable . . . varies from one time to another, from one research tradition to another, and from one set of politics to another" (Davies, 1999: 13).

We are two White women of working-class backgrounds; one over seventy, and one who is over forty; one of Eastern European Jewish heritage and one of Catholic Portuguese heritage. We recognize the contextualized and ideological dimensions of literacy. Our awareness of our place in the world has led us to this work. Our life experiences both with classism and ethnic bigotry and our long term participation in critical multicultural teacher education have moved us to be allies to underrepresented groups and social activists in our work with children and adults.

Critical multicultural analysis is a frame for teaching literature and constructing curriculum and spaces to take up issues of diversity and social injustice by problematizing children's literature: It is literary study as social change. It prepares teachers to analyze the ideological dimensions of reading and studying literature. Readers, young and adult, can address issues of social transformation and justice through their reading. By uncovering systems of meaning that perpetuate social inequities, readers can reposition themselves in the world and envision new intellectual spaces, breaking ground for constructing new social worlds. Critical multicultural analysis creates a site for re/construction.

Our audience is diverse. We have written this text for experienced teachers, advanced undergraduate and graduate students, teacher educators, literacy researchers and scholars of children's and young adult literature.

The cover of our text is a representation of Maria José's family home in São Miguel, Açores, where she lived the first seven years of her life. This image is based on photographs of her father Jacinto and sister Conceição, all taken by her brother José during the 1970s. This context is where Maria José learned about how power was exercised within her family as well as the power relations that her parents and siblings experienced in this island community. It was in this house where Maria José was first socialized to participate in the world.

Her family owned only one mirror that was approximately the size of this book. It was hung up high on the kitchen wall, for the taller members of the family to use during grooming activities. However, she caught glimpses of her reflection in the windows of the kitchen door, which looked out into a small yard, packed with plum, pear, peach, and fig trees. It was through the front windows that she first peered out to look at the farmers returning from the fields in the late afternoon, the fishermen selling the daily catch, the neighbor children gathering for play, or the neighbor women engaging in dialogue. The door opened out into the world of her community. The carpet of flowers made by her father from flower petals and greens, in preparation for the passing of a religious procession, evokes the sacredness and social transformative possibilities of everyday life. Within this house, a construction site of sorts, her parents guided Maria José and her siblings in the deconstruction and reconstruction of unjust ways of being in the world.

Overview of the Book

Our theoretical framework of critical multicultural analysis has had a great influence on how we organized this text. Multiple U.S. histories and their sociopolitical contexts anchor the book chapters. We consider how genres, words, images, perspectives, social interactions among characters, and story closures shape how stories get told. We apply our theoretical framework to trade books published in the United States and Canada, clustered as text collections, reflecting particular cultural themes, genres, and storylines. We analyze these texts and others, both literary and nonliterary, alongside each other and other texts.

Throughout the book we review the research on multicultural children's literature and re/consider its pedagogical possibilities and dilemmas. At the end of each chapter, we provide recommendations for classroom application, classroom research, and further reading, as well as bibliographies of the works cited. At the end of the book, we have compiled appendices on children's book awards and publishers; created diagrams of the power continuum and the theoretical framework of critical multicultural analysis; and generated lists of children's literature journals and online resources.

Chapter 1 grounds and frames our book. We introduce critical multicultural analysis and define "critical" and "multicultural." The theories we draw on are explicated and connected. We describe the role of genealogical (historical) work in re/contextualizing children's literature. The power positions of domination, collusion, resistance, and agency are explored. The assumptions that we bring to this project about literature, authors, reading, children and critical analysis are considered.

In Chapter 2, we reflect on the window metaphor and provide a historical overview of the constructions of childhood alongside children's literature. The key historical developments in children's literature are outlined and publishing trends are explored. We apply some common approaches to literary study to a children's book, *Leon's Story*, thinking about how they position the reader, the text, and society.

In Chapter 3, we historicize everyday and school literacies practices, as they developed in Western Europe and the United States. We use the literacy resources of code breaker, text pariticipant, text user, and text critic (Luke & Freebody, 1999) to analyze how literacy is depicted in children's literature.

The definition of culture is deconstructed and reconstructed in Chapter 4, creating a space to retrace the development of the literary category of multicultural children's literature, and to review its scholarship. We reveal the scholarly silence of class in children's literature and advocate for bringing class into the critical dialogue on race and gender. Class is an overlooked social construct, even though it is central to the U.S. context. (We demonstrate how class works with race and gender in books when we analyze children's literature about Chicano/a migrant farmworkers in Chapter 7.)

Chapter 5 examines the discourse of multicultural children's literature by locating the discursive threads of otherness and self-esteem, and naming issues of invisibility and silences. We consider the theoretical constructs of ideology, identity, subject positions, and power, and theorize a power continuum, using a multi-layered lens to examine how texts embody power relations.

Chapter 6 offers a historical sketch of how race has been socially constructed over time. We deconstruct the American Dream and propose that we consider the United States as a diaspora, creating a space for examining the complexities of power. We particularly focus on the history and sociopolitical context of Mexican American participation in migrant agricultural work as well as a review of Mexican American representation in children's literature, which we utilize in Chapter 7, in analyzing the text collection that represents this culture/power experience in children's literature.

In Chapter 8, we consider how genres shape how stories get told as well as influence the reader's expectations of the text. In Chapter 9, we consider the story of Cinderella as a genre and explore its structural elements. We offer a cross-cultural and cross-temporal analysis of multiple variants of this storyline, showing its endurance across place and time. The Cinderella folk tales are implicated in the social construction of gender.

We analyze the cultural theme of hair in Chapter 10 against the controversy surrounding a White teacher's use of the children's book, *Nappy Hair*, by Carolivia Herron. In Chapter 11, we revisit the sociopolitical dimensions of critical multicultural analysis by considering the pedagogical implications of *what we read* and *how we read*. We review the research literatures on the teaching of multicultural children's literature and use our theoretical/pedagogical framework to speak to the possibilities, dilemmas, and challenges addressed. We end the chapter with the possibility of children writing their own stories, as a way to talk back to publishing practices, and capturing and analyzing their own language use in action.

We invited Mingshui Cai, Patrick Shannon, and Junko Yokota to respond to our theoretical framework. At the end of the book, you will find our negotiated dialogue, constructed from an ongoing e-mail exchange.

While the book may be read in any order, we deliberately organized it to guide the reader in developing an understanding of the constructs and practices of critical multicultural analysis. Our intent is not to standardize the reading process but to make our critical reading public, as a way to "scaffold conscientização" (Sleeter, Torres & Laughlin, 2004).

We have been working together on this book for several years. During this time, we grew together theoretically and pedagogically, experiencing our theoretical leanings in many ways: It was a decolonizing experience. Our writing changed over time. Our language became explicitly political. In reading multiple drafts of this text, we found our layered selves, our multiple understandings. We do not want to contradict ourselves, but given our multiple subjectivities, questions are inevitable. This is not a final text, but rather a work in progress, leading us to rethink the teaching of children's literature. We invite you, the reader, to read and apply this text critically and multiculturally.

References

Botelho, Maria José. (1998). *The postmodern untangling of critical multiculturalism from multicultural children's literature: Creating space for critical literacy.* Unpublished manuscript, University of Massachusetts, Amherst.

Botelho, Maria José. (2004). *Reading class: Disrupting power in children's literature.* Unpublished dissertation, University of Massachusetts, Amherst.

Davies, Bronwyn. (1999). What is feminist poststructuralist research? Examining texts of childhood. In Barbara Kamler (Ed.), *Constructing gender and difference: Critical research perspectives on early childhood* (pp. 13–31). Cresskill, NJ: Hampton Press.

hooks, bell. (2000). *Where we stand: Class matters.* New York: Routledge.

Lakoff, George & Johnson, Mark. (1980). *Metaphors we live by.* Chicago: University of Chicago Press.

Luke, Allan & Freebody, Peter. (1999). A map of possible practices: Further notes in the four resources model. *Practically Primary* 4(2), 5–8.

Shor, Ira. (1992). *Empowering education: Critical teaching for social change.* Chicago: The University of Chicago Press.

Sleeter, Christine. (1998). Teaching Whites about racism. In E. Lee, D. Menkart, & M. Okazawa-Rey (Eds.), *Beyond heroes and holidays: A practical guide to K-12 anti-racist, multicultural education and staff development.* Washington, DC: Network of Educators on the Americas.

Sleeter, Christine, Torres, M. N. & Laughlin, P. (2004). Scaffolding conscientization through inquiry in teacher education. *Teacher Education Quarterly*, 31(1), 81–96.

Acknowledgements

The poet Antonio Machado says that we make the road by walking. The road to this work has been long and arduous, but I have not walked alone: Great companions walked with me along the way. My two beloved mentors, Sonia Nieto and Masha Kabakow Rudman, accompanied me. Their research and teaching are central to my work. Thank you to Masha for the invitation to co-write this book because it created a space for us to think, learn, and write together, time that I will always cherish. Thank you to Sonia for the many invitations to teach multicultural education, experiences that deepened my understanding of how power works in the United States.

Thank you to Professors Cathy Luna and William Moebius for their thoughtful participation during my doctoral studies, mentoring that greatly contributed to this book project.

Thank you to my dear mentors at the Ontario Institute for Studies of Education at the University of Toronto: Dean Jane Gaskell and Professors Dennis Thiessen, Tara Goldstein, Doug McDougall, and Normand LaBrie. Their inspiration and support over the past several years was instrumental in the completion of this work. What a blessing it is to have my beloved OISE colleagues in my life: David Booth, Linda Cameron, Patricia Chow, Sarah Cohen, Jim Cummins, Mary Kooy, Lisa Leoni, Miriam Patterson, Rubén Gaztambide-Fernández, and Padma Sastri. Thank you to Shelley Stagg Peterson, my cherished OISE "buddy," for her support and interest in this book. Thank you to Eunice Jang and Julie (Jules) Kerekes for their love and understanding. I am so blessed to have them. They will be forever in my heart.

Thank you to my wonderful graduate assistants: Ed Dixon, Agnes Kieltyka, Chyleen Shih, Yamin Qlan, and MinKyeong Suk. Their many contributions enriched this work.

My mother and father nurtured in me a great sense of social responsibility. They taught me about collaborative power through their sharing of resources and social power. Thank you to Annie, Jesse, José, and Conceição, my loving siblings, for being embodiments of our parents' teachings. Their love sustains me.

My beloved family, Jim and our children Emma and Elihu, has nourished my heart and soul. Jim has been a loving and supportive companion on this road. I hope this book makes a difference in the world because my children are the reason I took this trip in the first place.

This collaborative book project would not have been possible without the financial support from the University of Toronto Connaught Start-Up Grant.

Maria José Botelho

First and foremost I must acknowledge the steady competent support of my assistant, Kathy Boron, without whom I could not have completed my work. She helped me in every phase of the research and writing. She grappled with the foibles of the computers, helped in the editing, and managed the many tasks that I could not tackle.

I owe a debt of gratitude to those scholars and colleagues whose work has informed and guided me over the years. Sonia Nieto has been a friend as well as colleague and has always encouraged me in my work. Debbie Reese, Rudine Sims Bishop, and OYATE have all been gracious in their responses to my queries.

Sara Young has worked by my side in studying children's literature and the direction we are going in our thinking. We have co-taught, conferred, and bounced ideas back and forth.

My daughter, Reva Rudman, has contributed ideas, opinions, and emotional support to me in ways too numerous to mention, including bringing to my attention authors and titles I might otherwise not have seen.

I am indebted to all of my students, especially those in my Issues in Children's Literature classes over the years. Their questions and research spurred me to probe more deeply into the numerous texts and reviews that led to several of the chapters in our book. Some of the many names are John Raible, Patty Bode, Martha Morgan, Marisa Campbell, Nia Taylor, Diane Mercomes, Tara Nappi, Eileen Gould, and Tina Bisanti.

I beg forgiveness of those whose names I have not included here. I fear that there are many I have overlooked. Suffice it to say that this has been a collaborative project from the beginning and will continue to be so.

Masha Kabakow Rudman

We are grateful to Naomi Silverman, our wonderful editor, whose belief in this project was unending.

Thank you to Mingshui Cai, Patrick Shannon, and Junko Yokota for their generosity and insightful contributions during our online dialogue.

CHAPTER 1

The Metaphors We Read By[1]: Theoretical Foundations

The metaphors of mirrors and windows have often framed the scholarship of multicultural children's literature. Children need to see themselves reflected so as to affirm who they and their communities are. They also require windows through which they may view a variety of differences. Books are one way they learn about the world. Once these foundations of story and society are internalized, literature can become a conduit—a door—to engage children in social practices that function for social justice. Literary works focusing on African Americans, Native Americans, Latino/a Americans, and Asian Americans are strongly based on the black/white paradigm that is historically rooted in U.S. power relations. The publication of children's literature by and about people of color was a response to biased sociopolitical and publishing practices that contributed to the underrepresentation of people of color in U.S. public education and children's literature.

Critical multicultural analysis of children's literature (Botelho, 2004) demands a shift from the dominant paradigm of race relations between African Americans and European Americans to one that combines the U.S. power relations of class, race, and gender together. Critical multicultural analysis of children's literature acknowledges that all literature is a historical and cultural product and reveals how the power relations of class, race, and gender work together in text and image, and by extension, in society. (We appreciate the power of image and consider it consistently alongside text. For the purpose of conciseness, we will use text to be all encompassing and inclusive of image.)

Critical multicultural investigations of children's literature focus on the analysis of power relations as factors in the trends of what gets written, illustrated, and published. In other words, meanings found in children's books are not exclusively derived from language but also from institutional practices, power relations, and social position (Weedon, 1997). Children's books offer windows into society; they are sites for struggle among shifting, changing, overlapping, and historically diverse social identities (Shohat, 1995).

Critical multicultural analysis deconstructs hierarchical power relations around which language plays a critical role. The analysis centers on the sociopolitical function of linguistic and visual signs. Stephens (1999: 57) maintains that "The form and meanings of reality are constructed in language: by analyzing how language works, we come nearer to knowing how our culture constructs itself, and where we fit into that construction." We do not live outside of language. How we use language constructs who we are as people, as cultures, and as a society. Language circulates the dominant ideologies of gender, race, and class.

Paul du Gay, Stuart Hall, Linda Janes, Hugh Mackay, and Keith Negus (1997) analyze the Sony Walkman as a way to illustrate how to conduct cultural studies. Their study is instructive because it demonstrates how culture works in contemporary society. Du Gay (1997b: 3) argues that "the biography of a cultural artefact" can only be studied when the process of its articulation is made visible by locating a host of cultural processes. Articulation refers to the process of "connecting disparate elements together to form a temporary unity." Literature is a cultural artifact. Thus, cultural artifacts come to be through a combination of processes and linkages that emerge from particular times and places. He asserts that there are five principal cultural processes: representation, identity, production, consumption, and regulation. These processes considered together complete a circuit, "the circuit of culture." The circuit of culture helps to show how critical multicultural analysis makes these cultural processes visible and highlights its capacity to disrupt power relations.

The analysis of the representation process shows that meaning does not come directly from words but instead is re/presented in language (written or visual). Thus cultural meaning is established through representation, drawing on literary and nonliterary texts (imbedded with discourses) that play a central role in fixing the meaning in literature: Dominant meanings get encoded in books. These cultural meanings offer particular subject positions, which are associated with social identities. Identity is the interface between subject positions and historical and sociopolitical circumstances (Woodward, 1997). Drawing attention to subject positions invites readers to actively construct their own identities, while at the same time taking action in the constructing of society. Children's books are encoded with particular meanings during their production process, meanings that are constructing identification between the books (cultural artifacts) and particular groups of readers (consumers). In focusing on production, we need to look at the cultural meanings that are imbedded in the literature by examining the textual influences (e.g., genre, focalization, story closure) as well as sociopolitical and historical considerations.

How is the book made culturally meaningful? Du Gay (1997a: 4) argues "in thinking about the production of culture ... we are also simultaneously thinking about the culture of production." This attention to the culture of production connects us back to representation and identity, while bringing up questions of consumption. Meaning does not begin or end with the book, but is instantiated or made meaningful through reading. The circuit of culture highlights the dynamism of meaning making; it is an ongoing process. Du Gay (1997a: 5) argues that this encoding of particular meanings in products, in this case, in literature, is not where the story ends, but that "meanings are actively made in consumption." In reading the book, the reader can actively resist the subject positions offered by the text and take up new ways of being in the world. Thus the reader is not regulated in how he/she can be in society, but is an active member of society, co-constructing as it changes over time.

The circuit of culture demonstrates that meaning making is a dynamic process: writers encode particular meanings in books and readers often receive them inadvertently, but it is through reading/consuming that meanings are actively made. Critical multicultural analysis calls attention to the reading process. If they are conscious of this process, readers can detect how these messages or ideologies try to regulate their lives, and their society. They can interrupt ideologies that privilege particular groups over others. Critical multicultural analysis calls attention to how identities are constructed, how texts are constructed, how society is constructed, and how language/discourse creates us as much as we create it.

The circuit of culture demonstrates the matrix of discourses that have a hold on us and society: Meaning making is not sent from "one autonomous sphere and received in another autonomous sphere" (du Gay, 1997a: 10), but in a process of dialogue.

Reading against culture disrupts bounded and timeless notions of culture; it is an interruption of the status quo. Critical multicultural analysis is an invitation for readers to be researchers of language. Thus, readers are given opportunities to actively investigate how language works and the hold culture has on them because, as Roland Barthes (1977: 146) contends "the text is a tissue of quotations drawn from the innumerable centres of culture." He further maintains:

> A text is made of multiple writings, drawn from many cultures and entering into mutual relations of dialogue, parody, contestation, but there is one place where this multiplicity is focused and that place is the reader, not, as was hitherto said, the author. The reader is the space on which all the quotations that make up a writing are inscribed without any of them being lost; a text's unity lies not in its origin but in its destination.
>
> (Barthes, 1997: 148)

Critical multicultural analysis focuses on the reader as the midwife of meaning. The theoretical constructs of discourse, ideology, subjectivity, and power lead the reader to locating how the power relations of class, race, and gender are exercised in text.

A critical multicultural analysis focuses on the "constructedness" of literacy practices and knowledge (Wooldridge, 2001). The way we read books can further encode coercive power interactions if we wittingly or unwittingly accept the messages in the text and images. Because texts are socially constructed they can be deconstructed. This unpacking of the textual layers helps the reader become more conscious of the decisions that the author and/or illustrator made, foregrounding the choices and omissions. This process leaves the reader poised to pose critical questions, much like the ones proposed by Nathalie Wooldridge (2001: 261):

- What (or whose) view of the world, or kinds of behaviors are presented as normal by the text?
- Why is the text written that way? How else could it have been written?
- What assumptions does the text make about age, gender, [class], and culture (including the age, gender, and culture of its readers)?
- Who is silenced/heard here?
- Whose interests might best be served by the text?
- What ideological positions can you identify?
- What are the possible readings of this situation/event/character? How did you get to that reading?
- What moral or political position does a reading support? How do particular cultural and social contexts make particular readings available? (e.g., who could you not say that to?) How might it be challenged?

Children are invited to read and reread the text, taking stock of their reactions and responses. The point of view of the story is considered because the perspective determines the position(s) of power from which the reader "sees" the story. The social processes among the characters are explored to determine how power was exercised along the continuum from domination and collusion to resistance and agency. The story ending is considered in this process, examining the assumptions imbedded in the story's closure. The illustrations may be analyzed to determine how the text and images work together as well as to take stock of how power is represented in them. The genre of the text is closely examined because these conventions influence how the story gets told. They have an impact on the reader's expectations for the text.

Children's literature is read against its sociopolitical context. Readers ascertain what cultural themes are imbedded in the work. They search for ways in which the sociopolitical situations of the characters shape these themes. The text is considered within its historical context over time. In addition, it is important to discern the prevailing ideologies/worldviews about class, race, and gender.

We grappled with many ways of naming our theoretical framework. We considered "critical analysis" and "multicultural analysis;" both designations fell short of what we are trying to accomplish through these dynamic and disciplined reading practices. "Critical" and "multicultural", together, captured our analytical lens because they are the best words we have available to us at the present time. "Critical" demands reading beyond the text and making connections between the local and sociopolitical/global and the personal and the political, all grounded by historical analysis. It calls attention to the power imbalance in society as well as its organization. "Critical" implores us to pay attention to the social work of language because how we use language shapes perceptions and social processes. "Multicultural" acknowledges the multiple histories among us; the dynamism, diversity, and fluidity of cultural experience; and unequal access to social power. Critical multicultural analysis requires inward and outward examination, recursively.

Theories inform theories, and through their application, we theorize practice. Theories are dialogical (Cummins, 2000). Our theoretical framework builds on Masha's (1995) issues approach to children's literature and Sonia Nieto's (1997, 1999, 2004) research on Puerto Rican children's literature and multicultural education. Maria José's (2004) dissertation research on critical multicultural analysis of children's literature anchors this book project. Masha argues for a critical reading of the social issues such as gender and heritage. Sonia demonstrates how cultural specificity contributes to the analysis of the Puerto Rican experience in children's literature. She advocates for multicultural education that is anti-racist, basic, and critical education for all children, that is pervasive and dynamic, grounded by social justice imperatives. Maria José's doctoral thesis develops the theoretical and pedagogical foundations of the critical multicultural analysis of children's literature.

Like some social scientists, we consider children's literature as social transcripts. Sherry Ortner (1991) claims that the United States' great ethnography is in the form of literature. Maxine Greene (1988: 184) refers to literature as "an encounter with the text [that] relates very closely to the experience of qualitative research, since it makes so very clear that the meaning of any situation is always a meaning for particular human beings with different locations in the world." Critical anthropology (Abu-Lughod, 1991; Behar, 1993; Dirks, Eley & Ortner, 1994; Goode & Maskovsky, 2001; McLaren, 1999; Moss, 2003; Ortner, 1991, 1994, 1998) and critical ethnography (Carspecken, 1996; Goodall, 2000) contribute to a complex reading of children's literature because critical anthropological practices show the complex workings of culture and demonstrate that cultural themes come from power relations, rooted in particular historical and sociopolitical conditions.

The cultural studies of Stuart Hall (1996) and Paul du Gay (1997a & b) and colleagues (du Gay, Hall, Janes, Mackay & Negus, 1997) have complicated our understanding of identity and cultural production. Their scholarship has deepened our understanding of the unfolding of cultural identity as well as how cultural artifacts become meaningful over time.

The political criticism of Terry Eagleton (1996) grounds critical multicultural analysis. He maintains that literary theory is a political endeavor. He advocates for literary study that is grounded in democratic impulses. He argues that literature is a social construct that is historically, sociopolitically, and discursively rooted in social ideologies that maintain power relations. The critical literary criticism of children's literature by Peter Hollindale (1988/1992), Peter Hunt (1992), Roderick McGillis (1996), Lissa Paul (1998), and John Stephens (1992) greatly contributes to our theoretical framework. These literary theorists bring Eagleton's understandings about literature and literary theory to children's literature, as well as drawing on critical discourse analysis.

Michel Foucault's (1972, 1980) definitions of discourse (which James Gee [1999] draws from), knowledge, and power, further support critical multicultural analysis. His genealogical work reveals how power structures shape and change the boundaries of "truth." Thus Foucault notes that truth is no longer unchanging and universal, but the perpetual object of appropriation and domination. The feminist poststructuralism of Bronwyn Davies (1999, 2000) and Chris Weedon (1997) bring feminist thought to Foucault's work. Their research on subjectivity and agency are important contributions to critical multicultural analysis. The critical discourse analysis of Norman Fairclough (1989, 1992), James Paul Gee (1999, 2001a & b), and Allan Luke (1995, 2002) demonstrate how language, power, social groups, and social practices work together. Their work highlights how language use or discursive practices are implicated in social practices and processes.

The New Literacy Studies of David Bloome (1987, 1989), Colin Lankshear (1997), and Brian Street (1993, 1995) move away from the concept of literacy as an autonomous activity to literacy as an ideological activity, shaped by historical and sociopolitical circumstances. The critical pedagogies of Paulo Freire (1970/1985), Colin Lankshear and Peter McLaren (1993), and Ira Shor (1992) create the circumstances to enact critical literacy, leading students to "read" their sociopolitical situation.

Critical literacy offers tools for students to examine how society exercises power over who they are and what they want to become. The edited books by Sandy Muspratt, Allan Luke, and Peter Freebody (1997) and Barbara Comber and Anne Simpson (2001), respectively, focus on the application of critical literacies in classrooms across educational contexts and political borders. These theorists contribute to the theoretical framework that underpins our approach to literary study. Literary theories are ideological (Eagleton, 1996) and dialogical. We use critical multicultural analysis as a way to clarify and ground our theoretical/pedagogical/sociopolitical position as well as to speculate on new territories.

Paulo Freire's (1970/1985) work tells us that liberatory literacy education can provide tools for social change. If we identify the cultural origins of assumptions, we are poised for action or praxis. A Freirian perspective demands the problematizing of children's literature. Praxis is defined as the naming of an issue, conflict, or contradiction, critically reflecting on the issue, and transforming it through practical application. The reflection takes the shape of dialogue with other people and with other texts. This dialogue is recursive and creates new spaces for unlearning and learning.

Our sampling of children's literature is not comprehensive but rather includes texts that serve as illustrations for the particular conceptual perspectives, historical trends, and cultural themes that we analyze.

Our intention is not to standardize interpretations of these texts but to make our reading public. We do not want to impose our meaning making of the texts, but rather expose the social implications of our meaning making. We invite the reader to read all texts critically. We invite the reader to find seeds for applying critical multicultural analysis through these chapters.

Throughout the book we conduct literature reviews to reflect the scholarly dialogues about particular aspects of children's literature. Literature reviews can extract or decontextualize the conversation from historical and sociopolitical factors. Genealogical analysis, as conceived by Michel Foucault (1977), offers possibilities for situating these "dialogues." Going beyond historical inquiry, this analysis shows the instability of events and speaks to the specificity of those actions as manifestations of struggle among power relations, revealing conflict, contradiction, and events as products of multiple processes. Genealogical analysis proceeds in two dimensions: a deconstruction of events as well as a reconstruction of associated power relations to these events. Genealogical analysis opens up a space for speculation and dialogue, unsettling suppositions about "what culture is and how it works" (Dirks, Eley, & Ortner, 1994: 6). A genea-logical analysis of multiculturalism in children's literature demonstrates how multiculturalism is conceived and constituted in U.S. society.

Genealogical analysis grounds our literature reviews of multiple def-initions of culture, the history of multiculturalism in children's literature, the sociopolitical context of children's literature, the scholarship of multi-cultural children's literature, the discourse of children's literature, and reading the intersectionality of class, race, and gender in children's litera-ture. Critical multicultural analysis of race, gender, and class ideologies in children's literature reveals the historical and sociopolitical dimensions of culture.

Rosaura Sánchez (1992) concludes that the comprehensive analysis of any cultural product is incomplete without contextualizing it within history and society. In addition, Kirby Moss (2003: 112) advocates for "recontextualizing" because it is essential "to lure cultural experience and group identity out of their common presentations by moving deeper into postmodern and critical explorations of authority and representation." The act of recontextualizing shows how people are working against "essentialized boundaries of assumptions." They do this, he argues, as a "basic necessity to define themselves and their experience in relation and in contrast to the way they are perceived to be defined." Catching cultural actors in action shows how they exercise power in their everyday lives. Moss contends that as we struggle "to understand people as they experience their race, class, and subjective identities in general, we see contradictions and paradoxes to ingrained discourses and constructions, not splinterings from some mythical whole, but people constantly search-ing through their actuality for some type of whole" (Moss, 2003: 113). We have conceptualized these processes as re/contextualizing, calling attention to the dynamism, recursivity, reflexivity, and depth required in situating social practice.

We bring particular assumptions about literature, authors, reading, and readers to the critical multicultural analysis of children's literature. We believe that all literature is a cultural and historical product, emerging from a particular place and time, and reflecting particular cultural and temporal contexts. Stories are social constructs offering a selective version of reality, told from a particular focalization or viewpoint. Authors position readers to respond in particular ways through the decisions they make about choice of genre, language use, point of view, and other literary devices. Literary texts are "reflections of historically bound ideologies" (McGillis, 1996). Texts reproduce the dominant values of a culture at a particular time. Therefore, the sociopolitical context shapes the writing, illustrating, and publishing of children's books.

Furthermore, we argue that reading is a sociopolitical activity, shaped by the reader in conjunction with many sociopolitical influences upon that reader. The critical multicultural analysis of children's literature takes into consideration the institutional component from within which we read, the power relations involved, and their implications for social justice. We concur with Roderick McGillis (1996) that all reading is political, and that critical analysis functions in two ways:

1. to set out clearly the political or ideological position of the text one is reading, and
2. to clarify one's own ideological position.

(McGillis, 1996: 103)

Finally, readers will feel included or excluded depending on the author's presentation and the sociopolitical context, both of the book and the circumstances in which the reading is taking place.

As readers, we must interrogate the power structures that discriminate against certain groups and privilege others. We acknowledge that literature speaks to readers on a personal and emotional level (see Rudman, 1995). Beyond this, as a society, we must confront race, class, and gender relations, the impact of history, and other social issues. Children can understand and grapple with the painful realities of anti-social behavior and thought.

In her "Ideologies in Children's Literature: Some Preliminary Notes," Ruth B. Moynihan (1988: 93) argues that "stories told or written for children are often indicators of the dominant values within a society. Various times and cultures reveal various attitudes, not only toward children but also toward life and society."

What is suitable for children to know and when and how can they be informed? A critical multicultural analysis examines how literature represents power and how the reader can connect those messages with issues of social change and justice. Critical multicultural analysis of children's literature equips the reader with strategies to unmask dominant ideologies, integrate what they know about themselves with what they learn about others, and translate their reading and thinking into social action. Children's literature can be a tool for creating a historical, sociopolitical imagination in young readers, and teachers and other adults can serve as important role models of resistant reading.

The pedagogical/literary category of multicultural children's literature, when it is defined as literature containing and pertaining to people of color, or out of the mainstream of society, distorts the social issues of race, class, and gender, and distracts us from addressing social oppression. Without the critical component, multicultural children's literature disallows the problematizing of children's literature, reading, childhood, and the enterprise of publishing children's books. We believe that children's literature should affirm the diversity of our society.

Publishing trends, a history of the phenomenon known as children's literature, definitions of reading, and a firmly grounded perspective on how literature impacts society, support our work. We are interested in the issues of censorship, what gets defined as a classic, and how to use sociopolitical and ethical filters in order to examine literature. What is implicit in the term, "critical multicultural analysis," is that we need to examine the nexus of power in text and images, and by extension, in society. We are also interested in naming the implied audience of the text and the social practices rendered.

Children's books can be tools for discussing social and emotional issues (Rudman, 1995). All too often, well constructed language and illustrations mask underlying messages in texts. The exercise of coercive power often appears artfully and can be internalized by unwitting readers. On a daily basis we are lulled by aesthetic texts around us, often distracting us from their sociopolitical impact. For example, Maria José, who is usually perceptive about the workings of power, was lured by the aesthetic elements of an everyday text, a lawn.

Maria José was traveling with her colleague David down Bloor Street West in Toronto, on the way back to the University of Toronto. They had just participated in a dialogue on critical literacies. With colleagues, they tried to reconcile aesthetic and critical engagement with texts. Maria José had reminded the group that critical and aesthetic response can exist together. David eloquently supported this stance. As they traveled down Bloor, the beauty of a stately building's landscape arrested Maria José's senses. She pointed out to David the greenness of the lawn, juxtaposed with variegated and multicolored plants, and enclosed by a wrought iron fence. It was lush beauty in the middle of a traffic jam.

The aesthetic qualities of a text can engage us emotionally and experientially (Misson & Morgan, 2006). The lawn resonated with Maria José. The greenness echoed back to the valley in which Maria José lived in during her early childhood. The green exuded calm and life. The lawn created a moment of tranquility in a bustling part of the city.

According to Ray Misson and Wendy Morgan (2006: 213), aesthetic texts "lead us to apprehend certain aspects of the world by creating a structure of textual experience . . . that leads us to think and feel in particular ways." Apprehension creates "a stronger interpretative element in reading these texts, more room for the reader to expand her or his understanding" (Misson & Morgan, 2006: 214). This interpretative expanse leaves room for readers to hold different interpretations of the text as well as broaden their understanding.

David critically read the lawn and shared his analysis with Maria José, expanding her aesthetic response. Since this gated edifice belongs to an insurance company, he wondered about its extravagant use of money and asked who benefited from this opulence. What was the social function of this beauty? The fence and locked gate kept all passersby from the lawn's lushness. This experience is one example of how aesthetics can obscure sociopolitical consequence, much like beautiful language and artwork in children's literature.

All children (young and old) have the capacity to be critical multi-cultural readers. They can be invited to engage in ongoing dialogue with authors and illustrators as they listen to or read children's literature. They can insert themselves into the story and can question its point of view, the social processes among characters, and its ending. Children can analyze the positions of power the illustrations or photographs provide and ascertain if the illustrations affirm or contradict the messages in the text.

Children's social location, age, historical knowledge, and prior experi-ence with the cultural themes and genre of the text shape how the children make sense of the story. The group dynamics adds another layer. With support from teachers and other adults, older siblings, and peers, children become more and more adroit at critically engaging with text and images. Group dialogue can greatly contribute to the children scaffolding each other socially and textually, as they enjoy and problematize books. Can the enjoyment of texts exist alongside critique? Is this combination an oxymoron?

Many adults are concerned that critical analysis will "break the magic of" or "ruin" the story, getting in the way of children enjoying the aesthetic experience of books. From our work with children as young as preschool to high school age, we have witnessed the pleasure they experience in sharing their different observations and interpretations of familiar child-ren's books. Critical multicultural analysis creates spaces for children to connect texts to their life experiences, other texts (literary and non-literary), and the world.

Oftentimes the level of engagement in classroom dialogue and critical response to literature through multimodalities (e.g., drama, visual arts, poetry, and music) heightens children's participation in the reading of the text and increases their pleasure with and understanding of the text. They participate actively and collaboratively across texts and images. Inter-textuality is central to this work: Children see that the text's meaning is constructed and reconstructed in interaction with the text, each other, and the world. The critical analysis leads to reconstruction of the text's messages and spaces for apprenticing with new ways of being in the world. The teacher and student roles are reconciled because everyone is actively involved in the reading process. Teachers are no longer keepers of textual meaning.

Through critical analysis, children, Barbara Comber (2001: 8) argues, acquire "repertoires of literacies ... aesthetic, ethical, cultural, moral stances, views about knowledge, ways of working, organising (sic), thinking and interacting." She continues:

> Critical literacy makes children's interests central, because it involves discussing with children how texts work and how they work in the world. It is in all children's individual and collective interests to know that texts are questionable, they are put together in particular ways by particular people hoping for particular effects and they have particular consequences for their readers, producers and users.
>
> (Comber, 2001: 9)

When readers interact emotionally and intellectually with books, their aesthetic stance creates space to consider the texts' cultural assumptions. However, children need support in cultural critique (Cai, 2008). Critical multicultural analysis offers a critical scaffold for reading power in children's literature.

Classroom Applications

- What metaphors do children associate with reading? Guide children in deconstructing these associations. What do the metaphors tell them about their processes as readers?

Recommendations for Classroom Research

- Take stock of how you teach children how to read. Use Chapter 3 (in this text) to name the literacy practices prevalent in your teaching. Which ones are present? Which ones do you need to bring into your work?

Suggestions for Further Reading

Bloome, David. (2007). Words and power. *Language Arts*, 85(2), 148–152.

Cai, Mingshui. (2008). Transactional theory and the study of multicultural literature. *Language Arts*, 85(3), 212–220.

Comber, Barbara. (2001). Critical literacy: Power and pleasure with language in the early years. *Australian Journal of Language and Literacy*, 24(3), 168–183.

Edelsky, Carole & Cherland, Meredith. (2006). A critical issue in critical literacy: The "popularity effect." In Karyn Cooper & Robert White (Eds.), *The practical critical education: Critical inquiry and educational practice.* Dordrecht, The Netherlands: Springer.

Misson, Ray & Morgan, Wendy. (2006). *Critical literacy and the aesthetic: Transforming the English classroom.* Urbana, IL: National Council of Teachers of English.

Weedon, Chris. (1997). *Feminist practice & poststructuralist theory* (2nd ed.). Malden, MA: Blackwell.

References

Abu-Lughod, Lila. (1991). Writing against culture. In R. G. Fox (Ed.), *Recapturing anthropology: Working in the present* (pp. 137–162). Santa Fe, NM: School of American Research Press.

Barthes, Roland. (1977). The death of the author. In *Image-music-text* (S. Heath, Trans., pp. 142–148). New York: The Noonday Press.

Behar, Ruth. (1993). *Translated woman: Crossing the border with Esperanza's story.* Boston: Beacon Press.

Bloome, David (Ed.). (1987). *Literacy and school.* Norwood, NJ: Ablex Publishing.

Bloome, David (Ed.). (1989). *Classrooms and literacy.* Norwood, NJ: Ablex Publishing.

Botelho, Maria José. (2004). *Reading class: Disrupting power in children's literature.* Unpublished dissertation, University of Massachusetts Amherst.

Cai, Mingshui. (2008). Transactional theory and the study of multicultural literature. *Language Arts*, 85(3), 212–220.

Carspecken, Phil Francis. (1996). *Critical ethnography in educational research: A theoretical and practical guide.* New York: Routledge.

Comber, Barbara. (2001). Critical literacy: Power and pleasure with language in the early years. *Australian Journal of Language and Literacy*, 24(3), 168–183.

Comber, Barbara & Anne Simpson (Eds.). (2001). *Negotiating critical literacies in classrooms.* Mahwah, NJ: Lawrence Erlbaum Associates.

Cummins, Jim. (2000). *Language, power and pedagogy: Bilingual children caught in the crossfire.* Clevedon, ME: Multilingual Matters.

Davies, Bronwyn. (2000). *A body of writing 1990–1999.* Walnut Creek, CA: AltaMira Press.

Davies, Bronwyn. (1999). What is feminist poststructuralist research? In Barbara Kamler (Ed.), *Constructing gender and difference: Critical research perspectives on early childhood.* Cresskill, NJ: Hampton Press.

Dirks, Nicholas B., Eley, Geoff, & Ortner, Sherry B. (1994). Introduction. In N. B. Dirks, G. Eley, & S. B. Ortner (Eds.), *Culture/power/history: A reader in contemporary social theory* (pp. 3–45). Princeton, NJ: Princeton University Press.

du Gay, Paul. (1997a). Introduction. In P. du Gay (Ed.), *Production of culture/cultures of production* (pp. 1–10). London: Sage/The Open University Press.

du Gay, Paul. (1997b). Introduction. In P. du Gay, S. Hall, L. Janes, H. Mackay & K. Negus (Eds.), *Doing cultural studies: The story of the Sony Walkman* (pp. 1–5). London: Sage/The Open University Press.

du Gay, Paul, Hall, Stuart, Janes, L., Mackay, H. & Negus, K. (1997). *Doing cultural studies: The story of the Sony Walkman.* London: Sage/The Open University Press.

Eagleton, Terry. (1996). *Literary theory: An introduction* (2nd ed.). Minneapolis: The University of Minnesota Press.

Fairclough, Norman. (1989). *Language and power*. New York: Longman.

Fairclough, Norman. (1992). *Discourse and social change*. Cambridge, UK: Polity Press.

Foucault, Michel. (1972). *The archaeology of knowledge and the discourse on language*. New York: Pantheon.

Foucault, Michel. (1977). Nietzsche, genealogy, history. In D. F. Bouchard (Ed., Trans.), *Language, counter-memory, practice: Selected essays and interviews* (S. Simon, Trans., pp. 139–164). Ithaca, NY: Cornell University Press.

Foucault, Michel. (1980). *Power/knowledge: Selected interviews and other writings, 1972–1977*. New York: Pantheon.

Freire, Paulo. (1970/1985). *Pedagogy of the oppressed* (Myra Bergman Ramos, Trans.). New York: Continuum.

Gee, James Paul. (1999). *An introduction to discourse analysis: Theory and method*. New York: Routledge.

Gee, James Paul. (2001a). Critical literacy as critical discourse analysis. In *Critical perspectives on literacy: Possibilities and practices* (pp. 2–14). 46th Annual Convention of the International Reading Association.

Gee, James Paul. (2001b). What is literacy? In Patrick Shannon (Ed.), *Becoming political, too: New readings and writings in the politics of literacy education* (pp. 1–9). Portsmouth, NH: Heinemann.

Goodall, Jr., H. L. (2000). *Writing the new ethnography*. Walnut Creek, CA: AltaMira Press.

Goode, Judith & Maskovsky, Jeff. (2001). *The new poverty studies: The ethnography of power, politics, and impoverished people in the United States*. New York: New York University Press.

Greene, Maxine. (1988). Qualitative research and the uses of literature. In R. R. Sherman & R. B. Webb (Eds.), *Qualitative research in education: Focus and methods* (pp. 175–189). London: The Falmer Press.

Hall, Stuart. (1996). Who needs 'identity'? In S. Hall & Paul du Gay (Eds.), *Questions of cultural identity* (pp. 1–17). Thousand Oaks, CA: Sage.

Hollindale, Peter. (1992). Ideology. In Peter Hunt (Ed.), *Literature for children: contemporary criticism*. New York: Routledge.

Hunt, Peter. (Ed.) (1992). *Literature for children: Contemporary criticism*. New York: Routledge.

Lakoff, George & Johnson, Mark. (1980). *Metaphors we live by*. Chicago: University of Chicago Press.

Lankshear, Colin. (1997). *Changing literacies*. Philadelphia, PA: Open University Press.

Luke, Allan. (1995). Text and discourse in education: An introduction to critical discourse analysis. In M. W. Apple (Ed.), *Review of Research in Education 21, 1995–1996*. Washington, DC: American Educational Research Association.

Luke, Allan. (2002). Beyond science and ideology critique: Developments in critical discourse analysis. In M. McGroarty (Ed.), *Annual Review of Applied Linguistics, 22* (pp. 96–110). New York: Cambridge University Press.

McGillis, Roderick. (1996). Class action: Politics and critical practice. In *The nimble reader: Literary theory and children's literature*. New York: Twayne Publishers.

McLaren, Peter. (1999). *Schooling as a ritual performance: Toward a political economy of educational symbols and gestures* (3rd ed.). New York: Rowman & Littlefield.

Misson, Ray & Morgan, Wendy. (2006). *Critical literacy and the aesthetic: Transforming the English classroom*. Urbana, IL: National Council of Teachers of English.

Moss, Kirby. (2003). *The color of class: Poor Whites and the paradox of privilege*. Philadelphia: University of Pennsylvania Press.

Moynihan, Ruth B. (1988). Ideologies in children's literature: Some preliminary notes. In Betty Bacon (Ed.), *How much truth do we tell the children: The politics of children's literature*. Minneapolis: Marx Educational Press Publications.

Muspratt, Sandy, Luke, Allan, & Peter Freebody. (Eds.). (1997). *Constructing critical literacies: Teaching and learning textual practice*. Cresskill, NJ: Hampton Press.

Nieto, Sonia. (1997). We have stories to tell: Puerto Ricans in children's books. In Violet J.

Harris (Ed.), *Using multiethnic literature in the K-8 classroom* (pp. 59–93). Norwood, MA: Christopher-Gordon Publishers.

Nieto, Sonia. (1999). *The light in their eyes: Creating multicultural learning communities.* New York: Teachers College Press.

Nieto, Sonia. (2004). *Affirming diversity: The sociopolitical context of multicultural education* (4th ed.). Boston: Pearson/Allyn and Bacon.

Ortner, Sherry. (1991). Reading America: Preliminary notes on class and culture. In *Recapturing anthropology: Working in the present.* Richard G. Fox. Santa Fe, NM: School of American Research Press.

Ortner, Sherry. (1994). Theory in anthropology since the sixties. In N. B. Dirks, G. Eley, & S. B. Ortner (Eds.), *Culture/power/history: A reader in contemporary social theory* (pp. 373–411). Princeton, NJ: Princeton University Press.

Ortner, Sherry. (1998). Identities: The hidden life of class. *Journal of Anthropological Research,* 54(1), 1–17.

Paul, Lissa. (1998). *Reading otherways.* Portsmouth, NH: Boynton/Cook Publishers.

Rudman, Masha K. (1995). *Children's literature: An issues approach* (4th ed.) New York: Longman.

Sánchez, Rosaura. (1992). Discourses of gender, ethnicity and class in Chicano literature. *The Americas Review,* 20(2), 72–88.

Shohat, Ella. (1995). The struggle over representation. Casting, coalitions, and the politics of identification. In Román de la Campa, E. Ann Kaplan, & Michael Sprinker (Eds.), *Late Imperial Culture.* New York: Verso.

Shor, Ira. (1992). *Empowering education: Critical teaching for social change.* Chicago: The University of Chicago Press.

Stephens, John. (1999). Analysing texts for children: Linguistics and stylistics. In Peter Hunt (Ed.), *Understanding children's literature: Key essays from the international companion encyclopedia of children literature* (pp. 56–68). New York: Routledge.

Stephens, John. (1992). *Language and ideology in children's fiction.* New York: Longman.

Street, Brian V. (Ed.). (1993). *Cross-cultural approaches to literacy.* New York: Cambridge University Press.

Street, Brian V. (1995). *Social literacies: Critical approaches to literacy in development, ethnography and education.* New York: Longman.

Weedon, Chris. (1997). *Feminist practice & poststructuralist theory* (2nd ed.). Malden, MA: Blackwell.

Woodward, Kathryn. (1997). *Identity and difference.* London: Sage/The Open University Press.

Wooldridge, N. (2001). Tensions and ambiguities in critical literacy. In Barbara Comber & Anne Simpson (Eds.), *Negotiating critical literacies in classrooms* (pp. 259–270). Mahwah, NJ: Lawrence Erlbaum Associates.

Endnote

1. Title inspired by Lakoff and Johnson's (1980) text, *Metaphors We Live By.*

CHAPTER **2**

The Historical Construction of Children's Literature

Children's literature contains experiences that are different from children's everyday worlds. It offers a window into society and creates a space where children can meet people across lines of social difference (e.g., cultural, class, language, sexuality, age, ability, and geography), providing vantage points from which readers can view multiple lives. Critical multicultural analysis invites children to examine the social construction of difference, linking their experiences to broader sociopolitical practices (Lystad, 1980; McGillis, 1996).

Like ideology, socialization can be coercive or collaborative, constructive or destructive. If, on the one hand, peers, parents, and teachers pressure children, or the community serves to smooth down edges, capitulate to stereotypes, and/or cut off thought and debate, then this kind of socialization is harmful. If, on the other hand, children's exposure to diversity and the opening up to new ideas or to varying and even conflicting perspectives raises awareness of different rules, conduct, and thought, then this type of socialization is advantageous. This is not a question of deciding whether or not to engage in socialization; it is the process of examining how to "do" society, and in this doing or participation, everyone is an active partner.

Historicizing Children's Literature in a Sociopolitical Context

A historical backdrop is one of the filters that we have chosen through which to examine children's literature and its development in the United

17

States from the mid-1900s to the present. We will, however, also look at how some British influences have contributed to the shaping of U.S. children's book publishing.

The development of children's literature parallels the development of the concept of childhood as a social construction. In examining both the history of childhood and children's literature, we link the literature aimed at children with the social, political, and economic ideologies of the time. Definitions of childhood vary throughout history, from culture to culture, and across socioeconomic class. Karen Lesnic-Oberstein (1999) builds on the work of the French social historian, Philippe Ariés, to argue that "childhood" and "family" "function within cultural and social frameworks as carriers of changeable social, moral, and ethical values and motives" (Lesnik-Oberstein, 1999: 17).

How childhood is defined greatly influences what adults want children to know, learn, and experience through literature. These definitions have evolved based on the socioeconomic position of the child and family. Even in the days of the bards and their wanderings through medieval towns and villages, there was a distinction between stories for the upper and lower classes. The reality was that the rich stayed rich and the poor remained poor. It was this understanding that sparked the stories about virtuous poor people and the greedy, avaricious, wicked rich (Leeson, 1985: 24–25). Literature, especially in the form of ballads, often glorified robbers and rebels, thus serving as a subversive element, paving the way for later tales such as *Robin Hood*, which challenged the social hierarchy of the times.

Published stories (the record of the times) take us to England after the Renaissance. In the 1400s, literature for children existed as instructional text; the words rendered in print were meant to teach skills, concepts, and cultural norms. Early books (hornbooks) were made of wood and covered with animal skin to help them endure wear. They contained alphabets, numbers, and prayers that adults selected and deemed "good" for children to know. But the children who learned from these books were few in number, relegated to the classes of families who could afford to purchase them, and to those who did not have to labor all day and had the time and means to devote to education.

In the late 1400s, William Caxton, a prominent and successful publisher, realized that literature based on the oral tradition would sell to those people who could read and who could afford to buy books. *Reynard the Fox, The Fables of Aesop, Robin Hood,* and *King Arthur* were among the first books he published. Although they were not labeled as children's books, they soon found their way to this audience.

By the 1500s, we see the advent of "chapbooks" which were small books constructed out of paper. Peddlers sold these "cheap" books from their wagons and at fairs, markets, and festivals. Chapbook stories were written forms of legends, ballads, and brief histories of the times. They remained popular in the United States through the 1700s.

Spiritual Milk for Boston Babes (1646) was the first book written for children in the United States. The first primer, *New England Primer*, was published in 1687. John Locke (1693), rejecting Puritans' belief in original sin, theorized how children learn, theories that further appeared in the development of children's literature. He believed that children were rational and pliable, and were *tabulae rasae* or blank slates. He argued that children should enjoy learning through games and picture books, instead of mundane lists of letters, syllables and words. He believed that this joyful early childhood education was crucial for their character formation. John Newbery, a publisher and author, was greatly influenced by Locke's theories (Murray, 1998).

Starting in 1744, John Newbery pioneered in the publishing and selling of books for children. He wrote books that were entertaining and unthreatening to children and contained useful information for parents. He included brief essays in the introductions of his books with instructions to parents on how to raise their children. The field of book selling proliferated at this time. The spread of literacy had great influence in the development of the concept of childhood and children's literature (Morgenstern, 2001).

It was during this time that the social myth of the American Dream was emerging on both sides of the Atlantic. It was greatly to the benefit of the upper class to hold out the view that, if a child who was poor was passive, obedient, deferential, and played by social rules, he or she would rise out of poverty and reap great rewards.

In the American colonies as well as in England in the early 18th century, versions of Defoe's *Robinson Crusoe* and his "noble savage" helper, Friday, circulated to adults and children. The portrayal of people of color was rare, and when it occurred was filled with stereotypes. Another example of this phenomenon is James Fenimore Cooper's *The Last of the Mohicans*, which fueled the notion that no living Native Americans existed in the United States, a misconception that continues to this century.

This was a time of rapid growth of the middle class. It was also a time when books were used to serve the particular needs of the different classes. Reformers admonished the rich to eschew idleness, and sang the praises of the virtuous poor. Deliberately didactic stories were popular and authors' intentions were recognized and praised as "so godly, so rational, so unreservedly good for their select audience" (Leeson, 1985: 57).

Especially given the phenomenon of the Industrial Revolution, Leeson goes on to report that in the early nineteenth century the middle and upper classes in England were anxious about the possibilities of the rise of the lower class and were particularly concerned that their learning to read might cause trouble. To address this problem, a number of religious reformers (like Hannah More) on both sides of the Atlantic produced pamphlet-sized books, called "Tracts," designed for the sole purpose of communicating morals, and aimed at the lower classes, particularly children. These tracts were distributed among the poor in order to persuade them of their respectful and rightful positions as servants to the upper classes (Leeson, 1985: 58–59).

Material wealth was the goal of the middle class. Children's books helped to support this goal for the children of the affluent. "The question was how could one develop a system of education which would do that for the children of the middle class, while simultaneously teaching the children of the poor not to aspire to the same things? Given these middle class attitudes and the total hostility of the ruling class, education for the poor barely developed. . . . Even the more enlightened felt a limit must be put on the education of the working classes" (Leeson, 1985: 64).

Lamb's *Tales from Shakespeare* appeared in 1806. In the early 19th century a number of juvenile magazines were published, largely containing Christian moral instruction, but occasionally addressing the issue of slavery. They were generally short-lived, and aimed at the affluent White population. In her overview of these publications, Phyllis Settecase Barton (1998), referring to one particular magazine, comments: "In general, the tone of the magazine was benevolent – reminding children to obey their mothers and to be kind to animals; however, stories written about Indian, Eskimo, and Negro minority [sic] children were thoughtlessly patronizing" (Barton, 1998: 11). Another inexpensive weekly newspaper-magazine, ". . . was filled with vengeance, violent justice, and racial slurs. Indians were savages and Negroes Dimwitted" (Barton 1998: 11). This sort of treatment was the rule in the many inexpensive magazines made available for children to read.

An outspokenly anti-slavery periodical, *The Juvenile Magazine*, appeared in 1811, and it ceased publication after four issues in 1813. It was the product of Arthur Donaldson who founded a free school in Philadelphia for Black children. He wanted the periodical "to supplement the textbooks and lessons used in his school, to publicize his efforts and his educational philosophy, and to provide a forum for condemning slavery, for describing the achievements of blacks, and for arguing the need to educate black children" (Kelly, 1984: 256). Donaldson printed a sketch of the Black poet, Phyllis Wheatley, in his last issue, as well as a chronology of slavery in the South. Unfortunately, the financial needs of the school forced the premature cessation of the periodical.

In the mid-to-late 1800s, Puritan primers were still used to teach children religious beliefs and morals, as well as to show children how they should conduct themselves according to their socioeconomic group mores. But alongside the deliberately didactic volumes were retold versions of folk tales, legends, and fairy tales of the European writers Charles Perrault, Jacob and Wilhem Grimm, and Hans Christian Andersen. It is notable that the versions were not of the English folk, but of an imported and refined variety.

Meanwhile, the primary audience for books for young readers was the children of the middle class. Although some writers forecasted the end of the Empire and even called attention to the treatment of the poor and of people of color, for the most part these populations were ignored in print.

The American Anti-Slavery Society published a pointedly anti-slavery journal aimed at children in 1833. *The Slave's Friend* contained a variety of genres to show children the appalling conditions of slaves in the United States. According to Kelly (1984: 408), the journal "took pains to show the wickedness of slave-holders, the nobility of the black race, and the hypocrisy of a nation that called itself Christian but permitted one human being to won another." This journal first printed *The Black Man's Lament, or How to Make Sugar*, by Amelia Opie. This journal for children called attention to the cruelty of the African slave trade. This periodical also succumbed to financial stress, as well as to the threatening disapproval of the anti-abolitionist movements.

By the middle of the 19th century, conditions for the working poor had worsened and the children of the poor barely had any schooling available to them. Nevertheless, Sunday schools and a few day and factory schools somehow managed to teach more and more poor children how to read. Inexpensive magazines began to circulate with stories snatched from established authors, as well as others with radical messages, morals that were gentler than the strict religious tenets bound up with the Puritans, mounting to a large group of what many people called "trash."

Children eventually were part of the audience who read these "penny dreadfuls" and their literacy skills developed more extensively. Then, in 1850, a law was passed in England to support the setting up of free libraries. There was enough of a supply of children's literature in these institutions to make a difference to the young working class child.

Our Young Folks, which circulated from 1865 to 1873, combined an anti-slavery stance with a strong middle-to-upper middle class Protestant morality. Readers were encouraged "to pity those less fortunate and to exercise appropriate charity" (Kelly, 1984: 331). High aesthetic quality was its hallmark, for example, Winslow Homer's illustrations appeared frequently, as did music by Mozart, Beethoven and Schumann (Kelly, 1984: 332). The magazine printed many genres including nonfiction, with a number of pieces staunchly anti-slavery and pro-Union. However, much of the writing was somewhat patronizing in terms of the representation of Black characters. Similarly, Native Americans were represented with condescension, as were Jews.

Both in England and the United States the middle to late 19th century saw such milestones in children's literature as Lewis Carroll's (1865) *Alice's Adventures in Wonderland,* Louisa May Alcott's (1868) *Little Women,* George Macdonald's (1872) *The Princess and the Goblin,* Mark Twain's (1876) *The Adventures of Tom Sawyer,* Joel Chandler Harris's (1880) *Uncle Remus* tales, Robert Louis Stevenson's (1883; 1885) *Treasure Island* and *A Child's Garden of Verses,* Rudyard Kipling's (1894) *The Jungle Book,* and Helen Bannerman's (1899) controversial *Little Black Sambo.*

Although some of these books contained characters that were other than White, Protestant, and middle class, the audience was largely from that group, and in general the plots and characterization reflected the lack of concern for "the other" as anything more than an oddity or an exceptional character out of place in a relatively homogeneous society.

In the United States at the end of the 19th century, Andrew Carnegie played an important role in making books accessible to the children of the poor. The first library children's department was created with the opening of the main branch of The Carnegie Library of Pittsburgh (CLP) on November 5, 1895. According to Michael Lorenzen (2002), Carnegie had no access to education because he worked long hours as a laborer. However, Colonel Anderson, his benefactor, started a small library of 400 books, which he lent on Saturday afternoons to local boys. This is how Carnegie educated himself.

> Carnegie wrote in his 1920 *Autobiography of Andrew Carnegie:*
> This is but a slight tribute and gives only a faint idea of the depth of gratitude, which I feel for what, he did for me and my companions. It was from my own early experience that I decided there was no use to which money could be applied so productive of good to boys and girls who have good within them and ability and ambition to develop it, as the founding of a public library in a community. . . .
> (Carnegie, 1920/1986: 47)

Further, Carnegie is quoted as saying, "In a public library men could at least share cultural opportunities on a basis of equality" (*New York Times,* Jan. 8, 1903: 1). His libraries made it more possible for children of the poor to acquire and practice their literacy skills by gaining access to real books as more and more were published for child audiences.

Nevertheless, despite the opportunities the libraries gave to children who were poor, schools were still inadequate places for their education, and the industrialization of the United States and Britain made their education a low priority.

Partly to counteract the stereotyping of Black children, and mostly to change Black people's attitudes about themselves, Black adults designed the first children's periodical for Black children in 1919. *The Brownies' Book* (1921–1922) was produced by the NAACP, the National Association for the Advancement of Colored People, under the auspices of W.E.B. DuBois, Jessie Redmond Fauset, literary editor, and Augustus Granville Dill, business manager, (Kelly, 1984). The magazine was 15 cents a copy and was produced monthly. Its focus was on African American children. It contained short stories, poems, biographies of prominent Black people, and news items. Five issues had contributions by Langston Hughes. The cover illustrations as well as those inside the book were by African-American artists. Many photographs were used as illustrations.

The published material represented the diversity of the Black population in appearance, settings, class affiliations, and attitudes. *The Brownies' Book* was canceled after only two years. In its last edition, W.E.B. DuBois wrote, "We have had an unusually enthusiastic set of subscribers. But the magazine was begun just at the time of industrial depression following the war, and the fault of our suspension therefore is rather in the times, which are so out of joint, than in our constituency." (Kelly, 1984: 354). The last issue was released in December 1921. In 1996, Diane Johnson-Feelings wrote a book called *The Best of Brownies*, thus bringing to the attention of contemporary children some of the material from the original publication.

In her dissertation, Violet Harris (1986) reports that the founders had a number of objectives in creating this periodical. These included familiarizing Black children with their own history, helping them to realize the normalcy and appreciate the beauty of being "colored." It included the hope that Black children would be exposed to "models of behavior" that would support individual and group participation in a racist society. According to Harris, the magazine's editors created a publication that would contribute to shaping the "refined colored person" through a diverse assortment of genres like biographical sketches, monthly columns, fiction, and poetry.

Barton (1998: 14) is of the opinion that "gradually the stereotypical view of the Negro in children's books was replaced with a more factual and truthful literature." She cites as an example the publication of textbooks such as *Negro Boys and Girls*, by Emma E. Akin, and *The Child's Story of the Negro*, by Jane Dabney Shackelford.

This perceived progress notwithstanding, Nancy Larrick stunned the publishing world with her article: "The All-white World of Children's Books" in the September 11, 1965 *Saturday Review*. In it she reported on a study she conducted that led to the conclusion that there were very few children's books written, illustrated by, or containing people of color. Dorothy Broderick (1973), in her groundbreaking book, *Image of the Black in Children's Fiction*, analyzes the treatment of Black characters in various ways and raises many serious points.

Although by the 1950s, teachers, librarians, and other professionals were beginning to understand the problems caused by the great gaps in children's knowledge base and representation, it was becoming clear that the needs of modern children were not being met. The audiences for most of the books were primarily White children reading about White worlds. Even today, when approximately 5,000 new titles of children's books are published annually, people of color are represented in less than 10 percent of the books. However, a growing number of writers and artists of color are being acknowledged and rewarded for their talents.

Literary scholars over the years have opened readers' minds to different ways of looking at literature. Some of these focus strictly on the text; others admit to ideologies that drive them socially as well as cognitively. Teachers and librarians have a wealth of topics and themes to offer their readers. Sometimes the subject matter is sensitive and controversial. Sometimes what one group deems constructive is judged to be harmful, dangerous, and inappropriate by another. Over the years many books (such as *Roll of Thunder, Hear My Cry* by Mildred Taylor, *Bridge to Terabithia* by Katherine Paterson, and *Sylvester and the Magic Pebble* by William Steig) that have won awards have also been challenged and/or banned. Certainly, selection plays a role in accumulating a library, but one person's selection is another person's censorship, and the reasons for selection or rejection vary as widely as the ideologies of the people in charge of selection.

The American Library Association annually lists the books that were banned across the United States, and ascribes such reasons as "offensive language," "promotes religious viewpoint," "sexually explicit," "violent," "homosexuality," "challenging authority," "age appropriateness," and "occult," among a long list. These challenges occur locally and are attended to in various ways by local librarians and teachers. Sometimes the books are removed from the shelves or placed on a "secured" shelf with special permission required for young readers to borrow.

Selection depends on many different perspectives and often would benefit from multiple readings in order to make the decision of whether or not to purchase a book, and how to offer it to young readers once it has been selected. Some adults may fear that children below a certain age level will not be able to handle painful material and, therefore, may withhold the book from potential readers.

We have chosen *Leon's Story*, by Leon Walter Tillage, to demonstrate some of the possibilities attendant upon multiple readings through several lenses, because different ways of reading lead to different interpretations of texts. Because this story brings the reader up close to the dehumanizing social practices endured by Leon's family and the African American community, questions about the "appropriate" age of the readership may arise.

Multiple Analyses of *Leon's Story*

Leon Walter Tillage is the son and grandson of sharecroppers. He has been employed as school custodian at The Park School, Baltimore, Maryland for the past thirty years. During an annual school assembly, he shares his story with the seventh graders. Although she is not indicated as co-author on the book cover, Susan Roth, a parent of one of the students in the school and a published author, persuaded Mr. Tillage to tape record his story so that she could set it into print. Leon's narrative provides a window into the life of the African American community in rural North Carolina during the pre- and early Civil Rights era.

What follows is a multi-layered analysis of *Leon's Story* to demonstrate how different lenses shape the interpretation of the text. In juxtaposing literary, developmental, reader response, feminist, multicultural, and critical multicultural analysis, we pose critical questions about how the reader, the text, and society are positioned.

Literary Approach

The literary approach focuses on the aesthetic aspects of the text (e.g., plot, character development, setting, length and complexity of sentences, word choice, word order, figures of speech, and illustrations). Although the emotional impact of the piece of literature is an important component of the aesthetic analysis, implicit in this approach is that literary works should transcend race, class, and gender and should, in essence, retain a fixed meaning over time and despite contexts.

Focusing on the stylistics of the text, most of the reviewers of *Leon's Story*[1] foreground the use of concise and unadorned language as the key ingredient of the book, remarking on the "spare language," "quiet restraint," "uplifting you-are-there narrative," "no rhetoric, no commentary, no bitterness . . . none of the rambling oral history," "poignant first-person account," "simply and straightforwardly told," "documentary-style clarity that adds to its effectiveness," and "moving personal narrative."

The understated language is certainly one of the compelling features of the writing. To examine this quality using a critical multicultural analysis, one might interpret it as a deliberate avoidance of artificiality, a sign of not succumbing to membership in the established group of professional authors. Or conversely, this style could serve to empower the reader and narrator at the same time, by inviting the reader to reject those details and extensions that might have been included by a more verbose author. This could have the effect of the reader's joining the writer in constructing the narrative by means of the author's particular discourse community.

One message conveyed by Leon's lack of detail about atrocities and resistance might be that Leon does not want to offend privileged readers by laying blame. However, a possible implication could also be that the facts are strong enough to make readers confront their own privilege and complicity in acts of racism. Leon's mother attempted to obtain redress through legal action, demonstrating that the family tried to appeal the father's murder through the system of justice. The fact that this attempt failed miserably is expressed in low-key commentary: "Now it would be different, but in those days it didn't matter what you felt about the crime, because what could you do about it? It's not that we accepted my father's death, we cared, but we just minded our own business and stayed out of the spotlight because nothing was going to be done about it anyway" (Tillage, 1997: 70).

On the other hand, Leon is explicit about the possibilities afforded African Americans by education, even though his father is skeptical of the benefits. Perhaps he is influenced by his audience of young scholars at The Park School; it may be, however, that his ability to read and write constituted a significant personal achievement to him.

For the most part, the story is told in standard English. But sometimes, in rare instances, Leon uses the double negative construction of vernacular Black English. For some readers, that might be jarring and confusing. What is the impact of his code switching? Does he use it for emphasis? What drove the authors (Leon Walter Tillage and Susan Roth) to choose the few double negative statements in the book and maintain standard English for the most part, or is there no intentionality here? If there is intent or not, what is the impact on the reader?

Part of the aesthetic appeal of this story is that it is in the form of the first person narrative. This format provides an intimacy difficult to achieve in other genres. The assumption is that first-person narratives are closer to the "truth" and convey a "purer meaning." The information is transmitted directly rather than mediated through a narrator. Leon is providing us with his selective perspective. He is clearly addressing an implied reader with expressions like "you see . . ." and by the explanatory and conversational phrases he inserts. He is assuming that the implied reader is sympathetic.

Keep in mind that this text is a product of Leon's school presentations. He has a sense of the audience, what the audience already knows, and is familiar with the social tenor of the school.

What are the implications of a first-person narrative? In literary terms, it is designed to personalize and to invite empathy on the part of the reader. John Stephens (1992: 57) maintains that a first-person narrative

> inscribes ideology either (a) by strategically disclosing that the narrator is unreliable, whereby the text constructs an oppositional world view, notions of what is right, or a right way of seeing and encoding; or, (b) by situating readers in a subject position effectively identical with that of the narrator, so that readers share the narrator's view of the world or are convicted of error when/if the narrator is proved to be in the wrong in any sense.

In other words, the first-person narrative can make the reader either support or disagree with the narrator. Leon does not use the details of his personal life to endear the reader to him. Unlike many first-person narratives, *Leon's Story* does not include information about his growing up and family, or everyday events. The "Afterword" informs us that Leon was married twice, had three children, and works with his brother at the school. We also learn that his mother is thriving and is the first female deacon of her church.

As with many works of literature, this one is a mixed genre, combining oral performance with negotiated autobiography/first-person narrative/memoir. We wonder about what kind of story would have been written if Mr. Tillage had collaborated with someone else, or had written the story himself. We also wonder about how much Ms. Roth changed the original text. She is careful to inform readers: "We have tried very hard to be faithful to and respectful of Leon's own precise voice. All editing was done with his participation and approval. We tried to restrict the changes to bridging the gap between the spoken word and the written word" (Tillage, 1997: 104).

Certainly this project brought two people together across social lines and different storytelling and writing experience. Part of the power of the narrative resides precisely in the decision to include only the elements of Leon's life that situate the story and the reader in the events and climate of the American South in the years leading up to and including the Civil Rights Movement.

Developmental Approach

A developmental approach assumes that there is a clinical way of assigning emotional and cognitive factors to a child's act of reading a book that will be predictable and uniform across age groups. The danger here is in rigidly defining stages or patterns, assuming that every child at a certain age will react and respond in the same way as every other child of that age, and that this behavior is consistent and predictable.

Gaile Sloan Cannella (1997) cautions against assuming a common human developmental pathway that disregards the myriad differences among children. Children demonstrate a wide range of changes and variations shaped by the interplay of biological, historical, sociopolitical, environmental, and cultural factors.

The Park School teachers have made the decision to include Mr. Tillage's story in the seventh grade curriculum. The school has made an assumption about the developmental appropriateness of this kind of information for twelve-year-olds. However, now that the story is in print, it is not possible to control the age range of the readership. The simplicity of the language might invite a younger audience. On the other hand, the graphic cruelty depicted here might constitute an overwhelmingly difficult burden for younger readers to manage.

Reader Response Approach

While the developmental approach tries to match the text with the growth stage of the reader, the reader response approach inserts the reader into the text. The partnership of the individual reader and the text requires readers' interactive contribution. Within this approach in responding to *Leon's Story*, readers could draw on personal incidents of bullying and overt cruelty that might help them to empathize with Leon's situation. However, focusing exclusively on the personal individual experience and bypassing the sociopolitical impact could trivialize institutionalized racism or oppression.

In the most favorable of circumstances, readers fill in the gaps of particular texts, drawing on their own knowledge and personal experience. Reader response theory claims that readers personally create meanings from their lived experience. John Stephens (1992: 68) argues:

> In my view, the present habit of stressing reader-focused approaches to text in combination with advocacy of identification with focalizers [main characters], inconsistent as this may be, is a dangerous ideological tool and pedagogically irresponsible. It fosters an illusion that readers are in control of texts whereas they are highly susceptible to the ideologies of the text, especially the unarticulated or implicit ideologies.

Bronwyn Davies (1993/2003: 155) echoes Stephens' position but adds that although it is not sufficient in and of itself, reader response is necessary along with other more critical approaches to reading:

> Although I would see this as one necessary dimension of reading, I also regard it as a dangerous form of reading if it is the whole rather than one part. If students can import unreflective sexism and oppressive and limited forms of thought into the text and then see that as an authoritative reading of that text, texts can only confirm the legitimacy of the oppressive world they live in.

Mingshui Cai (2008), in his seminal article in *Language Arts*, defends transactional reader response theory and makes a case for the expansion of the notion of multicultural awareness into the aesthetic component of this theory. Eventually, combined with an expanded efferent stance (i.e., gathering information), he argues for the feasibility and importance of incorporating a critical multicultural stance into the reading process.

Feminist Approach

The feminist approach focuses on gender relations depicted in any text. Like the other ideologically positioned approaches, it asks who has power and who does not. However, looking exclusively at how women are treated in *Leon's Story* might misrepresent the book's sociopolitical context. A feminist reading might focus on Leon's mother and her perspective as well as her involvement in the events of the community. It is likely that an entire other book could be written about his mother's story. It would be interesting to find out how she became the deacon of the church, and how looking back on it from her current place in history, she might have changed what she said to her children. But to impose a focus on a character that does not figure largely in the story would be a distortion.

A feminist critique might examine more closely the role of women within the family. It might also question the apparently casual dismissal of the two women to whom Leon was married. On the other hand, Leon has eight brothers and sisters, but he does not include much information about his brothers or about himself. His mother emerges with enormous agency at the end, but after all, in this book it is not any individual's story; it is Leon's recounting of U.S. society at a particular time and place, and to apply a feminist analysis here could distort the text and ignore the influence of race and class.

Early feminist approaches often fail to show how gender intersects with race and class. This is unfair to the feminists who go beyond simple focalizing on gender in isolation from other power relations. There exists now a group of scholars like bell hooks (2000), Patti Lather (1991, 2007), and

Chris Weedon (1997), who critique how power is distributed, and advocate for a multi-layered analysis of gender relations by looking at gender, race, and class together.

Multicultural Approach

A multicultural approach applied to *Leon's Story* examines how African American characters and community are depicted. As readers, we are invited into this personal story about a sharecropping family in a particular historical period. Leon's mother sometimes cooked for the Johnsons (the White owners of Leon's family's home). When she cooked collard greens she would take home the discarded liquid to make a soup. Leon comments that the part of the greens that was most healthy was the liquid, and it was a big joke that the White owners' children were less hardy than their workers partly because of the difference in their diets.

Leon and the other sharecroppers' children walked a long distance and attended a school that required them to fire up the pot bellied stove, draw water from the well, and eat lunches, usually of beans or white potatoes, that their families managed to provide them.

We also learn about the culture of the White community, whose children ride a bus to a school housed in a big beautiful building with steam heat and a large kitchen. Mr. Johnson, a White property owner, has an attitude not far removed from having been a plantation owner. In contrast, Mr. and Mrs. Clark are kind and cordial to the Black community and to its children in particular. The Black children work in the fields all summer, but the White children lie in the shade and never have to work to help their families.

Church every Sunday, to which Leon's mother took dinner, was an important part of their lives. Recreation time was sitting around the fire in the evenings, listening to the elder people talking about family members, family history, cooking, washing clothes with lye soap, and their work on farms. Unlike the White families, they had no radio or other means of entertainment, except that on Saturdays Leon and his siblings did go to the movies.

Using a multicultural perspective the reader gathers information about cultural practices and mores of all the characters in the story. This group is part of the larger community, and represents Leon's experiences and economic status as well as his activities of daily life. In our view, it is important to recognize and value culture, without isolating it from other factors such as power, history, and politics. Cultural elements are interesting and informative but, when left unexamined and unchallenged in terms of power, do not yield as much insight into the impact and political ramifications of their struggles as when combined with context and sociopolitical lenses. Their cultural practices are largely shaped by historical and socio-political factors.

Critical Multicultural Approach

Leon begins his narrative with how ashamed he is to be Black and ends the story with how proud he is to be honored by The Park School with a scholarship fund and other recognitions. The implication is that this is a character that developed, much because of history and changing attitudes, and also because of his involvement in civil rights marches and demonstrations. He does not merely talk about civil rights action, he participates in it. On the one hand, Leon seems compliant, even complicit, and on the other hand, by bringing up the injustices in what appears to be a seemingly acceptant stance, he plants within the reader the seeds of outrage at the inhumanity of racism.

A critical multicultural analysis locates how power is exercised, circulated, negotiated, and reconstructed. In the process of creating the published text, Ms. Roth, a privileged professional member of the community, acknowledges the authority of Leon's lived experience. Although this is the first time his story has been set down in print, Leon has chosen to tell the story repeatedly to the children of The Park School. In doing so, Leon exercises agency and influences his audience by exposing racism and encouraging the listeners to connect the present to the past.

Ms. Roth, one member of Leon's audience, recognized the power of his story and suggested widening his audience by setting his story into print. It is to her credit that she honored Mr. Tillage's perspective rather than injecting her own. Thus this narrative, albeit in the guise of a personal story, avoids being reduced to Leon's story only. It is Leon who paves the way for the reader to be immersed in the events of the time and the feelings of the characters. It personalizes the events, but we must not stop there. Critical multicultural analysis demands that we look at the historical and sociopolitical layers of this narrative, as well as the social interactions among the characters.

Leon is a rare person. He has the capacity for empathizing even with the enemy, without excusing the enemy's behavior. Despite the cruelty and injustice, he never becomes a martyr. He never diminishes injustice, but recognizes the complexities of the human condition, and, that in some ways, White people were victims of a racist system too. That Leon endured is miraculous. That he is able to tell his story so piercingly is a gift to the reader.

The book not only raises the spectre of the coercive power of the Klan and the collusion of the government, but it also showcases collaborative power of Leon and his family. At the beginning of the book, Leon explains the sharecropper system and how it institutionalizes economic oppression. Leon provides the reader with a practical understanding of the power of education, without leaving it abstract. He provides examples. He comments on the consequences of his family's lack of education: "If they kept you uneducated, you weren't qualified to do anything but work on the farm" (Tillage, 1997: 10).

In a few words, Leon also demonstrates how the plantation-power structure deprived the sharecropper of some basic needs such as running water and electricity. The culture of the plantation is graphically drawn, and the coexisting culture of the family with strict rules, strong values, and regular interaction with the community, mostly through the church, also communicated. This culture is not exoticized or romanticized. It provides information to the reader and a context for the action of the story.

The family shows resistance that might not have been visible to the owners, that included a strong immediate and extended family cohesion, regular, communal church attendance, and provision of healthful food like the liquid from collard greens, the benefits of which the owners were unaware. When it seems as if the parents are colluding by telling their children ". . . that's the way it's supposed to be. You'll never equal up to the Whites" (Tillage, 1997: 27), Leon immediately explains how different his parents' attitudes (speaking from their perceived place in the world) were in those days and how today he would respond differently to his son.

Throughout the book, while he does not speak bitterly, he does point to injustice. After reporting on the murderous acts of a constable who had killed two Black brothers, Leon comments, "Both brothers in one night. It was never, never investigated or nothing" (Tillage, 1997: 61). Mr. Johnson, the landowner, pretends to be a kind, considerate man, who tells Leon's family to hide when he expects the Klan to ride that night. Leon is not a fool. He knows that Mr. Johnson is, in actuality, in collusion with the Klansmen.

By the 1950s, Leon reports ". . . we were learning that we weren't suppose to be living like this regardless of what our parents said . . . we knew it was time for change" (Tillage, 1997: 87). If the book were to be divided into sections of domination, collusion, resistance, and agency, this section would reflect resistance. In the end, we learn of Leon's consistent, secure position of 30 years duration as custodian at The Park School in Baltimore. In telling his story in person and on paper, Leon continues his "quiet protest." Through his participation and agency, he has affirmed his own power, and has taken and continues to take responsibility for social change.

Reading children's literature with a critical multicultural lens guides us to examine how power is exercised. We realize we have choices and that knowing these choices can help us see our own power, as well as see how we are implicated in the circulation of power. It invites us to co-construct history and society but, even before that, to actively construct who we are, and to keep on asking questions.

Critical multicultural analysis is a framework for teaching literature and constructing curriculum. It urges the construction of spaces in which to examine issues of diversity and social justice by problematizing children's literature. It is literary study for social change. Readers, young and adult alike, can grapple, inquire, and engage with issues of social transformation and justice through their reading. Stephens (1992: 8) reminds us that children's literature socializes children "to take part in society and act purposively [sic] within its structures." He argues, "Texts do not exist in a vacuum, but are context-dependent. They are produced within, and to an extent by, particular social formations, and they seek, explicitly or implicitly, to inculcate particular social values and attitudes available at the time of production" (Stephens, 1992: 69). By uncovering systems of meaning that perpetuate social inequities, readers can reposition themselves and envision new intellectual spaces, new social worlds.

Thus, we explore critical approaches to analyzing literature that involve active participation on the part of the reader. Reader response, feminist, multicultural, and critical analyses all require readers to question, problematize, deconstruct, and engage with text in ways that are not pre-packaged, standardized, or even predictable. Combined, they all demand attention to power and to the examination of social and institutional practices. Together, they have implications for pedagogy, and they all have ramifications for social action. Critical multicultural analysis brings all of these lenses together and connects our reading to personal, interactive, complex, multicultural, sociopolitical, and historical factors.

Classroom Applications

- Invite children to bring in books (and other texts like music, oral stories, photographs, visual arts) or generate lists of texts from their childhood. Take notice of patterns across the grades. Juxtapose lists across the class. What are some similar experiences? What are some differences? What social factors contributed to the similarities and differences?
- Examine multiple versions of *Little Black Sambo*. What elements of the original storyline and illustrations have endured over time? Why do some of the same characteristics still exist? What are the issues? How does it differ from *Babar* or *Curious George* or *Uncle Remus*? What constitutes a controversy?

Recommendations for Classroom Research

- Analyze your classroom or school library. Take inventory of the cultural representations in the books and genres that stock your shelves. Take notice of the images in the children's literature. How is the artwork presented in the texts and on the covers? What images are found in the texts? Who is represented? What are they doing? Note differences in gender, race or ethnicity, and social class. How are various social groups depicted? What are the storylines present in these texts? Which cultural experiences and genres are not present on your shelves? In what ways can you diversify your collection? Borrow books from school and local libraries? Donations? Children's stories published in the classroom?

Suggestions for Further Reading

Hunt, Peter. (Ed.). (2004). *International companion encyclopedia of children's literature.* New York: Routledge.

Hunt, Peter. (Ed.). (2005). *Understanding children's literature.* New York: Routledge.

Lurie, Allison. (1990). *Don't tell the grown-ups: The subversive power of children's literature.* Boston: Little, Brown and Company.

McGillis, Roderick. (1996). *The nimble reader: Literary theory and children's literature.* New York: Twayne Publishers.

Murray, Gail S. (1998). *American children's literature and the construction of childhood.* New York: Twayne Publishers.

Zipes, Jack. (Ed.). (2006). *The Oxford encyclopedia of children's literature.* New York: Oxford University Press.

References

Children's Books

Tillage, Leon Walter. (1997). *Leon's story.* Illustrated by Susan L. Roth. New York: Farrar, Straus & Giroux.

Secondary Sources

Barton, Phyllis Settecase. (1998). *The Pictus Orbis Sambo: Being a publishing history, checklist and price guide for The Story of Little Black Sambo.* Sun City, CA: Pictus Orbis Press.

Broderick, Dorothy. (1973). *Image of the Black in children's fiction.* New York: R. R. Bowker Co.

Cai, Mingshui. (2008). Transactional theory and the study of multicultural literature. *Language Arts, 85*(3), 212–220.

Cannella, Gaile Sloan. (1997). *Deconstructing early childhood education: Social justice and revolution.* New York: Peter Lang.

Carnegie, Andrew. (1920/1986). *Autobiography of Andrew Carnegie.* Boston: Northeastern University Press.

Davies, Bronwyn. (1993/2003) *Shards of glass: Children reading and writing beyond gendered identities.* (Revised Edition.) Cresskill, NJ: Hampton Press.

Harris, Violet. (1986). *The Brownies' book: Challenges to the selective tradition in children's literature.* Unpublished dissertation, University of Georgia.

hooks, bell. (2000) *Where we stand: Class matters.* New York: Routledge.

Kelly, R. Gordon. (1984). *Children's periodicals of the United States.* Westport, CT: Greenwood Press.

Lather, Patricia Ann. (1991) *Getting smart: Feminist research and pedagogy with/in the post modern.* New York: Routledge.

Lather, Patricia Ann. (2007) *Getting lost: Feminist efforts toward a double(d) science.* Albany: State University of New York Press.

Leeson, Robert. (1985). *Reading and righting: The past, present and future of fiction for the young.* London: Collins.

Lesnik-Oberstein, Karin. (1999). Defining children's literature and childhood. In P. Hunt (Ed.), *Understanding children's literature: Key essays from the international companion encyclopedia of children's literature* (pp. 15–29). New York: Routledge.

Lorenzen, Michael. (2002). Deconstructing the philanthropic library: The sociological reasons behind Andrew Carnegie's millions to libraries. Retrieved on September 12, 2007, from *www.michaellorenzen.com/carnegie.html.*

Lystad, Mary. (1980). *Dr. Mather to Dr. Seuss: 200 years of American books.* Boston: Schenkman Publishing Co.

McGillis, Roderick. (1996). Class action. In *The nimble reader: Literary theory and children's literature* (pp. 102–128). New York: Twayne Publishers.

Morgenstern, John. (2001). The rise of children's literature reconsidered. *Children's Literature Association Quarterly, 26*(2), 64–73.

Murray, Gail S. (1998). *American children's literature and the construction of childhood.* New York: Twayne Publishers.

Stephens, John. (1992). *Language and ideology in children's fiction.* New York: Longman.

Weedon, Chris. (1997). *Feminist practice & poststructuralist theory.* 2nd ed. Malden, MA: Blackwell Publishers Inc.

Endnote

1. These reviews were gleaned from the Children's Literature Comprehensive Database

CHAPTER 3

Reading Literacy Narratives

The historical development of Western literacy practices is tied to cultural contact, religious activity, trade, and conquest. The examination of this history demonstrates that literacy practices are social practices; that is, they are linked to human activity and interaction, to something we want to accomplish socially and politically. According to Jared Diamond (1999/1997: 215–216), "writing marched together with weapons, microbes, and centralized political organization as a modern agent of conquest." It is not known how many times writing evolved in human history. There is evidence that writing systems developed independently in Sumer (3000 B.C.E.), Mesoamerica (600 B.C.E.), China (1300 B.C.E.), and Egypt (3000 B.C.E.), all socially stratified societies with centralized political institutions. Diamond speculates on whether writing systems were copied as they spread, or whether they inspired other groups to invent their own systems of writing. The Roman alphabet, which we use today, is a product of "a long sequence of blueprint copying" (Diamond (1999/1997: 226). Writing for personal use emerged when writing systems became standardized and easier to decipher, facilitating access.

The history of reading, as developed in Western Europe, emerged with the invention of the alphabet and the development of writing by the ancient Greeks (80 B.C.E.). Orality was part of ancient reading practices, even during private reading, because of the unseparated lines of text. Readers depended on "the enhanced short-term memory that pronunciation afforded to recognize words within undemarcated strings of letters and to combine them to access higher orders of meaning" (Saenger,

1999: 11). Silent reading (no tongue and lip movement) was not common. The wealthy echelons depended on educated slaves to read to them.

It was not until the seventh century that Celtic monks introduced word separation and syntactic punctuation into Latin and Greek texts. These text innovations facilitated silent reading because they "communicate[d] directly with the eyes of readers" (Saenger, 1999: 12). The word-separated text format remained a unique phenomenon of the British Isles until the tenth century. By the twelfth century the word-separated and punctuated texts spread across Western Europe. The introduction of printing with movable type (after the twelfth century) and the use of the vernacular represent the major developments that contributed to the increase of people who could engage in silent reading in countries such as England and France.

In the sixteenth and seventeenth centuries the production of print materials increased dramatically. The availability of written materials contributed greatly to mass literacy. The opening of schools in the mid-1800s standardized the processes of reading and writing, as well as contributed to stripping away of people's cultural and linguistic practices (Bernard, 1999; Spring, 2004).

Historicizing School Literacies

The following historical sketch, constrained by its linear representation of the past, generalizes practices over time and across contexts. These ages of practices speak to the pervasive policies and practices of the time, keeping in mind that many school communities and individual teachers were subversively pushing at these narrow definitions of reading and affirming children's linguistic experiences. Patrick Shannon's (1989) and Jan Turbill's (2002) historical work anchors the following overview of literacy education development in public schools. Kathy Hall's (2003) analyses of the psycholinguistic, cognitive-psychological, sociocultural, and sociopolitical perspectives of literacy further contribute to this sketch. It is important to note that homeschooling practices and independent schools were in existence, as well as children who were speakers of underrepresented varieties of English. English language learners were not having the same experiences as children who had access to the language of power, standard American English. In addition, it is difficult to untangle how class, gender, and race play a part in these trends. Certainly race and class are tangled up with language diversity issues.

Policies, pedagogies, research, publishing practices, and child development theories have greatly shaped the teaching of school literacies over time. Prior to the mid-1600s, literacy education was the charge of the family in the British colonized sections of northeastern and southeastern sections of the United States. Families were expected to teach children how to read. By the mid-1600s, Massachusetts established the first publicly-funded schools for large communities. Fifty to 100 years later the rest of New England and other colonies instituted grammar schools to teach children Protestant responsibilities, including the memorization of Bible verses.

Hornbooks and the *New England Primer* were the main texts used during these first 150 years of public schooling. With John Newbery's *A Little Pretty Pocketbook*, children's book publishing, as considered in chapter 1, unfolded with great momentum. However, Shannon maintains that there is little evidence that these texts were used in the teaching of reading. What he notices is that the instructional materials of this period possess a change in tone, a reflection of how children were perceived.

During the 1800s, reading education emphasized word identification over meaning and oral reading over discussion. The spelling method dominated the teaching of reading during the first half of this century. Children learned the names of letters, spelled and pronounced lists of two- and three-letter nonsense syllables, and then spelled and pronounced lists of a variety of words before they began to read sentences orally.

By the latter part of the 1800s, most urban teachers shifted their focus to syllables and pronunciation of words. Rural teachers continued with the spelling method of reading for many more years. William Holmes McGuffey's *Eclectic First Reader for Young Children*, one of the most successful textbooks, promoted a phonics approach to reading, increasing children's recognition of words.

The teaching of writing during this period comprised three activities: children gained mastery of pen use as they formed letters, copied words and text, and reproduced their work. Writing supplies were scarce. Teachers often fashioned supplies out of local materials.

Horace Mann advocated for the word method during the 1840s and 1850s, but it did not take root until the late 1860s and 1870s. This shift in teaching required a change in the role of the teacher from overseer and drillmaster to "interpreters of culture" (Finkelstein, 1970, as cited in Shannon, 1989). The word method began with the children's experience and their naming those experiences. This exercise brought familiar words into children's classroom learning. Then teachers and children engaged in discussion about their meaning. Oftentimes, the word method was undermined because some teachers combined word method textbooks with phonics instruction. The word became the focus of instruction and not how the word related to children's lives. Thus, prior to 1880, reading instruction was reduced to reading aloud, with the teacher selecting bits of passages for children to read aloud and offer support with pronunciation (Finkelstein, 1970, as cited in Shannon, 1989).

As we stated earlier, some teachers were "interpreters of culture" and were committed to literacy teaching that was a "natural consequence of children's study of their physical and social environment" (Shannon, 1989: 11). Progressive educators like Colonel Francis Parker tried to institute this pedagogy in Quincy, Massachusetts. Parker endorsed the word method because he believed children could learn to read as they learned to talk. He advocated for an integrated approach to language arts teaching. He believed grammar and phonics teaching could wait until children had an understanding of written language and were deemed intellectually ready.

Joseph Mayer Rice's research (1893, as cited in Shannon, 1989) offers a window into the continuum of literacy across school contexts. Rice surveyed 36 cities in 1892. He found that school literacy teaching could be divided into three categories: first, "mechanical reading instruction" (reduced to "calling off words"); second, programs in transition (the language arts curriculum divided into subjects of reading, penmanship, and grammar); and third, "scientific" and "progressive" approach (literacy learning and thinking are unified by "the laws of psychology").

According to Shannon, since the late 1920s, the challenge for reading experts has been how to encourage teachers to use the scientific directions incorporated in teachers' guidebooks. For the past 85 years plus, reading experts and commercial publishers have dictated reading practices because of the prevalence of basal readers in schools. Shannon argues: "It often seems that the materials are using teachers rather than teachers using the materials" (Shannon, 1989: 29).

Jan Turbill's article, "The Four Ages of Reading Philosophy and Pedagogy," offers a historical context for understanding how school literacies developed after the 1950s. This historical sketch is useful in recontextualizing teaching practices in order to deconstruct the ideologies implicit in pedagogy.

From the 1950s into the early 1970s, what Turbill calls "The Age of Reading as Decoding," school literacies practices centered on teaching the following skills: directionality, visual and aural discrimination, letter-sound relationships (phonics), and word recognition. During this period, reading was taught in isolated, decontextualized lessons. It was believed that once children mastered these lessons, comprehension would follow. Spelling, handwriting, and written composition were taught in isolation from each other.

A cognitive-psychological perspective of reading grounds this age of literacy as a series of cognitive skills, processes that just happen in children's heads. This literacy pedagogy privileges the systematic and sequenced teaching of reading, governed by developmental stages that standardize the reading process for individual children. Commercially produced curriculum (basal readers) is the mainstay in these classrooms, anchored by scope and sequence charts. The focus is on the mechanics of written language, especially phonemic awareness, phonics, spelling, grammar, and vocabulary.

During the mid-1970s, "The Age of Reading as Meaning Making," reading became understood as a process; that is, children continued to learn how to read long after grade 2, and they learned to read by using reading for learning. Children read more from kindergarten through grade 6. The increase in children's trade book publishing contributed to these reading practices (as we consider in this chapter). The focus was on reading for meaning, using the cueing systems (i.e., graphophonic, syntactic, and semantic). The reading process was made visible and public through metacognition (thinking about the thinking). Phonics learning became heavily aligned with special education. Research or library skills were introduced in upper elementary grades.

Literacy as a psycholinguistic guessing game (Goodman, 1967) characterizes this period. This perspective acknowledges all children's predisposition for language learning, since language is a form of human expression. Process writing and whole language focus on the learner as meaning-maker and on the learner's interaction with the text. Classroom learning is more collaborative and peer interaction is fostered. The four language modes, that is, reading, writing, listening, and speaking, are integrated. The children are encouraged to use their schemata (prior knowledge), metacognition, and metalanguage (thinking about the language). The focus is on personal development and transformation.

"The Age of Reading-Writing Connections," a period that began in the early 1980s, introduced computer technology to school contexts. This period of time marks an increase in the production of reading programs and children's literature. Large print materials (e.g., Big Books) became available. Teachers and children read more together and independently. The writing process became a focus in schools. All children were encouraged to emulate writers, with young children approximating the writing process with drawings and scribbles and invented spelling. Invented spelling became foundational in early childhood classrooms. Children were invited to make connections among reading, writing, and spelling, since the goal was for children to read books and be immersed in the language of books. Emergent literacy was recognized; that is, the literacy practices children acquire during the first decade of their lives. Children were exposed to multiple texts. The shift from reading and writing to literacy reflected the integration of the language modes (e.g., speaking, listening, reading, and writing).

This era recognizes the sociocultural dimensions of literacy learning, while the psycholinguistic and cognitive-psychological perspectives focus on the child as an individual reader engaged in personal and isolated construction of meaning. Both perspectives also privilege the mind over the social or contextual aspects of learning. Cognitive-psychology, in particular, considers culture as one of many variables that influence meaning making. The sociocultural perspective places culture at the center of literacy learning. Literacy is deemed as a set of social practices that children, families, and communities engage in. Literacy learning is regarded as processes that are intellectual, emotional, motivational, and social. Multiliteracies (New London Group, 1996), the literacies that children practice in schools and out of school, are acknowledged.

The early 1990s, "The Age of Reading for Social Purpose," was a period marked by information explosion and a shift to school literacies that offered high levels of literacy to all children so that they could be employable citizens, as well as possess the ability to read and write in a range of contexts. Literacy was used to develop knowledge and understanding, and to achieve personal growth. Multiple literacies were recognized, that is, children's home and community (everyday) literacies were considered within the classroom context. Literacy was defined as the integration of speaking, listening, and critical thinking (e.g., problematizing texts) with reading and writing, processes that would contribute to the development of knowledge and understanding, as well as personal growth. Literacy was recognized as purposeful, flexible, and dynamic.

Literacy processes are not just cognitive processes or a set of skills stored in people's heads. Literacies are social practices, connected to and constructed by everyday practices and many contexts (e.g., home, school, work, community, and society). There are many social practices and policies that influence a child's access to written language.

The No Child Left Behind (NCLB) Act of 2001 is a U.S. federal law proposed to improve education for children who are underserved by schools, through a system of accountability based on standardized tests scores. The Reading First initiative of this legislation has dramatically changed the literacy teaching of children in kindergarten through grade 3. These policies undermine young children's cultural and linguistic knowledge and teachers' professional judgment, and get in the way of children learning to read and write. As a matter of fact recent reports indicate that the Reading First initiative has failed to raise children's reading scores (Dillon, 2008).

Critical literacy researcher Allan Luke (2000) maintains that the distribution of social power, that is, who possesses control over institutions, resources, and dominant discourse within society, largely determines education reform. The NCLB Act punishes rather than supports schools and lower income children, helps further an agenda of privatization of public schools, and further institutionalizes classism and racism. Because the NCLB law requires assessment in the form of standardized testing, it reduces literacies to reading only and sequenced skill-based instruction (Teale, Paciga & Hoffman, 2007), thereby establishing a stronghold, affecting classroom teaching and learning. Cognitive-psychological perspectives of literacy largely inform the NCLB law.

Literacy Defined

The above historical sketch demonstrates that literacy practices are not a fixed set of practices. They are socially constructed and always in flux, depending on many sociopolitical factors. Literacies are not autonomous but ideological; the sociopolitical context shapes the ideologies and power relations in which they take place (Street, 1993). Roz Ivanic (1998: 65) maintains "literacy is not a technology made up of a set of transferable cognitive skills, but a constellation of practices which differ from one social setting to another." Literacy practices are social practices because we use them to take action in and respond to our everyday participation with our families, communities, society, and the world. We draw on a wide array of literacy practices, shaped by exposure, experience, and access.

According to James Gee (2001), literacy is discourse. Gee suggests that our primary socialization is with our families, peers, and communities where we learn our "primary discourse." People learn "secondary discourses" within social institutions like schools, workplaces, stores, government offices, churches, and businesses. Secondary discourses develop from primary discourses. Gee (2001: 6) maintains that "literacy is control of secondary uses of language (i.e., uses of language in secondary discourses)."

There are many types of literacy. Gee conceptualizes them as follows:

- Dominant literacy is control of a secondary use of language used in what he calls "dominant discourse."
- Powerful literacy is control of a secondary use of language used in a secondary discourse that can serve as a meta-discourse to critique the primary discourse or other secondary discourses, including dominant discourses.

(Gee, 2001: 6)

What Gee means by "control" is that the reader has some degree of being able to "use" or "function with" the discourse. "Mastery" is defined as having "full and effortless control" (Gee, 2001: 6). He states: "one cannot critique one discourse with another one (which is the only way to seriously criticize and thus change a discourse) unless one has meta-level knowledge [thinking about the knowledge] in both discourses. And this meta-knowledge is best developed through learning, though often learning applied to a discourse one has to a certain extent already acquired." He concludes that powerful literacy ultimately involves learning, and not just acquisition. Thus, critical reading increases power and flexibility the more it is practiced.

Our theoretical position moves reading and writing away from an exclusively cognitive model which positions literacy as an internal, individual, psychological act, to literacy as a sociocultural, multiple, and political practice. All language modalities and literacy practices inform each other. For example, speaking can inform reading, and writing can inform reading. School literacies tend to privilege reading and writing over the other modalities.

Our contention is that any approach that excludes the social and political dimensions of reading maintains and reproduces dominant power relations. We advocate for a shift away from the psychological defin-ition of literacy to one that includes a social activity that takes place in a particular context, with particular people, involving particular relations and structures of power, values, beliefs, goals, purposes, interests, econo-mic, and political conditions. Texts, oral and written, are discursive sites, sociopolitical products imbued with units of language that move within a discursive grid. A critical multicultural reading, then, involves reconstruc-tion of subjectivities and repositioning the reader as a researcher of language and creator of meaning.

The conceptual framework of the four resources model of literacy practices (Luke & Freebody, 1999) features the practices that support strong and critical readers, writers, and artists. This model does not repre-sent a continuum or a linear process, but rather a dynamic family of practices. The four resources are code breaking, text participating, text using, and text critiquing. They are used depending on the literacy event, type of text, and children's prior literacy experiences. This resource model is not bound to a developmental or pedagogical schedule; it honors what children know.

Code breaking (cognitive-psychological) is not learned first, in isolation from the other literacy practices. Code breaking is learned as children engage with text participation, text use and text analysis. Code breaking includes alphabetic and letter-sound knowledge. While the teaching of phonics is an important part of literacy learning, it is problematic to begin there. Phonics assigns a fixed sound value to each letter, a difficult matter in the English language. In English, there are more speech sounds than there are letters (i.e., 26 letters to 42 to 44 sounds in spoken English) because we have different letters and letter combinations to represent the same sound. In addition, many languages have contributed to the English language (through cultural contact and conquest); often the spelling patterns reflect the original spelling. Lastly, there are many varieties of spoken English, with different accents producing different pronunciations and speech sounds. We need to ask ourselves "Whose phonics do we teach?" (Wilson, 2002). Maria José will use her name as a text to consider the complexities of these literacy practices (Botelho, 2007).

Her name is illustrative of the possibilities of code breaking practices: Maria José /Ma ree ya/ /Jzu ze/ can teach children about the letter-sound relationships in the Portuguese language, while affording many opportunities to compare to English letter-sound relationships. Exploring names creates spaces to negotiate and practice how to say children's names.

Text participation (psycholinguistic) takes children inside the text. Text participants understand and construct meaningful written, visual, and spoken texts from prior experiences. Children are invited to interact and to ask questions of the text. The role of the teacher is to deepen understanding by posing questions that were not explored, and to seek multiple perspectives. Returning to a name-based investigation, consider that families give their children names which reflect gender, culture, religion, history, family names, and the parents' hope for their children's futures. Some questions to explore: What are the origins of your name? What does it mean? What does your name tell others about your cultural heritage? Do you know your name in another language? Do you have a nickname?

Maria José's name was Maria José de Sousa Botelho. When her family immigrated from São Miguel, Açores to Massachusetts in 1969, her name was reduced to Maria Botelho. She is named after her paternal grandmother. De Sousa was part of her mother's maiden name and "de" signifies that she is from both families, and not just from the Botelho side. The Portuguese tradition was to name baby girls Maria, symbolizing their devotion to the Virgin Mary. José means God will increase. Botelho is an old Portuguese name, meaning ancient corn measure.

The text user (sociocultural) reads not only to understand and participate but also to make use of the text by considering form, purpose/function, and audience. Names create spaces for text-using practices. Children can complete a two-column list: On the left side, make a list of all the names they can remember being called, including nicknames. On the other side, next to each name, list the people who used it and identify the context. In addition, invite children to sort classmates' names according to roles (e.g., oldest child in the family, sisters) and activities (e.g., dancers, soccer players).

Maria José is called Maria, Maria José, Mary Jo, MJ, and Maria Josephine. All of these names represent her. Her immediate family and Canadian colleagues call her Maria José. Her American colleagues and friends call her Maria. Her Canadian family calls her Mary Jo. Some friends call her MJ.

The text critic (sociopolitical) understands that texts are not neutral; that is, they represent particular worldviews and silence other perspectives, as well as influence how people perceive themselves in the world. The text critic steps back from the text and analyzes the explicit and implicit messages in the text. Return to the name list: What do the children notice? Any surprises? In what ways have their names been changed? In what ways did their names remain the same? What are the significances of these changes and/or non-changes?

Maria José became another Maria for the sake of bureaucratic expediency. Little did government and school officials know that they severed Maria José from her namesake, her paternal grandmother. But her family complied. In school and in her neighborhood, she tried to encourage teachers, classmates, friends, and neighbors to say her full first name. Many pronounced José as the Spanish /Ho'zā/, a beautiful name, but not her name. As a young adult, she became a U.S. citizen. Maria José decided to change her name to Maria Josephine Botelho, discouraging any further mispronunciations of her name. Maria José's name change was an instance of her taking action and deciding what she wanted to be called, but it was also an instance of conformity to the sociopolitical practice of Anglicizing and culturally sanitizing first and last names. She reclaimed her full first name during her immigration to Canada. Maria José also is her academic name. Maria Josephine is her legal name, the one you will see on her U.S. passport. Names are texts that can help children see how language works as well as how language and power are bound together.

Analysis of Literacy Narratives

Literacy narratives are books that depict characters engaged in the language modes of speaking, listening, writing, reading, representing, and viewing. A critical multicultural analysis of these texts can uncover the implicit definitions of literacies imbedded in the books, as well as highlight prevailing assumptions about literacy practices. The goal is to locate a variety of texts showing a range of literacies, including literacies as tools for social change. We want to move beyond prevalent middle-class definitions of reading and writing for pleasure, entertainment, and information, to literacy practices that honor children's out-of-school literacies as well as value the interconnectedness of the four literacy practices as resources for learning and participating in the world.

Children's literature plays an essential role in the cultures of childhood and school. The following three studies examine the central characters' interactions with texts and literacy events (i.e., literacy). In the first small study, Wilma Kuhlman and Mary Lickteig (1998) assign three categories that reflect these encounters: "desire for literacy," "power of literacy," and "wonder of literacy." The first category, desire for literacy, relates to the central characters' motivation to become literate, seeking literacy through their own choice. This category locates the characters' power of taking action. However, this category can obfuscate some of the factors that have kept characters from literacy learning. Racism and socioeconomic oppression, family illiteracy because of poverty, and lack of access to literacy teaching and printed materials are manifestations of power relations. While it is important to examine the characters' motivation to learn to read and write, we also must consider the characters' resistance to reading and writing, naming the underlying factors contributing to the resistance. Lastly, there is a danger in thinking that passionate desire for literacy is enough; it does not mean that the reader will apply that reading in any way.

The power of literacy, the second category, signals the main characters' transformation because of their involvement with reading and writing. The transformation is at the individual level. Readers also need to learn about examples of the power of literacy to organize and create change, especially noticing the role literacy can play in the exercise of collaborative power.

The last category, wonder of literacy, is about the central characters' enjoyment of literacy activities. In other words, they find pleasure or important information through reading and writing. What is key here is to see a wide representation of the wonder of literacy. For example, pleasure can come from critical multicultural analysis and not be exclusive to reading without disturbing the status quo. The wonder can lead to using multiliteracies and other modalities (e.g., visual, gestural, linguistic), challenging generic conventions, connecting to other texts, and locating the sociopolitical and historical contexts of the children's book.

These categories, as the authors maintain, are not mutually exclusive, but work together, with one foregrounded and others evident in the background of the story. While these categories are useful places for preliminary analysis, Kuhlman and Lickteig's explications fall short of the complexities of these literacy practices. Their interpretations are individualistic, extracting the interaction from a sociopolitical context. Literacy narratives offer opportunities to question the commonsensical associations we attach to literacy practices and invite readers to reflect and deconstruct them.

The second study builds on Howard Gardner's theory of multiple intelligences and the sociocultural frameworks of early literacy development. Gardner's theories call on the diversity of human intelligence, but do not consider issues of access to and training within these modalities of learning. In her dissertation research, Jennifer K. Geringer (2001) locates instances of multiple literacies (e.g., language, cognitive, physical, natural, aesthetic, affective, and social) as represented in 55 award-winning picture books for children that were published between 1993 and 2000, the period that Gardner's theories gained credibility in universities and school communities. Geringer models her research project on Hoffman's (1993, as cited in Geringer, 2001) study, a project that analyzed literacy images across children's texts published between 1971 and 1990. Using a traditional definition of literacy as reading and writing, Hoffman notes that there is an increase of literacy images in books for children. The images reflect literacy strictly as reading and writing practices. Hoffman advocates for research to examine broader definitions of literacy and whether those literacies are portrayed. Geringer addresses this recommendation.

Geringer categorizes the literacy events "as brief, descriptive or developed, depending upon the level of importance placed on the literacy act and its role in the story" (Geringer, 2001: 1). She finds that most of the representations fall within "traditional" definitions of literacy, with reading events outnumbering instances of writing. She also noticed a significant frequency of literacy events as "multiple and multi-layered [the interconnectedness of multiple literacies and their use across intelligences; multimodality]" within the text sample, evidence of the new understandings about literacy in the field of education. Natural, aesthetic, physical, and social were the most prevalent multiple literacies. Geringer's study documents the social expansion of literacy images.

In Frank Serafini's (2004) study, "Images of Reading and the Reader," he argues that the literary representation of reading and readers may influence the literacy learning and teaching of elementary school children. After reading *Wolf!*, by Becky Bloom, to a group of school-age children, Serafini found a disconnection between the portrayal of reading processes and contemporary literacy theories. The text centers on the wolf's "ability to pronounce words and read aloud fluently" (Serafini, 2004: 611). This mismatch impelled Serafini to examine how picture books depict reading and readers. This study was guided by two questions: (a) "What images of reading and the reader are portrayed in the text and illustrations of contemporary picture books? (b) Is there a difference between the images of readers and reading portrayed in children's picture books and those portrayed in transactional, reader-response theories?" (Serafini, 2004: 611). This investigation led Serafini to also consider the implications of these representations of school literacies and teachers' expectations for child readers.

In *Wolf!*, written by Becky Bloom and illustrated by Pascal Biet, a hungry wolf learns to read so he can participate in "a farm for educated animals." The cow, duck and pig constantly read. This pro-reading story perpetuates middle-class norms of reading for pleasure. As the wolf becomes a stronger reader, he assumes particular practices that admit him into this bucolic farmyard. He first practices school reading skills using a contrived text of controlled vocabulary and sentence structure. He then exercises his choice and chooses texts from a local library and bookstore. The message here is that practice will lead to fluency and skills-based reading competence. To tell stories dramatically, the wolf enlists oral language for reading. His attire changes as his reading abilities change over time, signaling that reading is a social practice that vests the reader with particular cultural capital. The wolf discovers the power of literacy because it rewards him with social acceptance and power.

According to Serafini's findings, the texts in his study reduced the reading process to oral fluency and expression, sounding out words without mistakes, letters and sounds, and sight words—reading as only a part-to-whole, cognitive process. The children's books analyzed also represented environmental print contributing to early literacy learning; recognized emergent literacy; acknowledged the escapism from reality that reading offers; taught new things and met new people; and honored the emotional qualities of reading (e.g., symbol of love, comfort, and affection)—all sociocultural processes. Finally, reading was depicted as a requirement for democratic participation as well as a transformative event that could heal and change people in significant ways. The ability to read was equated with power and cultural capital processes (i.e., reading providing social mobility). According to Serafini, the role of prior knowledge in the reading process was missing from the text collection.

As Serafini maintains, critically analyzing representations of literacy in children's literature can create spaces to expand our definitions of reading. For example, it is not reduced to "closeted bookworms" or that pleasure can only be derived from fiction reading. What we noticed from this text collection is that there were no informational texts included as reading for pleasure. Informational texts can bring the reader lots of joy. The bookworm representation needs further consideration: Bookworms are privileged with time and book resources. Literacies should not dominate a child's life; they are social practices. For example, the protagonist in *The*

Gardener, by Sarah Stewart and illustrated by David Small, uses writing to communicate and to stay connected to her family in the countryside while she lives with her uncle in the city.

In the next section, we analyze literacy narratives, a text collection that we assembled from the Comprehensive Children's Literature Database and in consultation with local librarians. Selected themes emerged from multiple readings of the text collection (primary sources) alongside literacy histories and secondary sources as we analyzed the literacy events. Literacy is central to or plays a part in each text. We have chosen representative texts to explore each cultural theme and examine the implicit definitions of reading and other literacy practices across the text collection.

This is not an exhaustive analysis. There are many books that represent children engaged in multiliteracies (i.e., speaking, listening, writing, reading, representing, and viewing). For example, there are many biographies of famous writers and poets, and diary- and letter-type texts that warrant analysis. We decided to focus on the language modes of reading, writing, and speaking. We conducted critical multicultural analyses of the text collection representing the emerging cultural themes: African Americans and the struggle for literacy; adult/family literacy; English language learners; "reluctant"/ "struggling" readers and writers; emergent literacy; access to books and school literacies; orality; writing; and critical literacy. These themes are cultural because they come from particular historical and sociopolitical circumstances (Carspecken, 1996). These cultural themes speak to literacies as social practices associated with literacy events. For example, literacy practices such as accessing online catalogues and compiling lists of titles are associated with the social practice of borrowing books from the public library (literacy event). The text collection reflects the historical and sociopolitical implications of literacy practices.

African Americans and the Struggle for Literacy

Every form of oppression imposes silence. The great divide between orality and written literacy was socially constructed (Willis, 1995). The institution of slavery left its mark on the access for African Americans to acquire print literacy, silencing the community and contributing to its oppression. Several children's books that document the lack of and struggle for access to the language of power. (It is important to keep in mind that Native peoples were also stripped of their many languages.) The following texts, historically organized, create spaces to examine how race and class work with language, with African American history as a backdrop. The texts show how code-breaking and text-using literacy practices are crucial to full participation in a society whose language of power is centralized and maintained through print modalities. In a number of books, members from the African American community organize and teach other members, as a way to escape inhumane conditions.

Underlying *Nightjohn*, by Gary Paulsen, narrated by twelve-year-old Sarny, is the social power of the written word; so socially important that the White oppressors go to great lengths to withhold literacy from the slaves, making the teaching of reading and writing forbidden by law. Reading is so socially important that the slaves are willing to risk their lives to acquire it. This text brings the reader up close to the brutality of slavery.

In Gary Paulsen's *Sarny*, the young slave girl continues her story. As a ninety-four-year-old woman living in a nursing home in Texas, Sarny writes down her personal history. In the final days of slavery, reading spreads through the whole plantation. The story is a portrait of a strong woman who appreciates the social power of literacy and who gives back to society what her mentors have given to her. This text invites questions about how power is exercised and gained.

The next two texts show how members of the White community were allies to slaves and shared their literacy practices (cultural capital). In *Up the Learning Tree*, by Marcia Vaughan, Henry Bell, a slave child, risks his fingers getting cut off when he secretly learns how to read and write, first by eavesdropping on White children in a schoolhouse, and second, with the help of a young White teacher from the North. Even when the teacher is found out, the protagonist, Henry, continues his struggle for literacy as a way to escape slavery.

In *Alec's Primer*, by Mildred Pitts Walter, based on true events, a plantation owner's granddaughter teachers Alec Turner how to read letters, words, and sentences—illegal practices for slaves. When the plantation owner's wife discovers Alec's secret, she slashes his face with her whip. Alec is determined not to give up his primer and escapes from slavery by joining the Union Army during the Civil War. As a free man, he becomes a landowner in Vermont.

After Reconstruction, in *More Than Anything Else*, by Marie Bradby, nine-year-old Booker T. Washington wants to read the "secret in . . . books." He works from dawn until dusk in salt works with his brother and father. In his community of Malden, West Virginia, only a few people know how to read, but Booker maintains that "If I had a chance, I could do it." Race and class are implicated here. He has no access to schooling and literacy materials. The book jacket claims that this story is a "tribute to dreaming." He shows a desire for literacy, a motivation to become literate, but we must ask why he and other community members are labelled illiterate in the first place. How do U.S. race and class relations figure in this story?

Based on a passage from Richard Wright's autobiography, *Black Boy*, in

Richard Wright and the Library Card, by William Miller and illustrated by Gregory Christie, seventeen-year-old Richard borrows a White man's library card so he can access books from the local library. At the time in the 1920s, African Americans were banned from using libraries, which at that time were for Whites only. Richard reads prodigiously. He connects the lives that he has read about to his own and notes the same forms of suffering and longing for freedom as he experiences. Books offer him new possibilities for being in the world, learning about what it means to be free and summoning the strength to persevere.

In *Leon's Story*, Leon's father was left at the mercy of Mr. Johnson, partly because he could not read. Leon comments that even if his father had an education, he could only work on the farm because of the color of his skin. The Black community was relegated to farm work. Lack of access to literacy and formal education was one way racist practices were institutionalized.

Adult Literacy

Socioeconomic oppression contributes to the theme of adult literacy. Poverty bars access to and experience with dominant discursive practices. While these texts dispel the myth that all adults can read, especially all White adults, they focus on the individual, as if illiteracy were innate to these characters. The social factors that created these situations are avoided in these stories; it is as if the poverty the characters live was individually created. In what ways is illiteracy the lack of access to functional written literacy practices? Why are the other literacies adults practice in everyday life not recognized? Illiteracy is not a matter of intelligence but a symptom of sociopolitical factors. We must understand a person's literacy experiences against a broader context and ask: In what ways do school policies and teaching practices get in the way of people learning to read and write? In what ways does poverty, recognizing that race and gender are implicated, shape people's access to literacy? Code-breaker and text-user practices offer parents opportunities to support their children's learning of school literacies. In addition, these literacy practices broaden adults' employment possibilities. But are these literacy practices enough to actively enable participation in a democratic society? The goal is not just to skill unskilled groups. That is not enough. The four literacy practices model offers possibilities for adults and children to use literacies as social tools, for social transformation. Code-breaking and text-using practices lead to adults "functioning" in a society and not restructuring the power base.

Multiliteracies pedagogies (New London Group, 1996) recognize the everyday literacies of children and families. Is illiteracy possible within a multiliteracies framework? What is the equation of literacy: is it print literacies associated with the language of power? What about other modalities? Everyday literacies tend to be less recognizable and valued than the literacies associated with "doing" school. We cannot assume that people are not engaging in literacies. We should consider people's linguistic knowledge and the literacies associated with their families, communities, and work, as well as the social conditions that diminished their access to school literacies. The following texts perpetuate the myth that literacy is reading and that reading is code breaking, with meaning locked in the text. The language modes of speaking and writing, for example, are not enlisted for the learning of reading.

Jeremiah Learns to Read, written by Jo Ellen Bogart, is an idealized story of illiteracy. Elderly White farmer, Jeremiah, knows how to construct fences and prepare pancakes, but does not know how to read. The story, cast perhaps at the turn of the twentieth century, promotes the idea that illiteracy is a problem of the past. While Jeremiah gains support from a local teacher in a one-room schoolhouse, the reader never learns about the process and the hard work involved in learning to read.

Young Harry, in *Mr. George Baker*, by Amy Hest and illustrated by Jon J. Muth, narrates the story about his one-hundred-year-old African American neighbor, George, who takes an adult literacy class at Harry's school. George is a former jazz musician. The text portrays the friendship between a child and older person and their similar experiences of going to school: they carry the same book bags and use the same books, and both are learning to read. George's illiteracy needs consideration beyond the text. While it is endearing that both George and his young neighbor attend class at the same school, they are at opposite ends of formal schooling. It is never too late to learn to read, but we must consider the social factors that got in the way of George accessing school literacies in the first place as well as take stock of the literacies that George knows.

In the next several stories, the young protagonists support their parents in learning to read. Literacy learning is categorized as code breaking and text using practices. In *Papa's Stories*, written and illustrated by Dolores Johnson, young Kari enjoys her Papa's stories varying each time he "reads" a book. She grapples with the notion of literacy as an expression of intelligence, especially when she discovers that her father cannot read. Finally, Kari offers to help her father read but he has already made a good start with Kari's mother serving as his tutor. When her father is able to read the book word for word, Kari finds that she prefers his earlier renditions of the text (e.g., from *Little Red Riding Hood* to "*Little Miss Too-Big-for-Her-Red-Britches*"). Perhaps the intent here is to have young readers appreciate creativity as well as word for word reading.

In *Read for Me Mama,* by Vashanti Rahaman, Joseph, a young African American boy, loves to read. The librarian selects an easy book and a hard book for Joseph to enjoy at home. Because his mother is often tired from her work as a maid, a neighbor friend reads to Joseph. When the friend moves away, his mother admits she is unable to read and learns from a church member that she can take adult literacy classes at the local library. Mama becomes a capable reader, largely because she wants to be able to read to her son.

In *Just Juice,* by Karen Hesse, nine-year-old Juice is the middle child of five sisters of a poor family. They live in a small mountain town. The family experiences difficult times: Pa is unemployed, food is scarce, and Ma, who is diabetic, is expecting her sixth child. Juice feels challenged at school because, unlike her sisters, she still has difficulty reading. She stays home often where she is happy helping Pa in his machine shop in the yard: Juice is talented with her hands. Fairly early in the story, it becomes evident that Pa cannot read. Because he is unable to read official documents the family almost lose their home. In one of the final scenes, Ma gives birth and Juice is the only one at home to read the sugar monitor. The family survives these hardships because of their family interdependence and community support. Along with her father, Juice comes to learn about the social purpose and power of literacy.

The 11-year-old protagonist of *All Joseph Wanted,* by Ruth Yaffe Radin, details the daily challenges of an adult who is not functionally literate. Joseph convinces his mother that she needs support that an adult literacy course can provide. The reader comes to understand the frustrations, barriers and burdens adults face who cannot read. What about writing? What about the other language modes that can inform the learning of reading as well as the ones central to participating in a democratic society?

English Language Learners

The most powerful cognitive tool that children have is their first language. The U.S. Census Bureau projects that an estimated 40 percent of the school-age children by the year 2030 will need the teaching of English as an additional language. Children who speak nonstandard varieties of English will continue to need support with standard English development (Delpit & Dowdy, 2002). While cross-cultural and cross-linguistic contact is at its high in human history, language diversity has always been a reality in the United States (Spring, 2004); it is that we now recognize its presence.

Access to one's primary discourse or language is a human right (Botelho et al., in press). Keeping children away from their first language is another form of dehumanization. As Gee suggests above, secondary discourses develop from primary discourses. A child's primary discourse can inform English language learning as well as function as a meta-discourse to critique the first language and additional language learning. The difficulties that English language learners experience in schools are socially constructed because, often times, schools do not respect and draw on the linguistic and cultural resources children bring to school. Linguistic diversity is obscured by language and literacy policies and practices that attempt to undermine what children already know about language and the world. In Chapter 6, we further consider this theme because many of the protagonists in the text collection about Mexican American migrant farmworkers are English language learners.

Speaking, visually representing and writing are key language modalities reflected across these texts about English language learners. Some of the sub-themes that exist include friendships across cultures; child as translator (placing the child in adult role) and the role of the teacher in additional language education. We focus on the texts that represent teacher and student interactions with teachers who listen, interpret children's art and approximations of English, and scaffold children's speaking. (See also Chapter 6.) Some of the texts make visible the complex cognitive work that English language learners are engaged in on a daily basis.

In Aliki's *Marianthe's Story One: Painted Words*, written and illustrated by Aliki, Marianthe initially communicates with other children through her drawings. In the second story, *Marianthe's Story Two: Spoken Memories*, accessed by flipping the book over, Marianthe tells her teacher and classmates through speaking and writing about her family's lived experiences with war, famine, and immigration. Her teachers validate what she knows linguistically and culturally through inviting her to draw and speak what she knows, modalities that lead her to writing. She learns to speak, read, and write in English.

Hassan, a young Somali refugee, tells his story to his classmates through impressionistic watercolor paintings. In *The Color of Home* by Mary Hoffman, Hassan represents his home with warm colors before the soldiers invaded his village during a violent civil war. Through these watercolor representations the young protagonist conveys the message that his family "left all the colors behind in Somalia" but that the meaning of home eventually extends to his new surroundings.

Inspired by her own experiences in a New York City immigrant community, Josephine Nobisso portrays a young girl's initial days in a multicultural classroom as she tries to communicate her experience in Naples, Italy. Josephine augments her English with vocal expressions, body language, and occasional prompts from the teacher to help her convey her story. The teacher builds on Josephine's multimodal meaning making. After sharing her story verbally, she is invited to capture it in writing. In *In*

English, Of Course the young protagonist dispels some misconceptions about Italy, but some cultural stereotypes are rendered in the images of children from other cultural backgrounds.

I Hate English, by Ellen Levine, affirms attachment to one's language of origin. Mei Mei feels silenced and out of place in New York. She hates the sounds and appearance of English where "The letters stand alone and . . . bang against each other . . . Not like Chinese." She loves to write and speak in Chinese. Although there are many people in Chinatown who look and speak like her, she feels alienated and alone. She gets solace from helping out in a community center where some children speak Chinese, and others speak both English and Chinese. She discovers that she likes arithmetic because it is neither Chinese nor English.

One day a woman comes to the center to help Mei Mei learn English. She introduces Mei Mei to some children's books which challenge Mei Mei to start to learn English. However, she is afraid that she will be unfaithful to her origins and her language if she learns English. The loss of language is equated with the loss of culture and identity. Eventually, Mei Mei is willing to be convinced that English is a pathway to a parallel and satisfying second culture while she retains what she loves in her first culture, and that she will always have choices to make that are in her control. The teacher models respect and patience as she introduces the new language and culture to Mei Mei.

"Struggling" Readers and Writers

Randy Bomer and Katherine Bomer (2001) argue that the "struggling" label implies that all "struggling readers" are challenged by the same aspects of the reading process. They maintain that struggling is not failing, but demonstrates the child's intention and effort. The struggle is typically not named by the child reader, but is determined by grade-specific expectations that attempt to standardize and sequence literacy learning. Bomer and Bomer assert that anyone can struggle. What is prevalent across these experiences is that the loss of meaning is always implicated in the struggle (Bomer & Bomer, 2001: 89). In what ways do school literacies policies and practices create/contribute to these difficulties?

Cognitive-psychological perspectives of literacy attribute success and failure to individual difference and discount the influence of accessible social and cultural resources and institutional practices (Luke & Freebody, 1997). The struggle is left with the individual child, a struggle that could well be institutionally and pedagogically constructed. Psychological approaches to literacy learning standardize and sequence learning, conceptualizing learning as stages that are universally experienced by all children. This perspective decontextualizes the difficulties and inexperience a child might have, as well as dismisses the child's experience and does not build on what the child already knows. It is easier to blame the child than the system, isolating the child from sociopolitical factors that created the circumstances. There is a focus on synthetic phonics and decontextualized skills teaching, with no purpose and context for learning, reducing literacy learning to reading with code breaking as the prevalent practice. When children are permitted to use language modes with which they have experience, they offer a foundation for learning. The following texts enlist text participant and text user practices alongside code breaking practices.

In *Just Juice*, the main character is deemed a reluctant reader. It is only when her ability to read saves her mother's life and helps her family keep their house that she learns the purpose for reading and that it can afford the reader with social power.

In *Marvin One Too Many*, written by Katherine Paterson, first grader, Marvin, cannot read. He comes to reading at a slower rate than his classmates. The family rallies around. He gets support from his father by reading with him. He gets support from his sister when they play school and she constructs flash cards for him to sound out. Marvin begins to read when he encounters words that represent his own life. For example, he lives on a farm, so the word "cow" is relevant to his experience. School literacies gradually become accessible for Marvin when they are no longer disconnected from his lived experience.

The text, *Once Upon a Time*, by Niki Daly, reinforces the effectiveness of having someone (Auntie Anna) who appreciates the young child (Sarie) and to whom she can confide. Sarie moves from stammering and feeling sick when she is called upon in school to read aloud, to reading the *Cinderella* story clearly and easily. Her week-long practice with Auntie Anna with a book that she is interested in, the Cinderella story, does the trick. The story is set in South Africa but it could be any place where a child is jeered at for her school performance in reading aloud.

In *Thank You, Mr. Falker*, written and illustrated by Patricia Polacco, Trisha loves school, but like Sari, her difficulty with learning to read makes her feel inadequate. It is not until fifth grade that a new teacher helps her with her reading disability. In what ways did institutional practices contributed to this disability? Mr. Falker uses individualized teaching and invites Trisha to manipulate written language with different materials. Assumptions about knowledge are imbedded in the story: "Knowledge is like the bee that made that sweet honey, you have to chase it through the pages of a book!" Young Trisha comes to love school again and her experience as an artist is affirmed. She overcomes her reading disability and accesses school discourse through visual arts, a language mode that she knows well.

Emergent Literacy

The emergent literacy theme recognizes the range of literacy practices children engage with, reflecting their dynamic participation in language activities over time. Literacy learning occurs through participation in sociocultural activities that are based in culturally significant circumstances. Emergent literacy is connected to communities of practice, with community defined as a shared set of social practices that vary among members. The differences are historically, sociopolitically, and discursively shaped through access, exposure, experience, and apprenticing. Books about emergent literacy demonstrate that text participant and text user practices lead to code breaking, with multiple language modes valued.

In *Book!*, by Kristine O'Connell, a small child joyfully romps with his new book, finally getting his mother to read to him before he falls asleep, snuggled against the book in his bed. This is a lovely introduction to the joys of owning a book. The illustrations are purposefully of a family of color to aid in the dispelling of stereotypes.

A young child is asked by her teacher to go home and write a story in Steven Kroll's *Patches Lost and Found*. Even though writing does not come easily to the child, the teacher does not give her a prompt or invite her to tell the story to get her started on this project. When she loses her guinea pig, Patches, Jenny has her lived experience to draw from. She uses drawing and writing to locate her pet. The process of searching for Patches leads Jenny into writing the story of how he was lost and found. She uses images and words, one after another, in her search, which demonstrates how a text can be constructed. This story has implications for pedagogy: everyday life is used for literacy learning because stories live among us. The child is transformed by these literacy practices.

In *When Will I Read?*, written by Miriam Cohen and illustrated by Lillian Hoban, first grader Jim wonders when he will finally learn to read. Through actively noticing the print in his environment he comes to realize that he can read. The teacher in this story is encouraging and creates many invitations to literacy learning (e.g., labels throughout the classroom and the writing down of children's stories). This story speaks to reading as a process, supplying many wonderful examples of young children using reading and inquiry in their play throughout the classroom.

The "26 Fairmount Avenue" books, an autobiographical early chapter book series by Tomie DePaola, offer glimpses of a young boy's desire to learn how to read and write. If we use the category of desire, we assume that Tomie is naturally wanting to read and write. He grows up in a middle-class family, is school literate and has access to reading, writing, and art tools. There is a danger in assuming that when children have exposure to print and positive self-image, they will automatically succeed at reading and writing, and if that is not the case, the child tends to be blamed.

In *26 Fairmount Avenue*, the first book in the series, Tomie looks forward to his first day of kindergarten and to learning to read. Eagerly, he asks his kindergarten teacher, "When do we learn how to read?" She responds: "Oh, we don't learn how to read in kindergarten. We learn to read next year, in first grade." Tomie says, "Fine . . . I'll be back next year." He leaves the school and heads home. He returns home and waits for his parents, "holding one of [his] mother's big books, staring at it, hoping that I could learn to read by myself" (DePaola, 1999: 35).

Tomie DePaola indicates his opposition to what really are senseless rules. He is willing to compromise and abide by them. Because of the loving support of his extended family, he feels enabled and supported. The school scenarios depicted are rule-bound. For example, Tomie's name is spelled T-O-M-I-E. The schoolteachers insist that he must spell his name T-O-M-M-Y, and he obediently does so for seven years. The school tries to shape his literacy practices. Taken for granted in the stories is that Tomie can remain a child for a while. At home, there is no pressure for him to be independent; but he is encouraged to grow at his own pace.

In *Here We All Are*, the second book in the series, Tomie pronounces: "I know what I want to be. . . . I want to be an artist when I grow up. I want to draw pictures and write stories for books and sing and tap dance on the stage" (DePaola, 2001: 13). His entire extended family supports his interests by giving him drawing and writing supplies for his birthday and Christmas.

In *On My Way*, he challenges the reading practices of his first grade teacher. He "borrows" the reading text reader and masters it by asking family members and friends to assist in his practice. He returns the book to his teacher and surprises her with his newly acquired competence. She is so impressed with his ability that she signs off on a permission slip so he can have access to more books from the local public library.

Access to Books

The Library by Sarah Stewart, illustrated by David Small, tells the story of Mary Elizabeth Brown, a woman for whom books are an obsession and who has the economic means to maintain this passion. According to the text, she was born "skinny, nearsighted, and shy." Her only recreation is reading and she retains this single interest for her entire life. There is no reason a child reader would want to emulate Elizabeth's behavior. If the book's intention is to invite children into the world of reading, then it fails. Nowhere is there any indication of the titles of the books. Elizabeth's decisions are impulsive and not made with thoughtful care. She has the privilege of time and leisure. Who is the audience for this book? It may be very gratifying to elderly, upper-class, financially-secure readers. The implication here is that reading is a passive act and an isolating activity. It does not matter what books you read or how you read them.

Reading is depicted as if it were an insatiable appetite. This story might turn children off to reading: Who wants this kind of life? Who is taking care of this child? Where is her money coming from? The reader never meets her family. Where did her elderly friend come from at the end?

The Library is well intentioned but depicts, as the norm, a woman of means who seems to be anti-social and isolated. Reading should not be portrayed as uncontrollable consumption of books. What about other forms of reading?

While books only surround Elizabeth, in contrast, in *The Old Woman Who Loved to Read*, by John Winch, animals, tools, fruit, flowers, and the accoutrements of everyday farm life surround the older protagonist. Although the old woman loves to read, she is too busy managing her daily existence to spend much time with her books. When the dead of winter finally comes, the old woman does take the opportunity to catch up on her reading. The old woman reads practical books on weaving and craft making. The pile of books next to her and the list of books in the end papers demonstrate a variety of reading materials for different purposes. Some of the books are nonfiction and some are fiction. There is evidence that she uses the reading to improve her skills as a farmer.

Access to School Literacies

The role of the teacher is central to literacy learning. In the texts about English language learners (see Chapter 6), and emergent readers and writers, the interactions between children and teachers provide insights into the roles constructed by particular literacy pedagogies. Chapter 10 offers some guiding questions for the teaching of reading as a text, analyzing teacher and child roles in lessons, the source of knowledge, and what children are learning about their place in the world (Wooldridge, 2001).

It is telling that *The Year of Miss Agnes*, by Kirkpatrick Hill, is dedicated to Sylvia Ashton-Warner and other subversive teachers. Most of the teachers, who have come to this one-room school in an Alaskan fishing community, leave quickly thereafter. Miss Agnes is different in many ways. She is particularly different in the practices she uses to teach all of her students. She is respectful of the culture of the community. She manages to reach not only every child, but every adult in the community.

Fred (short for Frederika), a ten-year-old girl, is the narrator. Even though a child tells this story, there is an invitation for the reader to read between the lines. She describes the language experience approach Miss Agnes uses: The books the children write become their texts. Miss Agnes also reads aloud regularly from classic books such as *Robin Hood*. What Miss Agnes does is affirm the linguistic resources the children bring. She respects the children's life experiences and they become part of the invitations for learning. She teaches the children American Sign Language because one child is deaf. The children learn it with ease. Miss Agnes professes that schools are not just for children: "we have to keep learning all of your life" (Hill, 2000: 64). She integrates the curriculum and teaches the children about the rest of the world, while validating their own experience: "With Miss Agnes the world got bigger and then it got smaller" (Hill, 2000: 75). She understands the children's language and insists that there are many ways of speaking. The community worries that they are going to lose Miss Agnes after her one-year contract, but she comes back. She affirms children's multiliteracies by identifying children's experiences with different language modalities (e.g., drawing, American Sign Language, music, writing, and dancing).

In *Don't Say Ain't*, by Irene Smalls, Dana learns that she can maintain her two varieties of English and use them appropriately, depending on the situation. She learns that language is context dependent. She has some good models to draw on, since her teacher has successfully demonstrated her ability to speak both in Ebonics and standard English, depending on the social context. The teacher affirms the child's home literacies while helping the child to succeed within the school context to master school literacies and the language of power.

Orality

Everyone has access to oral language, but it depends on the language and language variety that determines the level of social power afforded the speaker. Orality is central to writing and reading but often is isolated from these language modes. Storytelling helps disseminate a culture's stories, values, and histories.

In *Keepers*, by Jeri Hanel Watts, young Kenyon loves listening to his ninety-year-old grandmother's stories. He also loves playing baseball. Little Dolly informs him that the family needs a keeper of stories and legends: "The Keeper holds onto the past until she can pass it on to the next." Kenyon volunteers for this important role but Little Dolly reminds him that keepers are typically girls.

For his grandmother's ninetieth birthday, Kenyon wanders from shop to shop in his town in search of a special present. A new leather baseball glove catches his eye and he buys it, thereby spending the money he saved for his grandmother's gift. He comes to realize that the perfect gift for his grandmother is writing down the stories she has told him over the years, capturing storytelling in print and carrying it on by a younger generation. Storytelling offers intergenerational learning and respect for elders, affirming a sense of community.

Storytelling brings a group of people together at an open-air market in *The Storytellers*, by Ted Lewin. The book shows a panoramic view of the marketplace. We meet many of the vendors who remind the reader of one of the benefits of their work: "We are lucky to work where we can see the sky." They also remark on how easy their work is in comparison to their neighboring vendors. The storytelling commands respect; the community values the storytelling as they lean into the stories. The story communicates the power of apprenticing between elders and the younger generation, in this case, between a grandfather and grandson. The discourse is not everyday language; it is an art form, a theatrical performance, passing on historical information.

William Miller wrote *Zora Hurston and the Chinaberry Tree*, a short biography of Zora Neale Hurston, an African American anthropologist, folklorist, and author. We learn about her gender-segregated community in Eatonville, Florida, the first all-Black, incorporated town in the United States. Her parents have different ideas about what she can do and who she can be in this small town. It is Zora's mother who invites her to dream and look beyond where she lives as she climbs the chinaberry tree, "one branch at a time." Zora crosses gender lines and observes and asks questions about what she sees and hears, (the groundwork practices of anthropological fieldwork). On her death bed, Zora's mother encourages her "to always remember what she had learned . . . [because] stories . . . kept their people alive." This text speaks to the power of oral stories for remembering history and maintaining culture, especially underrepresented cultures. Orality and listening are significant language modes.

Writing

Many children's books portray the writing process as a subtext. The metafictive or self-conscious devices call attention to different genres of writing (e.g., poetry, letters, diaries, journals). Writing can help characters name their realities and gain control of their lives through naming, synthesizing, connecting, and questioning their lived experiences (Goode, 1999), as well as allowing children to explore how language works.

Max's Words, by Kate Banks, depicts a young boy's decision to collect words from magazines, newspapers, and the dictionary, as a way to rival his brothers' stamp and coin collections. Smaller words lead to larger words. The word collection is used to label his daily activity and surroundings, and inspire storytelling, especially when the words take the shape of what they represent. His brothers organize their collections into stacks, resulting in piles of money and stamps, but when Max puts his words together he creates thoughts and stories and even his cynical brothers are impressed.

The Boy Who Loved Words, by Roni Schotter, reflects the same sentiment. The young protagonist, Selig, loves words and jots them down on pieces of paper. The children in his class make fun of Selig and call him "Wordsworth" and "Oddball." The latter name disturbs him and leads him to seek his life's purpose, at the advice from a magical genie, which leads him to new adventures with words. He collects words that sound melodious and contribute to good thoughts. He discovers the purpose for his passion for words by sharing and distributing words for community members to utilize in their everyday practices. This storyline challenges the literacy practice of "controlled" and "limited" vocabularies because it impedes literacy development and creative speaking, writing, and thinking.

The next two novels in verse portray the role of writing in helping children gain control of their lives, as well as the role that teachers can play in this process. In *Love That Dog*, by Sharon Creech, Jack, an elementary school student, unlearns assumptions about literacy learning and tells his story through journal entries of his growing acceptance of poetry writing: "I don't want to because boys don't write poetry. Girls do." His teacher, Miss Stretchberry, introduces several poems by well-known poets that transform Jack's views of poetry. These poems inspire Jack; he incorporates some of the poems' words and structures into his own work. Miss Stretchberry displays Jack's poems alongside other children's in the classroom. Jack's poems become an intertext, a blend of lived experience and voices from the other poems.

This story demonstrates the writing process and capitalizes on poetic sources of inspiration. Jack is exposed to different models and draws as well from his personal life. His journal is a catchall for these experiences, both literary and lived, and a space for Jack to tease out his questions about poetry writing. Miss Stretchberry creates multiple invitations for Jack to experiment and encourages him through her feedback and posting of his work.

Jacqueline Woodson's *Locomotion* is a series of poems written by eleven-year-old Lonnie. His parents are deceased, and he is separated from his sister Lili. He lives in a foster home and exercises his poetic spirit, with the guidance of his teacher, Ms. Marcus, through his writing at school. Lonnie writes poetry about all the issues that he thinks about in formats from rap to haiku to sonnet and many other poetic structures in between. He writes about his undirected energy, mixed-up emotions, daily observations and experiences, as well as his bittersweet memories of his family before a fire took his parents' lives because, as Ms. Marcus says, "write it down before it leaves your brain." The poems develop subtly from beginning to end, reflecting both specific school writing assignments and his emerging competence and comfort with poetic expression. Lonnie writes about racism, grief, loss, and growing up. Class and gender are implicated among these poems. He writes to survive his life. The protagonists in these novels in verse practice code breaking, text participating, text using, and text critiquing, speaking to the power of critical writing.

In *América is Her Name*, by Luis J. Rodríguez, América and her family are undocumented immigrants, living and working in Chicago. She aspires to be a poet and to belong in this place that deems her "illegal." Mr. Aponte, a Puerto Rican poet, visits her class and encourages the students to write poetry by using process writing and their home language as a resource: "There's poetry in everyone . . . Don't worry about spelling or grammar—that will come later. Write in Spanish or English, whichever feels comfortable."

América's father, who is unemployed, tries to discourage her from writing because it "won't pay the bills." Class, gender, and race are implicated here. If this story were used alone it would be problematic just as any single book would be, because there is a danger of perpetuating stereotypes about the Mexican American community. América's situation is one representation. There are many stories be told about Mexican Americans: They are not all undocumented immigrants, poor, unemployed, or abusers of alcohol. Nor are Mexican American communities replete with criminals.

The Gardener, by Sarah Stewart, illustrated by David Small, contains memorable characters and a deep sense of the hard times of the Depression. The father loses his job, and the family reluctantly decides to send Lydia Grace to the city to stay with her Uncle Jim, who owns a bakery, and who never smiles. The book contains evidence of several genres: letter-writing, realistic fiction, and picture book, making it a genuine hybrid and acknowledging how unproductive it is to label this text as a single genre.

The story is told through a series of letters that Lydia Grace, a child who is unflappable, creative, and resourceful, writes home to her grandmother and the rest of her family. Subtle messages appear through the illustrations, such as the fact that Uncle Jim's two valued workers, who are also his close friends, are African American. Lydia Grace makes an important contribution to her uncle and his friends, and they reciprocate. Left unsaid are the causes and impact of the Depression, but discussion can lead to questions, conversations, and research about this period in U.S. history.

Critical Literacies

Critical literacies acknowledge the role that language plays in social processes; they connect language use to the power relations of the socio-political context. Critical literacies pedagogies make visible how children are offered multiple subject positions through the discourses imbedded in the texts and images to which they have access. If children are taught from early childhood onward that language and texts are sites for ideological struggle, they learn to resist dominant messages that dictate who they are, who they should be, and what they can do and not do. Few texts reflect text critic practices among the characters. We located three titles, with two that have anthropomorphic farm animals. Typically, animal characters distance the reader from the issues grappled with in the text.

The cows on Farmer Brown's farm protest the work conditions and issue their complaint via typewritten letters in *Click, Clack, Moo*, by Doreen Cronin. The cows go on strike and the chickens join the effort. Farmer Brown enlists the help of a neutral party, Duck. The hilarious text exemplifies the process of negotiation and the role that writing can play in such work.

In the sequel, *Giggle, Giggle, Quack*, Cronin continues the story of the farmyard animals whose literate activities create problems for Farmer Brown. He goes on vacation and leaves his brother Bob in charge of the farm, but with an admonition: "keep an eye on Duck. He's trouble." Unfortunately, Bob is no match for the wily duck and his animal friends.

Once Upon a Cool Motorcycle Dude, written by Kevin O'Malley, show-cases the negotiation processes of collaborative writing and the possibilities for critical writing. A young girl and boy create a fairy tale together but challenge and "rewrite" each other's gendered renderings. They both try to overcome storylines that portray girls in pretty and passive roles and boys full of brawn.

Unless they are able to read and write for social change and justice, readers and writers will find themselves confirming and perpetuating existing meanings determined by dominant ideologies. While we must consider what children read, we concur with Peter Hunt (1992), that we should also consider "how they think about what they read." A critical multicultural analysis brings ideologies into a sharper relief and fosters critical multicultural consciousness and social change. Critical multicultural analysis is powerful literacy because it utilizes literacy for "reading" the discourses that have created us, as well as aligning ourselves with subjectivities (ways of being in the world) and discourses that will mobilize us toward democratic participation in society.

Classroom Applications

- Ask children to investigate home literacy practices and create a class book based on their findings. (See Compton-Lilly, 2004 for guidelines.) Compare these practices with what they do at school. What are the similarities and differences? Invite the children to represent their findings through multimodalities (e.g., visual arts, photography, poetry, speaking, digital technologies, dance). Use these assignments as windows into children's lived experiences outside of school.
- After children do a critical reading of a passage or children's book, invite them to create a visual representation of their process as critical multicultural analysts.
- Examine language use in Doreen Cronin's children's books that are diaries of different animals such as a worm, spider, and fly (e.g., *The Diary of a Worm*). These texts depict the possibilities of journaling as ways to document and name everyday occurrences. The entries are told from the perspective of a worm, for example, which invites the reader to consider how language use is specific to the animal's experience.
- Analyze texts about libraries. Consider issues of access and social function. Here are some titles to begin with:
  - *The House of Wisdom* by Florence Parry Heide and Judith Heide Gilliland.
  - *A Library for Juana: The World of Sor Juana Inés* by Pat Mora.
  - *The Librarian of Basra: A True Story from Iraq* by Jeanette Winter.
  - *My Librarian is a Camel: How Books are Brought to Children Around the World* by Margriet Ruurs.

Recommendations for Classroom Research

- Take stock of your literacies history. Create two columns on one sheet of paper. Make a list of your home literacies on the left side of the paper and school literacies on the right side. Which modalities were recognized within each context? Compare and contrast both lists. What are the similarities and differences? What do the similarities and differences signify? How can this reflection inform your teaching of literacies and children's literature? What questions emerged from this analysis?
- Analyze in what ways are multimodalities are represented in children's books. What are the explicit and implicit ideologies about these multiple forms of expression as reflected in these texts? Share your findings with your students.

Suggestions for Further Reading

Barton, David. (2007). *Literacy: An introduction to the ecology of written language.* Malden, MA: Blackwell Publishers.

Booth, David. (2007). *Reading doesn't matter anymore: A new way to look at reading.* Toronto: Pembroke/Stenhouse Publishers.

Cervetti, Gina, Pardales, Michael J. & Damico, James S. *A tale of differences: Comparing the traditions, perspectives, and educational goals of critical reading and critical literacy.* Retrieved on November 7, 2006, from www.readingonline.org.

Gee, James. (2008). *Social linguistics and literacies: Ideology and discourses.* (3rd ed). New York: Routledge.

Larson, Joanne. (2005). *Making literacy real: Theories and practices for learning and teaching.* Thousand Oaks, CA: Sage.

Larson, Joanne. (Ed.). (2007). *Literacy as snake oil: Beyond the quick fix (New literacies and digital epistemologies).* New York: Peter Lang.

Meacham, Shuaib J. & Buendia, Edward. (1999). Modernism, postmodernism, and poststructuralism and their impact on literacy. *Language Arts,* 76(6), 510–516.

Pahl, Kate & Rowsell, Jennifer. (2005). *Literacy education: Understanding the New Literacy Studies in the classroom.* Thousand Oaks, CA: Paul Chapman.

Shannon, Patrick. (2007). *Reading against democracy: The broken promises of reading instruction.* Portsmouth, NH: Heinemann.

References

Children's Books

Aliki. (1998). *Marianthe's Story One: Painted Words; Marianthe's Story Two: Spoken Memories.* New York: Greenwillow.

Banks, Kate. (2006). *Max's Words.* Illustrated by Boris Kulikov. New York: Farrar, Straus & Giroux.

Bloom, Becky. (1999). *Wolf!* Illustrated by Pascal Biet. New York: Orchard Books.

Bogart, Jo Ellen. (1997). *Jeremiah learns to read.* Illustrated by Laura Fernandez & Rick Jacobson.

Bradby, Marie. (1995). *More than anything else.* Illustrated by Chris K. Soenpiet. New York: Orchard Books.

Cohen, Miriam. (1996). *When will I read?* Illustrated by Lillian Hoban. New York: Yearling.

Creech, Sharon. (2001). *Love that dog.* New York: HarperCollins.

Cronin, Doreen. (2000). *Click, clack, moo: Cows that type.* Illustrated by Betsy Lewin. New York: Simon & Schuster Books for Young Readers.

Cronin, Doreen. (2002). *Giggle, giggle, quack.* Illustrated by Betsy Lewin. New York: Simon & Schuster Books for Young Readers.

Daly, Niki. (2003). *Once upon a time.* Illustrated by author. New York: Farrar, Straus & Giroux.

DePaola, Tomie. (1999). *26 Fairmont Avenue.* New York: G. P. Putnam's Sons.

DePaola, Tomie. (2001). *Here we all are.* New York: G. P. Putnam's Sons.

DePaola, Tomie. (2001). *On my way.* New York: G. P. Putnam's Sons.

Hesse, Karen. (1998). *Just Juice.* New York: Scholastic.

Hest, Amy. (2004). *Mr. George Baker.* Illustrated by Jon J. Muth. Cambridge, MA: Candlewick Press.

Hill, Kirkpatrick. (2000). *The year of Miss Agnes.* New York: Margaret K. McElderry Books.

Hoffman, Mary. (2002). *The color of home.* Illustrated by Karin Littlewood. New York: Phyllis Foselman Books.

Johnson, Dolores. (1994). *Papa's stories.* Illustrated by author. New York: Macmillan.

Kroll, Steven. (2001). *Patches lost and found.* Illustrated by Barry Gott. New York: Winslow.

Levine, Ellen. (1989). *I hate English*. Illustrated by Steve Björkman. New York: Scholastic.

Lewin, Ted. (1998). *The storytellers*. Illustrated by author. New York: Lothrop, Lee & Shepard.

Miller, William. (1994). *Zora Hurston and the chinaberry tree*. Illustrated by Cornelius Van Wright and Ying-Hwa Hu. New York: Lee & Low.

Miller, William. (1998). *Richard Wright and the library card*. Illustrated by Gregory Christie. New York: Lee & Low.

Nobisso, Josephine. (2002). *In English, of course*. Illustrated by Dasha Ziborova. New York: Gingerbread.

O'Connell, Kristine. (2001). *Book!* Illustrated by Maggie Smith. New York: Clarion Books.

O'Malley, Kevin. (2005). *Once upon a cool motorcycle dude*. Illustrated by Carol Heyer & Scott Goto. New York: Walker & Co.

Paterson, Katerine. (2001). *Marvin one too many*. Illustrated by Jane Clark Brown. New York: HarperCollins.

Paulsen, Gary. (1993). *Nightjohn*. New York: Delacorte Press.

Paulsen, Gary. (1997). *Sarny: A life remembered*. New York: Delacorte Press.

Polacco, Patricia. (1998). *Thank you, Mr. Falker*. New York: Philomel Books.

Radin, Ruth Yaffe. (1991). *All Joseph wanted*. Illustrated by Deborah Kogan Ray. New York: Macmillan.

Rahaman, Vashanti. (1997). *Read for me, Mama*. Illustrated by Lori McElrath-Eslick. Honesdale, PA: Boyds Mills Press.

Rodríguez, Luis J. (1997). *América is her name*. Illustrated by Carlos Vásquez. Willimantic, CT: Curbstone Press.

Schotter, Roni. (2006). *The boy who loved words*. Illustrated by Giselle Porter. New York: Schwartz & Wade Books.

Smalls, Irene. (2003). *Don't say ain't*. Illustrated by Colin Bootman. Watertown, MA: Charlesbridge Publishers.

Stewart, Sarah. (1995). *The library*. Illustrated by David Small. New York: Farrar, Straus & Giroux.

Stewart, Sarah. (2001). *The gardener*. Illustrated by David Small. New York: Farrar, Straus & Giroux.

Tillage, Leon. (1997). *Leon's story*. Illustrated by Susan L. Roth. New York: Farrar, Straus & Giroux.

Vaughan, Marcia. (2003). *Up the learning tree*. Illustrated by Derek Blanks. New York: Lee & Low Books.

Walter, Mildred Pitts. (2004). *Alec's primer*. Illustrated by Larry Johnson. Middlebury, VT: Vermont Folklife Center.

Watts, Jeri Hanel. (1997). *Keepers*. Illustrated Felicia Marshall. New York: Lee & Low.

Winch, John. (1997). *The old woman who loved to read*. New York: Holiday House.

Woodson, Jacqueline. (2003). *Locomotion*. New York: G. P. Putnam's Sons.

Secondary Sources

Bernard, H. Russell. (1999). Languages and scripts in contact: Historical perspectives. In D. A. Wagner, R. L. Venezky & B. Street (Eds.), *Literacy: An international handbook* (pp. 22–28). Boulder, CO: Westview Press.

Bomer, Randy & Bomer, Katherine. (2001). *For a better world: Reading and writing for social action*. Portsmouth, NH: Heinemann.

Botelho, Maria José. (2007). *Naming practices: Defining critical multicultural literacies*. Orbit, 36(3), 27–30.

Botelho, Maria José, Cohen, Sarah, Leoni, Lisa, Chow, Patricia, & Sastri, Padma. (in press). Respecting children's cultural and linguistic knowledge: The pedagogical possibilities and challenges of multiliteracies in schools. In M. L. Dantas & P. Manyak (Eds.), *Learning from/with diverse families: Home-school connections in a multicultural society*. New York: Routledge.

Carspecken, Philip Francis. (1996). *Critical ethnography in educational research: A theoretical and practical guide.* New York: Routledge.

Compton-Lilly, Catherine. (2004). *Confronting racism, poverty, and power: Classroom strategies to change the world.* Portsmouth, NH: Heinemann.

Cope, B. & Kalantzis, M. (Eds.). *Multiliteracies: Literacy learning and the design of social futures.* New York: Routledge.

Diamond, Jared. (1999/1997). Blueprints and borrowed letters. In *Guns, germs, and steel: The fates of human societies* (pp. 215–238). New York: W. W. Norton & Company, Inc.

Delpit, Lisa & Dowdy, Joanne Kilgour. (2002). *The skin that we speak: Thoughts on language and culture in the classroom.* New York: New Press.

Dillon, Sam. (2008). An initiative on reading is rated ineffective. *The New York Times,* May 2.

Gee, James. (2001). What is literacy? In P. Shannon (Ed.), *Political, too: New readings and writings on the politics of literacy education* (pp. 1–9). Portsmouth, NH: Heinemann.

Geringer, Jennifer K. (2001). *Visiting the lightbulb lab: Images of multi-layered literacies in children's literature.* Unpublished dissertation, University of Wyoming.

Goode, Erica. (1999). Can an essay a day keep asthma or arthritis at bay? *The New York Times,* April 14.

Goodman, Kenneth S. (1967). Reading: A psycholinguistic guessing game. *Journal of the Reading Specialist,* 4, 126–135.

Hall, Kathy. (2003). *Listening to Stephen read.* New York: Open University Press.

Hunt, Peter. (Ed.). (1992). *Literature for children: Contemporary criticism.* New York: Routledge.

Ivanic, Roz. (1998). *Writing and identity: The discoursal construction of identity in academic writing.* Philadelphia, PA: John Benjamins.

Kuhlman, Wilma & Lickteig, Mary. (1998). Literacy as change agent: Messages about reading and writing in children's literature. *Journal of Children's Literature,* 24(2), 84–93.

Luke, Allan. (2000). Critical literacy in Australia: A matter of context and standpoint. *Journal of Adolescent & Adult Literacy,* 43(5), 448–461.

Luke, Allan & Freebody, Peter. (1997). Shaping the social practices of reading. In S. Muspratt, A. Luke & P. Freebody, *Constructing critical literacies* (pp. 185–225). Cresskill, NJ: Hampton Press.

Luke, Allan & Freebody, Peter. (1999). A map of possible practices: Further notes in the four resources model. *Practically Primary* 4(2), 5–8.

McCall, Cecelia. (1989). A historical quest for literacy. *Interracial Books for Children Bulletin,* 19(3 & 4), 3–6.

New London Group. (1996). A pedagogy of multiliteracies: Designing social futures, *Harvard Educational Review,* 66, 60–92.

Resnick, Daniel P. & Gordon, Jay L. (1999). Literacy in social history. In D. A. Wagner, R. L. Venezky & B. Street (Eds.), *Literacy: An International Handbook* (pp. 16–21). Boulder, CO: Westview Press.

Saenger, Paul. (1999). The history of reading. In D. A. Wagner, R. L. Venezky & B. Street (Eds.), *Literacy: An International Handbook* (pp. 11–15). Boulder, CO: Westview Press.

Serafini, Frank. (2004). Images of Reading and the Reader. *The Reading Teacher,* 57(7), 610–617.

Shannon, Patrick. (1989). *Broken promises: Reading instruction in twentieth-century America.* Westport, CT: Bergin & Garvey.

Spring, Joel. (2004). *Deculturalization and the struggle for equality: Brief history of the education of dominated cultures in the United States* (4th ed.). Boston: McGraw-Hill.

Steiner, Stanley & Joy. (1999). Navigating the road to literacy. *Book Links* (March), 19–24.

Street, Brian. (1993). *Cross-cultural approaches to literacy.* New York: Cambridge University Press.

Teale, William H., Paciga, Kathleen A. & Hoffman, Jessica L. (2007). Beginning reading instruction in urban schools: The curriculum gap ensures a continuing achievement gap. *The Reading Teacher,* 61(4), 344–348.

Turbill, Jan (2002, February). The four ages of reading philosophy and pedagogy: A framework for examining theory and practice. *Reading Online,* 5(6).

Willis, Madge Gill. (1995). African American communication tradition—Oral and literate. In Osayimwense Osa (Ed.), *The all White world of children's books and African American children's literature* (pp. 55–73). Trenton, NJ: Africa World Press, Inc.

Wilson, Lorraine. (2002). *Reading to live.* Portsmouth, NH: Heinemann.

Wooldridge, Nathalie. (2001). Tensions and ambiguities in critical literacy. In B. Comber & A. Simpson (Eds.), *Negotiating critical literacies in classrooms.* Mahwah, NJ: Lawrence Erlbaum Associates.

CHAPTER 4

Deconstructing Multiculturalism in Children's Literature

Culture is one of the most complex words in the English language (Eagleton, 2000). How we define culture shapes how we understand social difference and the literary category of multicultural children's literature. Confining the definition of culture to "the complex whole" of values, customs, beliefs and practices, which make up the lifeways of a particular group (Tylor, 1871/1958) does not take power into account. Culture, as the complex whole, is a mismatch with our globalized world.

Culture and power are bound up together. Placing a text within its sociopolitical context opens up the dominant cultural assumptions imbued in its language and images. The definition of culture with which readers align themselves shapes their reading in particular ways, and certainly influences what they deem worthy of notice and analysis (Eagleton, 2000). Embracing a more complex view of culture repositions readers as researchers and creators of language, literature, literacies, and society. We need to situate cultural analysis within larger analyses of sociopolitical contexts and processes. Children's literature is a product of culture as well as evidence of power relations; it is a social transcript of the power relations of class, race, and gender.

Critical multicultural analysis builds on Clifford Geertz's (1973) understanding of culture, which historically views social life as symbolic and meaning making; it is "a web of meaning" encoded in a culture's symbolic forms such as language and literature. Sherry Ortner (1994) maintains that Geertz's great contribution to the theoretical construct of culture is that culture is not something locked inside people's heads, but rather is embodied in public symbols, symbols through which the members of a society communicate their worldview, value-orientations, ethos, and all the rest to one another ... Culture is a product of acting social beings trying to make sense of the world in which they find themselves, and if we are to make sense of a culture, we must situate ourselves in the position from which it was constructed.

(Ortner, 1994: 374–275)

A Geertzian concept of culture invites us to read culture as text for its underlying assumptions while others highlight its dynamism.

Marietta Saravia-Shore and Steven F. Arvizu (1992) and Brian Street (1996) define culture as a verb, demonstrating that culture is a historical and sociopolitical process. Saravia-Shore and Arvizu maintain that culture is a "dynamic, creative, and continuous process" (1992: xvii). Like Street, they further define it as the active interaction of opposing systems of values, beliefs, practices, norms, conventions, and power relations, which have been shaped by the sociopolitical history of a nation in the interests of its privileged members.

Sonia Nieto and Patty Bode (2008) define culture as "the values, traditions, worldview, and social and political relationships, and worldview created, shared, [negotiated], and transformed by a group of people bound together by a combination of factors that can include a common history, geographic location, language, social class, religion, or other shared identity" (171). Like Nieto and Bode, we align ourselves with a definition of culture as not static, isolated, permanent, inflexible, or bounded by hard perimeters, but dynamic, relentlessly changing, and influenced by historical, sociopolitical, and economic factors. Culture is thus learned, and not biologically determined, sociopolitically constructed, "porous" (Rosaldo, 1989), and always dialectical. History and the workings of power such as domination, collusion, resistance, and agency exist at its center. To try to separate culture from this interplay of power systems is to suggest that racism, classism, and sexism do not exist or that these political forces do not shape culture.

James Paul Gee's definition of "Big D" Discourses inserts power relations and how power is exercised into the meaning of culture. According to Gee (1999), Discourses are "socially accepted associations among ways of using language [e.g., speaking, listening, writing, reading, representing, and viewing], of thinking, valuing, acting, and interacting, in the 'right' places and at the 'right' times with the 'right' objects (associations that can be used to identify oneself as a member of a socially meaningful group or 'social network')" (17). Integrating Discourse into the concept of culture injects its definition with the processes of how power is exercised, as well as foregrounding diversity, multiple and shifting identities, contradictions, and the sociopolitical systems of class, gender, and race. It is locating "large-scale ideological formations." Examining culture as a sociopolitical critique of these power networks makes visible how race, class, and gender work in the U.S. context and exposes their global implications. Critical multicultural analysis of race, gender, and class ideologies in children's literature reveals the historical and sociopolitical dimensions of culture.

By examining the sociopolitical factors that contributed to the history of multiculturalism in children's literature, we retrace the institutional practices that led to the history of underrepresentation of various cultural groups in children's literature. In constructing a historical analysis of multicultural children's literature, that is, of the power relations and knowledge central in establishing the discourse of multicultural children's literature, the resistance and agency of communities of color and their allies are foregrounded, as they demand representation in children's literature.

The History of Multiculturalism in Children's Literature

All literature is a product of culture. Multicultural children's literature has been defined as literature by and about people of color. It is bound to the history of all literature and multicultural education, and tied to trends in publishing. It is linked politically to social movements to include underrepresented populations.

In the United States, people of color were virtually invisible in children's literature prior to the 1960s. When they were rendered in text, for the most part, they were stereotypically represented. The literary category of multi-cultural children's literature developed out of this historical and socio-political context (Larrick, 1965/1995; MacCann & Woodard, 1985; Osa, 1995; Rudman, 1976/1995; Sims, 1982; Wader, 1997).

Charlemae Rollins, a librarian with the Chicago Public Library, com-piled *We Build Together*, an annotated bibliography of books about African Americans. The recommended books were for elementary and high school students. The National Council of Teachers of English published the first of three editions in 1941.

Reading Ladders for Human Relations, first published in 1947, is a book-list that grew out of an American Council on Education sponsored project to find materials and techniques for improving human relations, a goal of intergroup education, with an emphasis on interracial harmony and interpersonal relations. These annotated bibliographies are organized in "ladder" themes, "perhaps because [the editors] saw them as necessary steps to take along a continuum of ever-increasing contacts with others" (Tway, 1981: 3). The ladders include: growing into self, relating to wide individual differences, interacting in groups, appreciating different cultures, and coping in a changing world. Several editions were published over a 35-year span. These booklists, used by teachers, librarians, and parents, promoted better human relations dislocated from a historical, sociopolitical context. *Reading Ladders for Human Relations* was largely informed by intergroup education which devotes little attention to power relations.

In 1954, the social climate after the Supreme Court desegregation ruling in *Brown v. Board of Education* forced mainstream publishing houses to confront the prevalence of ethnic stereotypes in children's literature (Wader, 1997). African Americans were recruited to join the field of publishing as authors, illustrators, and editors. The New York Public Library began publishing an annual annotated bibliography, *Books About Negro Life for Children.* (In 1963, the title was changed to *The Black Experience in Children's Books.*) This bibliography was published intermittently until 1994, highlighting the expansion of multiethnic voices in children's literature. It was not until after Nancy Larrick's (1965) article, "The All-White World of Children's Books," which called national attention to this underrepresentation, that publishers took note of their practices of exclusion and stereotyping. The increase of multicultural representation in children's literature was a direct response central to the historical and sociopolitical reality of American children's literature.

Nancy Larrick's (1965) survey of 5,000 trade books published for children during 1962, 1963, and 1964, found that only 6.7 percent of the books had one or more Black characters. Many of these characters were featured as backdrop or rendered as slaves, servants, sharecroppers, migrant or menial workers. If the institutionalized omission of African Americans from children's literature was not challenged and dealt with, Larrick argued that "There seem[ed] little chance of developing the humility so urgently needed for world cooperation, instead of world conflict, as long as our children are brought up on *gentle doses of racism* [our emphasis] through their books" (Larrick, 1965: 2). Larrick's findings confirmed what the African American librarians Charlemae Rollins and Augusta Baker (Harris, 1993) had observed all along.

It is important to note that Nancy Larrick did not initiate concern about the invisibility of African Americans in children's literature (Harris, 1993). According to Violet Harris, Larrick's efforts overshadowed the work of Virginia Lacy, Charlemae Rollins, and Augusta Baker. Larrick used her situated social power to call attention to this invisibility: she was a White person with strong connections to the library and publishing worlds. The work of the Council on Interracial Books for Children (late 1960s through late 1980s), Masha Kabakow Rudman's *Children's Literature: An Issues Approach* (1976), and Rudine Sims' [Bishop] *Shadow and Substance* (1982) roused further attention to the biased practices of publishers.

Multicultural children's literature as a literary category emerged in the 1960s during the Civil Rights Movement and the growing attention to multicultural education and teaching. During the late 1960s and early 1970s activists in ethnic studies, multiethnic movements, and the African American community, frustrated with the slow pace of desegregation, demanded more community control over their schools with a goal of infusion of Black history into the curriculum (Banks, 1995).

As schools responded to the African American community's demands, groups such as Mexican Americans, Puerto Ricans, Native Americans, and Asian Americans, who also experienced institutional racism and classism, put pressure on schools for representation in the curriculum and school life as well. According to James A. Banks (1995), it was during this time that "a rich array of books, programs, curricula, and other materials that focused on the histories and cultures of ethnic groups of color was edited, written, or reprinted" (Banks, 1995: 10). In this next section we draw heavily on the historical sketch compiled by Rosa E. Wader (1997), featured in *The New Press Guide to Multicultural Resources for Young Readers*, and Kathleen T. Horning and Ginny Moore Kruse's (1991) chapter, "Looking into the Mirror: Considerations Behind the Reflections."

During the late 1960s and early 1970s, several organizations and awards promoted children's literature that reflected underrepresented cultural groups. In 1967, the Council on Interracial Books for Children was founded by a culturally diverse group of writers, librarians, teachers, and parents to advocate for anti-racist children's literature and educational materials, and to create a forum for the sociopolitical analysis of children's books. They sponsored a contest for "Third World Writers." (Walter Dean Myers, an African American writer, won this contest in 1968 and published his first children's book with Parent Magazine Press, a mainstream publisher.)

In the mid-1970s, the Council expanded its mission to include the interrogation of sexism, homophobia, ableism, ageism, classism, and language discrimination. Toward the end of the 1970s, this organization published books on Indian stereotypes, human and anti-human values in children's books, and guidelines for selecting bias-free textbooks and storybooks. These guidelines were distributed to libraries, national teaching associations and other agencies, and adults working with children. The Council's list, "*Ten Quick Ways to Identify Racism and Sexism in Children's Books*," is still used today. (Many books on the theory and practice of multicultural education have included this list as a resource for educators.) This group also produced filmstrips on such issues as unlearning stereotypes about Native peoples and Puerto Ricans, and on gender roles. They also produced *Interracial Books for Children Bulletin*, a quarterly publication, and on occasion, bimonthly when the Council published special issues. This publication focused on educational issues, critical reviews of children's literature and other teaching resources, and served as a gadfly to the established publishing houses.

During the 1970s and 1980s, many national organizations were formed to promote awareness about underrepresentation in curriculum materials and children's literature: The Japanese American Curriculum Project called attention to Asian American children's books; and, the REFORMA group of the American Library Association and the Center for the Study of Books in Spanish for Children and Adolescents at California State University, San Marcos requested authentic literature by Latina/o authors. Since 1985 the Cooperative Children's Book Center at the University of Wisconsin-Madison has documented the number of books written or illustrated by artists of color, containing characters of color. African American artists were the first group to be included in this documentation.

During this time, several new independent publishers opened their doors for business: Lollypop Power Press specialized in non-sexist multicultural and bilingual picture books; Arte Público Press, which focused exclusively on the U.S. Latina/o experience, with books in both English and Spanish; and, the Children's Book Press published books featuring underrepresented groups and languages. The materials available from these new publishers provided multiple perspectives, as well as storylines where the characters of color were at the center of the story, and not simply rendered in relation to White society.

Several new annual awards emerged during the 1970s and 1980s, bringing authors and illustrators of color into the fold. (See Appendix A for more children's book awards information.) The Coretta Scott King Award was established by the American Library Association for authors and illustrators of African descent whose works promote an understanding and appreciation of the "American Dream," as defined by Martin Luther King Jr.'s work for peace and world brotherhood. The Carter G. Woodson Award, from the National Council for Social Studies, encourages treatment of topics related to ethnic minorities and race relations.

In the meantime, writers and illustrators of color were recognized for their work through mainstream awards: Tom Feelings became the first African American artist to win a Caldecott Honor Award in 1972. Nicholasa Mohr became the first Puerto Rican writer to win the Jane Addams Children's Book Award in 1974. Virginia Hamilton was the first author of color to win the Newbery Medal award in 1975. Laurence Yep was selected as the first Chinese American author to receive a Newbery Honor Book Medal in 1975. Leo and Diane Dillon, an interracial couple, earned the 1975 Caldecott Award for illustrating *From Ashanti to Zulu*, by Margaret Musgrove, an African American author. Ed Young became the first Chinese American to win the Caldecott Award in 1990 for illustrating his retelling of *Lon Po Po: A Red-Riding Hood Story from China*.

In 1985, the Cooperative Children's Book Center, a children's literature library of the School of Education at the University of Wisconsin-Madison, began documenting the number of books by and about African Americans. In 1994, the Center added Asian Pacific/Asian Pacific Americans, American Indians, and Latinos to the list. The Center defines multicultural literature as books by and about people of color. They publish an annual publication, *CCBC Choices*, which provides publishing statistics and an annotated bibliography of noteworthy titles.

Oyate, an educational organization that focuses on the portrayal of Indigenous peoples in children's literature, was founded in 1987 and incorporated in 1990. This group's goal is for all children to learn "the truth of history" (www.oyate.org). Their website offers text analyses of selected books, a list of books to avoid, and announcements of workshops to assist teachers in uncovering anti-Indian biases in children's materials. In-house publications include *Through Indian Eyes: The Native Experience in Books for Children* (1987/1998/2006) and *A Broken Flute: The Native Experience in Books for Children* (2005), both edited by Doris Seale and Beverly Slapin, founding members of Oyate.

All of these organizations and awards mark some of the ways underrepresented groups and their allies struggle for equality and equity within the publishing world of children's books.

In Joel Spring's (2004) brief history of deculturalization, he documents the struggle for educational equality within the Native American, African American, Latino American, and Asian American communities, groups that have been historically silenced, and offers a historical background for understanding the narrow definition of multiculturalism in children's literature. He defines the process of deculturalization as a stripping away of one culture to replace with a dominant culture. Many scholars of children's literature (Harris, 1993, 1997; Huck et al., 2001; Mitchell, 2003; Norton, 1999; Temple et al., 2006; Tomlinson & Lynch-Brown, 2002), building on the scholarship of Rudine Sims Bishop (1992; 1997; with Cai, 1994), define multicultural children's literature as literary works that focus on African Americans, Native Americans, Latino Americans, and Asian Americans. These cultural groups have been demeaned or rendered invisible both in literature and society. Against this historical scaffold, the definition of multicultural children's literature developed and became accepted through its pedagogical application (Cai & Bishop, 1994) and publishing practices (Ford, 1994).

The Sociopolitical Context of Children's Literature

The publishing of children's literature does not occur in a vacuum. Children's literature is a social institution; it reflects our larger society. The writing, illustrating, and publishing of children's books are influenced by society whose institutions still discriminate against individuals based on their race, ethnicity, class, gender, language, age, ability, and sexual orientation. Critical multicultural analysis leads readers to "reading the world" (Freire, 1970/1985), as Geertz (1973) argues, "To see social institutions, social customs, social changes as in some sense 'readable' is to alter our whole sense of what such interpretation is . . ." (Geertz, 1973: 31). Extending the notion of text beyond the written word on paper draws our attention to how meaning is inscribed in practice and how, through discourse, institutions work and exercise power. Critical multicultural analysis connects discursive practices to institutional and political power structures: Its goal is to disrupt intellectual and social hierarchies and contribute to the "refiguration of social thought" (Geertz, 1973: 19). By using historical and sociopolitical lenses, critical multicultural analysis problematizes childhood, children's literature, reading, and the enterprise of publishing children's books.

When the world of children's books was all White, children who were not in the privileged majority felt invisible and demeaned. In the past twenty years, publishers have attempted to acknowledge, through their publishing decisions, the need for portraying diversity in books. In 2006, of the approximately 5,000 children's book titles published, 546 were by and/or about people of color (Horning, Kruse, Rudiger & Schliesman, 2006). The percentages are still skewed toward the White-Northern European-Protestant-middle-class society. However, there are several publishers like Arte Público Press, the Children's Book Press, Just Us Books, Lee & Low, and Shen's Books that focus particularly on publishing books featuring underrepresented populations. Some of the large publishers also have small imprints (e.g., Hyperion Books for Children's Jump at the Sun) and sections in their catalogs (e.g., HarperCollins and Scholastic) devoted to these cultural experiences. (See Appendix B for more information on small presses.)

There are more than 345,880 children's books currently available for purchase in the United States from 15,190 U.S. publishers (Bowker, 2005). This figure represents more than three times as many books available to children now than a decade ago. Information compiled by the Cooperative Children's Book Center (CCBC) indicates that out of the 5,000 new titles published every year in children's literature, the number of books by and about people of color has rarely reached more than ten percent. (In 2007, CCBC received 3,000 children's books out of the 5,000 new titles.)

The CCBC's definition of multicultural literature is "books by and about people of color" (Horning, Lindgren, Michaelson, & Schliesman, 2008: 3). The Center's statistics for 2007 indicate a decrease from the 2002 publishing activity (when the Center began disaggregating its statistics for children's books by and about people of color) of books with African/ African American (166 to 150 new titles), American Indian (64 to 44 new titles), Asian Pacific and Asian Pacific American (91 to 68 new titles), and Latino/a (94 to 59) themes. At the same time, in 2007, there was an increase from 2002 in the number of books (out of the above titles) created, that is, written and/or illustrated, by African/African Americans (69 to 77 new titles), American Indians (remained at 6 for both years, with an increase to 14 in 2006), Asian Pacifics/Asian Pacific Americans (46 to 56). Books written and/or illustrated by Latinos/as decreased from 46 to 42, with an increase to 50 in 2005. Given the publishing industry's increasing concentration in the hands of eight multinational corporations (Hade & Edmondson, 2003; Taxel & Ward, 2000) and despite the intermittent publishing increase during the past ten years, the power relations of class, race, and gender still have a hold on children's book publishing. (See Appendix B for more information on conglomerates.)

Publishing trends are shaped by the distribution of power in the United States. In some instances, the increase in publishing by writers and illustrators of color reflects independently owned small presses' publishing activity (e.g., Lee and Low, Just Us Books, Third World Press, The Children's Book Press, Cinco Puntos, Arte Público Press, and Shen's Books). Joel Taxel and Holly M. Ward (2000) propose that adults and children can "exert some form of economic pressure on publishers (possibly through a selected boycott) to publish the kinds of books our children need . . . [while] join[ing] our colleagues in the publishing industry in resisting the increasingly tyrannical bottom-line imperatives of the market" (Taxel & Ward, 2000: 58). Daniel Hade and Jacqueline Edmondson (2003) argue that children should be able to experience books "without being subject to the homogenized, synergized, commercialized texts dominating the children's book market today" (143). Young and adult readers' book selecting and buying habits can challenge these imperatives by placing "economic pressure" that can contribute to the redistribution of power.

The Scholarship on Multicultural Children's Literature

Violet Harris and Arlette Willis (2003) maintain that definitions of multicultural literature are fluid and linked to shifting historical, sociopolitical, and economic contexts. These definitions are influenced by developments in multicultural education, critical pedagogy, and critical literary criticism. From its historical developments, children's literature by and about people of color was a response to racist social and publishing practices that led to the underrepresentation and disempowerment of people of color in U.S. society, curricula, and children's literature. The scholarship of multicultural children's literature mostly focuses on the conceptualization of its definition.

Rudine Sims Bishop (1982) conducted one of the seminal studies on the "cultural substance" of children's literature, that is, how cultural values influence social interaction and people's lives. She surveyed books published by and about African Americans between 1965 and 1979, and published her findings in the National Council of Teachers of English publication, *Shadow and Substance*. She maintains:

> At issue is not simply "racial background," but cultural affinity, sensitivity, and sensibility .... The irony is that as long as people in positions of relative power in the world of children's literature—publishers, librarians, educators—insist that the background of the author does not matter, the opportunities for Black writers will remain limited, since they will have to compete with established non-Black writers whose perspective on the Afro-American experience may be more consistent with that of the editors and publishers and whose opportunities to develop their talents as writers have been greater.
>
> (Sims Bishop, 1982: 13–14)

Three considerations grounded Sims Bishop's analysis of 150 realistic fiction books featured in *Shadow and Substance*. The first consideration was the implied reader of the book. Who is the target audience of the text? Is the book written for White children about Black people? Is the book for Black children about Black people? She argued that the primary audience influences both the theme and content of the book. The second consideration was the tension between viewing the United States as a culturally homogeneous society and a population comprised of a diversity of many cultures. This period of time (1965–1979), Sims Bishop maintains, contains evidence of African American writers' and illustrators' reclamation of their culture. The third consideration examined the book's cultural perspective or focalization. Did the book reflect an insider's viewpoint of African American culture or was it an outsider's perspective? These guiding questions led Sims Bishop to organize the 150 books into the categories of social conscience, melting pot, and culturally conscious, which created a framework for her analysis.

The social conscience books reflected U.S. society prior to 1970. These books chronicle the interpersonal effects of desegregation: conflicts emerging when African American students desegregate White schools; how White children cope with prejudice and discrimination against African American friends; Blacks and Whites working together within the power structure of the time; and Black children becoming friends with White children.

The melting pot stories focused on racial integration. Twenty five per cent of the books were told from a White child's point of view. While 30 percent of the books portrayed racial integration, Black children as main characters were depicted in integrated settings outside of their families. The remaining 30 percent of the stories focused on Black children within the context of their families and communities.

The last category, culturally conscious, consisted of books that placed Black characters at the center of the story. These stories were told from their perspective. Some aspect of the text and images represented the African American experience.

These three categories emerged out of a particular place and time in children's literature and U.S. society. Sims Bishop's (1991) assertion is that "if you want authentic African American experience, go to the people who have lived it and who bring those life experiences to bear on creating literature for children" (Sims Bishop, 1991: 34–35). And once you become familiar with these experiences, Sims Bishop contends that readers will develop background knowledge of the African American culture, offering points of reference, as they encounter new books and authors.

The first and second editions of *The Black American in Books for Children: Readings on Racism* (1972/1985), edited by Donnarae MacCann and Gloria Woodard, further examined the portrayal of the Black experience in children's books, especially on early racist representations (e.g., *The Adventures of Huckleberry Finn*), twentieth-century fiction and biography, picture books, and international and legal issues. In the first edition of *Children Literature: An Issues Approach* (1976), Masha Kabakow Rudman advocated for a "critical, or issues, approach," that is, a "critical examination of the books in the light of how they treat contemporary social problems and conditions" (Rudman, 1976: 3). She devoted two chapters to literature about African Americans and Native Americans, building on the criteria developed by the Council on Interracial Books for Children. Comprehensive annotated bibliographies of good books about these cultural groups were included. (The third edition, published in 1995, combines these chapters and expands the notion of multicultural literature to looking at heritage in literature. Heritage is broadly defined to include all cultural groups, with special consideration of underrepresented groups.)

The All White World of Children's Books and African American Children's Literature, published in 1995 and edited by Osayimwense Osa, opens with Nancy Larrick's *Saturday Review* article (*op. cit.*) and explores issues of African American representation in text and illustration, orality and literacy, and multiple genres. One chapter looks at developments in African American children's literature since the sixties: While African American writers are represented in each genre, the author asserts that realism dominates the fiction of the 1990s as it did in the 1970s and 1980s.

These texts by Sims, MacCann and Woodward, and Osa, and one chapter by Rudman, focus on the specific history of the African American experience in children's literature and bring together scholarship that grounds the overall research of multicultural children's literature. These scholars highlight the issues of underrepresentation, misrepresentation, cultural authenticity, and the artist's social responsibility. This research lays the groundwork for defining multicultural literature as books about and by people of color.

The early studies of multiculturalism in children's literature focused on African Americans, Asian Americans, Latino Americans, and Native Americans. The term multicultural children's literature gained recognition in the late 1980s: *The Horn Book Guide* editors adopted the term alongside the categories of Afro-American and Black (Harris & Willis, 2003). Multicultural literature gained wider acceptance because of the scholarly (i.e., publishing of books and journal articles, and conference presentations), pedagogical (i.e., developments in multicultural education and whole language), and publishing activities (e.g., editing, book reviewing, awards). Multicultural literature's early definition focused on race and ethnicity. By the mid-1990s, the definition of multicultural literature expanded to include other groups and issues such as gender, class, sexual orientation, ability, age, religion, and geographical location.

In "Multiple Definitions of Multicultural Literature: Is the Debate Really Just 'Ivory Tower' Bickering?" Mingshui Cai (1998) argues that at the center of this debate is "how many cultures are included in multicultural literature" (Cai, 1998: 312). He identifies three principal definitions in the research of multicultural literature: (1) the focus on "people of color"; (2) the assumption that "multiple + culture = multiculturalism"; and, (3) the assertion that "all literature is multicultural." The issues of insider/outsider and cultural authenticity, deemed basic criteria for

evaluating multicultural literature, emerge from these definitional developments. Static and bounded notions of culture that essentialize these
cultural groups further complicate these debates.

People of Color

Along with Harris (1993; 1997), Sims Bishop (1993; 1997), Cai and Sims
Bishop (1994), Barrera, Thompson, and Dressman (1997), and Yokota
(2001), the Cooperative Children's Book Center (Lindgren, 1991) argues
that we must focus on the populations who have experienced exclusion
and marginalization such as African Americans, Native Americans, Latino
Americans, and Asian Americans. CCBC's working definition of multicultural children's literature is that it is literature by and/or about people
of color. Sims Bishop (1993) outlines three types of multicultural literature: culturally specific, generically American, and culturally neutral. Culturally specific literature speaks to a particular cultural experience, for
example, illuminating specific language, religious, and family differences.

Multicultural literature that is generically American portrays characters
of color but leaves out cultural specificity (e.g., books with universal
themes). Culturally neutral literature acknowledges people of color, but
focuses on other topics (e.g., informational books). While culturally
neutral and specific stories echo Sims Bishop's (1982) earlier classifications
of melting pot and culturally conscious books, generically American books
are dissimilar from social conscience stories, another category from her
1982 study, because social conscience books come out of the particular
historical conditions of desegregation, whereas generically American
books show African Americans integrated into U.S. society. All of these
categories speak to the book's focalization or point of view, which positions
the characters in specific power relations.

Cai and Sims Bishop (1994) offer new ways to categorize multicultural
literature into three classifications—world literature, cross-cultural literature, and parallel culture literature—in an attempt to reconcile the tension
between pedagogical and literary approaches to defining the term multicultural literature. They further argue that these terms are political,
"implying at the very least an intent to include the literatures of underrepresented peoples, American and otherwise, in the curriculum of schools
in the United States" (Cai & Sims Bishop, 1994: 62). Thus, all of these types
of multicultural literature focus on the historically underrepresented
communities.

Cai and Sims Bishop define world literature as literature that includes
literary works (e.g., folktales, fiction) of "other underrepresented groups
outside the United States" (Cai & Sims Bishop, 1994: 62). Cross-cultural
literature is "(1) literary works explicitly about interrelations among

people of different cultures, without apparent focus on the unique experience of any other culture or cultural group, and (2) those about people from a given cultural group by a writer from another cultural group" (p. 65). This category highlights the "gaps between the author's cultural perspective embodied in the literary work and the cultural perspective of the people his or her work portrays" (Cai & Sims Bishop, 1994: 65). Cai and Sims Bishop argue that many children's books fall under this category of multicultural literature.

Finally, parallel culture books are "written by authors from parallel cultural groups to represent the experience, consciousness, and self-image developed as a result of being acculturated and socialized within those groups" (Cai & Sims Bishop, 1994: 66). This last category showcases a culture's shared experience, its "collective subjectivity" (Eagleton, 2000). Cai and Sims Bishop argue that parallel culture authors are best qualified to represent their cultural experience and parallel culture literature best serves the goals of multicultural education.

Many scholars (Rochman, 1993; Schwartz, 1995; Shannon, 1994) caution against definitions that reduce multiculturalism to racial essentialism. According to Patrick Shannon, "Such treatment allows most teachers and students to stand apart from multiculturalism, as if it were only about The Other and not about themselves" (Shannon, 1994: 2). He argues that all books "demonstrate the complexity of multiculturalism" (Shannon, 1994: 3).

Sims Bishop responds:

> I would answer, first of all, that if multiculturalism has been equated with racial issues, it is not because Violet Harris or I have made it so. America is, and has been for centuries, a racialized society . . . That is why the canon is what it is. That is why the image of the African-American in "mainstream" American literature, including children's literature, for so long had been either pathetic or laughable or non-existent. It is because race matters that people confuse race and culture. Black people and other people of color have been segregated, discriminated against, and worse; and part of our designs for living, our cultures, have evolved out of the conditions under which we have lived.
>
> (Sims Bishop, 1994: 7)

Like Sims Bishop, Toni Morrison (1992) argues that the United States is a historically "racialized" society with its literature formed and shaped by the four-hundred-year-old African and African American presence. She maintains that this presence needs consideration: "The contemplation of this black presence is central to any understanding of our national literature and should not be permitted to hover at the margins of the literary imagination" (Morrison, 1992: 5).

Race and ethnicity are social constructions and should be at the center of any discussion about all literature, but it is a limited perspective all by itself, because racial oppression interfaces with classism and sexism. Hazel Rochman argues that "Too many lists of so-called multicultural books function only as a well-meaning spotlight—shining brightly but briefly on one cultural island or another, providing overdue recognition, yes, but imposing a different kind of isolation, celebratory but still separate" (Rochman, 1993: 14). In many ways multicultural literature as literature about people of color isolates these cultural groups from power relations.

Multiple + Culture – Multiculturalism

Rochman (1993) advocates for a definition that means "across cultures, against borders" while not just referring to people of color. Julia Candace Corliss (1998) calls for a "literature of diversity" that "reflects the broad range of human experience and global kaleidoscope of cultures" (5). She emphasizes literature about and by people of color because of the disparity in publishing practices.

Corliss includes European American literature when those books "add to the kaleidoscope of human experience and connect to an aspect of the overall theme of crossing borders" (Corliss, 1998: 5). Junko Yokota (1993) places emphasis on the "multi" part of the term multicultural and defines multicultural literature as "literature that represents any distinct cultural group through accurate portrayal and rich detail" (157).

More recently, Yokota (2001) rejects this definition and argues for a multiethnic literature because "a focus on ethnicity-related issues in litera-ture allows us to consider the sociopolitical, economic, and cultural issues shared by ethnic groups that lie outside the mainstream" (xiv). Yokota advocates for an expanded view of diversity, while "recogniz[ing] that different kinds of diversity are not necessarily parallel in their issues and that although some issues affecting a range of diverse group are the same or at least similar, others are quite different" (Yokota, 2001: xiv).

Cai (1998) argues, "If the issues of inequality, discrimination, oppres-sion, and exploitation are excluded from consideration when we try to define multicultural literature, there is a danger of diluting, or even decon-structing, the social, political concept that underlies the term" (313). He further states "a definition of multicultural literature should therefore draw a demarcation line between the literature of the dominant main-stream culture and that of marginalized culture" (Cai, 1998: 313). While the definitions by Rochman, Corliss, and Yokota are idealistic and do not acknowledge the privileging and punishing systems of class, race, and gender, distinguishing between dominant and dominated groups is also problematic: Power relations are rendered as dualisms. Power is a complex matrix. However, expanding the definition of multicultural literature to include other groups is important, because it acknowledges the fact that all groups originate from historical and sociopolitical associations and disassociations and that all literature is a cultural product.

Toward the end of the 1990s and early 2000s, the definition of multicultural literature expanded in some of the research. Frances Ann Day (1999) broadens the definition by including European American authors in her multicultural literature resource book for teachers. In her book, *Multicultural Children's Literature: Through the Eyes of Many Children*, Donna Norton (2001) never explicitly defines multicultural literature, but includes Jewish Americans in her study of multicultural literature. Daphne Muse (1997) contends that works of multicultural literature are "books that chronicle, acknowledge, and examine the values, perspectives, and experiences of groups that have been marginalized because of race, gender, ethnicity, language, ability, age, social class, religion/spirituality, and/or sexual orientation . . . [they are] works written for, by, and about people of all cultures and backgrounds" (1).

All Literature is Multicultural

Shannon's (1994) commentary on multicultural literature is that all people have multiple social memberships, and perhaps these identities can link people across social lines. Cai (1998) argues against this position because the sociopolitical basis for the creation of multicultural literature is undermined when this happens. Examining how all literature is culturally coded and the multiple identities of characters and readers, as well as embracing a wider understanding of power relations, rejects "the idea that a dominant White Anglo-Saxon Protestant culture is the single force of acculturation in the United States" (Allender & Adams, 1999: 33). All literature is multicultural, showing the complexities of intercultural relations as well as cultural hybridity; other social memberships work together with race. Multiple perspectives, cultural similarities and differences broaden our understanding of multiculturalism, while highlighting the complex web of power relations. Schwartz (1995) points out that Shannon's article, "I Am the Canon: Finding Ourselves in Multiculturalism," summons us to "struggle against the canon, a struggle to foster an inclusive multiculturalism within a full-fledged social analysis of the relations between language, culture, and power . . ." (Schwartz, 1995: 637). While all the scholars associated with the above definitions of multicultural literature are committed to multicultural education, their social analyses differ considerably.

Children's Literature and Critical Multicultural Analysis

Schwartz argues that multicultural children's literature is problematic in several ways:

1. it signifies that [W]hite is the normative term against which all other groups are defined as "Other";
2. it is an exclusive term that signifies a social group based on perceived differences and described in the idiom of biology as opposed to the idiom of culture;
3. ultimately, it leads to the exclusion of other issues that may be represented within multicultural children's literature, such as issues of class, gender, disability, religion, and sexual orientation; and
4. the use of terms such as "people of color" and "parallel cultures" may ultimately be more divisive than liberating and more disempowering than empowering within the full context of inequitable power relations in western capitalist society.

(Schwartz, 1995: 641)

While definitions of multicultural literature refer to the demand of historically marginalized groups to be heard and represented in the literary history of the United States, these conceptualizations can be divisive and essentializing. They assume a one-directional power base (i.e., oppressed and oppressor), that is, power is owned, while culture is static and bounded. These definitions isolate race from the power relations of class and gender, as if they do not influence racism. These explications do not take into account that social identities are multiple, contradictory, and shifting. The assumption imbedded in multicultural literature is that there is a single meaning coming from a single writer. Thus, language, culture, and power are seen as fixed and stable, but cultural difference is historically and sociopolitically constructed.

Prejudice and discrimination occur not just because people lack cultural information or contact, but also because there are institutional policies and social practices in place that are racist, classist, and sexist. If we agree that all literature is socially constructed, then we accept the understandings that texts are historically, socially, politically, and discursively constructed. In doing so, we no longer privilege middle-class, White, Anglo-Protestant Americans by assuming that their culture is monolithic and accepted as the norm and that all others are "Other" and separate from the norm. We also acknowledge that reading is a sociopolitical activity influenced by society's institutions that privilege some groups over others as well as by individual experiences, values, and biases. These are significant shifts from the conventional approach to literary study and multicultural criticism.

In the Council on Interracial Books for Children's *Human and (Anti-Human) Values in Children's Literature*, published in 1976, the authors conclude that any language decision, whether oral or written, is a political one that emerges from a particular sociopolitical context. A critical multicultural analysis of children's literature posits that all literature is a historical and cultural product, inscribed with the dominant ideologies of a particular place and time. Critical multicultural analysis builds on the scholarship that advocates for reading critically and multiculturally.

In 1976, the Council on Interracial Books for Children questioned the source of values imbedded in children's books. They argued that they were not from individual writers, but from society as a whole: "Children's books generally reflect the needs of those who dominate that society ... the prevailing values are supportive of the existing [power] structure" (Council on Interracial Books for Children, 1976: 1).Their criteria, they claimed, emerged from a particular time. Their values checklist brought race, gender, class, age, and the like together. The Council maintained that values were imbedded in the words and images.

Critical teachers, Bill Bigelow (1994) and Herbert Kohl (1995a), advocate for reading children's books that challenge the way things are and how we perceive the past. Bigelow outlines the key elements of critical multicultural curriculum and teaching. Kohl discusses the characteristics of "radical children's literature":

1. the major force in the story is the community, beyond the family;
2. the conflict involves a whole community, class, ethnic group, nation;
3. a wide range of collective action is present;
4. the presence of an enemy who has abused power and who is nevertheless a three-dimensional person or group of people, not an abstract force;
5. the story depicts comradeship as well as friendship and love; and finally,
6. there is not a compulsory happy ending or resolution of the problem. Hope and possibility are evident.

(Kohl, 1995a: 66–68)

Bigelow and Kohl promote reading and stories that stretch children's social imagination and complicate their understanding of power.

Several scholars in the field of children's literature advocate for reading children's literature against race, class, and gender ideologies, so readers can become aware of how these systems of power work in society (Ching, 2005; Hade, 1997a & 1997b; Harris, 1999; Harris & Willis, 2003; Mendoza & Reese, 2001; Nodelman & Reimer, 2003; Rogers & Soter, 1997; Schwartz,

1995; Yenika-Agbaw, 1997). (It should be noted that many of these scholars still use the literary category of multicultural children's literature.) They move away from simplistic definitions of culture and argue for bringing history, culture, and power together.

Critical multicultural analysis draws from the above multiple definitions of multicultural literature. It is grounded in the historical silence of under-represented groups, keeping this history of underrepresentation at the center, while bringing the interrogation of the complexities of power relations into the fold. It is grounded in a definition of multiculturalism that affirms diversity and resists the "comfort zone of multiculturalism" (Nieto & Bode, 2008; Jackson & Solís, 1995; Kanpol & McLaren, 1995) by going beyond affirmation and difference, and by examining hegemony and issues of social power. Critical multicultural analysis of children's literature examines the complex web of power in our society, the interlocking systems of race, class, and gender and how they work together. It focuses on the process of analysis rather than the simple presence of characters who are people of color.

Reading Class, Race, and Gender

Anthropologist Sherry Ortner (1991) argues that even though class is a reality in the United States, "class is not a central category of cultural discourse in America, and the anthropological literature that ignores class in favor of almost any other set of social idioms—ethnicity, race, kinship—is in some ways merely reflecting this fact" (Ortner, 1991: 169). Anthropological research, like other social science inquiry, tends to overlook class because it is a layer of reality that we do not talk about. The American Dream ideology contributes to this silence in public and academic discourse. Ortner notes: "The United States has glorified opportunity and mobility, and has presented itself as more open to individual achievement than it really is" (Ortner 1991: 171). The U.S. ideology around social mobility masks class, racial, and gender inequities, placing the blame of economic oppression on the individual. What happens, according to Ortner, is that class gets displaced into the discourses of ethnicity, race, and gender, with the latter two social identities greatly shaped by class.

Sarah Theule Lubienski (2003), a professor of education, claims that class is not explored in educational research because researchers tend to focus on the affirmative characteristics of diversity, a response to "blame the victim" research trends. Another reason, Lubienski offers, is our "national discomfort" with addressing the presence and endurance of classism in the United States and acknowledging our own class privilege.

As a society, we believe that domination is inevitable (Guinier & Torres, 2002). Furthermore, class definitions have moved away from the dualisms of the "haves" and "have-nots" to definitions that reflect the complexities of power relations. Lubienski maintains that social class has been over-looked in education research because "differing ethnic and language tradi-tions can be viewed in strictly positive lights, [but] it is hard to view diversity in wealth and power in the same way" (Lubienski 2003: 32). This research elision is present in the scholarship of children's literature.

In surveying the research on U.S. children's literature, we have found a lack of scholarship exists in the analysis of class (Krips, 1993; Wojcik-Andrew, 1993). (This is broadly the case throughout the world although some exists by British scholars examining British children's literature (Dixon, 1977, Leeson, 1977). In their research, the British literary critic Peter Hunt (1992) and the Australian literary critic John Stephens (1992) treat class broadly by analyzing ideology in children's literature.)

In the 1954 edition of *Reading Ladders for Human Relations*, economic differences are discussed as a way to expose young readers to a "wide range of economic privilege" (Heaton & Lewis, 1954: 83). The books recom-mended show how many people live under different economic circum-stances and how those class positions will lead the reader to recognize "the handicaps and privileges that exist for particular people in the com-munities in which students live" (Heaton & Lewis, 1954: 85). Class issues are relegated to the individual and never discussed as system of power.

The next edition (Crosby, 1963) of this reading sourcebook asks adults to consider books that deal with change by sharing the following questions with children: "What does change come from? What does change, in given case, do to people? How do people make changes? What is the role and responsibility of the individual in change?" (Crosby, 1963: 157–158). While these questions remain with the individual, they invite the reader to think about change as it is depicted in children's literature.

In the fifth edition, change is dealt with more specifically and linked to "changing historical, social, and economic conditions" (Reid, 1972: 262). The editors argue that the books included in this "reading ladder" will remind readers that change is inevitable because "life is not static." Social change is naturalized in this discussion as something that has a life of its own and that people are not the cause of its instability. The focus here is on how the characters endure change. In the sixth edition, edited by Eileen Tway (1981), economic differences reside with the individual. A complaint is issued that the rich are not depicted in children's books.

In the guidebook for parents, educators, and librarians, the Council on Interracial Books for Children (1976) examines class relations as values of elitism, materialism, and individualism. The value of conformity is part of this checklist because, as the Council maintains, conformity "discourages readers from questioning whether the 'usual' way of doing things is best for all people concerned. It serves to prop up the status quo" (Council on Interracial Books for Children, 1976: 21). In their values matrix, these values co-exist with other values for analysis such as sexism, ageism, and racism. The Council's work brings these power relations together and attempts to show the complexity of social identities and values.

The Council published two analyses of class issues in children's literature during the early 1980s. The first, published in 1982, is an investigation of how class and race work together in children's books about the American Revolution. Joel Taxel conducted the study and found that the books overwhelmingly presented the Revolution from the middle- and upper-class perspective. He comments:

> Although several books point out that colonial America provided unprecedented opportunity for personal advancement, they stop short of explicitly pointing out that this greater freedom was restricted to [W]hites, and even then, not to all [W]hites. And, of course, none mention that this "advancement" was achieved at the expense of Native peoples who were either killed or dispossessed.
>
> (Taxel, 1982: 8)

This perspective constructed a false universality of experience, masking the difference in participation and insight among other groups. Jan Goodman's study, published in 1985, examined a set of books on the U.S. economy and how it works. Her study revealed many distortions and incomplete information about U.S. capitalism in the interest of "indoctrinat[ing] our children with a pro-capitalist view" (Goodman, 1985: 8). These two studies substantiate the claim that children's literature contributes to the social legend that we live in a classless society, permeated with equal opportunity for all.

One study conducted by Patrick Shannon (1986) analyzed books from *The Reading Teacher*'s "Children's Choice" list to see if these books offered individualist, collectivist, or balanced perspectives. He discovered that 29 out of the 30 books examined provided an individualist message, an ideology linked to capitalism, while only one offered a balanced perspective (the protagonist pursued self-development but not at the expense of family and community commitments).

Herbert Kohl's (1995a, b, & c) critical essays on children's literature address issues of power, including colonialism, racism, sexism, and classism. He makes a plea for "radical children's literature," books that resolve conflict collectively and make visible the forces of power.

The Pleasures of Children's Literature (Nodelman & Reimer, 2003) is one of the only survey texts often used in the teaching of children's literature in undergraduate and graduate education (Huck et al., 2001; Norton, 1999; Russell, 2001; Temple et al., 2006; Tomlinson & Lynch-Brown, 2002) that considers class and ideology. Perry Nodelman and Mavis Reimer claim that texts written during the same time and place tend to have shared ideologies. Therefore, if readers know something about the cultural and historical context in which the book was written, they can make the connections to its temporal and cultural contexts. Nodelman and Reimer further maintain: "Readers can develop a better understanding of literature by learning something about the culture or period of history that produced it. They can also develop a better understanding of a culture or period of history by reading the literature it produced" (Nodelman & Reimer, 2003: 152).

The books that Nodelman and Reimer cite are products of British culture, but they pose some critical questions that are relevant to the U.S. context: Which class distinctions are important and how are they portrayed? What are the author's assumptions about social hierarchy? Is social inequality taken for granted? They also suggest that one way to get at the assumptions of a text is to have readers look at the story from the point of view of the story characters featured from the lower socioeconomic class. Assumptions can also be uncovered if we look at the story from the point of view of the characters of color and the women.

Nina Mikkelsen (2000), in her book, *Words and Pictures: Lessons in Children's Literature and Literacies*, addresses ideology in children's literature. She cites Peter Hollindale's (1988) work on ideology. Hollindale claims that ideology can explicitly or implicitly be rendered in text, and that language is inherently ideological. Mikkelsen outlines Hollindale's scholarship and invites the scholar/reader to think further about issues of elitism, authenticity, and censorship.

Diana Mitchell (2003) takes up the power relations of race, class, and gender in her book, *Children's Literature: An Invitation to the World*. She offers criteria, which echo the efforts of the Council on Interracial Books for Children, for evaluating the presence of class or socioeconomic bias in children's books. Many of the criteria deal with stereotypes about working class or poor people. Some of her guiding questions include: "Are middle- and upper-class authority figures shown solving the problems of the working class or poor? Are they seen as successful only if they embrace the values of the middle and upper class? Would the portrayal be hurtful to a child in the working class or living in poverty?" (Mitchell, 2003: 184). Mitchell uses the theoretical construct of power to ground her criteria. These criteria could also be used to examine stereotypes about people of color and women.

More recently, in *Interpreting Literature with Children*, Shelby A. Wolf

(2004) devotes a chapter to issues of culture and class. But the chapter falls short of any structural analysis of cultural and class relations. Culture and class are left with the families in the stories analyzed. Wolf uses a transactional lens for reading books about migrant workers. In transactional criticism, the reader's lived experience guides her or his response to the text. While Wolf mentions the value of a sociocultural interpretation of the text, that is, analyzing power, she does not take up this position in her chapter. She provides a fixed and stable definition of culture and, while class is shaped by work, the power system of class is overlooked. Intragroup cultural differences are defined as "a range of lifestyles," which, we argue are constructed by the power relations of class, race, and gender.

The dissertation research by Edward L. Starkenburg (1999) represents the most recent comprehensive examination of class issues in U.S. children's literature. He uses the class markers of appearance, authority, capacity for making choices, career, housing, knowledge, language, social mobility, money, possessions, and status feelings as analytical tools to identify class representation in five award-winning works of fiction. He locates several silences of the authors, that is, what the authors do not say about social class, which, he concludes, impacts the readers' understanding of how society is organized and how social class shapes this organization.

Starkenburg finds that authors do not acknowledge that social class exists or take a position on its presence. The sampled authors do not indicate that "life is good regardless of class status" nor that "hard work can mobilize and move people up the hierarchy" (Starkenburg, 1999: 159). The ideology of the American Dream was not central to his text sample, but Starkenburg maintains "our culture still clings to its message" (Starkenburg, 1999: 159). In summing up, Starkenburg claims that these silences translate into the position that social class is unavoidable, shaping people's lives, with minimal possibilities for overcoming these social circumstances. Overall, the characters go along to get along in a stratified system. These silences perpetuate dominant class ideology.

Starkenburg concedes that while he extracted class from the social triad of class, race, and gender to magnify how class is rendered in text, race and gender were implicated in the texts he analyzed. He strongly recommends further research as essential to our understanding of the interlocking systems of racism, sexism, and classism, research that looks at these power relations together, in order to understand and resist dominant class ideologies.

In contributing to this dialogue, our intent is to invite teachers, librarians, undergraduate and graduate students, teacher educators, and scholars of children's literature into a process of ideological deconstruction, grounding them in textual analysis that is based on the theoretical perspectives of feminist poststructuralism, critical theory, and cultural studies. They, in turn, can guide children in reading dominant discourses of race, class, and gender, and identify how ideology is rendered in the materials they read and are exposed to. Like Terry Eagleton (1996), we believe that all texts and literary theories are ideological, and that knowing this can be a source of power, enabling readers to identify the processes of their own social shaping. We acknowledge the power of literature to inform and inspire, and we believe that a critical multicultural perspective creates the opportunity and space for young readers to take a socially responsible stance and to be open to ethical decision-making.

In the next chapter, we reclaim the mirror metaphor as a reflection of how language use is a reflection of our society. The discourse of multicultural children's literature is investigated. We then consider the theoretical constructs that ground critical multicultural analysis. Power is considered against the multi-layered lens of critical multicultural analysis.

We theorize critical multicultural analysis of children's literature and discuss the theoretical constructs of discourse, ideology, subjectivity, and power because they lead the reader to locate how the power relations of class, race, and gender are exercised in text. We develop a continuum of how power is exercised as a tool for making visible the reading subject positions offered by the text. Lastly, we demonstrate how the multi-layered and recursive nature of critical multicultural analysis works.

Classroom Applications

- Invite children to represent their understandings of culture through drama, visual arts, poetry, music, digital technologies, movement, and other modalities. Compare and contrast their understandings across these texts. Collaboratively reflect on these perceptions, document new understandings, and identify dimensions for further inquiry.
- In groups of four, invite students to select a children's book to analyze, using a critical multicultural lens, focusing on class.
- Survey the awards that are particular to your region. Which genres are honored by these awards? Storylines? Cultural groups?
- Log on to a book award site and review the award winners over the years. (See Appendix A.) Which cultural groups and storylines were recognized? Which ones are missing? Compare winners across awards. Analyze these patterns against the history of children's literature (Chapter 1) and multiculturalism in children's literature (Chapter 3). What are the implied reader positions? What ideologies are imbued in these stories?
- Critically analyze the criteria for a particular book award through a

mock selection process. In what ways can you rewrite (i.e., revise and/or expand) these practices?

- Create a book award(s) to recognize texts that are overlooked by current book award practices.
- Invite children to examine the books that are available for purchase in the stores their families frequent. Which titles are present? Cultures? Storylines? Genres? Who does the book ordering for the store? Consider findings in class.
- Invite children to interview the local children's librarian about self-publishing practices. How many books does the library purchase that are self-published? Which genres are represented? Cultures? Languages? Consider findings in class.
- R. R. Bowker, the global manager of bibliographic information, reports that there has been a dramatic decline in the overall publishing of children's books (R. R. Bowker, 2007). Invite children to speculate on the social practices contributing to this decline.
- Invite them to take note of the types of texts available for children in large chain bookstores.

Recommendations for Classroom Research

- Examine the scholarship of gender and children's literature. In what ways are race and class taken up in this research? What is missing? What are the gaps?
- Examine the book selecting and buying practices of your school. Which publishers benefit from these practices? Reconsider these practices and collaborate with colleagues on restructuring them.

Suggestions for Further Reading

Ada, Alma Flor. (1990/2003). *A magical encounter: Latino children's literature in the classroom* (2nd ed.). Boston: Allyn and Bacon.

Bishop, Rudine Sims. (2007). *Free within ourselves: The development of African American children's literature.* Portsmouth, NH: Heinemann.

Cai, Mingshui. (2002). *Multicultural literature for children and young adults: Reflections on critical issues.* Westport, CT: Greenwood Press.

Fox, Dana L. & Short, Kathy G. (2003). *Stories matter: The complexity of cultural authenticity in children's literature.* Urbana, IL: NCTE.

Harris, Violet J. (Ed.). (1993). *Teaching multicultural literature in grades K–8.* Norwood, MA: Christopher-Gordon Publishers.

Harris, Violet J. (Ed.). (1997). *Using multiethnic literature in the K–8 classroom.* Norwood, MA: Christopher-Gordon Publishers.

McGillis, Roderick. (Ed.). (2000). *Voices of the other: Children's literature and the postcolonial context.* New York: Garland Publishing.

Osa, Osayimwense (Ed.). (1995). *The all White world of children's book and African American children's literature.* Trenton, NJ: Africa World Press.

Rudman, Masha Kabakow. (1995). *Children's literature: An issues approach.* New York: Longman.

Seale, Doris & Slapin, Beverly. (Eds.). (2005). *A broken flute: The Native experience in books for children.* Walnut Creek, CA: Altamira Press; Berkeley, CA: Oyate.

Slapin, Beverly & Seale, Doris. (1987/2006). *Through Indian eyes: The Native experience in books for children* (3rd ed.). Berkeley, CA: Oyate.

References

Allender, Dale & Adams, Pat. (1999). Multicultural literature: an essay. *Multicultural Perspectives,* 1(2), 33–37.

Banks, James. (1995). Multicultural education: Historical development, dimensions, and practice. In J. A. Banks & C. A. McGee Banks (Eds.), *Handbook of research on multicultural education* (pp. 3–24). New York: Simon & Schuster Macmillan.

Barrera, Rosalinda B., Thompson, Verlinda D. & Dressman, Mark (Eds.). (1997). *Kaleidoscope: A multicultural booklist for grades K–8* (2nd ed.). Urbana, IL: NCTE .

Bigelow, Bill. (1994). Good intentions are not enough: Children's literature in the aftermath of the Quincentenary. *The New Advocate,* 7(4), 265–279.

Bishop, Rudine Sims. (1991). Evaluating books by and about African-Americans. In M. V. Lindgren (Ed.), *The multicolored mirror: Cultural substance in literature for children and young adults* (pp. 31–44). Fort Atkinson, WI: Highsmith Press.

Bishop, Rudine Sims. (1993). Multicultural literature for children: Making informed choices. In V. J. Harris (Ed.), *Teaching multicultural literature in grades K–8* (pp. 37–53). Norwood, MA: Christopher-Gordon Publishers.

Bishop, Rudine Sims. (1994). A reply to Shannon the canon. *Journal of Children's Literature,* 20(1), 6–8.

Bishop, Rudine Sims. (1997). Selecting literature for a multicultural curriculum. In V. J. Harris (Ed.), *Using multiethnic literature in the K–8 classroom* (1–19). Norwood, MA: Christopher-Gordon Publishers.

Cai, Mingshui. (1998). Multiple definitions of multicultural literature: Is the debate really just "ivory tower" bickering? *The New Advocate,* 11(4), 311–324.

Cai, Mingshui & Bishop, Rudine Sims. (1994). Multicultural literature for children: Towards a clarification of the concept. In A. H. Dyson & C. Genishi (Eds.), *The need for story: Cultural diversity in classroom and community* (pp. 57–71). Urbana, IL: NCTE.

Ching, Stuart H. D. (2005). Multicultural children's literature as an instrument of power. *Language Arts,* 83(2), 128–137.

Cooperative Children's Book Center. (2008). *Children's books by and about people of color published in the United States.* Retrieved on May 15, 2008, from www.education.wisc.edu/ccbc/books/pcstats.htm.

Corliss, Julia Candace. (1998). *Crossing borders with literature of diversity.* Norwood, MA: Christopher-Gordon Publishers.

Council on Interracial Books for Children. (1976). *Human (and anti-human) values in children's books.* New York: Author.

Crosby, Muriel Estelle. (1963). *Reading ladders for human relations.* Washington: American Council on Education.

Day, Frances Ann. (1999). *Multicultural voices in contemporary literature: A resource for teachers.* Portsmouth, NH: Heinemann.

Dixon, Bob. (1977). Class: Snakes and ladders. In *Catching them young: Sex, race and class in children's fiction* (pp. 42–93). Bristol, UK: Pluto Press.

Eagleton, Terry. (1996). *Literary theory: An introduction.* (2nd ed). Minneapolis: The University of Minnesota Press.

Eagleton, Terry. (2000). *The idea of culture.* Malden, MA: Blackwell.

Ford, Michael Thomas. (1994). The cult of multiculturalism. *Publisher's Weekly*, July 18, 30–33.

Foucault, Michel. (1980). *Power/knowledge: Selected interviews and other writings, 1972–1977.* New York: Pantheon.

Freire, Paulo. (1970/1985). *Pedagogy of the oppressed.* New York: Continuum.

Gee, James Paul. (1999). *An introduction to discourse analysis: Theory and method.* New York: Routledge.

Gee, James Paul. (2001). What is literacy? In P. Shannon (Ed.), *Becoming political, too: New readings and writings in the politics of literacy education* (pp. 1–9). Portsmouth, NH: Heinemann.

Geertz, Clifford. (1973). Thick description: Toward an interpretive theory of culture. In *The interpretation of cultures* (pp. 3–30). New York: Random House.

Guinier, Lani & Torres, Gerald. (2002). *The miner's canary: Enlisting race, resisting power, transforming democracy.* Cambridge, MA: Harvard University Press.

Hade, Daniel D. (1997a). Reading children's literature multiculturally. In S. L. Beckett. (Ed.), *Reflections of change: Children's literature since 1945* (pp. 115–122). Westport, CT: Greenwood Press.

Hade, Daniel D. (1997b). Reading multiculturally. In V. J. Harris (Ed.), *Using multicultural children's literature in the K–8 classroom* (pp. 233–256). Norwood, MA: Christopher-Gordon Publishers.

Hade, Daniel & Edmondson, Jacqueline. (2003). Children's book publishing in neoliberal times. *Language Arts*, 81(2), 135–143.

Harris, Violet J. (Ed.). (1993). *Teaching multicultural literature in grades K–8.* Norwood, MA: Christopher-Gordon Publishers.

Harris, Violet J. (Ed.). (1997). *Using multiethnic literature in the K–8 classroom.* Norwood, MA: Christopher-Gordon Publishers.

Harris, Violet J. & Willis, Arlette I. (2003). Multiculturalism, literature, and curriculum issues. In J. Flood, D. Lapp, J. R. Squire, & J. M. Jensen (Eds.), *Handbook of research on teaching the English language arts* (2nd ed., pp. 825–834). Mahwah, NJ: Erlbaum Associates.

Heaton, Margaret M. & Lewis, Helen Block. (1954). *Reading ladders for human relations.* Washington: American Council on Education.

Hollindale, Peter. (1988). Ideology and the children's book. *Signal*, 55, 3–22.

Horning, Kathleen T. & Kruse, Ginny Moore. (1991). Looking into the mirror: Considerations behind the reflections. In M. V. Lindgren (Ed.), *The multicolored mirror: Cultural substance in literature for children and young adults* (pp. 1–13). Fort Atkinson, WI: Highsmith Press.

Horning, Kathleen T., Kruse, Ginny Moore & Schliesman, Megan. (2002). *CCBC choices 2002.* University of Wisconsin-Madison.

Horning, Kathleen T., Kruse, Ginny Moore & Schliesman, Megan. (2006). *CCBC choices 2006.* University of Wisconsin-Madison.

Horning, Kathleen T., Lindgren, Merri V., Michaelson, Tessa, & Schliesman, Megan. (2008). Publishing in 2007. In *CCBC choices 2007. University of Wisconsin-Madison.* Retrieved on May 15, 2008, from www.education.wisc.edu/ccbc/books/choiceintro08.asp.

Huck, Charlotte S., Helper, Susan, Hickman, Janet, & Kiefer, Barbara Z. (2001). *Children's literature in the elementary school* (7th ed.). Boston: McGraw Hill.

Hunt, Peter (Ed.). (1992). *Literature for children: Contemporary criticism.* New York: Routledge.

Jackson, Sandra & Solís, José (Eds.). (1995). *Beyond comfort zones in multiculturalism: Confronting the politics of privilege.* Trenton, NJ: Bergin & Garvey.

Kanpol, Barry & McLaren, Peter (Eds.). (1995). *Critical multiculturalism: Uncommon voices in a common struggle.* Westport, CT: Bergin & Garvey.

Kohl, Herbert. (1995a). A plea for radical children's literature. In *Should we burn Babar? Essays on children's literature and the power of stories* (pp. 57–93). New York: The New Press.

Kohl, Herbert. (1995b). Should we burn Babar? Questioning power in children's literature. In *Should we burn Babar? Essays on children's literature and the power of stories* (pp. 3–29). New York: The New Press.

Kohl, Herbert. (1995c). The story of Rosa Parks and the Montgomery Bus Boycott revisited. In *Should we burn Babar? Essays on children's literature and the power of stories* (pp. 30–56). New York: The New Press.

Krips, Valerie. (1993). A notable irrelevance: Class and children's fiction. *The Lion and the Unicorn, 17*(2), 195–209.

Larrick, Nancy. (1965). The all-White world of children's books. *Saturday Review, 48*(11), 63–65.

Leeson, Robert. (1977). *Children's books and class society: Past and present.* London: Writers and Readers Publishing Cooperative.

Lindgren, Merri V. & Cooperative Children's Book Center (Eds.). (1991). *The multicolored mirror: Cultural substance in literature for children and young adults.* Fort Atkinson, WI: Highsmith Press.

Lubienski, Sarah Theule. (2003). Celebrating diversity and denying disparities: A critical assessment. *Educational Researcher, 32*(8), 30–38.

MacCann, Donnarae & Woodard, Gloria (Eds.). (1972/1985). *The Black American in books for children: Readings in racism* (2nd ed.). Metuchen, NJ: The Scarecrow Press.

Mendoza, Jean & Reese, Debbie. (2001). Examining multicultural picture books for the early childhood classroom: Possibilities and pitfalls. *Early Childhood Research & Practice, 3*(2), 1–31.

Mikkelsen, Nina. (2000). *Words and pictures: Lessons in children's literature and literacies.* Boston: McGraw Hill.

Mitchell, Diana. (2003). *Children's literature: An invitation to the world.* Boston: Allyn and Bacon.

Morrison, Toni. (1992). *Playing in the dark: Whiteness and the literary imagination.* New York: Vintage Books.

Muse, Daphne (Ed.). (1997). *The New Press guide to multicultural resources for young readers.* New York: The New Press.

Nieto, Sonia & Bode, Patty. (2008). *Affirming diversity: The sociopolitical context of multicultural education* (5th ed.). New York: Longman.

Nodelman, Perry & Reimer, Mavis. (2003). *The pleasures of children's literature* (3rd ed.). Boston: Allyn and Bacon.

Norton, Donna E. (1999). *Through the eyes of a child: An introduction to children's literature* (5th ed.). Upper Saddle River, NJ: Merrill/Prentice Hall.

Norton, Donna E. (2001). *Multicultural children's literature: Through the eyes of many children.* Upper Saddle River, NJ: Merrill Prentice Hall.

Ortner, Sherry. (1991). Reading America: Preliminary notes on class and culture. In *Recapturing Anthropology.* Santa Fe, NM: School of American Research Press.

Ortner, Sherry. (1994). Theory in Anthropology since the sixties. In N. B. Dirks, G. Eley, & S. B. Ortner (Eds.), *Culture/power/history: A reader in contemporary social theory* (pp. 373–411). Princeton, NJ: Princeton University Press.

Osa, Osayimwense (Ed.). (1995). *The all White world of children's book and African American children's literature.* Trenton, NJ: Africa World Press.

Reid, Virginia M. (1972). *Reading ladders for human relations.* Washington: American Council on Education.

Rochman, Hazel. (1993). *Against borders: Promoting books for a multicultural world.* Chicago: American Library Association.

Rogers, Theresa & Soter, Anna O. (Eds.). (1997). *Reading across cultures: Teaching literature in a diverse society.* New York: Teachers College Press.

Rosaldo, Renato. (1989). *Culture and truth.* Boston: Beacon Press.

R. R. Bowker Company. (2005). *Children's books in print.* New Providence, NJ: Bowker.

R. R. Bowker Company. (2007). *Bowker reports U.S. book production rebounded slightly in*

2006. Retrieved on May 15, 2008, from www.bowker.com/press/bowker/2007_0531_bowker.htm.

Rudman, Masha K. (1976). *Children's literature: An issues approach*. Lexington, MA: D. C. Heaton and Co.

Rudman, Masha K. (1976/1995). *Children's literature: An issues approach* (3rd ed.). White Plains, NY: Longman.

Russell, David. (2001). *Literature for children: A short introduction* (4th ed.). New York: Longman.

Saravia-Shore, Marietta & Arvizu, Steven F. (1992). Cross-cultural literacy: An anthropological approach to dealing with diversity. In M. Saravia-Shore & S. F. Arvizu (Eds.), *Cross-cultural literacy: Ethnographies of communication in multiethnic classrooms* (pp. xv–xxxviii). New York: Garland Publishing.

Schwartz, Elaine G. (1995). Crossing borders/Shifting paradigms: Multiculturalism and children's literature. *Harvard Educational Review*, 65(4), 634–650.

Shannon, Patrick. (1986). Hidden within the pages: A study of social perspective in young children's favorite books. *The Reading Teacher*, 39, 656–663.

Shannon, Patrick. (1994). I am the canon. Finding ourselves in multiculturalism. *Journal of Children's Literature*, 20(1), 1–5.

Sims (Bishop), Rudine. (1982). *Shadow and substance: Afro-American experience in contemporary children's fiction*. Urbana, IL: NCTE.

Spring, Joel, (2004). *Deculturalization and the struggle for equality: Brief history of the education of dominated cultures in the United States* (4th ed.). Boston: McGraw-Hill.

Starkenburg, Edward L. (1999). *Social class depiction in selected award-winning children's narrative fiction*. Unpublished doctoral dissertation, University of Northern Iowa.

Stephens, John. (1992). *Language and ideology in children's fiction*. New York: Longman.

Stoffman, Judy. (2006). *Unbound: Print on demand has spawned a self-publishing epidemic. Toronto Star*, December 9.

Street, Brian V. (1996). "Culture is a verb." In D. Graddol (Ed.), *Language and culture* (pp. 23–43). Multilingual Matters/BAAL.

Taxel, Joel & Ward, Holly M. (2000). Publishing children's literature at the dawn of the 21st century. *The New Advocate*, 13(1), 51–59.

Temple, Charles, Martinez, Miriam, Yokota, Junko, & Naylor, Alice. (2006). *Children's books in children's hands: An introduction to their literature* (3rd ed.). Boston: Allyn and Bacon.

Tomlinson, Carl M. & Lynch-Brown, Carol. (2002). *Essentials of children's literature* (4th ed.). Boston: Allyn and Bacon.

Tway, Eileen (Ed.). (1981). *Reading ladders for human relations* (6th ed.). Urbana, IL: NCTE.

Tylor, Edward. (1871/1958). *Primitive culture*. New York: Harper & Row.

Wader, Rose E. (1997). Milestones in children's literature. In D. Muse (Ed.), *The New Press guide to multicultural resources for young readers* (pp. 12–17). New York: The New Press.

Wojcik-Andrews, Ian. (1993). Toward a theory of class in children's literature. *The Lion and the Unicorn*, 17(2), 113–123.

Wolf, Shelby A. (2004). *Interpreting literature with children*. Mahwah, NJ: Lawrence Erlbaum Associates.

Yenika-Agbaw, Vivian. (1997). Taking children's literature seriously: reading for pleasure and social change. *Language Arts*, 74(6), 446–453.

Yokota, Junko. (1993). Issues in selecting multicultural children's literature. *Language Arts*, 70, 156–167.

Yokota, Junko (Ed.). (2001). *Kaleidoscope: A multicultural booklist for grades K–8* (3rd ed.). Urbana, IL: NCTE.

CHAPTER 5

Theorizing Critical Multicultural Analysis of Children's Literature

Using language as a mirror, we can begin to understand how power is exercised in the U.S. context. Language use or discourse reflects and circulates dominant ideologies that are responsible for constructing current power relations. Critical multicultural analysis of children's literature focuses on the examination of power as a factor in what gets written, illustrated, and published. In other words, meanings found in children's books are not from language alone but from institutional practices, power relations and social position. Children's books mirror these power relations and offer windows into society; critical multicultural analysis magnifies these relationships, naming the institutional and personal location of the discourses from within which we read, the power relations involved, and their implications for social justice.

Poststructuralists and cultural studies theorists maintain that we can only make sense of reality through language (Watkins, 1999). Feminist poststructuralist theories demonstrate how language constructs subjectivity (Davies, 2000; Weedon, 1997). Language is not seen as possessing a fixed, stable meaning, but as possessing significance that is bound by its historical and sociopolitical context. People use language to define and contest the reality they exist in. Language is where and how power is reproduced, distributed and maintained. Oral and written language constitute text to be analyzed and challenged. Meaning is constructed within a complex web of power relations rather than words substituting for objects and actions. These meanings are temporarily fixed. Meaning is constructed and reconstructed through interplay between texts, readers, and contexts. Just like identity, meaning is a process.

The Discourse of Multicultural Children's Literature

When we untangle multiculturalism from "multicultural children's literature," it creates a space to question and challenge the text, and re-imagine the social worlds depicted in the book. It is reading that goes beyond stretching children's cultural imagination to reading that fosters a historical and sociopolitical imagination. Bringing a critical lens to the study of multiculturalism in children's literature invites readers to deconstruct dominant ideologies of U.S. society which privilege those whose interests, values, and beliefs are represented by these prevailing worldviews. Critical multicultural analysis is reading power within the complex web of social relations.

Critical multicultural analysis disrupts binary thinking, which simplistically examines issues of privilege and power. The binary oppositions of black/white and oppressor/oppressed mask power relations. Binary comparisons can be equated with dominant ideology because it does not show the complexities, contradictions, and shifting aspects of an issue. Rather, they mask and distort. For example, multicultural children's literature disallows the problematizing of the category of European American (Botelho, 1997a). There is an implied "fictive unity" (Medeiros, 1996) in this cultural label, as if all European Americans share the same history and socioeconomic privileging. Multicultural children's literature grossly lumps cultural groups, including African Americans, Asian Americans, Latino/a Americans, and Native Americans, and obscures intragroup and intergroup diversity and power relations.

In untangling the discourse of multicultural children's literature we can analyze how this literary category draws on the "discursive threads" (Rudd, 2000) of otherness and self-esteem. These discursive threads circulate in society and reinforce dominant worldviews, while being "resistant to internal criticism and self-scrutiny since uttering viewpoints that seriously undermine them defines one as being outside them" (Gee, 2001b: 2). (It is worth noting that the scholars whose research is linked to the conceptualization of multicultural children's literature never took up Schwartz's [1995] critique of multicultural children's literature as a literary category. It was only recently that Harris and Willis [2003] cited Schwartz's article in their consideration of the history of multiculturalism and children's literature. In historicizing developments in multicultural children's literature, Harris and Willis situate Schwartz's work within a postcolonial theory and criticism.) The deconstruction of the discursive practices of multicultural children's literature locates the invisibility and silences inherent in this way of looking at the world of children's literature, and by extension, U.S. society.

Otherness

Schwartz (1995) maintains that as long as multicultural children's literature is about "Otherness," it will not question the ideological hegemony of the dominant culture and will not interrogate the root causes of White privilege (Ulichny, 1996). (The "Other" is defined as people who are different linguistically, culturally, racially from the dominant White Anglo-Protestant culture.) If literature of the dominant culture is not interrogated, then we are ignoring the power structure that is in place, ensconcing "White privilege" in the perceptions of the reader, and relegating the notion of multiple perspectives to "the Other," and thus, inadvertently, to a lesser position.

The discourse of "Otherness" implies that identity is fixed and unified, unfolding over time with a stable core in place. Stuart Hall (1996) defines cultural identity as "superficial or artificially imposed 'selves' which a people with a shared history and ancestry hold in common" (Hall, 1996: 3–4); it is an unchanged "cultural belongingness." Implicit in "Otherness" is that culture is bounded and independent from other cultural influences: culture is static. If "Otherness" is critically and multiculturally analyzed, its essentialism is exposed and its sociopolitical construction located.

Identity is a process that is never complete. People are always in the process of becoming. Hall argues that

> identities are never unified ... increasingly fragmented and fractured; never singular but multiply constructed across different, often intersecting and antagonistic, discourses, practices and positions ... identities are about questions of using the resources of history, language and culture in the process of becoming rather than being: not "who we are" or "where we came from" so much as what we might become, how we have been represented and how that bears on how we might represent ourselves.
>
> (Hall, 1996: 4)

Identities are constructed within discourse: like race, they are social constructions, not biologically determined. Critical multicultural analysis creates a space for readers to ask if the subject positions constructed by the discourses imbedded in text are those that they want to be. Identities play a role in how we perceive ourselves sociopolitically.

The author and reader are constituted through the ideological dimensions of discourses circulating in society and text. As Cai (1998) maintains, insider artists can also misrepresent cultural experiences as do outsider authors and illustrators. However, the author's identity is a central consideration in the debate of what multicultural children's literature is and is not (Bishop, 1992; Cai, 1998; Cai & Bishop, 1994; Harris, 1993, 1997; Sims, 1982). These scholars argue that insider authors (those who have similar lived experiences as the book characters) are better suited to write about the nuances of their cultural experience. Marta I. Cruz-Janzen (1998) warns that cultural groups are not immune to intragroup power relations; stories can be "replete with biases."

The issues of cultural authenticity and insider/outsider are intertwined in the discourse of Otherness. We assume that insider artists will bring us closer to a stable and pure culture, which is an essentialist view of culture, obfuscating the fact that texts reflect "the complexities of specific historical moments when many discourses and reading [subject] positions register the complex intersections of actual social practice" (Griffiths, 1994: 80). Implied in authenticity is that the text closely corresponds to a stable cultural reality.

Our findings demonstrate that we cannot discount the cultural membership of the author. The insider authors and illustrators are more versed in or have more access to culturally specific discourses and histories than outsiders to the culture. These writers and artists tend to have a greater understanding of how language is used and how power is exercised within and outside the culture. Class, race, and gender power relations shape this cultural specificity, shaking up the notion of culture as stable and fixed; its dynamic, multiple, and shifting nature is made visible. Many of these writers bring the reader up close to the complexities of culture and its power relations.

We also acknowledge that no person can speak for or represent an entire group. We are all outsiders to a degree, unless we are specifically portraying ourselves. And even then our portrayal is a representation of our lived experience.

In "What is the Author?" Foucault (1984) proposes that the author is tied to institutional systems which shape all discourses at all times in any given culture. The institutional discursive practices are more central to the definition of author rather than the contribution from a particular text, generated by a particular individual from a particular culture. Barthes (1977) maintains, "Once the Author is removed, the claim to decipher a text becomes quite futile. To give a text an Author is to impose a limit on that text, to furnish it with a final signified, to close the writing" (Barthes, 1977: 147). Focusing solely on the author is adhering to the notion that an individual and/or a culture is the source of the meaning in the book. Looking at a collection of books written by the same author, and trying to get at the discursive threads throughout the books, is a way to see the discourses deployed into this writer's writings. These discursive threads are linked to social practice and institutions. Foucault (1984) helps us to understand the "author-function" further because he points to our society's fixation with and fear of the "proliferation of meaning," that is, we associate single meanings with single texts, without proceeding to acknowledge the reader and the context.

Self-Esteem

"Self-esteem" is another discursive thread woven into multicultural children's literature. Just like "Otherness," the discourse of self-esteem assumes a fixed, unified, and stable self. Diane Hoffmann (1996) claims that many assumptions imbedded in this discourse are cross-culturally plausible. The underlying assumptions include that

1. self-esteem is based on a person's awareness of him or herself as a unique individual with particular abilities, potentials;
2. it is directly dependent on so-called individual abilities, qualities, and performances, thus, completely ignoring the existence of different cultural models of learning; and
3. the assumption that the self-esteem of minority children in particular requires improvement.

(Hoffmann 1996: 560–561)

The discourse of self-esteem implies that there is an inherent link between dominated cultural status and low self-esteem. This perspective privileges the dominant culture by defining it as the norm, setting it as the standard of high self-esteem toward which underrepresented groups should struggle. While Hoffman's analysis is flawed by her definitions of culture and identity as fixed and bounded entities, her critique brings attention to this discursive thread's fixation with the individual, isolated from community, culture, and society, as well as recognizing dominant ideologies as sources of self-esteem. The discourse of self-esteem distracts us from recognizing and resisting the current arrangements of power.

This discourse requires that individuals construct their own edifice of self-esteem, that is, "how we evaluate ourselves and our characteristics" (Kohn, 1994: 273). Joseph Kahne (1996) writes:

> Those who emphasize the impact of structural factors on self-esteem judgments are oriented toward asking how social conventions and institutional arrangements affect individuals' self-esteem. If poverty, sexism, or other factors systematically constrain the self-esteem of whole groups of individuals, and if self-esteem is a goal, then

policymakers must find ways to address poverty, homelessness, sexism, and so on. If, on the other hand, improving self-esteem judgments is viewed as a means of promoting "socially desirable" behaviors, then policymakers can focus instead on raising the self-esteem of poor or homeless individuals.

(Kahne, 1996: 10)

The self-esteem discourse is slippery, tied to the dominant ideologies of class, race, gender, and individualism that contribute to the chipping away of self-worth. Alfie Kohn (1994) maintains that "a self-oriented approach may fail to help students believe in themselves because it overlooks the political and economic realities that offer far more meaningful explanations of why some children doubt or even despise themselves" (Kohn, 1994: 277). It does not create a space for individuals to consider how they are historically, socially and discursively shaped.

Invisibility

If we say that literature mirrors society through its text and images, then invisibility in children's literature requires a closer look. Patricia Alexander (1983) contends, "nonportrayal is much like passing in front of a mirror and seeing only 'nothingness.' Indeed, invisibility is a powerful statement of value. The message transmitted may be that as a culture you are of little value within the society—of little consequence" (Alexander, 1083: 212). Invisibility in children's literature is a quiescent prejudice.

The study of children's literature must question whose culture gets reflected, or not, and how often. Native Americans are cultural groups of color that are largely represented by the publishing houses (MacCann, 1993). However, they remain stereotypically rendered, many times left behind in historical times. The critical question "Are the non-rendered the lucky ones?" must be considered. As Hall argues, "identities are . . . constituted within not outside representation" (Hall, 1996: 4). When cultural groups' stories are published they can then begin to negotiate with publishers, readers, and society how to portray their identities in books.

The issue of invisibility demands cultural specificity, and historical and sociopolitical analysis. The cultural grouping of European Americans, for example, implies a common history and heritage that does not exist. (That can be said about any cultural group.) For example, to understand why there are not any children's books by or about Portuguese Americans published in the United States, one needs to consider the multiple historical and sociopolitical contexts of the Portuguese experience (United States and the predominantly working-class, immigrant experience; Açores and its agrarian economy; Portugal and its history of colonization; and the European Community). European American as a cultural identity prevents us from disclosing the more subtle socioeconomic and linguistic hegemony that exists in this country (Botelho, 1997a). The "European American" label contributes not only to the invisibility of the Portuguese in U.S. children's literature, but also to the lack of exposure to many cultural groups' experiences.

Silences

Michel Foucault maintains that "There is not one but many silences, and they are an integral part of the strategies that underlie and permeate discourses" (Foucault, 1980: 27). Jacques Derrida's (1980) work further provides insights into absence and silence. For Derrida, the unsaid and the unwritten can be just as important as what is said and written. Bronwyn Davies (1999) maintains that poststructuralist theory tries to locate these silences and examine "what work it is that they are doing" (Davies, 1999: 16).

In addition to the discursive threads of otherness and self-esteem, and the issue of invisibility, the literary category of multicultural children's literature distracts us from focusing on two social silences—how class and gender work with race. (As a society, we have many silences around issues such as ageism, heterosexism, and ableism, to name a few. While we acknowledge that these power relations intersect with class, race, and gender, they are beyond the scope of this book.) It is easier to focus on a bounded, fixed, and stable notion of culture because it is something we all agree we all possess, whereas social privilege based on gender-, class-, and race-based memberships is not something we can say we all have.

The interrogation of class alongside race and gender is a direct attack on U.S. power relations. George Lipsitz (1997) argues that

> by reinforcing ideologies that see social existence as primarily private and personal, our teaching discourages social theory . . . . This way of knowing about the world is a deficient approach . . . it is particularly inadequate for understanding social relations and the connections that link individual lives to broad social structures.
>
> (Lipsitz, 1997: 11)

Untangling multiculturalism from multicultural children's literature demands the study of social class, race, and gender as elements in text construction. (In her teaching experiences, Maria José has found that teachers and students have difficulty articulating and analyzing experiences and perspectives, especially defined by social class and race.) A critical multicultural analysis of children's literature offers opportunities to identify vocabularies to expose the historical and sociopolitical dimensions of these power relations as they are constructed in the text.

Critical multicultural analysis of children's literature foregrounds that race, gender, class, culture, and otherness are socially constructed and must be contested in efforts to create reading spaces that move against and beyond traditional sociopolitical boundaries, at the same time, mounting social critique for social change. Young and adult readers should know that unless they are able to read for social change and justice, they will find themselves affirming and maintaining dominant ideologies that privilege some groups over others. Bringing a critical lens to the study of multiculturalism in children's literature invites the reader to deconstruct dominant ideologies that have been instrumental in perpetuating social inequities and distributing power unequally in the United States. The discourses of class, gender, and race work together.

Theoretical Constructs

Contradiction, construction and practice frame critical multicultural analysis (Parker, 1999). By contradictions, we focus on what different meanings are at work in the text. We locate the contradictions and link them to dominant ideologies or social myths, recover dominated meanings, and highlight processes of domination, collusion, resistance, and agency. By examining the construction of texts, we ask how these meanings are constructed. We attempt to retrace how texts have been socially constructed. Finally, in critical multicultural analysis, we are concerned with what these contradictory systems of meaning are doing to us as people and as a society: we focus on the sociopolitical function of texts and issues of power.

People are defined in relationship to other people because discourses are always defined in relationship to other discourses. Critical multicultural analysis situates language in social and political contexts, as well as taking into account how authors and readers collude with or challenge dominant ideologies. In the process of critical multicultural reading, power is located and a site is created for social justice and social transformation. Critical multicultural analysis can contribute to our deconstructing and reconstructing ourselves and society. It focuses on how language in books works to position readers in particular power relations. The theoretical constructs of discourse, ideology, subjectivity, and power ground critical multicultural analysis and offer tools for uncovering dominant messages in children's books by locating how the power relations of class, race, and gender are exercised in text and images.

Discourse

James Paul Gee (2001) defines discourse as a social practice comprised of ways of being in the world. Discourse is "a socially accepted association among ways of using language, of thinking, and of acting that can be used to identify oneself as a member of a socially meaningful group or 'social network' " (Gee, 2001: 1). The distinction between discourses and texts is that discourses are worldviews or ideologies, whereas texts, oral or written, contain discourses. Gee (2001) highlights several points that are crucial to understanding discourse:

1. Discourses are inherently "ideological."
2. Discourses are resistant to internal criticism and self-scrutiny since uttering viewpoints that seriously undermine them defines one as being outside them.
3. Discourse-defined positions from which to speak and behave are not, however, just defined internal to a discourse, but also as standpoints taken up by the discourse in its relation to other, ultimately opposing, discourses.
4. Any discourse concerns itself with certain objects and puts forward certain concepts, viewpoints and values at the expense of others.
5. Discourses are intimately related to the distribution of social power and hierarchical structure in society. Control over certain discourses can lead to the acquisition of social goods (money, power, status) in a society.

(Gee, 2001: 2)

Consequently, discourses that translate into the acquisition of social goods and power are "dominant discourses" and groups who use them with great facility are "dominant groups." How we come to these discourses throughout our lives is through a combination of acquisition (acquiring through exposure, imitation, and trial and error) and learning (learning through teaching). Gee offers a caveat: "We are better at what we acquire, but we consciously know more about what we have learned" (Gee, 2001: 4). Critical multicultural analysis makes the reader conscious of dominant discourses. Gee's (1999) definition of the little "d" discourse deals with the specific details about language, showing how language use becomes social and political practices with material consequences.

David Rudd's (2000) analytical tool of discursive threads is central to critical multicultural analysis as a way to uncover how texts draw on discourses in society. Rudd sums up the usefulness of discursive threads as follows:

1. discourses circulate in threads or fragments not in a "whole" form;

2. the metaphor of thread exemplifies how texts are weavings of many discourses and brings attention to the "texture of the text";
3. discursive threads capture the dynamic nature of discourses: it is "not simply a lump of language" but discursive practices (a thread captures the activity of language whereas discourses shape people and people shape discourses); and,
4. discursive threads reinforce discourses or create new discourses.

Through a critical multicultural lens, the study of literature becomes a study of discursive practices and the political and social ramifications underlying them. How do we recognize ideology, the conduit of power, in children's books? Peter Hollindale's (1988) and John Stephens' (1992; 1994 a & b; 1999) scholarship in ideological critique of children's literature offers guidance. Stephens applies critical analysis to children's books; he constructs a strong theoretical grounding that includes children as people who are invited to conduct critical textual analysis. He elevates children's literature to a position worthy of study and analysis by situating it in the landscape of critical literary theory.

Ideology

Discourse is inherently imbued with ideology: Ideology is inseparable from discourse and discourse is constituted from ideology. Stephens asserts that "the discourses of children's fiction are pervaded by ideological presuppositions, sometimes obtrusively and sometimes invisibly" (Stephens, 1992: 1–2). He further states that "the discourse of a narrative fiction yields up both a story and a significance" (Stephens, 1992: 2). Ideology is imbedded in both. Stephens states that the ". . . story comprises what we might roughly think of as what certain characters do in a certain place at a certain time, and discourse comprises the complex process of encoding that story which involves choices of vocabulary, of syntax, or order of presentation, of how the narrating voice is to be oriented towards what is narrated and towards the implied audience" (Stephens, 1992: 17). He further argues that the significance inferred from the text, "its theme, moral, insight into behaviour, is never without an ideological dimension or connotation" (Stephens, 1992: 2). Since these implicit messages or ideologies can shape readers' attitudes and worldviews, it is imperative that readers read resistantly.

Hollindale (1988) identifies three aspects of ideology: It can be deliberately or implicitly rendered in the text, and is inherently ideological. First, the most tractable ideology discloses the writer's explicit social, political or moral beliefs. Books that openly promote socially progressive messages are part of this category. Hollindale suggests that overt ideological representations pose problems for the writer: explicit advocacy tends to incite reader resistance to the message(s). Therefore, the more covert or implicit ideology is, the more interpretatively demanding it is for the reader.

Hollindale's second category is "passive ideology." This ideology is the implicit representation of the writer's unexamined assumptions. Hollindale argues that these hidden messages demand a critical analysis from the adroit reader. This passive ideology is the taken-for-granted values of society: that is, what people perceive as the "norm." These values permeate the text. Stephens (1992) maintains that the implicit ideology of children's literature has been clouded by discussions and controversies about the concept of the implied reader—largely created by the text's own narrative construction such as point of view.

Lastly, Hollindale maintains that ideology is inherent within language, while he defines ideology as "the words, the rule-systems, the codes which constitute the text" (Hollindale, 1998: 14). He argues that ideology in language works to contain conflicts and to confine meaning making to the attitudes and interests of dominant social groups.

The author and reader are constituted through the ideological dimensions of discourses circulating in society and text. Stephens invites us to look at the interactions among the characters in the stories in terms of their reception of each other's messages, and in so doing, he asks us to look at ourselves as readers. He invites the reader to contemplate "the Implied Author/Implied Reader pair as a construction within texts which has little, if any, narrative function, but which operates principally as the bearer of implicit social practices and ideological positions" (Stephens, 1992: 21). Ideology is not all coercive. We need ideologies that are in the interest of all people and which advocate for the equitable re/distribution of resources. We must consider the ideologies that are compatible with a democratic society.

Subjectivity

Feminist poststructuralism theorizes that subjectivity is socially and discursively constructed, rather than being innate or natural. Chris Weedon (1997) defines subjectivity as "the conscious and unconscious thoughts and emotions of individuals, their sense of self, and their ways of understanding their relations to the world" (Weedon, 1997: 32). An individual's subjectivity is not simply an identity, but one's sense of self that is always in flux, responding to the discourses available to one in a specific historical, sociopolitical context. Language, a signifying system, contributes to this process. By examining the ideological dimensions of a text, the reader can become aware of the subject positions it creates.

Stephens recommends analyses that consider the wide array of meaning systems within children's books such as the visual and textual features, issues of focalization or perception (Who sees?), as well as the unity of the text (e.g., spatio-temporal representation, point of view, intertextuality, and sense of closure). He claims that narrative structure, and especially closure, is an ideologically powerful component of texts, since aesthetic completeness and the sense of an appropriate story ending spill over into affirmations of the discourse's thematic conclusions. But an open ending can still be ideologically powerful by evoking particular values and assumptions by its very evasion of them (Stephens, 1992: 44).

The reader is best equipped when multiple reading strategies are available, including "an interrogative engagement with the implied reader" (Stephens, 1992: 69–70), the "implied reader" being the reader's role implicit in the text, which is linked to the dominant discourses. Stephens claims that texts create estranged or distanced subject positions when the following textual constructions are present: multiple protagonists are present; the main character misunderstands a situation; character development shifts over time; the text is playfully self-conscious (Stephens, 1992: 70).

Readers are often constructed intertextually, that is, out of a dialogue between the literary text and other literary and nonliterary texts. Discourses make available particular subject positions. Readers can resist the position constructed by the text and create alternative or resistant reading positions that support more collective values or worldviews. For example, they can interrupt reading subject positions that privilege some people over others based on race, class, and gender, and speculate on new ways to enact power relations that are socially just.

Power

Power is an important element in any critical multicultural examination of text. Foucault (1972) maintains that power is exercised and not owned, with power circulating within what he calls fields of discourse, which he defines as the relationship among language and social institutions, subjectivity, and power. Foucault is important to our work because, as he argues, we create discourses as much as they create us. It is within this discursive grid that we learn about how we may or may not access power, how to exercise this power as well as how power is exercised on us. Foucault's work foregrounds language and power and how it positions people.

Foucault explores power relationships that are involved in constructing reality. He argues that the following questions must be asked:

Who exercises power? How? On whom? Who makes decisions for

me? Who is preventing me from doing this and telling me to do that? Who is programming my movements and activities? Who is forcing me to live in a particular place when I work in another? How are these decisions on which my life is completely articulated taken?

(Foucault, 1995: 41)

Foucault maintains that the question of "who exercises power?" is not "resolved unless the other question 'how does it happen?' is resolved at the same time" (p. 42). He asserts that even if you come to know who the decision-makers are, you still do not know how power was exercised. Michel Bakhtin's (1981) perspective about language is useful here because users of language exercise agency with each utterance as they appropriate their intention in the words they use.

Bakhtin views language as heteroglossia (many languages), a site of ideological struggle. He states that "the word in language is half someone else's. It becomes 'one's own' only when the speaker populates it with his [sic] own intention, his own accent, when he appropriates the word, adapting it for his own semantic and expressive intention" (Bakhtin, 1981: 294). At the center of critical multicultural analysis, we must ask what cultural statements author and illustrator are responding to. Texts and images are sites of sociopolitical struggle.

Bakhtin situates the person within a larger dialogical and ideological world. Within this world the self is constructed through dialogic relationships. While engaged in these dialogic relationships we borrow each other's words, using them to inform and drive our own thinking and learning. According to Bakhtin (1981), these relationships are mediated by language as we engage with texts, whether these are oral or written.

Critical multicultural analysis is the "discursive leveling of texts," a way of placing books in the total discursive field (Rudd, 1999), that is, placing children's literature alongside literary and cultural criticism, and other secondary sources, because discourses circulate everywhere, including in book reviews, research, theory, pedagogy, and the like. Therefore, what books "do" in the world cannot be explicated through text analysis only (Pennycook, 2000; Reese, 2000). Critical multicultural analysis of children's books makes sense of literature against a broader historical, sociopolitical context and the discursive landscape.

Theorizing Power

Race, Class, and Gender as Sociopolitical Constructions

Race, class, and gender are situated in discourse. They are inseparable from discourse and power. Ann Louise Keating (1995) argues that racial categories must be historicized to ascertain the relational processes of all racialized identities. She outlines four reasons for grounding race in history:

1. our conceptions of "race" are scientifically and historically inaccurate;
2. constant references to "race" perpetuate the belief in separate peoples, monolithic identities, and stereotypes;
3. racial discourse quickly degenerates into a "black/white" polarization that overlooks other so-called "races" and ignores the incredible diversity among people; and,
4. racial categories are not—and never have been—benign. Racial divisions were developed to create a hierarchy that grants privilege and power to specific groups of people while simultaneously oppressing and excluding others.

(Keating, 1995: 916)

Finally, she states that "at the very least, we should complicate existing conceptions of 'race'—both by exploring the many changes that have occurred in all apparently fixed racial categories and by informing students of the political, economic, and historical factors shaping the continual reinvention of 'race' " (Keating, 1995: 917). Race, class, and gender are ideologically and materially bound.

Antonia Darder and Rodolfo Torres (1999) argue that the study of race ignores the influences of capitalism, a class-based system. They write that "racism is an ideology that produces the notion of 'race' not the existence of 'races' that produce racism" (p. 186). They argue that just examining race "leads us further down a theoretical and political dead end" (Darder & Torres, 1999: 186). They advocate for a "plural conceptualization of 'racisms' and their historical articulations with other ideologies" (Darder & Torres, 1999: 185). This kind of theorizing challenges the black/white paradigm and demands historical specificity, thus exposing "the historically shifting and politically complex nature of racialization" (Darder & Torres, 1999: 186). They contend that the social problems experienced by racialized communities are not about " 'race' but rather about the intricate interplay between a variety of racisms and class" (Darder & Torres, 1999: 186). Darder and Torres propose that an analysis of these complex power relations will bear "a multiplicity of ideological constructions of the racialized Other" (Darder & Torres, 1999: 187). Thus "shattering the race lens" unsettles essentialist, unified, and ahistorical perceptions of power.

Power is an under-explored theoretical and social construct. Lani Guinier and Gerald Torres' (2002) work is instructive here. Building on Foucault's concept of power, they propose "a political race project." Political race highlights the central role race has in constructing social identities, processes, and structures, while infusing the concept of political race with power, which the authors claim, is missing from the current dialogue. Guinier and Torres contend that race works alongside class and gender. They add the term "political" to signal the collective interaction at the individual, group, and institutional levels. This shift is an attempt to reframe and situate conversations about race within historical and socio-political power relations. Linking race to power reveals that "the distribution of resources in this society is racialized and that this racial hierarchy is then normalized and thereby made invisible" (Guinier & Torres, 2002: 15).

People in U.S. society are racialized. Guinier and Torres invite us to think about race as a verb. As a verb, race captures the social processes by which people become raced in multiple ways, times, and across contexts. Those closest to these experiences along with their allies, they argue, should be the ones to guide the political race project. They add: "Race is instructive in identifying the workings of class, but it cannot be swallowed up into class" (Guinier & Torres, 2002: 49). Our charge is to explore how these power relations intersect.

Gloria Ladson-Billings and William F. Tate IV's claim that "race, unlike gender and class, remains untheorized" (Ladson-Billings & Tate IV, 1995: 49). We contend that the complexities of race power relations remain untheorized, with class and gender implicated in these social processes, as power relations that work together.

While Marxist analysis highlights the workings of class through socio-historical, dialectical analysis, foregrounding contradictions and conflicts, it also generalizes race relations and White privilege (Ladson-Billings and Tate IV, 1995). Marxist scholarship can be overdeterministic, with domination perceived as inevitable: Power is constituted as domination and alienation, which are passive subject positions.

As stated earlier, education and social science research tend to focus on the "positives" of diversity and/or conflate race with ethnicity and class. Reading race alone, class alone, or gender alone does not reveal how power is exercised. We agree with Ladson-Billings and Tate IV that we must keep in mind the impact of race on gender and social class. They propose untangling democracy and capitalism because, they claim, "traditional civil rights approaches to solving inequality have depended on the 'rightness' of democracy while ignoring the structural inequality of capitalism" (Ladson-Billings & Tate IV, 1995: 52). U.S. democracy was founded on capitalism.

Race, gender, and class are social constructions that establish socio-political and economic hierarchies or power relations among people. Children's literature is a microcosm of these ideologies. The construct of race was/is used to divide people into groups on the basis of particular hereditary characteristics. Gender was/is used to divide women and men in complex ways to confer different degrees of social power. Race and gender are socially constructed differences, not biologically based. Class is also socially made. Class was/is used to confer different degrees of power and opportunity based on people's birth, wealth, occupations, education, social networks, and social position. In the United States, we hold to the romantic belief that success and failure in life are determined by individual factors rather than sociopolitical circumstances. Roxana Ng (2003) defines class as "a process whereby people's lives are organized and transformed in terms of the relation and means of production. Although this transformation hinges on economic relations in a capitalist society, it is not simply an economic relation" (p. 211). The social processes of race, gender, and class converge in everyday life and "(re)organize" our lives. Ng proposes that class locates this (re)organization.

These social processes of race, gender, and class happen within discourses and are relational and context dependent. They emerge in microinteractions. The power relations of race, class, and gender are complex because they are historical, sociopolitical, multiple, contradictory, fragmented, and intersect; implicate the nexus of the language/power relations because they are ideological, discursive, and interdiscursive (draw on each others' discourses); and, are social processes because they are exercised, negotiated, circulated, transformed, fluid, porous, relational and generative. Power is exercised and generated in relation to race, class, and gender. Power is dynamic.

Guinier and Torres (2002) reject the inevitability of domination and speak to the generativity of human agency. Power is constituted in discourse and rendered natural or "that is the way things are" in texts. By looking at how language use creates power subject positions, "the focus is on the way in which the discursive practices constitute the speakers and hearers in certain ways and yet at the same time is a resource through which speakers and hearers can negotiate new positions" (Davies & Harré, 1990). We must rethink power to disrupt it in children's literature, and by extension, in U.S. society. Maria José's teaching and research have led us to the following understandings:

- it is not useful to argue about a hierarchy of oppression (Lorde, 1983);
- it is important to identify ways in which these power relations are similar to or different from each other, and how they work together;
- class/race/gender are interconnected; and,
- it is important to remember that we all benefit from interrupting coercive power relations.

Reading class, race, and gender we become more aware of these social processes and see how dominant discourses figure in these social ways, in social structures, and social change. Taking responsibility for our everyday interactions we become aware of how discourses position us in society, and how we are implicated in their circulation.

How Power is Exercised

Antonio Gramsci's (1988/2000) notion of hegemony, dominant groups' over others, is largely maintained by controlling society's beliefs and practices through the media it controls. Hegemony happens through ideas. Critical multicultural analysis of children's literature is a way to understand the workings of hegemonic relations, as well as considering ways of resisting dominant messages.

Critical multicultural analysis is reading power and exposing how power is exercised, circulated, negotiated, and reconstructed. Children's books are windows into society and the complexities of the power relations of class, race, and gender. Critical multiculturalism underpins this kind of analysis because it respects diversity and uses it as a resource for learning, by going beyond affirmation to solidarity and critique (Nieto & Bode, 2008), and by examining hegemony and issues of social power.

Critical multicultural analysis is about opening a space for agency as readers make sense of texts. This space is where social constructions are challenged and new ways of being and organizing society are actively constructed and reconstructed. Our challenge as readers is not to reproduce dominant readings but to interrupt them. Many scholars (Collins, 2000; Darder & Torres, 1999; Goode & Maskovsky, 2001; Guinier & Torres, 2002; hooks, 2000; Ortner, 1991 & 1998; Perrucci & Wysong, 2003) argue that class analysis must be integrated into the critical dialogue on race and gender, especially since class helps us to understand the deeper dimensions of racism and sexism. For example, Rosaura Sánchez (1992) argues for looking at ethnicity, gender, and class together in Chicano/a literature because these discourses are "a dialogue with a number of texts in Chicano literature, with critical theory, and with Chicano history" (Sánchez, 1992: 73). She continues: "one of the salient characteristics of Chicano literature is its dialogue with history and its focus on collective subjectivity" (Sánchez, 1992: 73).

Building on Foucault's (1972; 1980) understanding of discourse (a way of referring to or constructing knowledge about a particular topic or practice), knowledge, and power, we have identified four positions, which we believe form a continuum of how power is exercised (see Appendix C). In our critical multicultural analysis of children's literature, the positions that characters assume lie on a continuum from domination to agency. This continuum exists because of structural power inequities: We live in raced, classed, and gendered hierarchical arrangements in the U.S. society. It is important to note that power exercised in dominated and/or collusive ways is coercive in constitution. There is an assumption that there is "zero-sum power" (Guinier & Torres, 2002), that is, when one person or group has more power, there is less for everyone else. Power exercised from collusion to agency is constitutively collaborative. Collaborative power is not fixed or inevitable, but something that is created in social interactions, between or among people. Jim Cummins' (2003) discussion on coercive and collaborative microinteractions between teachers and English language learners is useful to understanding these power relations.

Domination[1], collusion, resistance, and agency are historical and sociopolitical possibilities available for selfhood, for being in the world. Discourses translate these social positions into the text and make available particular reading subject positions. These patterns of power relations are not fixed but fluctuate over time, depending on particular contexts and interactions among people. Our goal as readers is not to freeze or isolate these positions, but to demonstrate their fluidity by examining the social processes of power in texts and demonstrate how these positions are constructed. There are multiple and contradictory discourses within each position, especially the subject positions of collusion and resistance. With any of these positions, with the recognition that there is a power matrix or how it works, people may help themselves move along the continuum to agency. When people become aware of their power, they can share their privilege for social change. Critical multicultural analysis focuses on the processes of gaining power, instead of keeping static power relations. It assumes that human agents are responsible for how power is exercised and circulated, as well as functions as a tool for examining discourse in the text.

The first position in the continuum is that of *domination*. It is the exercise of *power over* social circumstances. This position's attributes include dehumanization, victimization, imposition from external sources, and unequal power based on race, class, and gender. Sometimes, the domination occurs de facto because of existing social constructs and systems. Sometimes, it is interpersonal and used to manipulate the behavior of the particular individuals. It is always dehumanizing: unequal voice, participation, decision-making, and access.

The second position is *collusion*. This position differs from domination, mostly in the characteristic of internalized oppression or domination. Collusion may be conscious or unconscious. Colluders remain silent even when they have knowledge of wrongdoing. Towards the end of the continuum of collusion, colluders become conscious of their *power to* take action, while conspiring with dominant ideologies to gain power to resist and gain agency. Domination and collusion can be conscious and/or unconscious. Resistance and agency must be conscious.

Resistance is active questioning; it is the quintessential power construct of poststructuralism. It is not haphazard nor purely reactive. It is an unwillingness to be universalized and essentialized. It is by definition oppositional to imposition and coercive power. It is speculative. It challenges discourses, or as Bronwyn Davies claims, resistance is the "shaking up" by new discourses.

Agency is initiation and *power*. Agency ideally resides with all classes, genders, and ethnicities. Agency is all-inclusive and complex. An agent can be an agent as well as another subject position. Being able to read multiple discourses is part of agency, as well as holding contradictory discourses. Agency is understanding; it is the ultimate subjectivity. Bronwyn Davies (2000) maintains that "agency is never freedom from discursive constitution or [constructedness] of self but the capacity to recognize that constitution and to resist, subvert, and change the discourses themselves through which one is being constituted" (Davies, 2000: 67). Davies argues that agency lies in knowing the composition of discourse and a shift in consciousness "through imagining not what is, but what might be" (Davies, 2000: 67). Everyone possesses and participates in multiple subject positions.

Self-reflexivity is when readers become aware of their constituted subjectivities and the subject positions offered by texts. This kind of reflexivity challenges discursive practices responsible for maintaining and perpetuating the power relations of class, race, and gender. Davies argues that agency lies in knowing the "constructedness" of discourse.

How people perceive their place in the world influences how they act in the world (Freire, 1970/1985; Tejeda, Espinoza, & Gutierrez, 2003). Subjectivity is a process of becoming. Social transformation can only occur when people develop a critical consciousness of power relations and possibilities for changing or undoing oppressive ways of social organization. Critical multicultural analysis provides a site for deconstruction and reconstruction. This space offers readers cognitive flexibility in how they perceive the world, by questioning and theorizing, and taking up collectively minded worldviews. It is reading toward a sociopolitical imagination and social change.

Critical Multicultural Analysis: Constructing a Multi-Layered Lens

Critical multicultural analysis is a multi-layered lens (see Appendix D) that is focused and refocused through a recursive process of analysis. At the center of this lens is the focalization of the story (Whose story is this? From what point of view? Who sees? Who is observed?). We analyze the characters' language use and its role in the social processes among the characters, considering that language use constitutes discourses, ideologies, and subject positions; the characters' social processes relate to U.S. power relations of class, gender, and race. The focalization(s) of the text offers particular reading subject positions, linked to class/race/gender discourses and ideologies. After examining the point of view of these texts, the social processes of the characters are considered (How is power exercised? Who has agency? Who resists and challenges domination and collusion? Who speaks and who is silenced? Who acts? And who is acted upon? Who waits? What reading subject positions are offered by these texts?). The end or closure of these texts will be the next layer of analysis (How did the writer close the story? What are the assumptions imbedded in this closure? Is the ending ideologically open or closed?). Critical multicultural analysis requires examination of the historical, sociopolitical, and discursive forces that have constructed these texts.

We draw on Norman Fairclough's (1992) three-dimensional process of discourse analysis: Any discursive "event" (i.e., any instance of discourse) is seen as being simultaneously a piece of text, an instance of discursive practice, and an instance of social practice. Discursive practices construct social processes or power relationships between people, as well as contribute to maintaining raced, gendered, and classed power relations or structures. Discursive practice contributes to reproducing society, that is, social identities, social processes, and knowledge/power structures, as well as transforming power relations. Discursive practice draws on conventions. We are interested in how race, class, and gender ideologies draw on each other—intertextuality (texts draw on other literary and non-literary texts) and interdiscursivity (discourses drawing on other discourses). Fairclough states: "it is the nature of the social practice that determines the macroprocesses of discursive practice, and it is the micro-processes that shape the text" (Fairclough, 1992: 86).

We record and analyze the "instances of discourse" (Fairclough, 1992) among characters. The units of analysis are determined by a shift in language use due to time, place, character, event, or perspective changes. We discern how discursive practices or language use shapes social processes or relations by enacting the subject positions of dominator, colluder, resister, and/or agent. The microanalyses demonstrate how characters exercise power along a continuum of domination, collusion, resistance, and agency in representative texts.

We selected representative or key texts across many genres to explicate the emerging cultural themes of a text collection. In locating cultural themes, topics that run through these stories and interactions, we make visible how words live among other words, and how these word associations are implicated in how society is organized. Words possess histories and worldviews.

The categories that guide our analysis are: focalization, social function, class/race/gender ideology, and reading subject positions of domination, collusion, resistance, and agency. The last category is what the discourse is doing to social processes among the characters.

Since most of the books in our analyses are picture books, historical and realistic fiction, fairy tales, and nonfiction narratives, we closely examine how these genres position the characters and the reader; what subject positions are offered by each genre; and, how these genres organize the reader's perceptions of reality by managing ideology. In many ways, genre is the material representation of ideology. Our analyses locate some of the historical, sociopolitical, and discursive influences upon these genres.

Critical multicultural analysis examines texts against a sociopolitical lens. What cultural statements (in literary and nonliterary texts) is this book responding to? (Myers, 1988) What dominant messages about race, gender, and class are imbedded in the book reviews, research, and other literature about these books? What is the sociopolitical context of the cultural theme present in the text?

The lens widens to look at texts historically (What are some historical developments of the cultural theme?). Since the texts are social transcripts of U.S. power relations, the following questions are considered: What are the prevailing dominant ideologies about class, race, and gender translated in the texts? In what ways does the discourse of the American Dream prevail? The multi-layers of critical multicultural analysis are immersed in the discourses of race, class, and gender. These layers of analysis make visible the subject positions offered by each text.

The next step is the "discursive leveling of texts," a way of placing books in the discursive field (Rudd, 1999); that is, placing children's literature alongside literary and cultural criticism, and other secondary sources, because discourse circulates everywhere, including in book reviews, research, theory, pedagogy, and the like. A critical multicultural perspective places children's literature into the discursive field. David Rudd's (1999) discourse analysis of Enid Blyton's books is instructive. Critics deem Blyton's books sexist, for example. Rudd argues that by simply labeling this body of literature sexist, we fail to see how the other discourses have their hold on this power relation, overlooking the dynamics of this particular discourse. Rudd's analysis demonstrates that Blyton's books explore sexism, and in some cases, challenge it. By focusing on the textuality of children's literature, critical multicultural analysis discloses how discourses are layered in the construction of the text.

Like Allan Luke (2002), we advocate for a critical multicultural analysis that "move[s] back and forth from analysis of text to analysis of social formation and institution, then, the text can only be made sense out of if we have sufficiently theorized power, political relations, material and historical change, and the social institutions under scrutiny ... theorized reading of the social world" (Luke, 2002: 5). The reading subject position offered by a critical multicultural analysis is constructed intertextually, by reading the narrative against particular literary and nonliterary texts, and generic expectations. Through these dialogic strategies, the reader challenges the ideologically raced, classed, and/or gendered text, exposing the processes whereby race, class, and gender are constructed and rendered natural in texts, and enabling alternative subject positions. Thus, the meaning of the text lies within the spaces between or among texts (Bakhtin, 1981) in interaction with the reader.

Classroom Applications

- Explore critical multicultural analysis through reading aloud, shared reading, and mini-lessons. Select a children's book that is well known by the class. Analyze the focalization, social processes among characters, closure, and genre and juxtapose the text against sociopolitical and historical conditions.
- Locate the point of view of the story. What happens when the perspective is substituted with another viewpoint (e.g., rich character with a poor one or first-person with third-person narrative)?

Recommendations for Classroom Research

- Analyze the power continuum and deepen its dimensions and/or reconceptualize its subject positions. Use the continuum to make sense of social processes between you and your students as well as among your students.

Suggestions for Further Reading

McCallum, Robyn. (1999). *Ideologies of identity in adolescent fiction: The dialogic construction of subjectivity.* New York: Garland Publishing.

Moon, Brian. (1999). *Literary terms: A practical glossary.* Urbana, IL: National Council of Teachers of English.

Nealon, Jeffrey & Giroux, Susan Searls. (2003). *The theory toolbox: Critical concepts for the humanities, arts, and social sciences.* New York: Rowan & Littlefield Publishers.

Nikolajeva, Maria. (2002). *The rhetoric of character in children's literature.* Lanham, MD: Scarecrow Press.

Rudd, David. (2000). *Enid Blyton and the mystery of children's literature.* New York: St. Martin's Press.

Stephens, John. (1992). *Language and ideology in children's fiction.* New York: Longman.
Stephens, John, Watson, Ken & Parker, Judith. (2003). *From picture book to literary theory.* Sydney, AU: Phoenix Education.
Trites, Roberta Seelinger. (2000). *Disturbing the universe: Power and repression in adolescent literature.* Iowa City: University of Iowa Press.

References

Alexander, Patricia. (1983). Portrayal of the culturally diverse in literature: A view of exceptionalities. *Integrateducation,* 21(1–6), 212–214.
Bakhtin, Michel M. (1981). Discourse in the novel. In M. Holquist (Ed., Trans.), *The dialogic imagination: Four essays* (C. Emerson, Trans., pp. 259–422). Austin: University of Texas Press.
Barthes, Roland. (1977). The death of the author. In *Image-Music-Text* (S. Heath, Trans., pp. 142–148). New York: The Noonday Press.
Botelho, Maria J. (1997a). *"Lisboa é Portugal e o resto é paisegen": The issue of invisibility in Portuguese children's literature.* Unpublished manuscript, University of Massachusetts Amherst.
Botelho, Maria José (1997b). *Multiple dialogues: The cultural borderlands of critical pedagogy.* Paper presented at the University of Massachusetts Ninth Annual Conference on Ethnographic and Qualitative Research in Education, Amherst, MA.
Cai, Mingshui. (1998). Multiple definitions of multicultural literature: Is the debate really just "ivory tower" bickering? *The New Advocate,* 11(4), 311–324.
Cai, Mingshui & Bishop, Rudine Sims. (1994). Multicultural literature for children: Towards a clarification of the concept. In A. H. Dyson & C. Genishi (Eds.), *The need for story: Cultural diversity in classroom and community* (pp. 57–71). Urbana, IL: NCTE.
Collins, Patricia Hill. (2000). Toward a new vision: Race, class, and gender as categories of analysis and connection. In M. Adams, W. J. Blumenfeld, R. Castañeda, H. W. Hackman, M. L. Peters, & X. Zúñiga (Eds.), *Readings for diversity and social justice* (pp. 457–462). New York: Routledge.
Cruz-Janzen, Marta I. (1998). Culturally authentic bias. *Rethinking Schools,* 13(1), 5.
Cummins, Jim. (2003). Challenging the construction of difference as deficit: Where are identity, intellect, imagination, and power in the new regime of truth? In P. P. Trifonas (Ed.), *Pedagogies of difference: Rethinking education for social change* (pp. 41–60). New York: Routledge Falmer.
Darder, Antonia & Torres, Rodolfo D. (1999). Shattering the "race" lens: Toward a critical theory of racism. In R. H. Tai & M. L. Kenyatta (Eds.), *Critical ethnicity: Countering the waves of identity politics* (pp. 173–192). New York: Rowman & Littlefield.
Davies, Bronwyn. (1999). What is feminist poststructuralist research? Examining texts of childhood. In B. Kamler (Ed.), *Constructing gender and difference: Critical research perspectives on early childhood* (pp. 13–31). Cresskill, NJ: Hampton Press.
Davies, Bronwyn. (2000). *A body of writing: 1990–1999.* Walnut Creek, CA: AltaMira Press.
Davies, Bronwyn & Harré, Rom. (1990). Positioning: The discursive production of selves. *Journal for the Theory of Social Behavior,* 20(1), 43–63.
Derrida, Jacques. (1980). *Writing and difference.* Chicago: University of Chicago Press.
Fairclough, Norman. (1992). *Discourse and social change.* Cambridge, UK: Polity Press.
Foucault, Michel. (1972). *The archaeology of knowledge and the discourse on language.* New York: Pantheon.
Foucault, Michel. (1980). *Power/knowledge: Selected interviews and other writings, 1972–1977.* New York: Pantheon.
Foucault, Michel. (1984). What is an author? In P. Rabinow (Ed.), *The Foucault reader* (pp. 101–120). New York: Pantheon Books.
Foucault, Michel. (1995). Strategies of power. In W. Truett Anderson (Ed.), *The truth about*

the truth: De-confusing and re-constructing the postmodern world (pp. 40–45). New York: G. P. Putnam's Sons.

Freire, Paulo. (1970/1985). *Pedagogy of the oppressed*. New York: Continuum.

Gee, James Paul. (1999). *An introduction to discourse analysis: Theory and method*. New York: Routledge.

Gee, James Paul. (2001). What is literacy? In P. Shannon (Ed.), *Becoming political, too: New readings and writings in the politics of literacy education* (pp. 1–9). Portsmouth, NH: Heinemann.

Goode, Judith & Maskovsky, Jeff. (2001). *The new poverty studies: The ethnography of power, politics, and impoverished people in the United States*. New York: New York University Press.

Gramsci, Antonio. (2000). *The Antonio Gramsci reader: Selected writings 1916–1935* (D. Forgacs, Ed.). New York: New York University Press.

Griffiths, Gareth. (1994). The myth of authenticity: Representation, discourse and social practice. In C. Tiffin & A. Lawson (Eds.), *De-scribing empire: Post-colonialism and textuality* (pp. 70–85). New York: Routledge.

Guinier, Lani & Torres, Gerald. (2002). *The miner's canary: Enlisting race, resisting power, transforming democracy*. Cambridge, MA: Harvard University Press.

Hall, Stuart. (1996). Who needs "identity"? In S. Hall & Paul du Gay (Eds.), *Questions of cultural identity* (pp. 1–17). Thousand Oaks, CA: Sage.

Harris, Violet J. (Ed.). (1993). *Teaching multicultural literature in grades K-8*. Norwood, MA: Christopher-Gordon Publishers.

Harris, Violet J. (Ed.). (1997). *Using multiethnic literature in the K-8 classroom*. Norwood, MA: Christopher-Gordon Publishers.

Harris, Violet J. & Willis, Arlette I. (2003). Multiculturalism, literature, and curriculum issues. In J. Flood, D. Lapp, J. R. Squire, & J. M. Jensen (Eds.), *Handbook of research on teaching the English language arts* (2nd ed., pp. 825–834). Mahwah, NJ: Erlbaum Associates.

Hoffmann, Diane M. (1996). Culture and self in multicultural education: Reflections on discourse, text, and practice. *American Educational Research Journal, 33*(3), 545–569.

Hollindale, Peter. (1988). Ideology and the children's book. *Signal, 55*, 3–22.

hooks, bell. (2000). *Where we stand: Class matters*. New York: Routledge.

Kahne, Joseph. (1996). The politics of self-esteem. *American Educational Research Journal, 33*(1), 3–22.

Keating, AnnLouise. (1995). Interrogating "whiteness," (de)constructing "race." *College English, 57*(8), 901–918.

Kohn, Alfie. (1994). The truth about self-esteem. *Phi Delta Kappan, 76*(4), 272–283.

Ladson-Billings, G. & Tate IV, William F. (1995). Toward a critical race theory of education. *Teachers College Record, 97*(1), 47–68.

Lipsitz, George. (1997). Class and consciousness: Teaching about social class in public universities. In A. Kumar (Ed.), *Class issues: Pedagogy, cultural studies, and the public sphere* (pp. 9–21). New York: New York University Press.

Lorde, Audre. (1983). There is no hierarchy of oppressions. *Interracial Books for Children Bulletin, 14* (3 & 4), 9.

Luke, Allan. (2002). Beyond science and ideology critique: Developments in critical discourse analysis. In M. McGroarty (Ed.), *Annual Review of Applied Linguistics, 22* (pp. 96–110). New York: Cambridge University Press.

MacCann, Donnarae. (1993). Native Americans in books for the young. In V. J. Harris (Ed.), *Teaching multicultural literature in grades K–8* (pp. 137–169). Norwood, MA: Christopher-Gordon Publishers.

Medeiros, Paulo de. (1996). Beyond the looking glass of empire: The colonization of Portuguese literature. In M. T. Carroll (Ed.), *No small world: Visions and revisions of world literature* (pp. 43–57). Urbana, IL: NCTE.

Myers, Mitzi. (1988). Missed opportunities and critical malpractice: New historicism and children's literature. *Children's Literature Association Quarterly, 13*(1), 41–43.

Ng, Roxana. (2003). Toward an integrative approach to equity in education. In P. P. Trifonas (Ed.), *Pedagogies of difference: Rethinking education for social change* (pp. 206–219). New York: Routledge Falmer.

Nieto, Sonia & Bode, Patty. (2008). *Affirming diversity: The sociopolitical context of multicultural education* (5rd ed.). Boston: Pearson/Allyn and Bacon.

Ortner, Sherry. (1991). Reading America: Preliminary notes on class and culture. In *Recapturing anthropology*. Santa Fe, NM: School of American Research Press.

Ortner, Sherry. (1998). Identities: The hidden life of class. *Journal of Anthropological Research*, 54(1), 1–17.

Parker, Ian. (1999). Introduction. In I. Parker & the Bolton Discourse Network (Eds.), *Critical textwork: An introduction to varieties of discourse and analysis* (pp. 1–12). Philadelphia, PA: Open University Press.

Pennycook, Alaister. (2000). *Critical applied linguistics.* Mahwah, NJ: Lawrence Erlbaum Associates.

Perrucci, Robert & Wysong, Earl. (2003). *The new class society: Goodbye American Dream?* (2nd ed.). New York: Rowman & Littlefield Publishers, Inc.

Reese, Debbie. (2000). Contesting ideology in children's book reviewing. *Studies in American Indian Literatures,* 12(1), 37–55.

Rudd, David. (1999). Fiction: Five run around together—clearing a discursive space for children's literature. In I. Parker & the Bolton Discourse Network (Eds.), *Critical textwork: An introduction to varieties of discourse and analysis* (pp. 40–52). Philadelphia, PA: Open University Press.

Rudd, David. (2000). *Enid Blyton and the mystery of children's literature.* New York: St. Martin's Press.

Sánchez, Rosaura. (1992). Discourses of gender, ethnicity and class in Chicano literature. *The Americas Review,* 20(2), 72–88.

Schwartz, Elaine G. (1995). Crossing borders/Shifting paradigms: Multiculturalism and children's literature. *Harvard Educational Review,* 65(4), 634–650.

Sims (Bishop), Rudine. (1982). *Shadow and substance: Afro-American experience in contemporary children's fiction.* Urbana, IL: NCTE.

Stephens, John. (1992). *Language and ideology in children's fiction.* New York: Longman.

Stephens, John. (1994). Signifying strategies and closed texts in Australian children's literature. *Australian Review of Applied Linguistics,* 17(2), 131–146.

Stephens, John. (1999a). Analysing texts for children: Linguistics and stylistics. In P. Hunt (Ed.), *Understanding children's literature: Key essays from the international companion encyclopedia of children literature* (pp. 56–68). New York: Routledge.

Stephens, John. (1999b). Maintaining distinctions: Realism, voice, and subject position in Australian young adult fiction. In S. L. Beckett (Ed.), *Transcending boundaries: Writing for a dual audience of children and adults* (pp. 183–198). New York: Garland.

Tejeda, Carlos, Espinoza, Manuel & Gutierrez, Kris. (2003). Toward a decolonizing pedagogy: Social justice reconsidered. In P. P. Trifonias (Ed.), *Pedagogies of difference* (pp. 10–40). New York: Routledge Falmer.

Ulichny, Polly. (1996). Cultures in conflict. *Anthropology & Education Quarterly,* 27(3), 331–364.

Watkins, Tony. (1999). The setting of children's literature: History and culture. In Peter Hunt (Ed.), *Understanding children's literature: Key essays from the international companion encyclopedia of children's literature* (pp. 30–38). New York: Routledge.

Weedon, Chris. (1997). *Feminist practice & poststructuralist theory* (2nd ed.). Malden, MA: Blackwell.

Endnote

1. Domination is an imperfect word to describe this subject position because it implies a fixed position of power. We considered using oppression or repression, but, while

more dynamic in meaning, they still do not capture the fluidity of this subject position. Privileging was another consideration, but some form of privilege is a consequence of all the subject positions. We have decided to use domination, but implore the reader to keep the dynamism of this coercive position in mind, while remembering that it exists because of the U.S. power structures of class, race, and gender.

CHAPTER 6

Doors to the Diaspora: The Social Construction of Race

Joel Spring (2004) states succinctly that "race is primarily a social construction" (Spring, 2004: 4). Spring goes on to sorrowfully point out that racism breeds violence and gives examples such as the Civil War, the Trail of Tears resulting in the deaths of thousands of Native Americans, the brutality leveled at African slaves, lynching, race riots, and on and on.

Many books for children have been written depicting the cataclysmic results of racisms. Some have capitulated to the myths of European American virtue and righteousness, while others have painted a more complex picture, helping readers to engage in active dialogue with the author, their peers, and concerned adults. This engagement, at its best, includes comparing histories, discerning ideologies, and questioning "factual" information.

Readers use critical multicultural analysis to interrogate the subject positions offered by the text and consider whether those positions perpetuate anti-democratic ideologies. In so doing they find themselves reflected, open themselves to viewing others, and unlock doors to offer alternative ways of organizing themselves as communities, cultures, and as a society. While a door invites readers to locate similarities and differences between themselves and those reflected in books, it also requires readers to understand how social difference is historically, socially, and discursively constructed. The door transforms diversity into a resource for action. The window provides access to each other's stories as a way to begin to understand how dominant ideologies have worked to shape who we are as people, as well as how we have contributed to their circulation. The window opens to a view of unlearning and relearning. The door leads to how language can be implicated in social processes.

While critical multicultural analysis provides a window into the representation of multiculturalism in children's literature, the door engages us with critical questions about culture, power, race, class, gender, and how children's books position the reader. Why are some groups underrepresented in children's literature? What social factors have contributed to their underrepresentation? In what ways have underrepresented groups resisted dominant ideologies and taken action?

This kind of reading has implications for resisting worldviews that privilege the dominant culture's interests of those afforded with more social power based on race, class, and gender. Doors create opportunities for re-imagining power relations and organizing for collective action. Critical analysis is an entryway to locating dominant discourses and examining how they position us as readers. It is also a door to discourses that will lead us to more equitable ways of being in the world. The door opens to a space that permits us to consider movements of people in complicated ways.

Multiple U.S. Histories

North America (i.e., Canada, United States, and Mexico) was populated in a variety of ways. Although the evidence is sparse and Vine Deloria Jr. (1995) convincingly opposes the theory of the land bridge as inconclusive, and because of the tenuous nature of the theory, we should remain open to other theories. Historians and archaeologists suggest that the first peoples probably came from Asia; about 40,000 years ago across the land bridge that they believe then existed. The migration continued, with most of the groups traveling south, most likely following herds of wild game. It is estimated that some groups of people reached the southern tip of South America about 10,000 years ago.

At about the same time, it is proposed by some anthropologists that the northern land bridge became an ocean, so subsequent potential settlers had to travel by sea. There is some evidence in pottery and games played by ancient groups which indicates that people from Japan, China, and India may have made contact of some sort with the people of the Americas thousands of years ago.

Whatever the policy for labeling people as Native Americans, it is clear that in the fifteenth century when Europeans began colonizing the Americas there were already several millions of Indigenous people inhabiting the land. By the time Christopher Columbus reached the West Indies, many different peoples lived in North, Central, and South America. They spoke many different languages and practiced a variety of religions. Some groups farmed, others fished, and still others hunted. There were artists, engineers, and astronomers. The Aztecs of Central Mexico, who inhabited great stone cities, had developed a complex civilization. Mayans and Incas also were skilled craftspeople, scientists, and builders. Perhaps sixteen million people comprised the Inca Empire, which was larger than any kingdom in Europe at that time.

The Indigenous people of the United States were the first persecuted ethnic group on this continent. The persecution began with Columbus and continued with later European invaders, settlers, and governments. Although many European immigrants who sought religious freedom themselves had been subjugated, they became oppressors of Native Americans. They denigrated the religions and lifestyles of the Native peoples and did all that they could to forcibly convert the "heathen" to Christianity.

In 1804, the Cherokee nation was forced, unlawfully, to relinquish all of its lands and possessions. President Andrew Jackson overrode the Supreme Court ruling in favor of the Cherokee nation and expanded the numbers of Native Americans who were forced to be removed to the West, including 13,000 Choctaws and 22,000 Creeks (Zinn, 1997: 105–106).

In 1887, the Allotment Act permitted the United States to divide all Indian lands into small allotments and make all land that remained after the Indians had received their shares available to White settlers.

Howard Zinn (1997) maintains that "the forces that led to removal did not come from the poor white frontiersmen who were neighbors of the Indians. They came from industrialization and commerce, the growth of populations, of railroads and cities, the rise in value of land, and the greed of businessmen. The Indians were to end up dead or exiled, the land speculators richer, the politicians more powerful" (Zinn, 1997: 103).

The European Americans pushed Indigenous peoples out of their homes in order to move westward and "settle" the land. They called themselves pioneers, when in fact they were invaders.

With the various Spanish incursions of the fifteenth century and continuing with English, Dutch, French, and Portuguese occupiers in the next several centuries, the population of the United States became a mix of Native peoples and Europeans. They were soldiers, religious people fleeing oppression, farmers, and fur trappers. There were also African slaves brought by Spanish settlers to the Caribbean beginning in 1517. The importation of slaves from Africa, mostly from countries on the west coast, introduced a large body of people who were not here for profit or adventure. They were not here of their own free will. Like the Native Americans, they spoke many different languages, came from divergent cultures, and practiced diverse religions.

In 1619, a Dutch ship brought the first African slaves to Virginia to work mostly in the cultivation of tobacco and rice. By about 1700 there were approximately 80,000 people of African origin in the colonies. The invention of the cotton gin in 1793 made slavery much more profitable. (It became feasible for much more cotton to be grown because of the ease with which the cotton gin could process it.) By 1860 there were almost 4 million slaves in the United States.

Spaniards came to the Americas first as conquerors and then as inhabitants. They brought African slaves to help with the hard work of cultivating the land and mining precious material. From 1819 to 1898, the United States acquired land controlled by Spain through a series of purchases and military conquests. It is noteworthy that, like the Native Americans and Africans, each of the Latino/a groups is different from the others in history, culture, and language (e.g., Brazilians speak Portuguese). Within each group, there is also wide diversity. The Latino/a population today of the United States includes approximately 21 million from Mexico, 3.5 million from Puerto Rico, 1.2 million from Cuba and 10 million from all other Latin American countries (U.S. Census Bureau, 2000b).

In 1917, Puerto Ricans were granted American citizenship without taking part in the decision. High unemployment on the island and unrestricted entry to the United States forced thousands of Puerto Ricans to seek work and better financial conditions on the mainland. Many Puerto Ricans go back and forth from the island to the mainland, and about one third resettle in Puerto Rico permanently.

Cubans are most readily welcomed into the United States when they claim political asylum. The 1 million Cubans residing in Florida are part of a vocal and active political community.

Since the seventeenth century, waves of people came as a result of searching for religious or political freedom, as victims of wars and socioeconomic oppression, or as seekers of economic opportunities and prosperity. Socioeconomic oppression and religious persecution were pervasive in Europe. Most of the European immigrants to the United States from 1607 onward were from England, Wales, Ireland, Belgium, Sweden, Norway, Finland, Holland as well as the French Huguenots, Dutch, Spaniards, and Portuguese Jews.

Five million people emigrated from Western Europe between the 1820s and the 1850s. This mass migration doubled the existing U.S. population. The Industrial Revolution forced many farmworkers out of their homes. In Ireland, two factors figured strongly in a surge of immigration: the conversion by the British landowners of farmland to sheep-grazing land (because the sale of wool was more profitable than the sale of produce) and the potato blights that destroyed a significant source of food. Certain socially made conditions allowed for the potato blight to spread; it was not the first famine to take place in Ireland nor was it just a natural disaster. English domination over the Irish offered a blueprint for the deculturalization of people of color in the United States (Spring, 2004).

At this time, many Irish people immigrated to the United States and became domestic servants and laborers on canals, roads, and railroads.

When the Irish arrived in the United States, like all immigrant groups who came because of economic oppression, they were met with racism. They were considered disposable labor compared to the valuable slave labor and given the most dangerous jobs (Ignatiev, 1995).

During this time, many people from Southern Germany and the German Swiss areas came for economic reasons and settled in great numbers in the Midwest and in Pennsylvania. They favored occupations such as butcher, carpenter, shoemaker, and other skilled work. In this same period, people continued to come from Great Britain. Some of them opened commercial enterprises such as textile mills and pottery factories.

Starting in the mid-nineteenth century, Chinese immigrants arrived on the West coast in response to the need for laborers to build railroads and work in mines. By 1880, approximately 105,000 Chinese laborers lived in the United States. They were often victims of violence and hatred. After the Civil War, new waves of immigrants, mostly from Western Europe, settled in the lands west of the Mississippi. This contributed to the wresting of more land from the Indigenous peoples.

In 1882, sentiment against Chinese immigrants reached such proportions that the Chinese Exclusion Act was passed, suspending Chinese immigration for the next ten years. (It was followed by more exclusionary laws that were not repealed until 1943.) At that time, Japanese immigrants were not banned, and from 1885 to the turn of the century, Japanese emigrated in large numbers, mostly to Hawaii and California. In 1890, about 2,000 Japanese lived in the United States. In 1907, because of pressure exerted by people afraid of losing their jobs to low-paid Japanese laborers, and because of an irrational fear of a "yellow peril," the United States and Japan negotiated what was euphemistically called a "gentlemen's agreement." The Japanese government agreed to forbid laborers to immigrate to the United States for a period of two years.

Anti-Japanese sentiment accelerated in the twentieth century and reached a height at the onset of the Second World War when internment camps imprisoned more than 110,000 Japanese Americans (only recently has Congress officially admitted wrong doing). With Hawaii becoming the fiftieth state in 1960 came greater acceptance of Japanese people. The 2000 census reported that there are almost 850,000 Japanese Americans living in the United States.

Not until the late nineteenth century did emigrants from Southern and Eastern Europe arrive. Availability of jobs in the United States was probably the major attraction. Steamship lines permitted travel at affordable cost. Italians, Poles, Czechs, Lithuanians, Finns, and Croats came largely for economic reasons. Many Jews fled Russia as a result of the pogroms (organized annihilation of entire settlements of Jews) and because of virulent and violent anti-Semitism in the other countries of Europe. Turks, Armenians, and people from the Balkans also came to escape religious and ethnic persecution.

In 1980, the pressure to admit people escaping from Vietnam, Laos, and Cambodia impelled Congress to pass the Refugee Act allowing thousands to enter. Although this act was intended to correct the imbalance of political forces affecting acceptance of refugees according to the World Refugee Survey of 1992, 99.8 percent of the refugees admitted to the United States since 1980 have come from countries hostile to the United States.

Working class immigrant groups in the twentieth century encountered suspicion, resentment, and rejection from people who had come before them. U.S. immigration laws reflected these biased attitudes. A literacy requirement for citizenship was imposed on all new immigrants, and restrictions were increased against Asian immigration. In 1924, the Johnson-Reed Act limited emigration from each country to 2 percent of the number in the United States in 1890, with the total not to exceed 150,000. This act was intended to sharply limit "undesirable" populations from immigrating in great numbers.

The quota system was eliminated in 1965. In its place, variable ceilings were set annually for immigrants from North and South America and from the rest of the world. By 1991, the United States was accepting more immigrants and refugees than all other countries combined: about 700,000 each year, about 140,000 of them being refugees. Most now come from Asia, Latin America, and the Middle East.

The 2000 U.S. Census Bureau (2000b) counted over 10 million Asian Americans (a three-million increase since 1990), about 35 million Latino/a people (a 13-million increase since 1990), about 2.5 million Native Americans (a half million increase from 1990), and about 34.5 million African Americans (constituting 4.5-million increase since 1990). European Americans constitute approximately 211 million of the total population of approximately 281.5 million (an 11-million increase since 1990). By 2050, it is estimated that U.S. demographics will shift in the following ways: the Latino/a and Asian/Pacific Islander populations may triple; African American population may increase by 70 percent; the European American population may increase by 9 percent; and the immigrant population probably will double (from 26 to 53.8 million). These projections are based on childbearing, mortality, and migration patterns but do not consider possible future changes in the ways people may identify themselves as they report their race and ethnicity (U.S. Census Bureau, 2000a).

The predictions about the changing demographics of the United States are coming true. It is expected that the Asian population will increase tenfold and Latino/as threefold in the next 50 years, and that by 2070, European Americans will probably be a minority. It is all the more necessary (albeit not sufficient), therefore, that children's literature reflect as many hues, backgrounds, and cultures as possible, so as to provide both mirrors and windows for young people as well as for adults.

We are trying to make visible the process of how this country was peopled and what happened when different cultural groups came together. The process was marked by the differences in and among the populations. Some groups, such as the Irish, came voluntarily but out of desperation. From the beginning, Native American nations lived in what is now the United States and remained as nations despite almost genocidal oppression. People whose homes originated from across the African continent were forced to come and were enslaved. These cultural groups represent decidedly different histories and sociopolitical situations. It is important for us not to idealize or essentialize these cultural groups. We need to acknowledge the diversity of experiences within each diasporic experience.

We are concerned about the oversimplification of the designation of race as the key element that distinguishes one group from another. We are firmly committed to the understanding that there is only one race, the human race, and that more than the differences of skin color, facial features, and characteristics of hair distinguish individuals from each other. On the other hand, we want to acknowledge that the social construct of race alongside class and gender and the values attendant upon them shape how we are organized as a society in the United States.

Deconstructing the American Dream

The discourse of the American Dream, an ideology historically rooted in the "founding" of the "New World," romanticizes the workings of capitalism and tries to avoid the power relations of race, gender, and class. This social myth developed at the same time as the decline of European feudalism (Wang, 2000). The American Dream promised the possibility that all Americans could attain material prosperity through their own initiative and hard work. The persistence of the self-made ideology, which fueled the "from-rags-to-riches" paradigm, enticed many generations of immigrants to attempt success in "the land of opportunity." But this self-made success had a social cost that continues to this day.

Jeffrey Louis Decker argues that the American Dream is "U.S. capitalism's master trope" (Decker, 1990: 1). He claims that, even though this social vision has been part of American culture since the mid-nineteenth century, the term emerged after James T. Adams (1931) published "Our American Dream," what Decker calls, "a treatise on how to make the Dream 'come true' " during the Great Depression (Decker, 1990: 1). This essay tried to defuse the class struggle and class consciousness emerging during this economic crisis in the United States, a crisis that was historically and politically made. The ideology of the American Dream blames socio-economic inequities on the individual. The American Dream represses historical memory and promotes a permeable power structure that supposedly benefits all people.

The United States as a Diaspora

The American Dream has summoned many immigrants to the United States. Immigration and diaspora are two ways to categorize these movements of people. Immigration signifies the moving from one country to another, to take up permanent residency. Many social factors contribute to people's departure from one country for another: ethnic cleansing, socio-economics and political circumstances, religious bigotry, and reunion with families and communities.

Voluntary emigration conjures up images of White Europeans (e.g., Irish, Jewish, Italian, and Portuguese) leaving their homelands. This image excludes many cultural groups. In many instances choice is implied in this term because of voluntary movement in response to economic oppression, or religious or political unrest. It is difficult to find appropriate terminology to explain the phenomenon of not-quite-voluntary relocation. Also needed is language to describe the implications of the homeland governments and their roles in the flight of their citizens. Because we think it accounts for this phenomenon, we have chosen the term diaspora, which acknowledges the integration of race, class, and gender, as well as considering multiple cultural experiences.

According to the fourth edition of the *American Heritage Dictionary of the English Language*, published by Houghton Mifflin, diaspora is "the dispersion or spreading of something that was originally localized (as a people or language or culture)." The diaspora construct rejects that there is one U.S. history, and considers not only diversity, but also social difference and its construction. With diaspora, the homeland has a vested interest in scattering the targeted population.

We are drawn to the United States as a locus of diaspora because this concept takes into account the multiple power relations people participate in: local, national, and global. The study of diaspora reveals social processes (e.g., negotiation and recreation) and their complexities and dynamism.

Diaspora creates a space to name race, class, and gender. Emma Pérez (1999) maintains that a "diasporic subjectivity" differs from an immigrant one. She claims that race cannot be as easily overlooked from diaspora:

> Diasporic subjectivity opens a space where people of color [can] negotiate a raced culture within many kinds of identities without racial erasure through assimilation, accommodation, adaptation, acculturation, or even resistance—all of which have been robbed of their decolonial oppositional subjectivity under the rubric of immigrant. Immigrants are expected to become part of the dominant culture; they are urged to adopt its habits and forget their own—to erase. Diasporas, on the other hand, intervene, construct newness, and call upon these complex diasporic subjectivities that "live inside with a difference".
>
> (Pérez 1999: 78)

The diaspora foregrounds the responses of peoples as they live through these sociopolitical processes and exercise power on a daily basis, in efforts to reconstruct themselves and reconstruct culture.

In thinking about the United States as a diaspora, we reject simplistic binary oppositions of the colonizing and the colonized in historical and contemporary times. Like Carlos Tejeda, Manuel Espinoza, and Kris Gutierrez (2003), we align ourselves with a complex view of these power relations by acknowledging:

1. the diversity of the European American population, that is, these cultural group experiences are shaped by social divisions based on ethnicity, class, language;
2. the social diversity of the dominant Anglo population;
3. the plurality of experiences among Indigenous peoples;
4. the social diversity of "involuntary immigrants" (Ogbu, 1991) from Africa, and their descendants. They came from a diversity of cultures, languages, and social associations.

Not all European groups have colluded with "colonial/neocolonial relations of domination and exploitation" (Tejada, Espinoza, Gutierrez, 2003) nor have all European groups been privileged by these conditions (hooks, 2000). Conversely, social domination is not experienced in the same way by all Indigenous peoples, African Americans, and other people of color.

The concept of diaspora considers these social circumstances and re/contextualizes these cultural experiences within their histories. History offers new possibilities for looking at our collective subjectivities (cultural identities) and examines how social difference is a consequence of power. Lawrence Grossberg maintains that "diaspora emphasizes the historically spatial fluidity and intentionality of identity, its articulation to structures of historical movements (whether forced or chosen, necessary or desired)" (Grossberg, 1996: 92). He continues: "Subjectivity as spatial is perhaps the clearest, for it involves taking literally the statement that people experience the world from a particular position—recognizing that such positions are in space rather than (or at least as much as in) time . . ." (Grossberg, 1996: 100). The construct of diaspora recognizes these dimensions.

Nation and culture develop out of social practice. Culture is the product of historical and sociopolitical processes. Nationhood is performed by the nation's members; it does not develop naturally over time but through historical and sociopolitical forces that contribute to its construction. Homi Bhabha describes these processes as "a double narrative movement"—both pedagogical and performative (Bhabha, 1990: 297). The pedagogical signifies the historical background (the tradition) of a people and the recognized identity of a nation. The performative process is the dynamic in which a nation's population participates in the construction of the country's collective subjectivity. Cultural products such as children's literature play a role in "narrating the nation" and must be studied against historical and sociopolitical contexts, with an awareness of the social construction of nation and culture. Critical multicultural analysis can peel away at the layers of these constructions.

In this chapter, we have examined the processes by which Europeans, Asians, Latinos/as, Native peoples, and African slaves came together under the umbrella of the United States. What follows is a re/contextualization of Mexican American representation in children's literature by examining the historical and sociopolitical circumstances of Mexican American participation in the U.S. farmworker system by historicizing representation over time. The social, discursive, and political constructions of genres, narrative processes (characterization), and story closure will be considered in this process of re/contextualization; that is, understanding this text collection against historical, sociopolitical, and discursive conditions.

The Historical and Sociopolitical Context of Mexican American Participation in the U.S. Migrant Agricultural Labor System

Although we acknowledge the rich culture of the Mexican people, for the purpose of this text, we are focusing on the contemporary Mexican American, from the time of the invasion and the annexing of Mexican territory by the U.S. army. The Mexican American experience began historically in 1848 with the Treaty of Guadalupe Hidalgo. This historical event marks a sociopolitical shift in identity. Before this date, the Mexican population was socially and economically diverse as well as geographically scattered. The response to U.S. conquest was also diverse (Almaguer, 1989): What came to bind the Mexican Americans to each other was a history of power relations between the dominant Anglo-American culture and the fledgling Mexican American culture. This history informs the rendering and interpretation of the Mexican American experience in children's literature. Economic and racial oppression, political inequality, and educational deculturalization mark this history. Mexican Americans were/are a heterogeneous group with class and cultural associations and disassociations, which dramatically shape/d the diversity in ethnic identification and social position. These historical processes are complex.

Mexican American historian Tomás Almaguer argues that "both the class and racial oppression of the Chicano, and of other colonized people of color, have stemmed from the organization of the economic structure of U.S. capitalism and from the labor relationships that generate from that particular mode of production" (Almaguer, 1974: 43). The migrant agricultural labor system is a by-product of economic exploitation.

Almaguer (1989) contends that the racial examination of the colonizing processes obscures the class divisions that existed prior to 1848 and hides "the class nature of this racial conflict" (Almaguer, 1974: 12). For example, according to Almaguer, these historical accounts fail to document the enslavement of the Indian population in the ranchero-based system. In addition, the class system in place before Anglo contact was greatly divided along racial lines. The focus on Anglo-Mexican relations overshadows the experiences of other underrepresented Southwest groups. The labor systems were complex: "These included the coercive labor system associated with the Mexican rancho economy, other pre-capitalist labor systems such as slavery and indentured servitude, the marginalized communal economy of the Indian population, and the free wage-labor system of the rapidly ascending capitalist economy" (Almaguer, 1974: 17). Almaguer (1989) maintains that it does not mean that Chicanos were on equal economic footing with the Anglo-American population, but that historical evidence shows that they were relegated to the bottom of the "emerging capitalist economic order" (Almaguer, 1989: 17). Mexicans became socially defined against blackness, which "destabilized [this] political alliance built out of resistance to an oppressive economic regime" (Guinier & Torres, 2002: 230). Mexicans did/do not fit into the black/white paradigm.

Overall, Mexicans were considered "more structurally assimilable" than other minority groups because they, for the most part, were a Christian people, spoke a romance language, had a politically powerful upper class, the female population intermarried with Whites, and, because of their Spaniard ancestry, were perceived as White. Their social position significantly changed with a great influx of immigrants in the early decades of the twentieth century. The significant feature of the twentieth-century Chicano experience in California is marked by "the proletarianization of the Mexican population that immigrated to the United States during the 1910s, 1920s, and 1930s" (Almaguer, 1989: 24). In these early decades of the 1900s, main conflicts occurred between the Mexican and Anglo-American working classes.

Mexico was/is a class and race divided society. In the earlier 1900s, Mexicans were "pushed north by the Mexican government's radical dismantling of traditional communal landownership, which forced 5 million rural Mexicans—over 97 percent of the campesino population—off their land" (Rothenberg, 1998: 32). The agricultural industry absorbed many Mexican documented and undocumented immigrants during this period. Rodolfo Acuña (1988) argues that "Mexican labor . . . built the Southwest" (Acuña, 1988: 141), especially the expansion in agricultural production. The immigration laws such as the 1908 Gentleman's Agreement and the 1924 Immigration Act, which excluded Asian labor, further facilitated the increase in Mexican agricultural labor. Many farmers preferred Mexican farmworkers because they were "more humble and you [got] more for your money" (Takaki, 1993: 321).

The First World War brought an increase in Mexican migration to the United States due to the labor needs of "the war economy." The U.S. government created programs to promote Mexican migration across the border. Many of these immigrants worked in agriculture. Mexican migration, motivated by this "push-pull process" (McWilliam, 1968 as cited in Gonzales, 1999: 114), accounts for one of the largest mass migrations in human history: Acuña (1988) maintains that one-tenth of Mexico's population migrated north from the early 1900s up to the Great Depression. The Mexican Revolution, which began 1910, created social, political, and economic forces that contributed to this influx of immigrants.

The Mexican International Railroad facilitated mass migration. According to Ronald Takaki (1993), the Mexican population in the Southwest swelled from approximately 375,000 to 1,160,000 between 1900 and 1930, with Mexican nationals as the majority. The greatest stream of people moved during the 1920s, when approximately half a million Mexicans entered the United States. Many of these people settled in Texas, Arizona, New Mexico, and California. During the Great Depression, Chicanas/os actively participated in labor struggles. For example, in 1933, 12,000 farmworkers in the San Joaquin Valley protested wage cuts. In 1929, the federal government passed the Deportation Act, which gave counties power to send Mexicans back to Mexico. Many U.S.-born citizens were sent back in the Immigration Bureau's many sweeps. Between 1929 and 1935, approximately 450,000 Mexicans and Mexican Americans were relocated to Mexico, one of the largest involuntary migrations in the United States.

During the Second World War, the possibility of farm labor shortages was imminent because many poor White workers were entering the military or finding better jobs in the war economy. The U.S. government instituted a "guest worker system" in 1942 called the Bracero[1] Program, a "managed migration" (Gonzales, 1999: 174). Over a 22-year period, this program brought 4 to 5 million Mexican workers into the United States to work in the agricultural industry (Rothenberg, 1998). This program supplied farmers with "cheap, docile, and disposable farm laborers from Mexico" (del Castillo & De León, 1996: 127). Manuel G. Gonzales (1999) claims that the duration of the Bracero Program speaks to the substantial power held by U.S. agribusiness.

While the Bracero Program was in place, it obstructed unionization efforts because it permitted a free flow of labor from the South. The U.S. government ended this program in 1965. The termination of this federal program created a space for the United Farm Workers (UFW) union, "the most ambitious unionization attempt to date" (Gonzales, 1999).

The United Farm Workers, first named the National Farm Workers Union, was founded in Fresno, California, on September 30, 1962 by César Chávez, a former migrant farmworker, and Dolores Huerta, a former schoolteacher. Since union activities accommodated families, women played a key role in securing better wages and work conditions, and access to health and dental care.

The Delano grape strike, initiated by a Filipino farmer's union, the Agricultural Workers Organizing Committee, was UFW's first project. Since most of the farmworkers in the area were Mexican, Chávez was invited to join forces. Greatly influenced by Gandhi and Dr. Martin Luther King Jr., he passionately believed in nonviolence. The UFW allied themselves with other trade unions and religious organizations. Along with these alliances, the UFW has organized, striked, boycotted, protested, marched, and fasted against unjust agricultural labor practices. To this day, the UFW struggles to organize farm labor.

The Chicano *movimiento* of the 1960s failed to include the farm-workers' concerns of labor exploitation in their cause (Rosales, 1997). *El movimiento* participants embraced a middle-class Mexican American agenda: education and social mobility, whereas the Mexican workers had "bread-and-butter concerns" (Rosales, 1997: 112). In addition, Arturo Rosales argues that "*movimiento* participants did not dwell on unioniza-tion because its success depended on a working-class consciousness that required collaboration with [W]hite workers—an unattractive option during these very nationalistic times" (Rosales, 1997: 112).

Documented immigration from Mexico in the 1970s averaged 60,000 per year. Pressure by agribusiness resulted in legislation to allow more Mexicans to enter the country as "guest workers." The human flow between the two countries can be attributed to economic factors, the decline of extended family networks, family reunification efforts, and anti-Indian policies and practices in Mexico. More women now immigrate with their families. In addition, many of the recent immigrants from Mexico are refugees from Central America (Gonzalez, 1999). The push-pull explan-ation no longer applies. Immigration patterns are more complex. For example, many families maintain dual residence, establishing "a trans-national migrant circuit" (Rouse, 1989 as cited in Gonzalez, 1999: 228).

Mexican Americans are the largest growing ethnolinguistic group in the United States. In the March 2002 "Current Population Survey" of the U.S. Census Bureau, Latinas/os[2] comprised 13.3% (37.4 million) of the U.S. population, of which 66.9% (25.1 million) were Mexican[3] people who mostly resided in the American Southwest. One-third of the Latina/o population was under age 18, with Mexicans/Chicanos having the largest proportion (37.1) of people under this age. One-quarter of Latina/o children lived in poverty. Latina/o families were more likely to live in poverty and be unemployed than "non-[Latina/o] White" families: Mexicans/Chicanas/os had the second highest rate (8.4%) of unemploy-ment, with Puerto Ricans experiencing the highest rate (9.6%).

Approximately 76 percent of Mexicans/Chicanas/os, who are full-time year-round workers, earned less than $35,000. Latinas/os have the lowest formal education attainment rate in the United States, with twenty-five-year-old and older Mexicans/Chicanas/os having the lowest proportion of people with a high school diploma, bachelor's degree or higher education. In a 2000 survey about languages spoken at home, over 28 million people (the U.S. population was 262.4 million), who were 5 years old and over, spoke Spanish or Spanish Creole (U.S. Census Bureau, 2000). Out of this total, 8,105,505 speakers of Spanish resided in California. Sánchez states:

"One of the salient characteristics of Chicano literature is its dialogue with history and its focus on collective subjectivity" (Sánchez, 1992: 73). The representation of the Mexican American experience in children's literature further illuminates the depiction of the migrant farmworker system.

The Mexican–U.S. border stretches two thousand miles across sand, scrub, brush-strewn yellow dirt, and the dark waters of the Rio Grande. Many of the characters in the text collection cross this border or refer to its presence as a marker that signals the socioeconomic divide that exists within and between Mexico and the United States. However, this border is sociopolitically made, and historically speaking, as Maria José Fernández (2003) maintains, the border crossed the people; that is, the American Southwest once belonged to Mexico and was taken over by military force by the United States.

In his most recent book, *Brown: The Last Discovery of America*, Chicano scholar Richard Rodriguez (2002) explains that brown is understood in Latin America as "a reminder of conflict": "I am made of the conquistador and the Indian" (Rodriguez, 2002: xii). North of the U.S–Mexico border, "the future is brown" (Rodriguez, 2002: 35). Brown becomes a verb—the "browning" of the United States. South of the border brown signals a history. Brown is beyond "the founding palette" of Red, Black, and White. The border is a metaphor for shifting identities and geopolitical status.

The Historical and Sociopolitical Context of Mexican American Representation in Children's Literature

Many scholars argue that Mexican American children's literature needs to be interpreted against a historical and sociopolitical backdrop of the Mexican American experience, starting in 1848, the political moment that is used to mark the beginning of Mexican American identity. But literature existed before this historical moment and continued after this conquest. It is worth noting that, most recently, Arte Público Press initiated the Recovery Project, a comprehensive program to reconstitute the literary history of Latinos/as in the United States from colonial times to 1960.

No Mexican American children's literature was published prior to 1940; however, an oral literary tradition was present before and after this historical period and a number folk tales were published as picture books. Unfortunately, cultural homogeneity and historical distortion pervade through the representation of Mexican Americans in children's literature. The stereotypic rendering began in 1940: It was a "pastoral view" (Cortes, 1992) of what Mexicans, not Mexican Americans, looked and acted like.

Between 1940 to 1970 approximately six books a year on Mexican American themes and content were published. The Council on Interracial

Books for Children (CIBC) (1975) argues that this number is inflated since many of the 140 books they surveyed were not about Chicano culture, but about Mexico and Mexicans "adventuring in the United States [and] about characters with Spanish names" (CIBC, 1975: 7). Of the 60 nonfiction books examined in this investigation, only 15 were about the Mexican American experience and the Southwest. Given these figures, a more accurate estimate for annual publishing would be about one to three books per year for this time period, Latino children's literature scholars Barrera, Liguori and Salas (1993) maintain.

In 1975 the CIBC initiated the first comprehensive study of the representation of Mexican Americans in children's literature. Their findings were published in the *Interracial Books for Children Bulletin* (1975). (The Council simultaneously published this survey in Spanish in *La Luz*, a magazine based in Denver, Colorado.) The survey included 200 children's books on Chicano/a themes, published from 1940 to 1970. Anglo writers wrote all the books examined. Out of the 200 volumes 140 books were fiction. CIBC's intent was to analyze books for racist and sexist content. The survey findings show a general pattern of cultural misrepresentation and stereotypic depiction.

Many of the strong undercurrents in these books reveal race and class biases. The common cultural themes include the "poverty plot," generated by two assumptions held by Anglo authors: "(1) the assumption of Mexican and Chicano quaintness, ignorance and inferiority; and (2) the assumption of Anglo benevolence and the unquestioned superiority of the Anglo American way of life"; "poor, ignorant, helpless Mexican is saved by a benevolent Anglo"; "Chicano gets his wish, but selflessly sacrifices it"; "striving Chicano (pushes for an education)"; and "adventures of the migrant worker," that is, Mexicans depicted as going north to the "land of opportunity," whereas Chicanos born in the United States are portrayed as "leading a rootless life following the crops" (CIBC, 1975: 8). Implicit in all of these recurrent themes is that acculturation is inevitable and the "only possible road to [a] better life" (CIBC, 1975: 8): A pressure to be "American," while leaving the Mexican American culture and Spanish language behind, is central to these texts.

The Spanish language and English language learning are carelessly treated in these texts: There are translation mistakes and the stereotypical portrayal of the English speech of people whose first language is Spanish. In these books, poverty is consistently one of the main characters and "a literary device" (Hade, personal communication, July 2002), that is, a technique to tell a story, and, as CIBC maintains, realistic fiction became a stereotype of a cultural group (CIBC, 1975).

A smaller study conducted by Shirley A. Wagoner, published in *The*

Reading Teacher in December 1982, examines books published since 1970, with the majority produced between 1970 and 1973. Wagoner claims only a handful of books were published after 1974. She outlines the recurring themes: family life and education. Stories portray families as large and close-knit. Education promises the fulfillment of personal and social goals. She found stories more complex than the books published prior to 1970; the texts feature three-dimensional protagonists constrained by their "cultural circumstances." The particularities of family life are interpreted as cultural ways, instead of the ways families respond to a racist and classist society. These books generally portray most Mexican Americans as migrant farmworkers, even though, in 1973, 80 percent of the Mexican American population lived in urban centers (Eiseman, 1973: 64 as cited in Wagoner, 1982).

During the early 1980s Mexican American culture was invisible in children's literature, but a shift occurred toward the second half of this decade and early 1990s. The shift can be attributed to a small number of Chicana/o writers who began writing for children (e.g., Gary Soto, Rudolfo Anaya, Sabine Ulibarrí, Carmen Tafolla, and Pat Mora) and Mexican-American-owned and small alternative presses' publishing activity. Their works of fiction reflected the complexities of the Mexican American community, cross-cultural friendships, biracial families, connections between traditional and contemporary themes, and blended story elements from multiple cultures, as well as including codeswitching in text and bilingual text (Spanish/English) editions.

This shift in writing captured the "subtle and not-so-subtle intra-group differences," foregrounding the commonalities that bind the Mexican American community as an ethnic group (Barrera, Liguori, & Salas, 1993: 223). The genres represented in these developments were fiction and poetry. According to these scholars, nonfiction representation offered a more balanced treatment of the Mexican American community during the 1980s and into the 1990s. European American authors wrote most of these texts. During this time, many omissions still existed in the areas of biographies and historical accounts. Rosalinda B. Barrera, Olga Liguori, and Loretta Salas (1993) argue that storylines exist to move along "the parade of cultural information," that is, Mexican American characters are superficially depicted, with European American children as the targeted audience (Barrera, Liguori, & Salas, 1993: 211).

Their survey of 1980 to 1991 marks a period of substantial improvement in the representation of Mexican Americans in children's literature. Barrera, Liguori, and Salas (1993: 208) recommend some "seeds for growing a 'new literature' " that they claim can considerably improve Chicana/o children's literature:

- this experience is diverse, complex and dynamic;
- authentic portrayal is based on particularities of this experience;
- insider writers play an important role in representing this experience;
- the literary potential of this experience has barely been tapped; and,
- Mexican American literature is a source of knowledge and learning for all children.

Their recommendations signal that the Mexican American experience is dynamic, diverse, complex, contradictory, multiple, and shifting, a complex definition of culture.

Who gets to write about the Mexican American culture? Oralia Garza de Cortes (1992: 123) notes that "authors from outside the culture have generally been more successful in writing nonfiction, which relies upon factual research and the quality of its presentation, than in depicting the subtle aspects of language, experience, and emotion necessary for a compelling work of fiction." In their study, Barrera, Liguori, and Salas (1993) locate misinformation or "cultural errors" as well as a cultural barrenness—an "acultural rendering," that is, the story includes some Latino names and a dash of Spanish words. Barrera, Liguori, and Salas (1993: 218) purport that "cultural authenticity will follow and flow naturally when the doors to children's literature are opened to writers from underrepresented cultures, when different perspectives and different voices are encouraged and supported." Insider authors may be more apt to portray power relations up close instead of stereotyping and/or decontextualizing people and their behaviors; they situate social processes. Capturing these social subtleties brings the reader closer to how the power relations of class, race, and gender are exercised in microinteractions.

Joined by Oralia Garza de Cortes, another scholar of Latino children's literature, Rosalinda B. Barrera (1997) conducted research on the Mexican American in children's literature from 1992 to mid-1995, a period marked by increased activity in multicultural publishing. The text sample consisted of 67 books published in the United States. They also examined 50 books published about Mexican culture and experience to garner any subtle information that would illuminate their analysis. At this point, the annual average increased from 6 books per year to 19. These scholars argue that this is a small increase given the growth in the overall multicultural children's literature publishing, and in U.S. children's publishing in general, and the increased growth of the Mexican American population.

In this early-to-mid-1990s survey, fiction outnumbers nonfiction by a ratio of 2.35 to 1. Eighty-two percent of the fiction books take place in contemporary times, and the remaining books deal with the past. Authors of Mexican American heritage created approximately a third of these titles

(23 books). Gary Soto, a Mexican American author, wrote almost half of these books (11 titles).

These books reflect an increased use of Spanish in the text: bilingual editions with English and Spanish texts alongside each other or "interlingual," incorporating Spanish words and phrases within the English text. With this increase in Spanish, also different dialects of Spanish are included.

Across their text sample they found the following themes: holidays/special days (e.g., Christmas, Day of the Dead, and birthdays), migrants, immigrants (documented and undocumented), and foods. While these developments demonstrate an increase of a more complex representation of Mexican American, some "chronic" stereotypes persist: "(a) Mexican Americans are an 'exotic' and 'foreign' people . . . (b) Mexican Americans are a readily identifiable group within a narrow band of society" (Barrera & Garza de Cortes, 1997: 135). The latter stereotype discounts the intragroup diversity of the Mexican American people: migrants and immigrants are one fraction of the whole. Thus a large portion of this cultural group remains invisible in the world of children's literature.

The Mexican American story includes more complex views of family life, while not submitting to the stereotypes that all Chicano families are large and splintered. These family portrayals have moved into urban contexts and not just rural, farm settings. While these stories move away from stereotyping family life, some distortions still endure: ethnocentricism (assumption that the dominant culture is superior), "overloading", romanticism, and "typecasting." "Overloading" is the return of the "cultural parade" where customs and traditions are strung together without a story line in place. The "myth of U.S. opportunity" is imbedded in these stories where the characters speculate on better lives in the United States. There also exists an overemphasis on the urbane Santa Fe style as representative of Mexican American culture. Romanticism signifies a lack of sociopolitical information to offer a deeper understanding of the social arrangements. Typecasting refers to recurring social positioning of Mexican Americans as particular character types in particular roles.

Barrera and Garza de Cortes (1997) attribute the more complex rendering of the Mexican American identity to the writing by insider authors. They cite a dearth of biographies about Mexican Americans who have made significant contributions to the Mexican American community and U.S. society, as well as the lack of histories of important events in the Mexican American experience.

In 1999, Rosalinda Barrera, with her collaborators Ruth E. Quiroa and Cassiette West-Williams, published their analysis of Mexican American children's literature produced from late 1995 to late 1998. Ninety-two books were identified for analysis, a 37 percent increase from the previous study and an annual increase from 19 to 31. Fifty-eight percent of the sample was fiction (54 books), with 22 percent biography, representing .5 percent of the total amount of children's books published annually in the United States. Nineteen books have bilingual text and 10 of the 19 have separate editions written in Spanish. The majority of the texts were written in English. Some of these books include a sprinkling of Spanish words and phrases, with glossaries providing translation for the new vocabulary.

The overarching theme in the primary grade books is the importance of family and intergenerational ties. Other themes include childhood memories, growing up and gaining confidence, cultural transition involving school, and celebrations. The books for middle school age readers consist of similar themes about family and family issues. Other themes were coming-of-age and survival struggles; intercultural conflict; overcoming personal issues; and cultural maintenance and change.

Most books, at both levels, take place in contemporary times. Gary Soto (7 titles), Pat Mora (4 titles), and Olivia Dumas Lachtman (4 titles) were the principal authors for this time period. One third of the children's books published in this period of time were produced by small independent publishers such as Arte Público Press, Piñata Books, an imprint of the aforementioned publishing house, and Children's Book Press. These small presses specialize in Latino and multicultural texts for children.

Barrera, Quiroa, and West-Williams (1999: 322) comment that the fiction published during this period is "a significant core of young adult fiction books which combine gripping content, cultural authenticity, and skilled writing." Among these texts is Francisco Jiménez's book, *The Circuit*. These scholars contend that Jiménez moves away from a romanticized depiction of migrant life, oftentimes rendered in children's and young adult literature. Jiménez conveys the interdependence of the family members with accuracy. He weaves Spanish words, phrases, and sentences, letting in the subtleties of the Spanish language, as only an insider can, note the scholars. *Gathering the Sun*, written by Alma Flor Ada and illustrated by Simón Silva, which conveys "respect and dignity for the nation's Mexican American migrant farmworkers," was also published during this period (Barrera, Quiroa, & West-Williams, 1999: 325). Originally written in Spanish, this book showcases the Spanish alphabet. *Migrant Worker: a Boy from the Rio Grande Valley*, written by Diane Hoyt-Goldsmith and photographed by Lawrence Migdale, also was published during this period. This photo-essay documents the hardworking life of Ricky, an eleven-year-old boy.

The Cooperative Children's Book Center (CCBC) publishes statistics on books about or by Latinos from 1994 to 2007. On average about 70 books have been published annually. CCBC attributes these steady publishing trends to an increase of books written by Latino/a authors and the publishing activities of small presses. In addition, the Américas, Pura Belpré, and Tomás Rivera awards have brought recognition to the work of Latina/o writers.

The historical and sociopolitical context of Mexican American representation in children's literature and the Chicana/o participation in the U.S. migrant farmworker system re/contextualizes these historical and sociopolitical conditions, which offers a backdrop to analyze the content of the text collection. Critical multicultural analysis also demands that readers consider the role form plays on the content of a text. In the next chapter, the social construction of genres as realistic fiction, poetry, picture books, nonfiction narratives, as well as the discursive shaping of characters and ideological implications of the story closure are examined in a text collection about Mexican American farmworkers.

Classrooom Applications

- Invite children to make a multimedia collage of representations of race in words and images (e.g., newspapers, advertisements, literature, TV commercials, music videos, etc.). Locate patterns across these texts.
- History is a representation of the past. How we use language in describing historical events positions people and communities in particular ways. For example, in what ways do the following words position the Irish and English during the famine of the mid-1800s: Irish famine, potato blight in Ireland, Irish Great Hunger, *An Gorta Mór*. Consider other historical events and deconstruct the language use associated with these occurrences.
- Conduct a critical multicultural analysis of children's books about the Irish Great Hunger. Examine how Irish, British, and American authors portray these circumstances. In what ways do these different renderings demonstrate the social construction of this catastrophe? Use Siobhan Parkinson's (2002) article, "Children of the Quest: The Irish Famine Myth in Children's Fiction," to guide your analysis. Follow this same process and consider another historical event from multiple perspectives.
- Locate nonfiction texts on different countries and/or cultural groups. Invite children to critically examine these renderings by analyzing the text and images. What images were chosen to represent the culture? What is the implicit definition of culture imbedded in the text? How

is the culture represented in the past? How is it represented in the present?

- Analyze texts about Native Americans in contemporary times because they are often rendered in the past. In what ways do these stories document the consequences of colonization as well as acknowledge the Native families' and communities' exercise of collaborative power?

Recommendations for Classroom Research

- In what ways have your personal, professional, and academic experiences been shaped by race? In what ways are class and gender implicated?
- Which cultures are present in your classroom, in your school community? Initiate a study group where different histories and sociopolitical situations of the communities you serve are considered. This work will inform your teaching and work with diverse families and communities.

Suggestions for Further Reading

Acuña, Rodolfo F. (2006). *Occupied America: A History of Chicanos* (6th ed.). New York: Longman.

Chomsky, Aviva. (2007). *"They take our jobs!" and 20 other myths about immigration.* Boston: Beacon Press.

Deloria, Vine. (1995). *Red earth, white lies: Native Americans and the myth of scientific fact.* New York: Scribner.

Ignatiev, Noel. (2008). *How the Irish became White* (revised ed.). New York: Routledge.

Kelley, Robin D. G. & Lewis, Earl. (Eds.). (2000). *To make our world anew: A history of African Americans.* New York: Oxford University Press.

Loewen, James. (2007). *Lies my teacher told me: Everything your American history textbook got wrong.* New York: Simon & Schuster.

Parkinson, Siobhán. (2002). Children of the quest: The Irish Famine myth in children's fiction. *The Horn Book Magazine* (November/December), 679–688.

Roediger, David R. (2005). *Working toward whiteness: How America's immigrants become white: The strange journey from Ellis Island to the suburbs.* New York: Basic Books.

Rothenberg, Paula. (Ed.). (2004). *Race, class, and gender in the United States: An integrated study.* New York: Worth Publishers.

Spring, Joel H. (2007). *Deculturalization and the struggle for equality: A brief history of education of dominated cultures in the United States* (5th ed.). Boston: McGraw-Hill.

Takaki, Ronald T. (Ed.). (2002). *Debating diversity: Clashing perspectives on race and ethnicity in America* (3rd ed.). New York: Oxford University Press.

Zinn, Howard. (2003). *A people's history of the United States: 1492–present.* New York: HarperCollins.

Zinn, Howard, Konopacki, Mike & Buhle, Paul. (2008). *A people's history of American empire: A graphic adaptation.* New York: Metropolitan Books.

References

Children's Books

Ada, Alma Flor. (1997). *Gathering the sun: An alphabet in Spanish and English*. Illustrated by Simón Silva. New York: Lothrop, Lee & Shepard.

Hoyt-Goldsmith, Diane. (1996). *Migrant worker: A boy from the Rio Grande Valley*. Photography by Lawrence Migdale. New York: Holiday House.

Jiménez, Francisco. (1997). *The circuit: Stories from the life of a migrant child*. Boston: Houghton Mifflin Company.

Secondary Sources

Acuña, Rodolfo. (1988). *Occupied America: A history of Chicanos* (3rd ed.). New York: Harper & Row.

Almaguer, Tomás. (1974). Historical notes on Chicano oppression: The dialectics of racial and class domination in North America. *Aztlan*, 5(1 & 2), 27–54.

Almaguer, Tomás. (1989). Ideological distortions in recent Chicano historiography: The internal model and Chicano historical interpretation. *Aztlan*, 18(1), 7–28.

Barrera, Rosalinda S. & Garza de Cortes, Oralia. (1997). Mexican American children's literature in the 1990s: Toward authenticity. In V. J. Harris (Ed.), *Using multiethnic literature in the K–8 classroom* (pp. 129–153). Norwood, MA: Christopher-Gordon Publishers.

Barrera, Rosalinda S., Liguori, Olga & Salas, Loretta. (1993). Ideas a literature can grow on: Key insights for enriching and expanding children's literature about the Mexican American experience. In V. J. Harris, *Teaching multicultural literature in grades K–8* (pp. 203–241). Norwood, MA: Christopher-Gordon Publishers.

Barrera, Rosalinda, Quiroa, Ruth E. & West-Williams, Cassiette. (1999). Poco a poco: Continuing development of Mexican American children's literature in the 1990s. *The New Advocate*, 12(4), 315–330.

Barrera, Roslinada B. & Quiroa, Ruth E. (2003). The use of Spanish in Latino children's literature in English: What makes for cultural authenticity? In D. L. Fox & K. G. Short (Eds.), *Stories matter: The complexity of cultural authenticity in children's literature* (pp. 247–265). Urbana, IL: NCTE.

Barrera, Roslinada B., Quiroa, Ruth E. & Valdivia, Rebeca. (2003). Spanish in Latino picture storybooks in English: Its use and textual effects. In A. I. Willis, G. E. García, R. Barrera, V. J. Harris (Eds.), *Multicultural issues in literacy research and practice* (pp. 145–165). Mahwah, NJ: Lawrence Erlbaum Associates.

Bhabha, Homi K. DessemiNation: Time, narrative, and the margins of the modern nation. In Homi K. Bhabha (Ed.), *Nation and Narration* (pp. 291–322). New York: Routledge.

Cortes, Oralia Garza de. (1992). United States: Hispanic Americans. In Lynn Miller-Lachmann, *Our family, our friends, our world: An annotated guide to significant multicultural books for children and teens* (pp. 121–154). New Providence, NJ: R. R. Bowker Company.

Council on Interracial Books for Children. (1975) Chicano culture in children's literature: Stereotypes, distortions and omissions. *Interracial Books for Children Bulletin*, 5(7 & 8), 7–14.

Decker, Jeffrey Louis. (1990). *The interpretation of American dreams: The political unconscious in American literature and culture*. Unpublished dissertation, Brown University.

Del Castillo, Richard Griswold & De León, Arnoldo. (1996). *North to Aztlán: A history of Mexican Americans in the United States*. New York: Twayne Publishers.

Deloria, Vine. (1995). *Red earth, white lies: Native Americans and the myth of scientific fact*. New York: Scribner.

Fernández, María José. (2003). Negotiating identity: Migration, colonization, and cultural marginalization in Lara Rios and Vicky Ramos' *Mo* and Carmen Lomas Garza's *In My Family/En Mi Familia*. *Children's Literature Association Quarterly*, 28(2), 81–89.

Gonzales, Manuel G. (1999). *Mexicanos: A history of Mexicans in the United States*. Bloomington, IN: Indiana University Press.

Grossberg, Lawrence. (1996). Identity and cultural studies. In Stuart Hall & Paul du Gay (Eds.), *Questions of cultural identity*. Thousand Oaks, CA: Sage.

Guinier, Lani & Torres, Gerald. (2002). *The miner's canary: Enlisting race, resisting power, transforming democracy*. Cambridge, MA: Harvard University Press.

Hade, Daniel. (2002). Personal communication. July.

hooks, bell. (2000). *Where we stand: Class matters*. New York: Routledge.

Ignatiev, Noel. (1995). *How the Irish became White*. New York: Routledge.

Nieto, Sonia. (2004). *Affirming diversity: The sociopolitical context of multicultural education* (4rd ed.). New York: Longman.

Ogbu, John. (1991). Cultural diversity and school experience. In Catherine Walsh (Ed.), *Literacy as praxis: Culture, language, and pedagogy* (pp. 25–50). Norwood, NJ: Ablex.

Pérez, Emma. (1999). Tejanas: Diasporic subjectivities and post-revolution identities. In *The decolonial imaginary: Writing Chicanas into history* (pp. 75–98). Indianapolis: Indiana University Press.

Rodriguez, Richard. (2002). *Brown: The last discovery of America*. New York: Viking.

Rosales, F. Arturo, (1997). *Chicano! The history of the Mexican American civil rights movement*. Houston, TX: Arte Público Press.

Rothenberg, Daniel. (1998). *With these hands: The hidden world of migrant farmworkers today*. New York: Harcourt Brace & Co.

Rudman, Masha K. (1995). *Children's literature: An issues approach* (3rd ed.). White Plains, NY: Longman.

Sánchez, Rosaura. (1992). Discourses of gender, ethnicity and class in Chicano literature. *The Americas Review*, 20(2), 72–88.

Sánchez, Sylvia Y. (1998). Storying in the Mexican American community: Understanding the story behind the stories and the cultural themes shared in Chicano novels. In A. Willis (Ed.), *Teaching and using multicultural literature in grades 9–12: Moving beyond the canon* (pp. 169–191). Norwood, MA: Christopher-Gordon Publishers.

Spring, Joel. (2004) *Deculturalization and the struggle for equality* (4th ed.). New York: McGraw-Hill.

Takaki, Ronald. (1993). El Norte: The borderland of Chicano America. In *A different mirror: A history of multicultural America* (pp. 311–339). Boston: Little, Brown & Company.

Tejeda, Carlos, Espinoza, Manuel & Gutierrez, Kris. (2003). Toward a decolonizing pedagogy: Social justice reconsidered. In Peter P. Trifonias (Ed.), *Pedagogies of difference* (pp. 10–40). New York: Routledge Falmer.

U.S. Census Bureau. (2000a). *Census Bureau projects doubling of nation's population by 2100*. Retrieved on January 3, 2007, from www.census.gov/Press-Release/www/2000/cb00-05.html.

U.S. Census Bureau. (2000b). *Population of race hispanic or Latino origin for the United States 1990–2000*. Retrieved on January 3, 2007, from www.census.gov/population/cen2000/phc-tl/tab01.pdf.

Wagoner, Shirley A. (1982). Mexican-Americans in children's literature since 1970. *The Reading Teacher*, 274–279.

Wang, An-Chi. (2000). The American dream in John Updike's Rabbit tetralogy. *NTU Studies in Language and Literature*, 9, 227–268.

Zinn, Howard. (1997). *A people's history of the United States*. New York: The New Press.

Endnotes

1. Bracero means "someone who works with his arms." The Bracero Program ran from 1942 to 1964, permitting U.S. farmers to contract Mexican farmworkers for seasonal work.
2. This U.S. Census Bureau survey refers to Latinas/os as Hispanics. Like Joel Spring and Sonia Nieto, we prefer the term Latina/o because Hispanic is "associated with Spanish cultural imperialism" (Spring, 2004: 75). Just like with Mexican American and Chicana/o, no consensus exists within the Latino/Hispanic community about which term to use (Nieto, 2004). These are complex historical and cultural associations.
3. The U.S. Census Bureau uses Mexican to signify someone who was born in Mexico or of Mexican heritage. We will use Mexican/Chicana/o instead to signal these cultural memberships.

CHAPTER 7

Leaving Poverty Behind[1]: The Social Construction of Class

Our goal for this critical multicultural analysis of children's books about Mexican American migrant farmworkers is to work toward a discursive leveling of texts; that is, reading these texts alongside literary and cultural criticism, and consulting other secondary sources. Reading these books against a broader historical, sociopolitical context will re/contextualize them and make visible the social implications of these texts.

In this analysis, we read books against the historical and sociopolitical context of migrant work in the United States (see Chapter 5). We historicize current representations of Mexican American migrant workers within the developments of the Mexican American experience as it is rendered in children's literature (see Chapter 5). Since many of these titles fall under the genre of realistic fiction, we consider how this genre textually reconstructs reality. We also consider the nonfiction narrative because, as readers, we need to challenge how accurately factual stories represent reality.

Through critical multicultural analysis, we analyze how power is exercised among the characters along a continuum of domination to agency. We connect these microinteractions among characters to the power relations of class, race, and gender.

The following critical multicultural analysis of children's literature about Mexican American migrant farmworkers involves the examination of a text collection juxtaposed with the historical and sociopolitical context of Mexican American participation in the U.S. migrant agricultural labor system. It also considers the historical and sociopolitical context of

153

Mexican American representation in children's literature, as well as the social and discursive constructions of genres, characters, and story closures.

Many of the characters in the books we studied hope to leave their poverty behind at the U.S./Mexican border. Readers can investigate what social power relations the characters immigrate into in the "land of opportunity."

A Critical Multicultural Analysis of the Text Collection

The study of children's literature is a social practice that can produce, reproduce, and circulate dominant cultural meanings as well as resist and subvert these prevailing ideologies. Children's literature invites readers to contend with power relations through its thick description of who we are and how we are organized as a society. Critical multicultural analysis of *The Circuit* and other titles in our text collection highlights that all literature is culturally coded; authors and readers are discursively, socially, and historically constructed; and that reading is a sociopolitical activity. Critical multicultural analysis disrupts fixed and bounded notions of culture, identity, class, race, gender, and power. It illuminates these social processes.

Critical multicultural analysis creates a space for adults and children alike to recognize their discursive constitution, as well as providing a site for resistance, subversion, and transformation of dominant class, race, and gender ideologies. Reading class, race, and gender in children's literature leads to reading how power is exercised in society. It calls into question the subject positions offered by the dominant discourses imbedded into children's books. A critical multicultural analysis of books about Mexican American migrant farmworkers explores how power is exercised and circulated in these stories by looking at how characters dominate, collude, resist, and show agency; it is a critical multicultural reading of the social myth of the American Dream.

Reconsidering Publishing Practices

Our text collection consists of 26 titles, published from 1992 to 2005. The stories are targeted at children from age 5 to young adult. The genres represented include nonfiction narratives, picture books that draw on the nonfiction genre, and realistic fiction, ranging from picture books to young adult novels. Numerous titles are autobiographical in origin.

Ten authors (Ancona, Ada, Dorros, Hart, Herrera, Jiménez, Mora, Rivera, Soto, and Viramontes) identify as members of the Mexican American culture and/or speakers of the Spanish language. Nine authors (Altman, Atkins, Brimner, Bunting, DeFelice, Hoyt-Goldsmith, Olson, Paulsen, and

Pérez) are European American. Pam Muñoz Ryan is of Mexican- and European-American heritage. European American authors wrote and took the photographs for the nonfiction narratives, with the exception of *Harvest*, which is written and photographed by George Ancona, whose heritage is Mexican American. Eight illustrators are of Latina/o heritage.

Small independently owned publishers such as Lee & Low, Children's Book Press, Arte Público Press, Bilingual Press, and University of New Mexico Press produced nine of the stories; conglomerate-owned publishers created seventeen of the texts. Houghton Mifflin, a member of The Blackstone Group, takes the leadership in publishing about Mexican American migrant farmworkers. They published Jiménez's two chapter books, two Spanish translations of these stories, and two picture books based on the author's first book, *The Circuit*. One of Jiménez's picture books is in bilingual text and the other has a Spanish edition. Most texts garnered culturally specific awards (e.g., Pura Belpré, Tomás Rivera, and Américas awards), thus bringing national recognition to these texts.

Analyzing the Text Collection

We have woven in book reviews and other texts about the texts. We have organized the text analyses by publishing date within the genre whenever relevant, because these texts are, in many ways, responses to each other. (See Appendix E for a chart of the publishing practices associated with this text collection.) How the power relations of class, race, and gender are enacted in children's literature about Chicana/o migrant farmworkers is the central question guiding this analysis. In addition, we consider the following questions:

- In what ways are the cultural themes imbedded in these texts constructed by these power relations?
- In what ways do the genre(s) and focalization shape how power is represented in each text?
- How do the characters exercise power?
- We have taken care to analyze the story ending as well: is it open or closed? Does it confirm, disrupt, speculate upon, or question the class, gender, and race ideologies imbedded in the text?

Generic considerations guide much of our analysis.

The text collection overturns the stereotypes often associated with the working poor, such as "lazy, uneducated, unlucky, abusive, dirty, immoral, criminal tendencies, and undisciplined," as Maria José and our colleagues Jane Kelley and Cynthia Rosenberger (Kelley, Rosenberger & Botelho, 2005) found when they examined the representation of poverty in children's literature. The text collection shows characters who are resource-ful, resilient, and family-minded, and whose responses are products of their lived experience. These children's books show how the characters exercise power within the specific historical and sociopolitical conditions of the migrant agricultural labor system.

The following cultural themes emerged from the particular power circumstances of the migrant farmworker system in the United States.

Cultural Themes

Critical multicultural analysis of the text collection foregrounds the follow-ing cultural themes:

- maintaining family bonds (family);
- negotiating Chicano/a/Mexican American/Mexican identity (identity);
- accessing formal schooling (education);
- learning English language and literacy (English language learning);
- including and maintaining the Spanish language (language);
- reflecting on undocumented and documented immigration (immigration);
- reconsidering migrant agricultural labor (work); and,
- establishing a sense of place (home).

These themes are cultural because the meanings are not locked in the words but come from particular historical and sociopolitical circumstances, shaped by the power relations of gender, class, and race. The cultural themes of education, language, and English language learning are central to this text collection.

Education/Language/Identity – Language and identity are central issues within the school context. The process of deculturalization, or the stripping away of one's culture, as Joel Spring (2004) documents in his historical research on underrepresented cultural groups in the United States, is evident in the characters' school experiences as they struggle to keep their first language, Spanish. According to Spring, the compulsory education law is not always enforced for Chicana/o children. He considers this lack of implementation one of the most discriminatory acts against this population of children. He further argues that the migrant worker system, initiated by U.S. farmers, contributes to the segregation of this cultural group. Spring maintains that language is the place where Mexican Americans, like other linguistically diverse groups, resist deculturalization policies and practices.

In the text collection, the incompatibility between school and migrant work is present, with migrant farm work taking precedence because families economically depend on their children's contributions to their livelihood. In many instances, according to Spring, "racism serves as a justification for economic exploitation" (Spring, 2004: 82). In the children's books these cultural themes are entangled with the discursive threads of power. Schools are the central context where characters' identities are constructed and contested.

The characters also exist in the U.S. diaspora, an experience contributing to their transnational identity formation. Anthropologist James Clifford (1997) explains: "the language of diaspora is increasingly invoked by displaced peoples who feel (maintain, revive, invent) a connection with a prior home" (Clifford, 1997: 310). Many of the characters possess a strong connection with Mexico, a relationship that shapes their identity in combination with their present community associations in the United States.

Family/Work – The text collection demonstrates how the migrant agricultural system, largely influenced by the power relations of class, race, and gender, greatly contributes to organization of the families in these stories. Race, class, and gender power relations can disrupt family and community systems, while some families organize, reorganize, and show resiliency and resourcefulness in response to these oppressive circumstances. The discursive threads of resiliency and resourcefulness are collective forms of power.

As analytical readers of these stories, we question whether it is socially just for families to endure poverty. While we all should be resilient and resourceful, especially as we exercise our power against dominant ideologies, these ways of being should not be left with the individual or family. We can connect these ways of exercising power to race/class/gender relations. There is a danger of isolating families' responses to poverty, that is, casting them as models of resiliency and resourcefulness, because it dislocates their experiences from the historical and sociopolitical conditions that shaped their living circumstances in the first place. Poverty is violence against children and their families. Children's literature scholar Eliza T. Dresang (1997) cautions readers:

> Does the presence of a fictional child who develops the inner strength to deal with a violent or potentially violent situation negate the apparent radicalism of writers who include topics once tacitly forbidden in children's texts? Do these books masquerade as different while using only a veneer of violence to overlay a content closely resembling the pastoralism of their predecessors?
>
> (Dresang, 1997: 133)

In looking at the migrant agricultural labor system, we consider how farm work shapes these families as well as how these families reorganize to take collective action against this system of social inequities.

The text collection represents a range of gender relations within the family, but certainly the machismo of the father and unconditional love of the mother are present in some of the texts. (According to the *Oxford English Dictionary* [2000], the word machismo originates from Mexican Spanish meaning "the quality of being macho, manliness, male virility, or masculine pride, or the display of this." When the machismo of the father leads to family instability, the mothers in some of the texts play a key role of keeping the family together. Chicano social scientist Manuel Gonzales (1999) warns that focusing on the authoritarian male, prevalent in studies about the Mexican family, leads to a "familial deficiency model" (Gonzales, 1999: 237). In general, these texts show interdependence between fathers and mothers, both working together and, in some cases, alongside their children to earn an income that will provide for the basic needs of the family. The text collection represents a community of heterogeneous families who live a diverse range of migrant experiences.

While all the parents are not formally schooled beyond grade 4, most of the families encourage their children to do well in school. These school experiences take the children further away from what the families know. Some of the characters devalue what parents know (e.g. knowledge related to the harvest cycle) and try to disassociate themselves from this knowledge. They understand too well the knowledge that has currency in the dominant culture; they are aware of the power/knowledge nexus. Some of the child protagonists try hard to succeed in school culture and at school literacies.

Immigration/Home – The border is present in most of these texts; it is like another character. The border signifies the geopolitical circumstances the characters immigrate into as well as the socioeconomic factors that influenced the border crossing. In his study of travel and movement in children's literature, John S. Butcher (2002) maintains that the push and pull and "the bright lights" influences, which contributed to this transnational movement, offer "the promise of a better opportunity" (p. 152). In the text collection, documented and undocumented immigration are represented against class and race relations in both Mexico and the United States. The families organize to make a homeplace for themselves, but the migrant circuit disrupts their efforts. These cultural themes (education/language/identity, family/work, and immigration/home) permeate the books by Francisco Jiménez.

Visiting *The Circuit*

Francisco Jiménez[2] has written four books about his family's experiences as migrant workers in the United States. The title story of *The Circuit* was initially written for adults and later reprinted in a couple of young adult short-story anthologies. More recently, it was published in "Some Consequences of Racial, Gender, and Class Inequality" in *Race, Class, and Gender in the United States* by Paula Rothenberg (2004). *La Mariposa* and *The Christmas Gift/El Regalo de Navidad*, two short stories from *The Circuit*, have been adapted and published as picture books. The characters are three-dimensional, their situation is realistic, and the conditions of the migrant work are conveyed with precision.

In the late 1940s, Papá dreamed of the long trek north. "cross *la frontera*, enter California, and leave our poverty behind." (Jiménez, 1997, p. 1). Thus the Jiménez family, Papá, Mamá, Roberto, and Panchito, crossed the Mexican/U.S. border in hopes of finding better living conditions as migrant workers. The family moves with the harvests of cotton, strawberries, and grapes, and the agricultural work of thinning lettuce and topping carrots. Depending on the needs and circumstances of the family, Mamá maintains the babies and the camp or contributes monetarily by picking, or cleaning and cooking for other farmworkers. Panchito and Roberto contribute to the family's livelihood. The two brothers' school attendance is disrupted by the harvest cycle: just when Panchito makes friends with one of his classmates, he has to move on; at one point when he develops a close relationship with a teacher, he has to move on; finally, when he becomes more comfortable with English, he has to move on.

La migra, the border patrol, is a constant shadow in their daily lives. The fear of deportation is real. Papá constantly reminds the boys that they must say that they were born in California. "Don't tell anyone," he instructs his sons, "even friends can turn you in." Even though foreshadowing is seeded throughout the book, the ending, where they are captured and deported, comes as a shock to the reader.

The Circuit tells of hard, hard times, love and resilience, and generosity of spirit. Simply classifying *The Circuit* as a multicultural children's book without analysis essentializes migrant farmworkers, the Mexican American family, and the author as insider. The factors that cause this family's poverty are complex. Approaching children's literature about Chicana/o migrant farmworkers with interest and respect is important but not sufficient.

According to Stephens (1992), one way the first-person narrative constructs a worldview is by "situating readers in a subject position effectively identical with that of the narrator, so that readers share the narrator's view of the world" (Stephens, 1992: 57). In this realistic, young adult novel, the narrator, Panchito brings us close to the socioeconomic circumstances of his family and the communities they find themselves in, and describes the condition of migrant work. Reading *The Circuit* only as a multicultural text may foster an unquestioned identification with the focalizer or the narrator, in this case, which makes the reader vulnerable to the ideological dimensions of the text. Stephens maintains that this kind of reading is "pedagogically irresponsible" (Stephens, 1992: 68). Critical multicultural analysis offers strategies for examining texts from "estranged subject positions" and rejecting simple identification with the main character(s).

Jiménez comments on the reasons why he wrote these stories:

> I wrote them to chronicle part of my family's history but, more importantly, to voice the experiences of a large sector of our society that has been frequently ignored. Through my writing I hope to give readers an insight into the lives of migrant farmworkers and their children whose back-breaking labor of picking fruits and vegetables puts food on our tables. Their courage and struggles, hopes and dreams for a better life for their children and their children's children give meaning to the term "American dream." Their story is the American story.
>
> (Jiménez, 1997: 115–116)

Jiménez is responding to the invisibility of migrant agricultural workers in everyday life, the sociopolitical landscape, and children's literature, especially Mexican American representation in children's and young adult books.

In leaving their poverty behind at the U.S./Mexican border, the story's characters slip into the American Dream. While Papá challenges the discourse layers of this social myth, in the end, he still believes in some aspects of its promise. Mamá defers their future to God's will. The American Dream lures this family, but their initial experiences in California defy its guarantees. While this short story collection offers "a wonderful representation of a culture that exists in the U.S. but is foreign to most Americans" (Ginsberg, 1998: n.p.), as readers, we can read these stories against the migrant work system that has a hold on this culture and how it controls this family's everyday experiences.

In the short story, "Learning the Game," Panchito describes how power is exercised within the *contratista* system. Panchito witnesses how Díaz, the brutal foreman maltreats Gabriel, a migrant farmworker, and learns a lesson from Gabriel's resistance against Díaz's oppressive work practices. In the end, Gabriel does lose his job, with real economic ramifications for him and his family back in Mexico. Gabriel took a great risk in resisting Díaz's dehumanizing practices and internalized oppression because the way he does business as a *contratista* is structurally supported by the migrant labor system. As a result of Gabriel's resistance Panchito learns to be an ally to Manuelito, a younger boy who lives in his camp, when Carlos, the camp bully, excludes Manuelito from the group. Panchito declines to play with Carlos:

> "If Manuelito doesn't play, I won't either," I said. As soon as I said it, my heart started pounding. My knees felt weak. Carlos came right up to me. He had fire in his eyes. "Manuelito doesn't play!" he yelled.
>
> ... He stuck his right foot behind my feet and pushed me. I fell flat on my back. My brothers rushed over to help me up. "You can push me around, but you can't force me to play!" I yelled back, dusting off my clothes and walking away.
>
> ... After a few moments, he cocked his head back, spat on the ground, and swaggered toward us, saying, "OK, Manuelito can play."
>
> (Jiménez, 1997: 77–78)

While Gabriel interrupts Díaz's domination, he is pushed out of "the game" of the migrant labor system. Panchito disrupts the oppressive cycle created by the camp bully. He refuses to collude with "the game" of domination and emulates Gabriel's resistance.

The Circuit ends abruptly. Panchito's memorization of the preamble to the Declaration of Independence is juxtaposed ironically with the beginning of the deportation process of the Jiménez family. Hardworking undocumented immigrants do not have the same rights as other workers. *The Circuit* invites the reader to re-examine equality; to question a government that preys on undocumented immigrants and condones substandard living conditions for migrant agricultural workers; to consider the dilemmas of education and child labor on a local and national level; to rethink U.S. immigration policies and their impact not only on undocumented immigrants, but also on the U.S. economy and food supply; and, to consider definitions of poverty and sociopolitical status versus individual responsibility for meeting the basic needs of all people. The hegemony of English as the language of social power contributes to the marginalization of Panchito's family.

The Christmas Gift/El Regalo de Navidad, based on the short story by the same name, is told in third-person narrative point of view, a shift from the first-person perspective of *The Circuit* from which it was drawn. It is almost Christmas and Panchito hopes against hope that he will receive his very own red ball as a gift. But it is not to be. Instead, he and his siblings receive bags of candy, all that his parents can afford. The only "extravagance" is an embroidered handkerchief for Mamá that Papá purchases for ten cents to help a young couple, who go from door to door, asking for help. In an act of thoughtfulness and understanding, Panchito genuinely thanks his parents for their gift.

It is noteworthy that the author changed the ending of the original story as it appeared in *The Circuit* and, for the picture book, added Panchito's ability to let go of his personal desires. In the picture book, the ending is closed, whereas in the short story, it is left open. The ending of *The Christmas Gift/El Regalo de Navidad* conflates the "spirit of Christmas" with the harsh socioeconomic conditions lived by Panchito's family. The spirit of Christmas dictates "making do" with what one has, but this family can barely provide for the basic needs of its members. The unresolved ending of the short story version calls attention to this family's situation and invites the reader to wonder about the social factors that constructed these conditions.

The setting and circumstances are more evident in *The Christmas Gift/El Regalo de Navidad*. Panchito and his family (mother, father, and four siblings), along with the other migrant workers, must move on from their unsuccessful stint at picking cotton. The weather has been too damp, and they have been eating only because of a kind and generous butcher who sells them meaty bones. In one illustration spread, a shopper chooses select fruit and vegetables from an outdoor grocery store stand, and on the other side of the fence, Panchito and Mamá salvage vegetables and fruit from the trash receptacles behind the grocery store.

Another fence divides a grower's property, a quilted agricultural landscape, from the small tent dwellings for the migrant farmworkers. These two scenes are the two omniscient narrator's perspectives, representing urban and rural inequities and social *fronteras* experienced by Panchito's family.

Young children are the targeted audience for both of these picture books. The third-person perspective brings resolution to these stories: The closures are complete. These two reconstituted stories demonstrate that children's literature are spaces for socialization (i.e., what we want young children to know and not know through children's books). Poverty is romanticized in these stories, focusing on families showing resourcefulness and resilience. While class/race inequalities are evident, they are not emphasized in the storyline. As a society, we believe these social problems are not appropriate for young children to experience (even vicariously in literature) but many children live these social inequities on a daily basis; these are realities for children who are poor.

In *Breaking Through*, the sequel to *The Circuit*, Jiménez chronicles his adolescent years, beginning with age 14 until his first day of college. This realistic fiction packaged as a young adult novel is told in the first person, with Panchito, his older brother Roberto, and their mother at the center of the stories. The family is detained by *la migra* and forced to leave the United States, but they find their way back to California. Mamá holds the family together, especially since Papá can no longer work because of back problems (a source of frustration for him).

This family's socioeconomic situation confronts the notion of the universal adolescent experience; its social construction is exposed as the family, especially the parents, challenge cultural experiences and expectations associated with this age group. For example, Panchito comments on how he does not have free time to cultivate close friendships or go out on weekends, because this is the time that Roberto and he work. American popular culture strains family ties. *Breaking Through* tells how teachers share their power and help Panchito navigate school literacies and culture. Race and class are central to this family's experiences.

Panchito and Roberto are invited by the school janitor to collude with White privilege: the family knows all too well that a lighter skin tone might win them higher status, especially if they can overcome their Spanish accent. But the family does not try "to pass" as White. The maintenance of their Mexican American heritage is more important. Their accented language signals their cultural membership. In her book review, Rochman comments that the author "writes about a harsh world seldom seen in children's books. Readers will discover an America they didn't know was here" (Rochman: 2001, n.p.). Jiménez reveals U.S. power relations as lived by him and his family.

Panchito [Francisco] works hard for his accomplishments in school. It is misleading to think about Panchito's resiliency separate from the hardships he and his family bear during these adolescent years. He and his family, especially Roberto and his mother, exercise collective power in many instances. Critical multicultural analysis requires that Panchito's and his family's responses to classism and racism be understood against these power relations.

Nonfiction Narratives

This genre claims to capture reality as it is, with the photography zooming in on the protagonist's circumstances. Often, photographs, like drawings and paintings, offer a vantage point to view the story, and to observe power relations.

In *A Migrant Family*, published in 1992, the author Larry Dane Brimner positions Juan Medina, the protagonist of this illustrated nonfiction narrative, in a harsh and brutal world with his very first sentence: "As darkness bleeds from the sky, Juan shivers at the 6:00 a.m. chill" (Brimner, 1992: 6).

Juan and his family are migrant workers, hoping to wrest a marginal existence on the promise of minimum wage. The book documents the difficult living conditions most migrant workers endure. The black and white photographs offer the reader a proximate perspective to view this family's migrant life, documenting great poverty. There is no "bright side" to this story.

Migrant labor dominates the life of this family. The story offers panoramic views of the broader context of the camp. The third-person perspective contextualizes the first-person point of view. The two focalizations are dialogic. Juan and his family refute and challenge stereotypes and social epithets. The family works together to survive.

Too often the workers fall prey to violent behavior on the part of outsiders. They have little recourse to U.S. law enforcement agencies. The makeshift camps are frequently cited for health code violations and forcibly disbanded. Because there is little regulation and because many migrant workers speak little or no English, they are easily victimized.

Although the conditions in the camp are oppressive, the money migrant workers can earn is far greater than a family could earn in many Mexican and Central American villages. The extraordinary poverty in their countries of origin is even more extreme than the conditions that they experience as migrant workers. Nevertheless, too many employers exploit the workers even to the point of withholding wages. Migrant workers who have undocumented status are the most vulnerable because they risk being reported by their employers to the Immigration and Naturalization Services.

Schooling is inadequate and often frustrating because it is interrupted by work availability, which depends on weather conditions and the harvest time of each crop. Most migrant families are constantly on the move. Programs have been initiated to help address some of these problems. The Encinitas Jobs Center in California helps both employers and workers. The Center issues library cards, helps with tax preparation, offers English classes, and provides employment services. While these community efforts offer relief, they do not represent structural change. Although agencies of this sort provide some support, it is clear that life for the migrant worker family remains difficult.

This book of photographs is one of the few in the text collection that confronts the sociopolitical context of the Mexican American migrant agricultural labor system. The poverty lived by this migrant family is portrayed in great detail, with no attempt to romanticize Juan's migrant experience. The text is an intertext of the migrant farm work conditions in San Diego juxtaposed with the wealthy community up on the hill: "They want us to work," Juan says. "And they want us to disappear" (Brimmer,

1992: 18), commenting on how the surrounding community wants their camp shut down.

The book reports that two young White men attacked the migrant workers and stole one laborer's money. Upon leaving, one of the assailants hurls an epithet, "Wetback." Juan is affronted by the word wetback, a racist/classist word for workers who cross the Mexican border, undocumented, to find work in the United States: "We have papers," he says. "We have a right to be here. Who are we hurting?" (Brimmer, 1992: 17).

Because of their precarious and liminal place in society, farmworkers mistrust U.S. law enforcement. Although they rarely earn more than a minimum wage salary, it is still more money than a family could earn in Mexico. Moreover, they do the kinds of jobs that nobody else will do.

Juan dreams of being rich, "but first, school." Many migrant children never complete high school: They are academically unprepared because of their nomadic existence and because of their child care and work responsibilities. In many cases, schools and teachers give up on them. In the end of the book, Juan has to set aside his notebook and go with his stepfather, Joel, to look for work.

School is a privilege that this family cannot always afford. This book shows the dilemma and contradiction between "the hope" and "the reality" of this migrant family, which demonstrates how race and class are inseparable in the migrant condition.

The sociopolitical framework that supports this system of oppression is exposed here through the third- and first-person perspectives. There are many culprits: the farmers who hire the migrant workers without providing suitable living quarters and wages; consumers who purchase the produce, expecting to pay minimum prices; the oppressive political and economic systems in workers' countries of origin; the communities surrounding the farms that are usually inhospitable to the workers; and, the economic system that governs farm profit.

Voices from the Fields: Children of Migrant Farmworkers Tell Their Stories, written and photographed by Beth S. Atkin (1993/2001), is a montage of portraits, poetry (some translated by poet Francisco X. Alarcón and the children interviewed), interviews, and factual information to show the sociopolitical layers of the life of migrant workers. She demonstrates the class, race, and gender issues confronted by the families showcased, and links those experiences to structural policies and practices. The text shows the diversity of situations among this population. Family devotion and the role of education in "escaping the fields and helping other family members" are the central messages (Atkin, 1993/2001/6). One of the values of the Mexican American family, shaped by historical and sociopolitical factors, is to "help each other for the good of the entire family even at the cost of the individual" (Atkin, 1993/2001: 6). Many of the children speak of their mothers' love and commitment to them.

The ideology of individualism is challenged throughout these pages as children speak about their commitment to their immediate and extended family. Victor Machuca states: "I think doing things like working together is important. It makes our family stronger" (Atkin, 1993/2001: 50). The last interview is of Mari Carmen López, who will attend college in the fall. She attended Yo Puedo Program (I CAN) (Perhaps this program could also include the collective "we" in their title.) but she claims that she "still [has] obstacles, like English" (Atkin, 1993/2001: 91). She further states that "always in my family, they've said how important education is, that not everyone is lucky enough to get one, and that we should always strive for the best" (Atkin, 1993/2001: 93). The discursive thread of luck is often associated with class mobility, ignoring the factors contributing to or hindering social mobility.

Migrant Worker: A Boy from the Rio Grande Valley, written by Diane Hoyt-Goldsmith (1996) and photographed by Lawrence Migdale, and *Harvest*, written and photographed by George Ancona (2001), are assembled as photo albums or scrapbooks. The color photography heightens the abundance present in the landscape and, in *Migrant Worker*, the "bright side story" and the hope education extends to the child.

Harvest, a photo-essay, juxtaposes rich land with poor people and introduces the reader to the migrant life of recent Mexican immigrants. The text is told in the third-person omniscient perspective with some interviews interwoven throughout the text. George Ancona documents the harvest of fruits and vegetables.

Ancona includes three interviews: one of a young mother, one of a retired farmworker, and one of a substitute teacher. The rest of the text describes harvest and family time on the farm, with the interviews bringing the reader up close to some of the hopes and concerns of these farmworkers. The young mother believes that hard work and education will reward her children. Isabel Sorio, a substitute teacher, wants her children to be educated, not deculturalized. She notes the dominating practices of migrant labor as a form of slavery.

The text ends with "*La lucha sigue!* The struggle goes on." The open ending signals the work that still needs to be done so migrant farmworkers' rights are protected. The United Farm Workers Union represents a small fraction of these laborers. The limited participation in the union leaves many agricultural workers vulnerable to unfair treatment and poor compensation.

These nonfiction narratives connect the personal to the political. They show how these families collaborate to survive the hardships produced and maintained by the migrant farmworker system, while at the same time adopting the discourse of education as the key to the American Dream. Narratives are dialogically constructed, addressing the specific living and working conditions of migrant farmworkers against a sociopolitical backdrop.

Picture Books

The picture book constructs an intertextuality between the textual and visual representations: the illustrations and text convey the relationship between the pictures and words. The illustrations contribute to the "position of power," the location from which to view the social interactions among the characters. All of these picture books draw from realistic fiction, told from the third-person point of view, with the exception of *Going Home*, which is told from the first-person perspective. The cultural themes present in these texts include education, home, work, and the effects of migrancy.

Amelia's Road, written by Linda Jacobs Altman (1993) and illustrated by Enrique O. Sánchez, is one of the first picture books to place the migrant child protagonist at the center of the story. The illustrations, textured acrylic-on-canvas paintings, give the reader a visceral sense of the setting. Amelia, the protagonist, hates the constant moving around that her family must do because of migrant farm work. There is no mention of the working conditions, the owners' participation, the manner in which working and housing arrangements are made, or workings of the migrant labor system. In some ways, as Hazel Rochman (1993) claims, this story functions as metaphor for migrant farmworker experience.

In the author's note at the end of the book, Altman does a credible job of describing the difficulties of migrant life. It is unfortunate that on the inside back flap of the book the migrant experience is trivialized by the statement "she identifies with migrant children because her family moved around often when she was young." Clearly the author empathizes with her protagonist, and probably understands the fears of not being accepted into new schools, making and losing friends, and adjusting to new neighborhoods and communities. But the experience of being forced to live in a succession of marginal dwellings is vastly different from a middle-class experience with a succession of comfortable homes. Children of academics, children of service people, and children whose families enjoy upward mobility and maybe reassignment to different locations do not compare to children who must move from shacks to tents to barrack-like accommodations and subsistence living. Their lives are not safe, private, or predictable.

This book is not a window into how families live in different ways, as suggested by one book reviewer (Wilde, 1993); the difference is sociopolitically made. Told through a third-person perspective, this is a story of a Mexican American family, who are migrant farmworkers needing to travel from field to field for work. Amelia is tired of moving around and wishes to stay in one place. She works alongside her parents three hours each morning and then goes off to school: "By the time she had finished her morning's work, Amelia's hands stung and her shoulders ached. She grabbed an apple and hurried off to school" (n.p.). The family perseveres without complaining.

The story shows workers in a respectful way, but the migrant worker system is not questioned; it functions more as a backdrop or scenery. While Amelia creates a place she will call home, there is a complete silence about the power structure of the socioeconomic system that perpetuates a dependence on the exploitation of migrant farmworkers. Amelia shows agency when she decides to make the spot under the old tree her sense of home, a place of her own.

Amelia is dissatisfied about the kind of knowledge that her father possesses: "Other fathers remembered days and dates. Hers remembered crops" (n.p.). The farmworker's knowledge has no value alongside school knowledge. Despite this, the ending of the story is filled with promise: "For the first time in her life, she didn't cry when her father took out the road map" (n.p.). Amelia takes charge of the situation and creates permanence amidst the instability. She has a special spot, "a place she can come back to," marking the return of the harvest cycle, but no economic change will happen for this family. This closed ending trivializes and contributes to the inevitability of the migrant experience.

Tomás and the Library Lady, written by Pat Mora (1997) and illustrated by Raul Colón, was inspired by a real life character, Tomás Rivera, who was a migrant worker and became a writer, professor, and chancellor of the University of California at Riverside. The illustrations, done in scratchboard overwashed in sun-drenched colors, create a dream-like atmosphere.

In this story, Tomás and his family spend winters in Texas and summers in Iowa as migrant farmworkers. The grandfather, who is an accomplished storyteller, sends Tomás to the library to gather more stories. The librarian invites Tomás into the library, supplies him with a refreshing drink of cold water, and offers him some books. The family appreciates the stories that Tomás reads to them. Tomás and the librarian develop a strong friendship over the course of the summer. When the family leaves to return to Texas, "the library lady" gives Tomás the gift of a new book. Told from a third-person perspective the text reflects the role libraries can play for migrant communities—a public home.

Although this story reveals little about the actual experience of migrant farmers, we see the support of the family, valuing of story, and the importance of a relationship with a key community member. The librarian is respectful of the child and his abilities, and genuinely interested in who he is. She sees him as an individual from a specific cultural group. The family is supportive of his interests. Unlike Amelia, Tomás is not devastated by his situation. He carries his sense of self with him.

The story's ending is left open with possibilities. What books will Tomás read? What stories will he tell? Tomás is the new family storyteller, which points to the family's future. But will Tomás' stories displace his grandfather as teller? Certainly the family values Tomás' ability to read, thereby giving him access to other stories. The danger is whether this access will devalue the stories Papa Grande has to tell. Will book knowledge be valued over lived experience and oral tradition?

Going Home, written by Eve Bunting (1996) and illustrated by David Diaz, told in first-person narrative, incorporates multiple focalizers, thus giving the story an interrogative edge. A migrant worker family returns to Mexico during Christmas time. Even though the family members are documented immigrants, they worry: "Are you sure they will let us back, Papa?" (Bunting, 1996: 5), a concern many of the characters express because of race relations in the Southwest. Opportunity is the underlying theme in this story.

On their journey back to Mexico, the children, Dolores and Carlos, discuss their parents' choice to labor in the fields. The family is in the United States "for the opportunities," Dolores, the oldest child, mimics her father. Carlos comments: "I don't see them getting many of these wonderful opportunities" (n.p.). Dolores is critical of the association between the United States and opportunities. On their first night in Mexico, the children gain an understanding of their parents' attachment to their homeland as they notice their parents' ties to family, community, and the landscape.

During their visit to Mexico, the townspeople comment on the opportunities education affords in the United States, admiring the children's ability to speak English and applauding the parents' decision to emigrate. Nevertheless, the ending is ambiguous with the possibility held out that if they succeed in the United States they may return to Mexico.

The challenges of going from school to school are captured in the last picture book that draws from realistic fiction. *First Day in Grapes* (2002), written by L. King Pérez and illustrated by Robert Casilla, reflects the Mexican American migrant experience. This text, told in the third-person omniscient position and first-person perspective, depicts Chico's reluctance about attending a new school again. He worries that kids will make fun of him. And they do.

His new teacher clearly is involved with the students: She plays baseball during recess. She notices that math is Chico's strongest subject and invites him to take on challenging problems. During lunchtime two fourth grade boys mock Chico because of his tortilla lunch. He stands up and, using his math knowledge, proceeds to pose math problems for the boys to solve. This interrupts their bullying efforts and rallies other students to Chico's side. Chico feels his power. In getting off the bus, he politely and pleasantly introduces himself to the "grouchy bus driver." These two situations speak to Chico's agency. He decides to resist the disrespectful ways some of the children treat the bus driver. Chico is a resister and an agent.

Linda Perkins (2002), one of the book's reviewers, claims that this text is "an insightful glimpse of another way of life and a reminder that different kids have different talents." We are concerned about the idea of viewing this situation as "another way of life;" rather, it is greatly shaped by race and class relations. *First Day in Grapes* demonstrates that this migrant family is exercising collaborative power to make their situation work against the difficult conditions created by the migrant agricultural labor system. The photographs and illustrations of nonfiction narratives and picture books offer a place from which to view the story. The next group of books uses poetic elements, which intensify the language use in these stories.

Poetry

Poetic elements deepen the language use in three picture books and two young adult novels. The first text, *Gathering the Sun: An Alphabet in Spanish and English*, is framed by the Spanish alphabet. It was first written in Spanish and then translated into English. The two picture books by Juan Felipe Herrera savor words in telling about his experience as an English language learner. *Crashboomlove: A Novel in Verse*, and *Downtown Boy*, also by Herrera, use footnotes to translate Spanish words or scaffold the reader's understanding of Spanish, techniques providing an in-text code switching. All of these picture books are hybrids of picture book, realistic fiction, and poetry genres. Herrera's young adult novels are told in free verse.

Gathering the Sun: An Alphabet in Spanish and English, told by Alma Flor Ada (1997), illustrated by Simón Silva, and translated into English by Rosa Zubizarreta, acknowledges and affirms the Spanish language. The text introduces the reader to the Spanish alphabet, providing a different view of the people who work the land, and offering some information about Californian agriculture, and Mexican culture and history. Barrera, Quiroa, and West-Williams (1999) maintain that "Respect and dignity for the nation's Mexican American migrant farmworkers, young and old, is equally conveyed by the text and art of this book focused on the Spanish alphabet." In order for this book to work as an alphabet book, it is the Spanish to which we must refer.

The poem "*Orgullo*/Pride" exemplifies the intent of this text: "*orgullosa de mi familia/orgullosa de mi lengua/orgullosa de mi cultura/orgullosa de mi raza/orgullosa de ser quien soy.* Proud of my family/Proud of my language/ Proud of my culture/Proud of my people/Proud of being who I am" (n.p.). For the most part the book is a celebration and affirmation of love, honor, and pride in self and family, and an appreciation of nature. It is a visually sumptuous representation of migrant experience, with little hint of inequity or strife. A feeling of permanence pervades. The illustrations indicate an abundance that could be misleading if this text is not read alongside other depictions of the migrant experience.

The young adult novels by Francisco Jiménez help the reader become intimate with the family and each member comes to life. In *Gathering the Sun*, the reader gets a sense of each family as caring and affectionate but the reader does not get to know the family. In this text, we have no idea how stable the position is, although it is as if the family were permanently located in a fairly comfortable situation: The people are consistently adequately dressed, living in permanent housing, surrounded by the nuclear family (mother, father, boy and girl), in possession of a good-sized, well-maintained pick-up truck. The book becomes a paean of praise for the fruit of the harvest.

In Jiménez's chapter books, it is clear that the family must move with the harvest. In addition, his young adult novels demonstrate the complexities of being a farmworker: the uncertainty, abuse, exploitation, disruptive nature of moving around, and the like. In *Gathering the Sun*, the "W" page is a thank you to the farmworkers for their harvest, the "Y" page connects the past and future of Mexican Americans, and the "Z" page closes the story with the message that ultimately nature is the one in control. The story closure of this Spanish alphabet book confirms that nature inevitably determines the harvest. This closed ending fails to consider that migrant agricultural work as an exploitive system of labor is socially made.

Poet Juan Felipe Herrera wrote *Calling the Doves/El canto de las palomas* (1995), illustrated by Elly Simmons, and *The Upside Down Boy/El niño de cabeza* (2000), illustrated by Elizabeth Gómez, to document his English language learning experience as a migrant child. These stories combine first-person narrative with lyrical language, realistic fiction, and magical realism. (Magical realism is a uniquely Latin American genre. It invites the real and the fantastical to exist side by side.)[3]

These two texts depict a loving family, with an affectionate father who is present. Book reviewer Annie Ayres (1996) maintains that these texts are "a welcome alternative to the usually bleak portrayal of the migrant farmworker experience, this is an inspirational self-portrait of a loving family" (Ayres, 1996). There are strong bonds between people, their work, and the landscape. Choice is implicit in both of these stories. The parents envision a new life for their son, with choice and some sacrifice.

The Upside Down Boy/El niño de cabeza addresses the power teachers can share with their students. Mrs. Lucille Sampson, Juan Felipe's third grade teacher, the teacher to whom the author dedicates this story, recognizes Juan Felipe's talents with words, art, and music. She offers many invitations for him to explore and expand these talents. Even though his teacher does not invite Juanito to use Spanish in his learning, not acknowledging his first language as a resource for learning, she shares with him a love for language and values the use of music as an entry point to literacy learning.

This story affirms the author's uneasiness about attending a new school. Education and English language learning are the cultural themes in this story. The author tells the next part of his life story when his family settles down so he can go to school for the first time. The text's vibrant language and illustrations capture his feeling of being "upside down" as he learns in a formal context and acquires a new language. At school his friend Amanda helps him with the English language.

Juanito is a second language learner. He is motivated to learn English: "If I learn them [alphabet letters and numbers] will they grow like seeds?" (Herrera, 2000: 10). The alphabet letters are the seeds of the English language. Juanito's teacher invites him to sing a song in English and recognizes his singing talent. His music leads him into poetry writing. While Mrs. Sampson's pedagogy values multiple language modes, it fails to acknowledge that a child's first language can be a resource for learning a second or additional language. Language and identity are bound together. Juanito's full selfhood was not honored in this classroom.

In *Crashboomlove: A Novel in Verse* (1999), the combination of Herrera's free verse and first-person narration capture the immediacy and force of the power relations experienced by sixteen-year-old César García, the novel's protagonist. Herrera pushes the boundaries of the genre of poetry to tell his story in the format of a novel. This series of poems takes the reader into the life of César García. César's father, Papi César, leaves the migrant circuit in California, deserts the young César and his mother, and joins his other wife and children in Denver, Colorado.

César's "school friends" too often lead him into trouble. Eventually, despite César's getting into trouble, his mother and teachers, who believe in him, help him to find a path for himself.

Herrera demonstrates here that poetry can be a medium for reality. The free verse heightens the insidious nature of racisms and classism and sexism in this setting. Its sparseness conveys the economically lean quality of poverty. Social interactions are fast and hard. Identity constructions are intergroup and intragroup processes. This text shows how the power relations extant at Rambling West High School in Fowlerville, California, try to swallow César García up whole.

César struggles as a Mexican American teenager in a hostile school situation, a context that is new for him. The free verse amplifies his liminal status within this school community. He is marginalized because of his migrant farmworker status as well as his Mexican cultural and language differences. Extreme peer pressure to participate in racist, classist, and sexist activity through verbal and physical violence is commonplace at this high school.

César tries to hide his Mexican identity and looks to the marketplace to create a common culture and mask his heritage:

> Xeng sits next to me and Miguel Tzotzil. Lunch.
> Show him my shoes.
> New Air Tigers Lucy bought me.
> Hide my tortillas in the wrinkled bag.
> (Herrera, 1999: 13)

The name brands offer new associations in the school context, which perpetuate intragroup racism and classism:

> Maxy Ortega snarls,
> Hollers to the new guy—Kick his butt!
> He's a scrapa, a wetback. Spits on me.
> (Herrera, 1999: 30)

Gang life becomes a microcosm of society. César colludes with intragroup racism, and because of peer pressure, beats up his friend Miguel Tzotzil. We also recognize that César wants to cease his participation in petty crimes, violence, and drugs.

Mama Lucy protests school practices that discriminate against her son César and alienate the Mexican American students. She intervenes at the end of the story and offers to teach afternoon and Saturday classes that will bring Mexican American students back to their culture. Another ally, Ms. Steiger, who is a teacher in the alternative school that César attends, uses the arts, especially writing, to humanize "problem students." She invites them to say the unspeakable, to write the undocumented:

> Ms. Steiger said, Write about who you are.
> Carlos Johnson laughed. Is something funny?
> She asked. How can I write about myself?
> I don't even know what I am.

> I don't know if I am Black.
> I don't know if I am Mexican.
> My parents never talk about it.
> That's it, Carlos. Write that.
> Ms. Steiger smiled a big smile.
> It was the first time
> I heard Carlos
> Talk in class. It was the first time
> I heard he was Mexican *and* Black.
>   (Herrera, 1999: 151)

Carl Johnson is the ringmaster of many of the altercations represented in this novel. Ms. Steiger guides him to name the internalized oppression that he has experienced. Mama Lucy and Ms. Steiger embrace these young adults whose fast-paced high school environment guarantees failure. This novel ends like the author's two other books, with Ms. Steiger creating a space for César and his classmates to find and hear their voices.

Downtown Boy (2005), a novel in verse written by Juan Felipe Herrera, is narrated by Juanito, the ten-year-old son of an undocumented migrant worker we familiarly know as "Papi," generically from the boy's point of view. The story opens with Juanito and his permanent resident mother, "Mami", trying to lead a new non-migrant life in the sometimes mean streets of San Francisco. Juanito's peripatetic Papi is often absent from the family's new life, no longer because of migrant work but ostensibly to seek a cure from the healing health spas of Mexico. In actuality, Papi is visiting his older children from a previous marriage with Mami's consent. Papi has two families, a thematic echo of his dual life in the United States and Mexico. "It isn't easy having two families," Papi later said to his son.

Alone with his Mami for much of the time, Juanito and his family's values are sorely challenged by some proto-gang related youth culture in the *barrio*, as Chacho, his *primo* (cousin) said, "This is the Mission. Nobody cares." The main struggle in the book is the effect constant moving has on the family, especially on Juanito. While his family life is characterized by a loving mother and father, the frequent absence of his father sets up a cultural and moral vacuum for Juanito which leads him into a world of pranks and petty thievery. Chacho uses slang like "Slickest", "toughest cat", and "Daddy-o", 50's patter that does not define him as a Mexican American per se, but as any American teenager in any American city or town. Chacho is a force to reckon with, immediately introducing himself as a dynamic agent of change on the first page of the book as he emphatically cajoles Juanito to join the boxing club. To Chacho, the most effective sign of agency is a strong right hook. Juanito recalls his father's words against the use of violence, hesitates, but finally relents and agrees to box. "Don't know what I'm doing here," Juanito says to himself later at the gym. This should be taken literally and metaphorically. Juanito does not want to become one of the Harrison Street Boys and what that represents but cannot entirely resist and adhere to his father and mother's instructions. "*Respeto*," his mother says, and "*Paciencia*." Respect and patience. "Chacho isn't patient," thinks Juanito, "Chumps are patient."

Papi and Mami moved to the city to provide a better, less transient life for their son. But the tradeoff was diminished financial security for a family accustomed only to migrant farm work. "There's no jobs for farmworkers in the big towns . . . But in big towns, there are beautiful schools!" said Papi to his son. Mami and Papi show a significant amount of agency in this move, but ultimately this capacity for positive change is limited by Papi's minimal English acquisition, undocumented status, and lack of formal education.

Juanito's Aunt Albina and Uncle Arturo represent the non-migrant entrepreneurial class. Albina runs La Reina Mexicatessen, a small Mexican-American deli, and Arturo runs the only tortilla-making machine in the Mission District. They are financially comfortable and an example of material success. Aunt Albina appears to exercise more independence in running her deli while Juanito's mother exercises less agency with her dependence on Papi's diminishing income. Classism and racism by the dominant American mainstream is largely veiled since very few Anglo-American characters are depicted outside the Mexican-American experience. There are ominous but brief brushes with welfare and immigration agents, but they loom largely more as anonymous threats than real characters. There is a continued sense of invisibility, a theme often repeated in the Mexican-American experience but also the critical necessity to be invisible as well. Maria, Juanito's friend and neighbor, is only allowed to leave her undocumented father's apartment to attend elementary school. Other than that, she must stay home, leading a life of invisibility. One day, after slipping each other surreptitious notes beneath each other's doors, she and Juanito decide to visit the beach together. They are surrounded by beachgoers and an amusement park at their back, but they still experience complete anonymity.

Although Mami came to the United States in the 1920s and has a green card, she has been living the life of the migrant worker accompanying her undocumented husband up and down the state of California. They live a neverending immigrant experience, one that seldom achieves the critical mass of time in one place and one place only to experience a true rooted landing. In this sense, they are neither American nor Mexican. Juanito narrates:

Mexico feels like a house
where we used to live
so long ago no one remembers it,
or knows exactly where it is.

We always seem to talk about it though. Papi goes back and looks for it,
but I don't think he's found it yet. Mami says
he knows where he's going
but I think he's lost
and doesn't know where the house
is anymore; he circles it.
Loses it again.
Why can't this be Mexico?

(Herrera, 2005: 77)

Fairly early on in the book we learn that Papi is not entirely healthy. He suffers from early onset diabetes. Diabetes, like mental illness and public policy, has invisible but vicious long roots that feed on the blood of a sufferer's life. In this way, the seeds for Papi's illness and subsequent double amputation were sown well before his son was born. Seen as metaphor, it was almost a product of predestination. Emotionally, Papi was severed from both his right and left legs long ago, walking on borrowed time. As an undocumented immigrant, he stood neither in Mexico nor the United States. And when he gave up the only life he knew in order that his son could receive a stable and rooted upbringing, he became incapacitated.

The remaining novels in the text collection combine realistic fiction and autobiographical elements to represent the Mexican American migrant farmworker experience.

Realistic Fiction

Steinbeck once said that he wrote books "the way lives [were] being lived not the way books [were] written" (as cited in Reef, 1996: 92). Like Jiménez's *The Circuit* and *Breaking Through,* all the texts in this section possess the social realism of John Steinbeck's *The Grapes of Wrath.*

Tomás Rivera's 1970 young adult novel, *y no se lo trago la tierra . . . And the Earth Did Not Devour Him,* first written in Spanish, is one of the first books to document the Mexican American migrant experience in great detail, an experience that was otherwise absent from the literary landscape. This text was newly translated and published by Arte Público Press in 1987, and reissued in 1995. The English translation is included in the second half of the book.

In his study of the undocumented immigrant representation in Chicano/a literature, Alberto Ledesma (1996) argues that Rivera's text is the first to pay attention to the undocumented immigrant experience, even though Rivera refers to protagonists as migrant farmworkers. Ledesma maintains that Rivera did this intentionally to deflect attention from the farmworkers' unauthorized status.

In Mexican culture there exists a social myth, based on religious superstition, that if you curse God's name, the earth will part and you will be swallowed whole. This belief is the basis of the title of Rivera's novel, a first-person narrative laced with multiple perspectives. The unnamed protagonist curses God's name out of desperation at seeing his family, friends, and community endure poverty. The twelve chapters connect isolated events in the novel, each one symbolic of a month in the migrant cycle.

This text describes the migrant experience in the 1950s, by showing how a community is exploited or discriminated against by farmers, shopkeepers, and even other Mexican Americans. The young boy, who remains nameless throughout the story, struggles for self-identity amidst exploitation, migrancy, death, disease, and social conflict.

In *Jesse* (1994), a semi-autobiographical, first-person narrative, Gary Soto, one of the most prolific Mexican American writers, tells the story of Jesse and his brother Abel. Jesse, a high school student, drops out of high school at Christmas during his senior year and moves in with Abel because his family life with his stepfather and mother is dysfunctional. He registers at City College, a local junior college in Fresno, California, during the Vietnam War era. Abel and Jesse work as migrant farmworkers on the weekend to pay for their food; housing is covered by their social security checks that they receive because of their father's industrial-related death. They resist White people's expectations for Mexican Americans, as one of the peripheral characters denounces: "White people only saw Mexicans as manual laborers" (Soto, 1994: 15). They attend college as an attempt to break out of the migrant circuit.

These two brothers work hard at school and at work. They are committed to each other and come to each other's help when necessary. Racist and classist assumptions about Mexicans and Mexican Americans as people and as students are challenged throughout the text. For example, one art student's work is not accepted because the teacher cannot believe a Mexican American student could create such good art.

In his art class, Jesse decides to paint the farmworkers' strike. He invites his mother to his class art show. She comments on Jesse's course of study:

> "*Ay, Dios mio*," she said, wiping her eyeglasses. "Is this what you're learning in college . . ."

. . . "Why can't you go into electricity? Angie's son is fixing radios and making good money. 'know he fixed the clock at St. John's? He got his wedding almost for free for that."

I shook my head no and led her to my drawing of striking field workers, which I had titled "*¡Huelga!*" The long dusty line of strikers curled out of view toward a sunset pink as a scar on a girl's knee. I didn't tell her that it was my drawing because I wanted her to like it a lot and then say, "This is really good, *mi'jo*. Who did this one?" But Mom wrapped her Juicy Fruit in an old coupon for Trix and said in Spanish, "*¡Mira!* These lazy people are giving us a bad name."

"Mom, they're strikers."

. . . "Is this what you and Abel go to school for?" . . .

(Soto, 1994: 125–126)

"Which one was yours?"

"What?"

"The pictures. Which one was yours, *mi'jo*?"

(Soto, 1994: 128)

Jesse lies and tells his mother that his painting is the one with the giraffe poking his head through the hedge. She is so pleased.

Jesse's mother colludes with racist and classist ideologies about what Mexican Americans can and cannot be. She wants her son to succeed in a world that only thinks of Mexican Americans as laborers. Jesse has other ideas for his future. He is conscious of the struggle within the farmworkers' community, which his mother interprets as a rejection of work opportunities. Jesse's mother's collusion comes from her position in society. He rejects his mother's expectations for the subject matter of his art, but never admits to being the artist of "*¡Huelga!*"

Jesse exercises collaborative power in helping his rich Mexican American friend with the college application process. Jesse shares his knowledge of how to apply to an institution of higher education as well as his writing talents. He co-writes Luis' personal statement by capturing in writing what he says. Leslie, a Vietnam veteran and friend to Jesse and Abel, is a White ally to them and the Mexican American community. The story ends with Abel's draft letter to go to Vietnam and Jesse imagining miles and miles of melons to harvest. The story closure questions how people could acquiesce to a socially unjust society: ". . . no one was getting up to set the crooked world straight" (Soto, 1994: 166).

Barefoot Heart: Stories of a Migrant Child, written by Elva Treviño Hart (1999), is an autobiographical account of the life of a child growing up in a family of migrant farmworkers. Elva Treviño Hart was born in south Texas to Mexican immigrant parents. She spent her childhood moving back and forth between a small, segregated south Texas town and Minnesota.

Hart faces racial prejudices in school. She finds a way not to be judged subjectively: "In math there was only one right answer . . . if I just did my very best, then I didn't have to fight, and I could get the best grade. I had finally found a place where being Mexican didn't matter" (Hart, 1999: 177–178). She therefore chooses to pursue mathematics, a field with cut and dry answers, even though she prefers English and reading.

Hart comments on the gender roles awaiting her after high school: "I saw that once I finished high school I had to leave and probably not come back except to visit. My parents expected no more of me than to be a local Mexican girl who married a local Mexican guy and became a *mamacita,* a *comadre,* a *tía,* and finally, an *abuelita* . . . it would be fine with them" (Hart, 1999: 207). Her focus in mathematics led her to a graduate program in computer science and engineering at Stanford University, followed by a twenty-year career as a computer programmer for IBM.

Hart's assimilation process separates her from Mexican culture and identity, and compromises the quality of relationships with her family. These consequences stem from survival strategies and choices made along the way. She experiences a "dual existence" as an adult.

Hart excels as a professional: "I had all the trappings of success. I was driving a Mercedes, flying all over the country on business, and vacationing in the Caribbean. As Gloria Steinem said, 'We were becoming the men we had always wanted to marry'" (as cited in Hart, 1999: 231). She becomes "a particular man." She buys into a class system that stratifies our society according to race and gender. It is not just "a man's world." It is a particular man's world—White middle- and upper-middle class man. She colludes with dominant class ideology, which severs her from her Mexican background.

Hart's life story is instructive because it demonstrates the tension between social and economic mobility and maintaining one's own cultural heritage. These two developments do not have be mutually exclusive, but can become so when moving up socially requires a person to by-pass or move away from the culture/power history they have lived, creating a cultural disconnection. The struggle is to improve one's socioeconomic situation while resisting dominant class ideologies, and working and living for collaborative power, and not just for personal wealth.

Hart quits her job at IBM and realizes her talents as a writer. She no longer lives the trappings of an affluent lifestyle, a desire that was an attempt to fill the void left by the poverty she lived as a child. Hart addresses that void through service and donates the profits from her autobiography for scholarship funds. The book closes with Hart embracing herself as "a Mexican American woman writer."

In *Esperanza Rising* (2000), Pam Muñoz Ryan builds her story on the life experiences of her maternal grandmother and the historical period of the early 1930s. Esperanza and her parents live a life of affluence in Aguascalientes, Mexico. Tragic circumstances force Esperanza and Mama to escape with their servants, Hortensia and Alfonso, and their son Miguel, to California, and settle in a Mexican migrant farm work camp. There they experience the challenges of hard work, acceptance by their own culture, and socioeconomic problems constructed by U.S. racist relations and the Great Depression. When Mama becomes ill with Valley Fever and a strike to protest working conditions threatens to uproot their new life, with the help of the community, the once-privileged Esperanza does everything she can to maintain life in the labor camp.

Ryan constructs this third-person narrative with multiple perspectives, creating a distance or estrangement for the reader to challenge the messages conveyed in the story. Esperanza's mother, an influential role model, the powerful voice of Marta, one of the strike organizers, and the dialogues between Esperanza and Miguel offer a critique of the life of farm labor. Esperanza's raised consciousness about her privileged past illuminates the social river that runs between Miguel and Esperanza. History provides the context for this story to unfold: the Great Depression and the repatriation of Mexicans and Mexican Americans to Mexico, the largest "involuntary migration" up to 1935.

Mama's lived experience amplifies the gender relations of the time, especially for an affluent woman. She cannot claim the family estate after her husband's death. She is not assigned housing because her family is not male-led. Eventually, Mama and Esperanza share living quarters with Hortensia's family.

Throughout this young adult novel, most of the interactions between Esperanza and her mother signal Esperanza's struggle to adapt to her new economic circumstances. Their conversations document her growing awareness of the privilege she enjoyed up to the border crossing. Imbedded in these dialogues are Esperanza's classist attitudes toward people who are poor. For example, she equates the poverty and the unclean train conditions endured by the peasants with thievery and untrustworthiness. Mama and Miguel provide ongoing commentary to Esperanza's classist and racist worldviews.

Esperanza marvels at the charity of Carmen, who is poor herself. She does not understand how Carmen can even think of others when her family has great need. Miguel responds: "The rich take care of the rich and the poor take care of those who have less than they have" (Ryan, 2000: 79).

Esperanza naively still cannot understand why Carmen has to take care of the beggar, when a farmer's market exists a few yards away. Miguel comments: "There is a Mexican saying: 'Full bellies and Spanish blood go hand in hand.' " He continues: "Have you never noticed?" . . .. "Those with Spanish blood, who have the fairest complexions in the land, are the wealthiest" (Ryan, 2000: 79). His observation shows Esperanza that class and race relations work together within Mexican society. Esperanza comes to understand her new social position; she and Mama are peasants now. To survive they exercise collective power with Hortensia's family and the rest of the migrant camp community.

Esperanza works hard to provide for Mama while she is sick. She witnesses other Mexican farmworkers laboring long hours in the fields. She is highly skeptical of the American Dream but Miguel has hopes:

> In Mexico, I was a second-class citizen. I stood on the other side of the river, remember? And I would have stayed that way my entire life. At least here, I have a chance, however small, to become more than what I was. You obviously can never understand this because you have never lived without hope.
>
> She clenched her fists and closed her eyes tight in frustration. "Miguel, do you not understand? You are still a second-class citizen because you act like one, letting them take advantage of you like that. Why don't you go to your boss and confront him? Why don't you speak up for yourself and your talents?"
>
> "You are beginning to sound like the strikers, Esperanza," said Miguel coldly. "There is more than one way to get what you want in this country. Maybe I must be more determined than others to succeed, but I know that it will happen."

> (Ryan, 2000: 222)

The next three realistic fiction narratives take place during the summer months of farming and harvest. All the protagonists are European American boys, one of working poor status, the other two of upper-middle- and middle-class standing, respectively.

These young men work alongside Mexican farmworkers. In each situation they come to know their work and living conditions. Books like Jiménez's *The Circuit* and *Breaking Through* should be read alongside these books from the White working-poor, middle-, and upper-middle class perspectives, so they can amplify the Mexican American migrant farmwork experience in these texts.

These books represent a shift in focalization. In analyzing these three texts, we examine how power is exercised among the characters as well as how power relations are perceived. Like Suzanne Fondrie (2001), we agree that readers cannot "ignore the way whiteness provides white characters status and privilege not accorded to other characters" (Fondrie, 2001: 9).

Fondrie provides two guiding questions that are useful to critical multicultural analysis: "How do the characters embody White privilege? And how does White privilege work with class?" (Fondrie, 2001: 10). While Fondrie is advocating "reading a new way," her recommendation does not take into account that power includes class and not just race relations, and that "multicultural aspects of children's literature" exist in all literature, because all literature is a cultural artifact or product.

Consequently, Peggy McIntosh's (1990) and Anne Marie Harvey's (2001) lists of White privilege are problematic because, in many instances, they conflate White privilege with class privilege. All White people do not benefit from all the privileges outlined on these lists because of ethnic bigotry and economic oppression. In many ways, these lists essentialize the White experience and obscure intragroup/intergroup diversity and the workings of class, reflecting particular White experiences.

In *The Beet Fields: Memories of a Sixteenth Summer* (2000), a young adult novel and memoir written by Gary Paulsen, the boy has contact with Mexican farmworkers in the first third of the book. This third-person narrative refers to Mexicans as a group most of the time or by gender and age, but never by name. Few Spanish words are imbedded in this text. Some microinteractions between the boy and the migrant workers exist.

The boy runs away from an abusive home situation and contemplates wealth, just like Juan Medina in *A Migrant Family*, as he is offered his first job on the road:

> When he'd started hoeing he dreamt of wealth, did the math constantly until the numbers filled his mind. Eleven dollars an acre, an acre a day; after ten days a hundred and ten dollars, twenty days the almost-unheard-of sum of two hundred and twenty dollars. More than a man made per month working in a factory for a dollar an hour—and he was only sixteen. Rich. He would be rich.
>
> But after the first day when his back would not straighten and his hands would not uncurl from the hoe handle and his blisters were bleeding, after all that and two-fifty for food, and three for the hoe, and fifty cents for the lodging, not to mention the hat and gloves, only a third of an acre had been thinned that first day, and he knew he would not get rich, would never be rich. By the second day he was

no longer even sad about not being rich and laughed with the Mexicans who would also never be rich but who smiled and laughed all the time while they worked. Now, on the fourth day, gloved, he just hoed.

(Paulsen, 2000: 6–7)

The Mexicans share their food, music, and social commentary with the boy: "They know we are not legal; we are like ghosts that they see but do not recognize. As long as we just work and do not go into town or make a difficulty we are all right and they leave us alone." (Paulsen, 2000: 43). He learns the work ethic of the Mexicans and questions the racist remarks he has heard about this cultural group in the past. The boy and the Mexicans exercise collaborative power as they share their meals together. With the encouragement of one of the Mexican men, the boy learns to capture pigeons from the barn rafters. Pigeons are a food source for the boy and the Mexican community.

After the hoeing is done, the Mexicans and the boy head down the driveway. The farmer stops the boy and offers him summer work, but the boy informs him that he is going with the Mexicans. The farmer replies, "But you're not a Mexican and I thought . . . well, let's try it another way. Can you drive a tractor?" (Paulsen, 2000: 49). The farmer does not offer stable work to the Mexicans because they are seen as disposable labor. The boy benefits from his White privilege and colludes with the farmer and stays on. Besides the predictable income, the boy remains behind because of possible romance with the farmer's daughter, whom he never sees again.

Gretchen Olson, a berry farmer, wrote *Joyride* (1998), a third-person narrative. Jeff McKenzie, an affluent seventeen-year-old, who lives in a neighboring city, decides to go for a joyride through the countryside. In the darkness, he happens to drive through farmland, leaving a farmer's damaged bean field behind. During that summer he works for the farmer to reimburse him for the damages. As a farmworker, he works alongside Mexican migrant workers, and becomes friends with one of the foremen, Macario. He comes to respect the migrant farmworkers, while, at the same time, recognizing his parents' and friends' racist attitudes.

The White working poor are stereotypically portrayed in this story. This class perceives the Mexicans encroaching on working class jobs as well as their town. Jeff's parents and his school friends are stereotypically portrayed as racist and classist rich people, while the Mexican farmworkers are rendered as good-natured. Jeff, the farmer's daughter Alexa, and Macario are the most fully embodied characters. The microinteractions among these characters are relational, revealing their assumptions about the world, thus offering the reader multiple subject positions.

Jeff is given some privileges early on the farm because he works hard, but also because he is White. He is assigned to drive the farm truck to make strawberry deliveries. His relationship with the farmer's daughter, Alexa, flourishes as they work on the farm together. Alexa challenges the gender roles assigned to her by her community: she is smart, athletic, and plans to work on the family farm when she grows up. Jeff's rich girlfriend Debbie, a walking stereotype tries to make him jealous by dating his tennis rival. She is divisive and colludes with gender power relations by wearing revealing clothing, being demanding, and playing the part of the submissive young woman.

In *Under the Same Sky* (2003), written by Cynthia DeFelice and told in a first-person narrative, fourteen-year-old Joe comes to understand his class and White privileges. His father wants him to learn what working is about, but his mother challenges this position, saying that Joe is still a child. The father answers that if he wants a motorbike, something a child would not desire, he is old enough to work. Joe begins working the fields, not really knowing much about the work or the Mexican community that assembled on his family's land from April until November. His father gives Manuel, one of the migrant workers, a lot of responsibility, which annoys Joe. He notices the high regard his father has for this young man. Joe's friends, Randy and Jason, make fun of Joe's plans to work part of the summer. Jason mocks Joe with racist and classist remarks: "*Señor* José, *amigo* . . . why you not working in the fields earning *muchos dineros?*" (DeFelice, 2003: 14). Joe denounces Jason's mockery.

Joe's contact with Mexican farmworkers makes him reconsider his desire to purchase a $900 motorbike: ". . . here was Luisa [one of the young Mexican farmworkers], working so she could send money home to her family, money for food and clothes and stuff like that. I felt like a real jerk working so I could buy what [his sister] LuAnn had just described as a toy" (DeFelice, 2003: 152). Joe's description of the farmworkers is humanizing; he places them on the landscape and connects their conditions to socio-political factors, in many ways, exposing how his family benefits from undocumented migrant farm labor.

Joyride and *Under the Same Sky* use the "under the same sky" metaphor to narrow the geographical and social distance between people and communities. The story closure connects two disparate places, urban and farming communities in *Joyride*: "[Jeff] looked at the sky—the same sky that stretched over a farm near Sheridan, Oregon. The same sky that looked over an oak knoll, an irrigation pond, a strawberry field . . . and a bean field" (Olson, 1998: 200).

In *Under the Same Sky*, Luisa asks Manuel to tell Joe that "she looking at the same sky" (DeFelice, 2003: 214). Joe thinks to himself: "I looked at the sky, at the sun that was also shining on Luisa in Sodus. I closed my eyes and let it warm my face . . . . Later that night, I sat under the maple tree and watched the stars come out, and then the moon, and felt Luisa watching them, too" (DeFelice, 2003: 215). The sky connects these young couples across social borders, social lines.

Concluding Remarks

Our critical multicultural analysis of children's literature about Mexican American migrant children's literature made visible how characters exercise power along the power continuum. All the characters exercise power, but the subject positions of collusion and resistance are more difficult to discern. The texts show raced and gendered expressions of class as characters interact with each other, offering multiple subject positions. In many instances the characters resist race, class, and gender ideologies and move toward collaborative power, but mostly within the family.

The focalization of the text shapes how stories are told. The texts with multiple focalizations construct a dialogic space for problematizing migrant farmwork. The single-focalized texts are less interrogative and require closer examination. The story closures contributed to the meaning of each story either by confirming the ideologies imbedded in the text or disrupting the prevailing explicit and implicit messages.

Each genre shapes how the stories are told, with hybrid genres, demanding more distancing strategies from the reader, especially the examination of the social construction of each genre. The cultural themes that emerge through critical multicultural analysis are expressions of U.S. power relations and are not intrinsic to this cultural group or the language in the texts. They situate how power is exercised within families, schools, communities, and society.

The poverty and marginalization experienced by migrant farmworkers call into question the ideology that everyone has equal access to the American Dream if they work for it. Penzenstadler (1989) speculates: "What would America be without the Dream? . . . If there had been no [B]lacks, [N]ative Americans, or Hispanics from whom Anglos could differentiate themselves, how would the American character have been delineated?" (Penzenstadler, 1989: 177). Mexican American literature questions the "Anglo American Dream—not only as to whether it is attainable by Mexican-Americans but as to whether it is worth attaining at all" (Penzenstadler, 1989: 177). Many Mexican immigrants trade in one form of oppression for another at the U.S./Mexico border. Reading class against culture makes visible how class, race, and gender work together within a cultural group's experience.

Classroom Applications

- Invite children to make a multimedia collage of representations of class in words and images (e.g., newspapers, advertisements, literature, TV commercials, music videos, etc.). Locate patterns across these texts.
- Construct a map of Mexico and the contiguous United States of America. Trace the journeys of three of the characters in the bibliography using this map. Discuss when each of the states were originally part of Mexico.
- Build on the research by Rosalinda B. Barrera and Ruth E. Quiroa (2003) and their work with Rebeca Valdivia (2003) by investigating how Spanish is re/presented in these texts. What is the function of Spanish in the text collection? The presence of Spanish can deconstruct, construct, and/or reconstruct culture in children's literature: English can conceal, while Spanish can reveal. Who is the implied reader for these texts? English language learners? Speakers of English?
- Conduct a critical multicultural analysis of the Judeo-Christian discourse circulating in the text collection. In what ways is the Judeo-Christian discourse implicated in some of these stories? How are the discursive threads of luck and good fortune linked to this discourse? What is this discourse doing in terms of how power is exercised, especially among the female characters?
- Complete a critical multicultural analysis of migrant farm work across cultures and over time. For example, how are European American migrant workers represented during the Great Depression? What are other migrant experiences represented in children's literature (e.g., Jamaican or Haitian farmworkers)? How are race, class, and gender depicted in these stories?
- Examine poverty in other work circumstances, especially across different historical and sociopolitical conditions.
- Analyze work across cultures. In what ways are class, race, and gender enacted in these texts? How is power exercised among the characters?
- bell hooks (2000) advocates that class might be the unifying force across other social differences. In what ways can class be read across culture?
- Biographies, like other genres, distort reality and need analysis. Oftentimes, the people and life work highlighted are rendered separate or isolated from the people that supported them (Kozol, 1975; Kohl, 1995c). Consider biographies about Mexican American migrant workers, especially depictions of the struggle within the migrant community. How do the biographies of César Cháves and

Dolores Huerta, for example, depict the struggle among the migrant community? What are these life stories doing to our understanding of the migrant labor system? What do different biographers foreground and background in their construction of Dolores Huerta's life, for example? How do these different versions affect the ideologies conveyed to the reader?

Recommendations for Classroom Research

- Compare recent migrant worker statistics with what the books are depicting. What gets portrayed or focused on? To reject cultural stereotypes, etc., does the story have to center on an individual or family experience extracted from the sociopolitical context that defines them? Is culture only seen in a vacuum? Look at Stephens' (1992) work to address the way stories are constructed and how these constructions perpetuate the status quo and social oppression.
- How is work depicted? How is leisure portrayed?

Suggestions for Further Reading

Acuña, Rodolfo. (1988). *Occupied America: A history of Chicanos* (3rd ed.). New York: Harper & Row.

Day, Gary. (2001). *Class.* New York: Routledge.

Del Castillo, Richard Griswold & De León, Arnoldo. (1996). *North to Aztlán: A history of Mexican Americans in the United States.* New York: Twayne Publishers.

Gibson-Graham, J. K. (1996). *The end of capitalism (as we knew it): A feminist critique of political economy.* Malden, MA: Blackwell.

Gibson-Graham, J. K. & O'Neill, Phillip. (2001). Exploring a new class politics of the enterprise. In J. K. Gibson-Graham, S. Resnick & R. Wolff (Eds.), *Re/Presenting class: Essays in postmodern Marxism* (pp. 56–80). Durham, NC: Duke University Press.

Gibson-Graham, J. K., Resnick, Stephen A. & Wolff, Richard D. (2000). Introduction: Class in a poststructuralist frame. In J. K. Gibson-Graham, S. A. Resnick, R. D. Wolff (Eds.), *Class and its others* (pp. 1–22). Minneapolis, MN: University of Minnesota Press.

Gibson-Graham, J. K., Resnick, Stephen A. & Wolff, Richard D. (2001). Toward a poststructuralist political economy. In J. K. Gibson-Graham, S. A. Resnick, R. D. Wolff (Eds.), *Re/Presenting class: Essays in postmodern Marxism* (pp. 1–22). Durham, NC: Duke University Press.

Giecek, Tamara S. (2007). *Teaching economics as if people mattered: A high school curriculum guide to the new economy* (2nd ed.). Boston: United for a Fair Economy.

hooks, bell. (2000). *Where we stand: Class matters.* New York: Routledge.

Kelley, Jane, Rosenberger, Cynthia & Botelho, Maria José. (2005). Recurring Theme of Poverty in Children's Literature. *The Dragon Lode,* 24(1), 25 30.

Lubienski, Sarah Theule. (2003). Celebrating diversity and denying disparities: A critical assessment. *Educational Researcher,* 32(8), 30–38.

Mantsios, Gregory. (2001a). Class in America: Myths and realities (2000). In P. S. Rothenberg (Ed.), *Race, class, and gender in the United States* (5th ed., pp. 168–182). New York: Worth Publishers.

Mantsios, Gregory. (2001b). Media magic: Making class invisible. In P. S. Rothenberg (Ed.), *Race, class, and gender in the United States* (5ᵗʰ ed., pp. 563–571). New York: Worth Publishers.
Ortner, Sherry. (1998). Identities: The hidden life of class. *Journal of Anthropological Research*, 54(1), 1–17.
Wojcik-Andrews, Ian. (1993). Toward a theory of class in children's literature. *The Lion and the Unicorn*, 17(2), 113–123.

References

Children's Literature

Ada, Alma Flor. (1997). *Gathering the sun: An alphabet in Spanish and English.* Illustrated by Simón Silva. New York: Lothrop, Lee & Shepard.
Altman, Linda Jacobs. (1993). *Amelia's road.* Illustrated by Enrique O. Sánchez. New York: Lee & Low.
Ancona, George. (2001). *Harvest.* Photography by author. New York: Marshall Cavendish Children's Books.
Atkin, S. Beth. (2000). *Voices from the fields: Children of migrant farmworkers tell their stories.* Photography by author. Boston: Little, Brown & Co.
Brimner, Larry Dane. (1992). *A migrant family.* Photography by author. Minneapolis: Lerner Publications.
Bunting, Eve. (1996). *Going home.* Illustrated by David Diaz. New York: HarperCollins.
DeFelice, Cynthia. (2003). *Under the same sky.* New York: Farrar, Straus and Giroux.
Dorros, Arthur. (1993). *Radio man/Don radio.* Illustrated by author. New York: HarperTrophy.
Hart, Elva Treviño. (1999). *Barefoot heart: Stories of a migrant child.* Tempe, Arizona: Bilingual Press.
Herrera, Juan Felipe. (1995). *Calling the doves/El canto de las palomas.* Illustrated by Elly Simmons. San Francisco: Children's Book Press.
Herrera, Juan Felipe. (1999). *Crashboomlove: A novel in verse.* University of New Mexico Press.
Herrera, Juan Felipe. (2000). *The upside down boy/El niño de cabeza.* Illustrated by Elizabeth Gómez. San Francisco: Children's Book Press.
Herrera, Juan Felipe. (2005). *Downtown boy.* New York: Scholastic.
Hoyt-Goldsmith, Diane. (1996). *Migrant worker: A boy from the Rio Grande Valley.* Photography by Lawrence Migdale. New York: Holiday House.
Jiménez, Francisco. (1997). *The circuit: Stories from the life of a migrant child.* Boston: Houghton Mifflin Company.
Jiménez, Francisco. (1998). *La mariposa.* Illustrated by Simón Silva. Boston: Houghton Mifflin Company.
Jiménez, Francisco. (2000). *The Christmas gift/El regalo de Navidad.* Illustrated by Claire B. Cotts. Boston: Houghton Mifflin Company.
Jiménez, Francisco. (2001). *Breaking through.* Boston: Houghton Mifflin Company.
Mora, Pat. (1997). *Tomás and the library lady.* Illustrated by Raul Colón. New York: Alfred A. Knopf.
Olson, Gretchen. (1998). *Joyride.* Honesdale, PA: Boyds Mills Press.
Paulsen, Gary. (2000). *The beet fields: Memories of a sixteenth summer.* New York: Delacorte Press.
Pérez, L. King. (2002). *First day in grapes.* Illustrated by Robert Casilla. New York: Lee & Low.
Rivera, Tomás. (1970/1995). *—y no se lo tragó la tierra. . . . And the earth did not devour him.* Houston, TX: Arte Público Press.
Ryan, Pam Muñoz. (2000). *Esperanza rising.* New York: Scholastic.
Soto, Gary. (1994), *Jesse.* New York: Harcourt, Brace & Company.
Viramontes, Helena María. (1995). *Under the feet of Jesus.* New York: Penguin Publishers.

Secondary Sources

Ayres, Annie. (1996). Book review of *Calling the Doves/El canto de las palomas*. *Booklist*, 92 (9 & 10).

Barrera, Roslinada B. & Quiroa, Ruth E. (2003). The use of Spanish in Latino children's literature in English: What makes for cultural authenticity? In D. L. Fox & K. G. Short (Eds.), *Stories matter: The complexity of cultural authenticity in children's literature* (pp. 247–265). Urbana, IL: NCTE.

Barrera, Roslinada B., Quiroa, Ruth E. & Valdivia, Rebeca. (2003). Spanish in Latino picture storybooks in English: Its use and textual effects. In A. I. Willis, G. E. García, R. Barrera, V. J. Harris (Eds.), *Multicultural issues in literacy research and practice* (pp. 145–165). Mahwah, NJ: Lawrence Erlbaum Associates.

Butcher, John S. (2002). Aspects of travel and movement in children's literature. *The New Advocate*, 15(2), 145–155.

Clifford, James. (1997). Diasporas. *Cultural Anthropology*, 9(3), 302–338.

Dresang, Eliza T. (1997). The resilient child in contemporary children's literature: Surviving personal violence. *Children's Literature Association Quarterly*, 22(3), 133–141.

Fondrie, Suzanne. (2001). "Gentle doses of racism": Whiteness and children's literature. *Journal of Children's Literature*, 27(2), 9–13.

Ginsberg, Sherri Forgash. (1998). Book review of *The Circuit*. *KLIATT Review*, 32(2).

Gonzales, Manuel G. (1999). *Mexicanos: A history of Mexicans in the United States*. Bloomington, IN: Indiana University Press.

Kelley, Jane, Rosenberger, Cynthia & Botelho, Maria José. (2005). Recurring Theme of Poverty in Children's Literature. *The Dragon Lode*, 24(1), 25–30.

Kohl, Herbert. (1995c). The story of Rosa Parks and the Montgomery Bus Boycott revisited. In *Should we burn Babar? Essays on children's literature and the power of stories* (pp. 30–56). New York: The New Press.

Kozol, Jonathan. (1975). Great men and women (Tailored for school use). *Learning Magazine*, (December), 16–20.

Ledesma, Alberto. (1996). *Undocumented immigrant representation in Chicano narrative: The dialectics of silence and subterfuge*. Unpublished dissertation, University of California at Berkeley.

McIntosh, Peggy. (1990). White privilege: Unpacking the invisible knapsack. *Independent School* (Winter), 31–36.

Penzenstadler, Joan. (1989). La frontera, Aztlán, el barrio: Frontiers in Chicano literature. In D. Mogen, M. Busby, & P. Bryant (Eds.), *The frontier experience and the American dream: Essays on American literature* (pp. 159–179). College Station, TX: Texas A & M University Press.

Perkins, Linda. (2002). Book review of *First Day in Grapes*. *Booklist*, 99(6).

Reef, Catherine. (1996) *John Steinbeck*. New York: Clarion Books.

Rochman, Hazel. (1993). Book review of *Amelia's Road*. *Booklist*, 90(2).

Rothenberg, Daniel. (1998). *With these hands: The hidden world of migrant farmworkers today*. New York: Harcourt Brace & Co.

Rothenberg, Paula. (Ed.). (2004). *Race, class, and gender in the United States: An integrated study*. New York: Worth Publishers.

Spring, Joel. (2004). *Deculturalization and the struggle for equality: Brief history of the education of dominated cultures in the United States* (4rd ed.). Boston: McGraw-Hill.

Stephens, John. (1992). *Language and ideology in children's fiction*. New York: Longman.

Wilde, Susie. (1993). Book review of *Amelia's Road*. *Children's Literature*.

Wilhem, James J. (1985). *Garland publications in comparative literature*. New York: Garland.

Endnotes

1. The main title of this chapter is inspired by Francisco Jiménez's book, *The Circuit.*
2. Jiménez was instrumental in editing *The Identification and Analysis of Chicano Literature*, the first volume of critical essays on Chicana/o literature. Bilingual Press published this collection in 1979. This collection demonstrated "evidence of the vitality of scholarship on Chicano literature" and its rightful place in American literary study (p. ii). He also edited *Poverty and Social Justice: Critical Perspectives: A Pilgrimage Toward Our Own Humanity*, a collection of essays on poverty, published by Bilingual Press in 1987. The intent of this volume was to show the origins of poverty, to speculate on possible solutions, and to challenge the reader "to confront and reflect upon the moral, philosophical, and religious dimensions of poverty" (p. 10).
3. Magical realism is based on Western views of reality, while creating a space for the representation of myths and beliefs of Indigenous peoples of Mexico and other Latin American countries (Wilhem, 1985).

CHAPTER 8

Genres as Social Constructions: The Intertextuality of Children's Literature

According to Webster's eleventh edition, genre is "a category of artistic, musical, or literary composition categorized by a particular style, form, or content." A genre is a classification within which there are prescribed or common elements that invite expectation on the part of the reader or viewer. Genres are imbued with ideologies and particular ingredients that are open to reconstruction and reinterpretation over time, that is, socially co-constructed by the author and reader.

A generic scheme invites a literary study with much emphasis on the structure of the story (also known as story grammar). Aesthetic quality, plot and character construction, setting, voice, and style constitute the primary elements of such criticism. In many ways, the genre shapes the readers' expectations for the text. Therefore, it is reasonable to look at how genres have been socially constructed, how these constructions shape what gets told, and in what manner. Each genre contains "categories set up by the interaction of textual features and reading practices which shape and limit the meanings readers can make with a text" (Moon, 1999: 81).

According to Nina Mikkelsen (2000: 45), "We must know about genres because they account for the way the world organizes literature." While genres are not institutions, Vincent Leitch (1991: 85) argues that "there are, of course, relations between genres and institutions, as, for example, the epic and the state, the drama and the church, the essay and the school, but such . . . institutions often employ and frequently regulate particular genres." Genres are social constructs, which get their definitions from institutions of teaching and learning, publishing, and book buying and borrowing.

Most children's literature courses and many textbooks are organized by genre. That is, the literature is divided into such categories as poetry, picture books, nonfiction (e.g., biography, journals, diaries, collaborative autobiography, and all informational books), realistic fiction, historical fiction, chapter books, science fiction, fantasy, and what some people call traditional literature (e.g., folktales, fairy tales, and myths). There is an almost endless list of sub-categories that may be considered, depending on the scope and intent of the course.

In many introductory or survey courses the genres are defined and exemplary titles are studied and discussed, but rarely are the genres challenged as to their efficacy and inherent ideologies. Terry Eagleton (1976), raising the issue of genre and ideology, is of the opinion that,

> In selecting a form, then, the writer finds this choice already ideologically circumscribed. He may combine and transmute forms available to him from a literary tradition, but these forms themselves, as well as his permutation of them, are ideologically significant. The languages and devices a writer finds to hand are already saturated with certain ideological modes of perception. . . .
>
> (Eagleton, 1976: 26–27)

Terry Threadgold (1989) asserts "to make genre, discourse and story 'visible' by teaching them is potentially to provide the means if not the certainty of subversion and change" (Threadgold, 1989: 107). Genres are a system of control over the writer and reader. According to Robert Hodge (1990),

> The classifications of texts are also classifications of people—readers and writers—and of what they write or read about and what they should think and mean. Clearly the concept of genre is crucial in understanding how literature is implicated in basic systems of social control.
>
> (Hodge, 1990: 21)

Any genre can contain or be a mixture of several genres, thereby forming hybrids. Each genre is a tapestry of discourses, woven with discursive threads. When we think of a particular genre we see the world through a particular prism. A "humor" classification will cue us to respond differently from a "horror" piece. And "science fiction" will help us to provide a different context than "historical fiction". Our expectations and responses can be shaped according to the genre clues that are emitted by the text. Genre organizes our perceptions and confirms our literary expectations.

Who or what, therefore, is in control of the text? Where does the source of the meaning lie? Is it the genre, the author-writer, or the reader? How do social and political practices and conditions influence the text? Roland Barthes (1977) and Michel Foucault (1984) contend that the author has little to do with the ultimate meaning of the text. Barthes believes in the reader's power, and Foucault in what is generated socially through the "author-function." Foucault brashly raises the possibility that "We can easily imagine a culture where discourse would circulate without any need for an author" (Foucault, 1984: 468) and where no one would worry about the identity of the true author or the authenticity of that person. Rather, the questions would be directed toward the process of the text and the "modes of existence of the discourse" (Foucault, 1984: 468).

The deconstruction and reconstruction of genres unmask power and speculate on their redistribution. Conventions, social agreements, and expectations influence what gets said and not said. Genres are one way to control human discourse and manage ideology; they are the material representation of ideology. But genres can be sites of resistance and struggle as authors experiment with genre blurring and hybridization. Thomas Beebe (1994) maintains: "If genre is a form of ideology, then the struggle against or the deviations from genre are ideological struggles" (Beebe, 1994: 19). Eagleton adds, "significant developments in literary form . . . result from significant changes in ideology" (Eagleton: 1976: 24–25).

Not only do authors use genre to reach and influence particular audiences, but also publishers make decisions based on their perceptions of who will constitute a market for their products. Sometimes publishers will even change the tenor of a book by refusing to buy a work unless it meets the classification of the popular trend at the time, for example, memoir rather than fiction.

Rather than supporting literary study organized narrowly by genre, we invite the reader to look at genres differently. It is artificial and potentially damaging to classify literature and make those classifications so rigid as to have particular expectations and meanings solely constructed by the classification. It is as erroneous to do this to literature, as it would be to people. It does not allow for individual differences or for deeper meanings to emerge. To analyze the impact of genre on both the writer and the reader it is imperative to look at how each genre has been socially constructed and how these conventions shape what gets told and how.

We have selected a few genres to explore and deconstruct in order to apply our theoretical scaffolding. We begin with poetry because it seems the most unlikely of genres to make political statements to children. Rhyme, rhythm, and space constraints would appear, at first glance, to be insurmountable obstacles. We end with traditional literature (folk and fairy tales) because, by definition, especially when it comes from the oral tradition, it is inherently socially shaped, but its translation sometimes works to the detriment of authenticity and respectful portrayal of its culture of origin.

Poetry

Poetry and picture books are the least restrictive genres in terms of content, and the most structured in terms of format. Poetry is usually the medium of emotion rather than fact. It may be light or heavy, but the language must be condensed and distilled to its barest possible essence. One of the attractive features of poetry is that even though there are many prescribed forms and formats, very often poets break the rules and strike out for themselves in new directions.

Poetry runs the gamut from songs and rhyming verse to narrative, and even epic formats. The definition of poetry is elusive and there is as much argument about the topic as there is over "What is art?" Some poetry is lighthearted and nonsensical, or it may convey the deepest emotions. It has frequently been relegated to the status of the elite and obscure. Some teachers and librarians have withheld it from children whose skills are deemed to be "inadequate" because of its sometimes-abstract symbolism, and ostensibly limited range of interest.

That situation has changed radically in the past ten to fifteen years. Many teachers now read aloud a wide range of poetry to their students and encourage them to savor the poetry with all of their senses. Poetry, more than any other genre, requires young readers to pay attention to language. It invites thought as well as emotion, and analysis as well as synthesis (Hunt 1992: 131). Because today's authors are increasingly pushing against boundaries of audience and form we are seeing poetry that expresses deep and complex emotions and takes into consideration such issues as class, gender, ethnicity, and culture. Poetry invites the reader to become a poet and to create many questions about the meaning and intent of the work. Contemporary poets tend to propel readers beyond their own situations and cultures so that their worlds are expanded and made fluid.

Naomi Shihab Nye, reflecting on the mystery of the disappearing honeybee and lightening bug in her book of poems titled *Honeybee*, comments on the importance of making contact with people across our nation as well as across the world, especially through the medium of blogs and the internet. ". . . nothing is random. No one alone" (Nye, 2008: 11). Nye is interested in everything about all people, and her poetry and anthologies reflect that interest. She has spoken out on the importance of addressing political issues as well as other social concerns in poetry as well as in life.

She treasures and reflects her Palestinian heritage (her father is Palestinian; her mother is German American) and she continuously explores other heritages and points of view.

The late June Jordan tackled politics head-on in the workshops she led for young aspiring poets and activists. Her work is described in a manual, entitled, *June Jordan's Poetry for the People: A Revolutionary Blueprint*, edited by Lauren Muller and the Poetry for the People Collective. The project ". . . rests upon a belief that the art of telling the truth is a necessary and healthy way to create powerful, and positive connections among people who, otherwise, remain (unknown and unaware) strangers" (Muller, 1995: 16).

A number of authors such as Sharon Creech, Karen Hesse, Juan Felipe Herrera, Pamela Porter, Cynthia Rylant, Mel Glenn, Virginia Euwer Wolff, and Jacqueline Woodson have pushed the boundaries of the genre of poetry to tell stories in the format of a hybrid novel.

The genre of the novel implies more explicit detail about plot, character development and interaction, description of the setting, and literary elements such as foreshadowing and rise and fall of the action. It usually requires a climax. Poetry demands a filling in of detail and mood on the part of the reader plus an understanding of the characters' feelings and thoughts as well as interpretations of symbolic language and its implications.

The elements in a novel are usually linear. In a poem there is no requirement for chronological or sequential reporting. Some critics complain that the quality of the poetry is not as exacting as it should be in these hybrid poetic novels, while others extol the imagery and emotion of the poetic impact. Joy Alexander (2005) proposes that the verse novel is typically constructed from a first person perspective and possesses cinematic qualities, with a succession of scenes presented to the reader, constructing reading as an "intimate conversation or even as eavesdropping" (Alexander, 2005: 270).

In Herrera's young adult novel, *CrashBoomLove: A Novel in Verse* (as noted on page 72), is a series of poems that takes the reader into the life of sixteen-year-old César García. César's father has deserted him and his mother, his "friends" too often lead him into trouble, and school is a mixed bag. Herrera, a noted poet, demonstrates here that poetry is not necessarily lyrical or disconnected from reality. The poetic genre heightens the impact of César's struggles as a Mexican American teenager in a hostile school situation, a context that is new for him. The free verse amplifies his peripheral status within this school community.

In an interview for the teacher's edition of *Out of the Dust*, Karen Hesse reveals that she selected free verse as her medium "because of the spare understatement needed to tell the story." She comments that she had written in the genre of poetry before she wrote historical fiction. But she found poetry such an all-consuming genre that she only felt able to tackle it when her growing daughters were no longer in constant need of her attention. She notes that "Billie Jo tells her story from a heart that doesn't waste a single beat, from a mouth that doesn't waste a single word." The story grows as the main character does. In journal format, each entry is dated; each stands on its own as a poem. The tension and emotions build, and even through the tragedy that occurs (Both Billie Jo and her father feel responsible for the mother's death.) and the hard, hard life she and her dad endure in the dustbowl, Billie Jo forgives, is forgiven, and survives.

The expectation of the genre of poetry is that symbols are used to take the place of phrases and sentences, language is allusive, and emotions appear to reign over logic. To go beyond the conventional there must be room for experimentation and deviation from the expected. Because of the sparseness of the language, there will be many things left unsaid, inviting the audience to fill in the gaps. Karen Hesse posits:

> If a writer included everything, the reader would be excluded from the creative process. The books most beloved by readers, I think, are ones that provide enough detail to anchor the story in the reader's mind and heart, but leave room enough for the reader to bring his or her self into the created reality. If the author gets the balance just right, readers are not shut out of the story by too much detail, nor are they left dangling because there is too little to bind them to the fiction. How is it that literature from other cultures, other historical periods, other worlds even, can be universal enough to resonate with the contemporary reader? The answer grows organically out of what the author omitted and what the author included.
>
> (Personal correspondence, July 17, 2001)

In response to the question, "What makes you decide to put what you're writing into the genre of poetry?" Jane Yolen says, "I don't. What I want to say chooses its form. But the condensed lyrical line has great power for me and so much of what I do comes out a poem." Her *Owl Moon* is an excellent example of the aptness of the combined poetic and picture book genres. The book provides a picture of the idyllic outing that a young girl and her father share while they are hoping to see and hear owls as they walk through the woods. A sense of respect pervades the entire piece: respect for nature, and for the opportunity for the father and his daughter to be together, sharing this very special experience. Without belaboring the issue, some young readers may acknowledge surprise that it is a father and daughter going on this outing, rather than a father and son. Gender roles are certainly not the focal point of the book, but provide another element of respect to consider.

Lee Bennett Hopkins is very careful to be inclusive in the content, potential audiences, and creators of the poetry in his numerous anthologies. Lee stays in touch with poets around the country who write for his compilations, sometimes on a given theme. They write about contemporary pleasures and problems, dysfunctional families, social mores, death, divorce, lifestyles, and whatever else children need help with.

Hopkins points out that poetry reflects society through the ages. Master poets like Walt Whitman and Carl Sandburg have written on these topics that remain as fresh today as when they were written. He includes these and other well established as well as new poets in his collection, *Hand in Hand: An American History Through Poetry*, published by Simon and Schuster. The book presents different points of view on U.S. history, and includes perspectives not always found in history books. For example, Sandburg's poem from "The People, Yes," ends with a child asking, "Suppose they'll give a war and nobody will come?" (Hopkins, 1994: 96). The poet invites children to question the decisions adults have made about waging war.

Another of the poems in this consistently provocative collection is by Myra Cohn Livingston, entitled "Paul Revere Speaks." In it, Revere acknowledges his many accomplishments that contributed to the war effort, but in the end, he proudly recounts his prowess as a silversmith, and concludes: "There are some things a man needs to be remembered by that only his hands can make" (Hopkins, 1994: 30).

Sometimes a nation's political climate is so pro-war that it takes courage to make a statement indicating that there are some contributions more glorious than adding to the war effort. Sometimes it is the poet whose lone voice helps to change attitudes in times of war. Hopkins believes that the genre of poetry lends itself to this kind of influence. It is his hope that teachers and librarians will integrate poetry into every area of the curriculum.

On the other hand, this collection of poetry also supports some of the established ideologies about the sanctity of history even when it was neither noble nor democratic. Felicia Dorothea Hemans' poem, "The Landing of the Pilgrim Fathers," not only omits the role of women in this enterprise, but also neglects any mention of the Indigenous population that already inhabited the land. And of course there is no mention of the prejudice the Pilgrims held against people who did not practice their religion in the same way the Pilgrims did.

One of the attractive elements of this book is the inclusion of so many points of view. Although some of the poems omit any mention of the effect of colonization on the Native Americans, Hopkins points out in his preface to the third section of the book, "Midst the need to grow there was bloodshed between frontiersmen [sic] and the Native Americans who rightfully fought for their land—a land they possessed long before 'white men' decided it was theirs" (Hopkins, 1994: 38).

Arnold Adoff has, for years, produced books of poetry that include African American and biracial children's experiences and feelings. His *Black is Brown is Tan*, first published in 1973, and reprinted in 2002, mirrors his (and his wife, the late Virginia Hamilton's) own children's lives with their combined maternal African American and Native American and their paternal Jewish American heritages. Adoff has collected anthologies of poetry written by people of color since the late 1960s. In his preface to the first edition of *The Poetry of Black America: Anthology of the 20th Century* (1973), he explains that one of the reasons he decided to compile this anthology was "To go beyond the racist textbooks and anthologies that were on the shelves and in the bookstores" (Adoff, 1973: xvi). This groundbreaking anthology, with an introduction by Gwendolyn Brooks, contains the works of Black poets from the nineteenth century to the present time. It remains an important comprehensive collection and model for anthologists seeking to provide an in-depth view of the history and development of Black poetry.

In the opinion of Peter Hunt (1992), poetry, out of all the genres, is the one that challenges our notion of comprehension. No single meaning is intended in a poem. Words, phrases, images, ideas, all convey different shades of meaning and a range of feelings. Poetry requires a careful consideration of each word, syllable, line break, and image. It makes us confront our notions of language and meaning. A well-crafted poem helps readers to examine and value the construction as well as the language of written literature.

Critical multicultural analysis requires that readers come to a genre informed about its conventions and ready to see how the form shapes the message, how the content fits the form, and how the individual author uses form and content to communicate his or her ideological position. The relationship of reader to author becomes more intimate because the thinking and feeling of the poet are conveyed directly, not implied as in some of the other genres. David Swanger (1999), in looking at a poem for its subversion of dominant paradigms, persuades us that it provides "a broadening of vision, a reinvention of the world, an invitation to the imagination" (Swanger, 1999: 16).

The Picture Book

One book that reflects Swanger's conviction is *Drummer Hoff*, adapted from a folk tale by Barbara Emberley, illustrated by her husband, Ed Emberley, who won the 1968 Caldecott Medal for the book's woodcut-illustrations. This hybrid, an excellent example of the blending of genres, can be classified as picture book, poetry, and allegory. It can be read as rhythmic verse, like a Mother Goose rhyme, with no obvious moral message. But if one looks closely and listens carefully, the picture of war emerges as a bloody, mutilating, and futile experience.

It is the story of a drummer in a nameless war. (The book was first published during the time of the Vietnam War.) Simple rhyming rhythmic text takes the reader through the measures necessary for firing a cannon. Various members of the military from General Border down to Private Parriage perform these preparations. It is explicit in the illustrations, though never mentioned in the text, that each one of them is maimed in some way, clearly as a result of injuries sustained in battle.

In the grand climax, Drummer Hoff, who still has all of his limbs intact and appears to be the youngest and the healthiest of the group, fires off the cannon. Leaving the actual firing in the hands of the lowliest member of the troop signifies the opposite of what one might expect in the order of rank. The resultant massive explosion of sound and color then leads to a last page showing the rusted and disabled cannon overgrown with flowers, leaves, and grasses, without even one person in sight.

These illustrations, following one upon the other, may evoke conflicting responses. On the one hand, the explosion of sound and color is exhilarating, and might indicate a triumphant, and even positive, feeling about the effects of the explosion. On the other hand, the cannon eventually rusts away and is buried by flowers in a field empty of people or the instruments of war. Although the ending is ambiguous for some people, a good argument can be made for the conclusion that war is futile.

This is a book that invites discussion with its many details that can be interpreted in several ways. The assumptions that picture books are exclusively for the very young, that bright primary colors signal light-hearted action, and that simple repetitive language cannot convey deep messages are certainly laid to rest here.

John Stephens (1992) helps us to see that intertextuality figures strongly in the reading of picture books. As readers, we come to a text with different social backgrounds, experiences, and abilities. We are familiar, in varying degrees, depending on our heritage, class, religion, and education, with different biblical and mythological stories, genre conventions, images, and historical and cultural information. We connect our understanding to what we read, and are able, in varying degrees, to draw inferences, clarify, and make sense not only of the texts, but also, the world.

While it is vital that this intertextuality takes place in any reading in order for the reader to exercise critical analysis, it is imperative in picture books. Picture books, by their very nature, provide dual sources of information and emotional response, so that the visual image is as important as (and sometimes more important than) the text.

Several scholars (Bader, 1976; Nikolajeva & Scott, 2001; Nodelman, 1988) have written guides to picture books, but William Moebius (1986) has provided us with a particularly provocative guide to picture codes. He comments on the frequency of the "phenomenon of intertextuality in picture books" (Moebius, 1986: 147) and helps us as readers to see how important it is to view the position, size, appearance, and location, among others, as traits of pictures that convey information, provide context, and shape our responses. It is also important to acknowledge that the relationship between the pictures and the text can make a difference on the impact of the book.

In his introduction to *Reading Contemporary Picturebooks: Picturing Text*, David Lewis (2001) raises the question of what constitutes text: ". . . if we speak of 'the text' of a picturebook, do we mean the words or words-and-pictures together?" For example, as we mentioned before, in *The Christmas Gift*, by Francisco Jiménez, the words describe the Mexican American migrant mother and child "looking for food in the trash behind grocery stores."

The illustration depicts the mother and son behind a grocery store collecting bruised and discarded produce, while in front of the market a White woman selects choice fruit for purchase. The text lets the reader into the lives of the main characters, while the illustrations, although they are somewhat sanitized and pretty, show the socioeconomic divide for this family. A fence, starkly in the center of the page, heightens this divide.

Pictures and words may complement each other, add different features, supplement information, or, on some occasions provide surprises that amount to contradictions. These conditions shape the relationship between the reader and the text as well. The more visually literate the reader becomes, the greater will be the amount of understanding and appreciation of the text as a whole.

In general, picture books contain a minimum amount of text and are designed for the youngest readers, sometimes for the child who has not yet begun to read independently. As John Stephens (1992) maintains, "Picture books can. . . never be said to exist without either a socializing or educational intention, or else without a specific orientation towards the reality constructed by the society that produces them" (Stephens, 1992: 158).

Children are never too young to be influenced by ideology. Too often it is implied, and conveys the existing norms with such subtlety that it becomes internalized without question. Stephens reminds us "In order to make sense to its viewers, a picture book will be grounded in some version of consensus reality and use conventional codes of representation" (Stephens, 1992: 158). We advocate that children become visually as well as textually literate as early in their lives as possible, aware of the conventions and of how those conventions are attached to ideologies.

Sometimes the story is not as important as the elements of the presentation forming the substance of the book. That is the case in the Caldecott Award winning *Joseph Had a Little Overcoat*, by Simms Taback. Taken from an old Yiddish folksong, it details the sequential progression of how Joseph, a farmer who is handy with a sewing machine, recycles an old overcoat. People, especially those who have grown up in poverty or in working class families, resonate to the moral that one of the greatest sins is wastefulness and that it takes stamina and ingenuity to "make do" in this world. The illustrations demonstrate the richness of Joseph's background alongside the real poverty in this small village in Poland. What Joseph wears and eats, as well as his community gatherings and celebrations portray his everyday existence.

He is also connected to the Yiddish cultural scene in the diaspora, examples of which appear in his home in numerous detail: clippings are displayed from two actual Yiddish newspapers of the era, as well as books, posters, and other artifacts that contain strands of cultural information. Allusions to authors Sholem Aleichem and I.L. Peretz, Sigmund Freud, and the philosopher Mendele Mocher S'forim, catch the readers' attention, as do a fiddler on the roof, snatches of the Yiddish alphabet, and occasional Yiddish words. Wise sayings are posted on the walls and photos of famous Yiddish performers are evident. Each page yields a cornucopia of references to rural community life, the influence of the U.S. Yiddish diaspora, and the intellectual, social, political, economic, and emotional content of Joseph's life.

This is a book aimed at an audience of more than young children. For readers to reap the benefits of all that is included here a knowledgeable cultural and historical guide would be needed in order to understand the settings and details of this complex textual weave. Someone who grew up in a family of Jews, imbued with Yiddish theater and music, and passionate about improving the plight of the working class would probably identify with and resonate to the many artifacts depicted on every page. The myriad photos of unnamed people include, for those in the know, Jewish entertainers, writers, leaders, and, one suspects, family members.

Two newspapers, The *Jewish Daily Forward* and The *Morning Freiheit*, appear several times. How many people know that these two newspapers were political rivals, with both of them espousing decidedly left-of-center political perspectives? Mendele Mocher S'forim, the philosopher whose book is pictured here, is one who deplored superstitious naive beliefs and practices. The song, "Tumbalalaika," takes up a double page spread and is clearly an important part of a joyful celebration: it is a Yiddish song combining the mundane with the metaphysical. (Some of the riddles in the song are: "What is higher than a house? What is faster than a mouse? What is deeper than a well? What is more bitter than gall?" And the answers are, "A roof is higher than a house; a cat is faster than a mouse; love is deeper than a well; death is more bitter than gall.")

What is not obviously here is the threat of pogroms (the organized murderous raids that decimated Jewish villages); the wrenching oppression and grinding poverty of the Jews and other peasants; the separation of families due to forced conscription into the Russian and Polish armies, and also as a result of emigration; and the political challenges to the dominance of the religion that were important factors in Russia and Poland at that time.

While these historical conflicts may not be deemed developmentally appropriate for young children, they do form an important rounding out of an accurate picture of Jewish life in the early 20th century. They figure largely in the stories of Tevye Milchiker by Sholem Aleichem which were later adapted into the play *Fiddler on the Roof.* These stories are alluded to several times in the illustrations for *Joseph Had a Little Overcoat.*

The same tale is told in *Something from Nothing*, written and illustrated by Phoebe Gilman. The story is identical to *Joseph Had a Little Overcoat*, except for a few minor elements: the setting is a small town, or shtetl, not a rural community, and much more information is provided about Joseph's family. In this book, Joseph is a little boy, and it is his grandfather, a tailor, who keeps recycling what was initially a baby blanket. The details of daily living, including practicing the religion, are depicted in the illustrations. There is no mention of the diaspora here, nor is there a hint of external oppression. The illustrations do provide subtle evidence, however, of the difficulties of daily life.

What can readers do if there is no informed guide to go beyond the words and pictures of the book? How can adults and children explore further what the cultural artifacts convey that are depicted in the text? How can adults help children to organize the information into a meaningful order? (Stephens, 1992: 85). How can they do this, especially when their prior knowledge does not possess what the text requires?

In *Joseph Had a Little Overcoat*, if the readers' experience does not include knowledge of Yiddish culture of the early twentieth century, where do they go to draw on intertextual knowledge? If their communities provide materials for cultural research, then they may be able to access information via established routes that are readily available. Interviewing people who have expertise, conducting library research, and exploring electronic search engines provide texts that interested readers may consult, especially if they have had the experience upon which they can build of organizing quests for information. Care must be taken to avoid the pitfalls that Stephens points out, of accepting, without critical analysis, the information acquired (Stephens, 1992: 85–86).

Currently, there are many picture books in circulation that an older audience would appreciate, and, indeed, which might be too sophisticated or challenging for younger children. *Terrible Things*, by Eve Bunting, is one such book. It is subtitled *An Allegory of the Holocaust* and it calls to mind the comments by Martin Neimöller, a Lutheran minister in the time of the Nazi domination, who regretted deeply not intervening earlier in the Hitler reign. Harry W. Mazal is the creator of the Mazal Library, one of the largest private collections in the world of Holocaust related materials including books, ephemera, microfilms, video-films, photographs, and the like with over 20,000 catalogued items. According to Mazal, Martin Niemöller said:

> When Hitler attacked the Jews I was not a Jew, therefore I was not concerned. And when Hitler attacked the Catholics, I was not a Catholic, and therefore, I was not concerned. And when Hitler attacked the unions and the industrialists, I was not a member of the unions and I was not concerned. Then Hitler attacked me and the Protestant church—and there was nobody left to be concerned.
>
> (*Congressional Record*, 14, October 1968: 31636)

Mazal states, "Although there are some variations that have been published on that famous quotation, the words shown above are the exact ones that Niemöller spoke in Congress."

The pictures in *Terrible Things* are black, white, and shades of gray pencil drawings of dark clouds and furry woodland animals. The Terrible Things (we never see what they really are) carry off each of the animal groups, for example, things with feathers, things with bushy tails, things with quills. We feel, along with little rabbit, a mounting sense of confusion and dread. Little Rabbit is enjoined from asking questions; his family just wants to stay out of any conflict with the Terrible Things. Of course, in the end, the Terrible Things capture the only remaining creatures, the White Rabbits, and there is no one to protect them. Only Little Rabbit remains, and he vows that he will warn the rest of the world that they must stand up to the Terrible Things and protect each other.

Allegory is a difficult genre to master. Too often it is cloyingly cute or simplistic, trivializing the large theme it is trying to present. That is not the case here. *Terrible Things* works very well to stimulate readers' questions and comparisons with real-world events.

For some young readers (and, indeed, for some older ones) there may not be the necessary information in their background to support a truly intertextual reading. Some knowledge of the Holocaust, and perhaps an acquaintance with Niemöller's message, would help make the text more broadly understandable. On the other hand, perhaps simply having had experience with bullying, harassment, bigoted language, or behavior might be sufficient to make the text meaningful. It could be accessible to young readers if an adult were there to guide the reading and support the reader. But it is certainly not too "easy" a book, even for adults.

The Summer My Father Was Ten, by Pat Brisson, a hybrid of memoir, realistic fiction, and picture book, is another book whose message about the exercise of power is so integrated into the plot that it never descends into tract, but always retains the quality of story. Here, a background containing an understanding of working class conditions and values, for example, work ethic, appreciating the fruits of one's labor, taking responsibility for one's actions, respect for elders, and immigrants' experience would help provide a context for the reader.

The young narrator brings to life the story that her father has told her year after year about the terrible mistake he made the summer when he was ten years old. Her dad and his friends were playing with a softball that landed in a garden that his elderly neighbor had lovingly and painstakingly grown and nurtured. In the process of retrieving the softball, without taking time to think about what they were doing, impulsively, the boys began throwing ripe tomatoes and anything else they could snatch from the earth, and eventually destroyed the garden. Too late, when the elderly man appeared and accosted them, her father came to his senses, and was horrified and ashamed. The next summer, and subsequently every summer of his life, he atoned for his behavior by creating a garden, first in partnership with his elderly neighbor, then on his own, and eventually with his daughter.

Subtly woven into this well-told story is a sense of the elderly man's isolation in a community where his language and origin are foreign, plus a view of a working class neighborhood in which few people have the time or impetus to care about a vacant lot. Although there seem to be no people of color in the neighborhood, cultural differences are implied and could provide discussion points for students.

The Other Side, by Jacqueline Woodson, is a picture book combined with enough text to also label it realistic or social justice fiction. Clover lives in a house on one side of a fence that divides the entire town. White people live on the other side, and both mothers warn their daughters not to climb over the fence because "It's not safe."

Eventually, the White girl who lives in the house on the other side of the fence moves from being called "that girl" to being acknowledged by her name, "Annie." Clover and Annie progress from behaving as wary strangers to becoming friends. Both girls are courageous. They are growing beyond their experience, and perhaps, beyond their fears. Both take risks; Clover is comfortably situated with her Black friends but there is the implied possibility of their rejecting her because of her friendship with the White girl. Annie is vested in her White privilege, but takes risks because of her wish to have a friend.

Through what the characters say and do not say, and what they do and do not do, the author and illustrator invite us to unpack the course of events and ask some questions about the implications of the situation. The title itself bears examination. Who is "the other?" "The other side" implies more than one opinion/view/judgment/attitude/truth. What are the "sides" here? What other metaphorical fences or walls exist today?

In looking more closely at the story, if Annie were not such a loner, would she and Clover have become friends? What would have happened if the author had placed Clover in the position of having to choose between her long-time Black friends and her new White friend? What if the author and illustrator had depicted Annie as also having some White friends? Would she have invited Clover to play? If Clover were alone would she have been the one who initiated the friendship?

Why is it that only Clover's mom sees and condones the friendship? Where is Annie's mom, and what is she thinking? Why is it that Annie crosses the fence, but the Black children never do? When does the story take place? According to the illustrations, the story is set in the 1950s. This was entirely the choice of the artist. The author has stated that she imagined it as a contemporary story. How far have we come as a society since the pictured setting of the book? What difference would it have made on the impact of the book if the illustrations depicted a contemporary twenty-first century setting?

The fence itself is an indicator of social division and domination. The acceptance of the fence and its implications of "never the twain shall meet" signals collusion on the parts of the families living on either side of the fence. The girls' resistance (albeit tentative) provides hope for eventual agency, not only for the children, but also even perhaps for their families.

How far the resistance and agency can extend is up to the reader and society.

These musings are meant to interrogate the possibilities beyond those already presented in Woodson's constructive and hopeful book. We recommend that readers acknowledge the author's stance and go on to form their own opinion. We suggest, as part of a critical multicultural analysis, that questions may be raised apart from, as well as stemming from what the author and illustrator have indicated in their text and pictures. This approach requires an informed social imagination on the part of readers and a willingness to inquire further into culture and history on their own. In this deceptively simple book it may be that different perspectives can be confronted as part of an understanding of the dynamics of interracial relationships and progress.

No Bad News by the African-American psychologist, Kenneth Cole, traces the development of Marcus, a young boy whose mother has determined that it is time that he walk by himself through his urban neighborhood to the barbershop to receive his usual haircut. The photography of John Ruebartsch illustrates this book. They are in black and white when they depict the boy's journey to the barbershop, and they are negative and frightening, even including an encounter with an angry teenager who knocks Marcus to the ground.

The community of people at the barbershop reassures Marcus about the good things going on in his neighborhood, and sure enough, on his way home, Marcus sees good things happening. He observes a loving family walking down the street, a gardener, music being played, all portrayed in color. And he is an active part of the good things.

Rather than assuming that "photos never lie" the author and illustrator demonstrate that the process of writing and illustrating is one of selection and decision making, analogous to the power of action and creation in everyday life. The subject matter and how to represent and interpret it are in the hands and minds of the author, illustrator, and reader.

Postmodern Picturebook

Bette P. Goldstone (2004) makes an excellent case for identifying the postmodern picture book as a new subgenre. She outlines and comments on a set of specific features that are calculated to surprise the reader, as well as to empower the reader to make new connections among the real world, the text, and the image. Goldstone summarizes the essential components of postmodern thought including nonlinearity where the reader cannot expect all of the components to be included or to be presented in logical order. Most postmodern picture books scoff at reality and tease both the reader and the subject matter. In fact, postmodern picture books most often contradict themselves on purpose. There is rarely a hierarchy of power or structure. Very often the attitude of the author and the invitation to the reader mock what has up to now been considered sacrosanct.

David Wiesner's retelling of the classic folktale, *The Three Pigs*, demonstrates the quintessential postmodern picture book. It begins in a conventional manner for two pages. Then instead of the wolf eating the little pig that had built his house of straw, the wolf's huffing and puffing blows the little pig off the page and out of the story. The text reads ". . . and ate the pig up" but the picture shows an empty handed and confused wolf. The same pattern is repeated with the second little pig and again there is a decided contradiction between the words and the images.

During the course of the story, the pigs naughtily disassemble the book, folding some of the pages into a paper airplane which they gleefully ride through the air into total white space after which they enter a different nursery rhyme, "Hey Diddle Diddle." They take a little side trip into a fairy tale replete with a dragon and a would-be dragon slayer. From the pigs' perspective, it is the dragon who needs rescuing, and again text and image contradict each other. With the help of the fiddler cat, the pigs and the dragon join blissfully and live in the now reconstituted house made of bricks.

Much that is unconventional and surprising about this book has to do with the blasting of expectations and overturning of conventional reading patterns. Almost every page invites readers to question and to join in the sometimes subversive fun. The absurd wins out over the commonplace.

Realistic Fiction

Fiction that reflects the feelings and concerns of contemporary young readers has gained popularity in the past 40 years. The burgeoning of realistic fiction can also be connected to developments in multicultural education because of its goal to acknowledge and affirm all children within the domain of the school and society. It is particularly in this genre that the metaphors of mirrors, windows, and doors have been applied. Children as individual readers need to see themselves and their issues and problems represented in books in order to feel validated. They also need to be introduced to the feelings and experiences of others in order to react empathically and humanely. They require models of behavior and response in order to function as productive citizens of a global society.

Fiction can run the gamut from the realistic or problem novel, through the historical, to the comic. For younger readers fiction is often in the form of chapter books, which tend to recount stories with a child as the main character, going through the ordinary episodes of typical childhood. For the older reader the situations become more problematic and even traumatic. There is no topic that is currently off limits, especially in young adult fiction. Authors often conduct a considerable amount of research in order to present an issue such as illness, abuse, or death in a way that satisfies psychological as well as societal criteria. Although by definition fiction is created rather than reported, it must always have the ring of truth and, when dealing with history, should not violate readers' knowledge of the past.

It was not until 1967, with the publication of the then seventeen-year-old S.E. Hinton's *The Outsiders* that the genre of the realistic young adult novel became established. Alleen Pace Nilson and Kenneth L. Donelson (2001) call this book, along with several others, "ground-breaking, preparing readers for the iconoclastic, taboo-breaking novels of today" (Nilson & Donelson, 2001: 74). *The Outsiders* deals with class warfare, gangs, and poverty, and does not end happily, although there is some hope that one of the protagonists, Pony Boy, will survive and overcome the tragedies, mostly because he will write about his experiences. Sociopolitical constraints figure strongly in the novel.

Current young adult novels carry on the tradition set by S.E. Hinton. In *The Absolutely True Diary of a Part-Time Indian* Sherman Alexie offers readers a wide range of emotions and a tragic/comic perspective not only of the fourteen-year-old protagonist, but also of life on the Spokane Native American reservation. Junior is the unlikely hero. He understands all too well the implications of issues such as alcoholism and racism coupled with poverty and death as they affect his people and himself. He manages to overcome significant physical disability as well as ostracism both from his friends and enemies.

The humor is often raunchy but never out of place. Even the most flawed characters are portrayed with some redeeming understanding. Forney's comic art enhances the reading experience. Junior's survival is truly heroic, but not unrealistic. The story follows Junior (aka, Arnold Spirit) in his struggles to secure a good education for himself. He and his family live on the Spokane reservation. He knows that in order to have a life for himself, away from alcohol and violence, he must leave the reservation. He does this reluctantly and only partially: daily he commutes the long distance (22 miles) from the reservation to Reardon, the all White neighboring community, and comes home at the end of the school day. Sometimes he has to walk, sometimes his father manages, despite being drunk, to drive him, and sometimes he catches rides with various drivers.

Despite his disabilities, Junior is a talented cartoonist and more intelligent than most of his peers. He is also exceptional at selectively making friends. Alexie tells the story of the reservation community, as well as Junior and his family, lovingly and respectfully.

John Stephens (1999) argues that one way to challenge the social authority of realistic narrative is by locating how the narrative form summons the reader to consider the text in close relationship with the real world. In many ways, realistic fiction persuades the reader to ignore the workings of language, blurring the line between reality and fiction. Stephens further states that "debates about realism are always actually debates about how we understand language to operate, and how the world is" (Stephens, 1992: 193).

Historical Fiction

Sometimes historical fiction provides more truth (as opposed to a collection of facts) than a work of nonfiction about the same era. In historical fiction history serves to authenticate the fictional past that the book is trying to create. A critical multicultural analysis of this genre opens up a space for the reader to have a dialogue with the past. Readers may look at how history is portrayed and may use the events depicted to excuse discriminatory behavior. (A person might justify this attitude by saying, "We can't criticize the behavior because that's the way it really was then.")

Mildred Taylor's *Roll of Thunder, Hear My Cry* and the other books in the series depicting the Logan family convey the strength of this African American family in the midst of bigotry and their struggle for survival in Mississippi in the mid-1930s. Cassie, age 9, is the narrator, and we get to know her well. We also gather insight into the rest of the family as well as members of the community, White and Black. The problems of a widespread racist society are addressed within the context of the plot. Every episode is believable. Although it is clear that the White people are the oppressors, the Black families are not unrealistically saintly, nor are any of the characters two dimensional.

Fact cloaked in fiction, when it is well done, leaves more of a lasting understanding than raw information, and promotes an internalizing of the situation. Any history, even when it is in the format of historical text, takes a stand, offers a perspective and particular decisions were made in its construction of the past.

Although racism or other oppression might have been endemic, and even tolerable to some members of a society, it is the responsibility of the author to communicate that evil never was and never will be right. Just because something happened does not mean it is acceptable. It is always possible for one or more of the characters, or for the author, to make a comment, react appropriately, or raise a question, so that contemporary readers are informed about the moral dilemma or the social injustice.

In *Walking to the Bus-Rider Blues*, by Harriette Gillem Robinet, the author draws upon her own lived experience, as well as the experience and history of her community. In her books, history is not simply a backdrop, but there is engagement with the historical moment. She personalizes the history, while at the same time, going beyond just the personal. The main characters are full-bodied and complex. We meet Alfa (the young narrator), Zinnia, Big Mama, the storekeeper, and the White police officer. Robinet provides a historical context for the resistance activities of this African-American community in Montgomery, Alabama. Towards the end of the book, the plot gets cluttered, but does not get in the way of the reader getting to know the community and its circumstances, and the interesting ramifications of the bus boycott for the Black community.

It was dangerous for Alfa to navigate the streets: bullies beat and rob him. It took longer on foot to get from one place to another. The author certainly intends to show the class stratification of the community: one of the thieves fits all the stereotypes, but comes from the middle class. It is an interesting comment on class, because the thieves, in both of the cases where the working class could be implicated, turned out to be from the middle and upper classes. With this window into class relations, the author brings the reader up close to the complexity of race relations.

Nonfiction

Eagleton (1996) claims that the distinction between "fact and fiction" is futile (Eagleton, 1996: 1–2). In *The Ideology of Form: The Nonfiction Novel*, Phyllis Frus McCord (1986) maintains that the distinction between literary and nonliterary texts has great consequence:

> The works that are defined as nonliterary, nonfictional, or "other" narratives, then are regarded as "true," factual or objective, and we fail to consider their fictional, ideological nature–that is, the structures they too impose on their materials and the "reality" they create rather than merely reflect.
>
> (McCord, 1986: 60)

Implied in nonfiction is that there is a reality out there that can be captured in language and that language is stable. The authority of the nonfiction book is dependent on the agreement among the participants, the writer, and the reader. Along with the reading of these nonfiction texts it is important for readers to look at the context of the society in which the books are situated and to query what the prevailing power base is, as revealed in the texts.

Biography

Like poetry and picture books, nonfiction also has few limitations in terms of content. Ostensibly, the primary ingredient is fact. Of course the author's perception of what constitutes fact is critical here. Perhaps even more important is what the author excludes as well as what he or she includes. For example, in a biography of Rosa Parks, depending on the author's perspective, the reader may or may not learn that Ms. Parks was a political activist for much of her adult life. She was ideal for the NAACP to focus on in their massive movement of protest. Her characteristics and impeccable background served well to provide the ideal situation from which Dr. Martin Luther King Jr. and other leaders could rally people from many communities. Thus they were able to organize a bus boycott and to bring the issues of racism to the attention of the world.

Often photos, rather than drawings, are used to convey a sense of authenticity, enhance the written information, and add visual documentation. Sometimes illustrations and text combined are designed to prevent the reader from questioning the representation. The reader needs to be on guard, particularly when the material is presented as a matter of fact. In fact, the selection of photographs as well as angles, details, and poses, all contribute to constructing a perspective as forcefully as a sketch or a painting might. However, just like any other form of illustration, photography is socially constructed and subjective.

Sometimes, particularly in biographies, journals, and autobiographies, it is clear that the author's point of view is slanted because of the effusive language and decidedly admiring tone, as well as the omission of anything controversial. In addition, biographical writing tends to extract the famous people from their communities so that they become larger than life. Wherever possible several biographies may be used to compare and contrast the different perspectives on a historical figure.

Biographies, like other genres, may distort reality and require analysis. Oftentimes, the people and life work highlighted are rendered separate or isolated from the collective currents of participation that supported the people in their activism (Kozol, 1975; Kohl, 1995). How do these life stories contribute to our understanding of people, their communities, and society? What do different biographers foreground and background in their construction of the same life story? How does this affect the ideologies imbued in the biography?

Certainly, in children's literature, it is satisfying to the reader to have the young protagonist emerge triumphantly as a result of his or her own talents. How can the social order then be reconstructed so that this is possible in fact, and not only because of the remarkable talents and energy of the individual?

Biographies of famous people often extol their talents without revealing anything about their flaws or foibles. Sometimes a third-person account omits the entire context of the person's community or larger universe. Such is the case with Helen Keller. As James Loewen (1994) protests, in *Lies My Teacher Told Me*, "Keller, who struggled so valiantly to learn to speak, has been made mute by history. . . . The truth is that Helen Keller was a radical socialist . . . Keller learned how the social class system controls people's opportunities in life . . ." (Loewen, 1994: 10–12). Loewen is concerned that children do not learn about Keller beyond her disabilities. Fortunately, the biography, *Helen Keller: Rebellious Spirit*, by Laurie Lawlor, makes clear that Helen's adult life was spent in the pursuit of causes such as world peace, better conditions for poor people, access to treatment for blind and other disabled people, the rights of children, and suffrage for women.

The personal perspective of memoir, autobiography, and biography need not conflict with a historical perspective. Informational books can contribute vastly to the store of knowledge young people need to become informed citizens. Diaries, photobiographies (such as Russell Freedman's award-winning book, *Lincoln: A Photobiography*), and the best of the nonfiction books are based on rigorous research. This involves consulting multiple scholarly sources including personal contacts with knowledgeable people. It requires investigating many perspectives and an openness to conveying facts that do not mask serious problems or controversial stances.

Any biography that presents the noted subject as a saint, omniscient, or independent of his or her community or family is seriously compromising the effectiveness of the book. Any author who chooses to write about the people of another country without indicating the political, social, and economic conditions of that country is not doing justice to the person or to the context, and is presenting a misleading picture.

Personal stories told in an intimate and heartfelt manner make the truth of the situation all the more compelling. These stories may take the form of oral history, which can offer people a way to talk back at the historical record. Or they may take the form of narrative, of memoir, or of reconstructed personal memories.

Leon's Story, by Leon Walter Tillage, as we considered it in Chapter 1, is an oral history told to and set into print by a sympathetic member of the school community in which Tillage works. *Bowman's Store*, by Joseph Bruchac, is a personal autobiographical exploration, a retracing of his past. *The Circuit* and *Breaking Through*, by Francisco Jiménez, as we analyzed in

Chapter 6, are reconstructed memoirs. All of these stirring works provide us with stories of those who might otherwise have been left out of the official record. Leon, of African American heritage, was a sharecropper's son in the depths of the Great Depression, in the heart of a land menaced by the Ku Klux Klan.

Francisco is a child of Mexican migrant workers. Although his nemesis is the grinding poverty common to all who crossed the border to work the land, not the active life-threatening hatred of the nightriders, both he and Leon experience abuse and oppression, yet both emerge with feelings of self-pride and determination to overcome social oppression.

Joseph Bruchac's family who do not identify themselves as such, but who are, in part, of Abenacki heritage, are working class, but are not physically assaulted. Like the other two, his story conveys openness of narrative, and the same sort of personal triumph at having survived and surmounted the odds.

It is important for young readers to have access to these books. They are not only inspiring, they are also an invitation to think and talk about what is usually left out of history and children's literature in terms of underserved and under-recognized groups and individuals. In all three of these well crafted, stirring autobiographies the protagonists focus on their own struggles and individual actions coupled with the loving support of their families.

In none of these books is there a hint of bitterness or complaint about racism or the structure of a society that permits and even embraces racist behavior and attitude. It seems as if the assumptions underlying the books accept as a given that economic injustice and racism exist and must be overcome by dint of personal effort. But the books also contain unmistakable evidence of the invidious oppression of the racism and classism endemic to the country.

They invite the reader to question why there were not more allies to intervene when injustices were being perpetrated. They also make clear, if in indirect ways, that injustice was not fought vigorously by members of the middle class, or by representatives of the government. They subtly call attention to the perception of many middle class members of the privileged majority that people of color are "good" when they accept blame or responsibility for their condition, and when they pull themselves up by their bootstraps, and are grateful for the opportunity to do so.

Sometimes an autobiography can help young readers to understand world events by personalizing and epitomizing the global situation and presenting it in the context of one person's experience. Such is the impact of *Anne Frank: The Diary of a Young Girl.* The enormity of the Holocaust is difficult to grasp. The actuality of one young girl's ordeal is much more palpable. This book has done more to open a period of history to young readers than multiple textbooks could ever accomplish.

Fantasy

Historical fiction and nonfiction raise the expectation on the part of the reader that the text is based on fact. Fantasy often disguises itself as unrelated to fact, lowering the reader's guard and inserting "information and values" that the reader internalizes. This is especially true if the fantasy is packaged aesthetically, enticingly, and cleverly.

Fantasy, according to Ruth Nadelman Lynn (1983:1) is "a broad term used to describe books in which magic causes impossible, and often wondrous, events to occur." Fantasy can be set in the real world that we inhabit or it can occur in a place or time invented by the author and governed by its own rules and values. Stephens (1999: 288) explains that, "In so far as fantasy writing comments on contemporary social practice, it does so by indirections, parallels, figures, even allegory." The author's deft touch is crucial in making the audience suspend disbelief. It must be totally credible for the events to happen in the context of the imagined setting.

Hybrids of fairy tales (a ubiquitous cousin to fantasy) and picture books abound, with each genre retaining its own special characteristics. Picture books rarely stand alone as genres. They are connected to other genres, depending on the perspectives of the artist and writer, and are shaped by discourses imbedded within the storylines.

Fantasy is not lack of truth. In order for it to work, it has to have a connection for the reader to a deep reality. We also have to remember that fantasy is not context free and that class, gender, and race figure as largely in a work of fantasy as in any other genre.

Genres carry with them certain characteristics. For example, fantasy often includes the creation of a new world that goes beyond ordinary earthly bounds, introducing characters with greater than human abilities. Usually magic plays an important part in the accomplishment of the hero's quest. Perhaps in response to the restrictions and narrow impositions that require rigid adherence to the rules of any genre, authors choose to go beyond a prescribed template.

For example, the Harry Potter books contain fantasy, myth, adventure story, and social narratives. Issues of class and values (e.g., competition, tenderness, honor, and devotion to or flouting "the rules") are raised. Members of the faculty of the Hogwarts School represent different ways of looking at behavior, history, and social responsibility. The Harry Potter series is not unique in this. Other fantasies, such as Philip Pullman's

Golden Compass, Susan Cooper's *The Dark Is Rising*, Lloyd Alexander's *Chronicles of Prydain*, and other series do the same.

Time Travel

Time travel, a possible sub-genre of historical fiction because of content and format, is also a sub-genre of fantasy since it is generally agreed that people cannot as yet travel back or forward in time. Time travel stories are not bound to everyday behaviors that are taken for granted in historical novels. These texts encourage a dual perspective: the time traveler to the time past or future, and the contemporary reader. *The Devil's Arithmetic*, by Jane Yolen, weds historical fiction to time travel when Hannah is transported to Lublin, Poland in the year 1942. She then suffers, with her family, the horrors of the ensuing Holocaust. The combination of fantasy and reality makes this book a vivid portrait through the eyes of a young girl, a book that resists classification as a single genre.

Science Fiction

Science fiction is aligned with some time travel stories as well as with fantasy. In this genre, authors may exhibit their sometimes uncanny sense of scientific possibilities, while at the same time retaining their imaginative creations.

The category of dystopias falls under the genre of science fiction. It includes constructing a utopia, usually assumed to be far in the future, aimed at remedying the ills of our modern day world and relying heavily on scientific innovations to carry out the workings of the new world. *The Giver*, by Lois Lowry, winner of the 1994 Newbery Medal, describes a society carefully designed to eliminate gender role discrimination, racism, over population, war, pain, violence, competition, and excesses of strong emotion and bad individual decisions. This society is managed by a group of elders with the aid of scientifically designed medications, clear rules, constant vigilance, and frequent publicly broadcast communication. The community is insulated against such distractions as color (everything in this world looks gray). Readers are invited to determine for themselves how important individual decision making is in their lives and what the cost is of loss of freedom.

Jonas, the protagonist in the story, has been assigned the position of "receiver", which sets him apart from his peers and imposes upon him all of the community's history and memories and sets him in opposition to the careful workings of the society. The ambiguous ending provides more fodder for discussion. Does sameness of color eliminate racism? Can forced pre-selection of occupations in the community balance gender roles? Does sameness eliminate competition? Does lack of pain and strong emotion prevent violence? Young readers can benefit from conversations about this utopia turned into dystopia. Science fiction is frequently merged with other genres such as fantasy and horror. Increasingly, social and ethical issues are raised in works of science fiction.

Traditional Literature

Traditional literature, including fairy tales, nursery rhymes, ballads, fables, folktales, legends, and myths might fall into the realm of fantasy if they were not transmitted orally across generations. They originated with the folk of all continents and formed a communications system among and within peoples long before the advent of print. They reflected values, morés, acceptable behavior, the consequences of behavior, the battle between good and evil, and the assumptions of responsible citizenry. Depending on when the folkloric collectors captured them and set them down in print, the tales reflected ongoing evolution in the society. They were originally intended for all of the members of a community, no matter what the age of the inhabitant.

Here again is the question of the author and his or her importance. Who are the authors of these tales? Is it the collectors? What about the minstrels and bards who circulated them? Also consider the folk people who transmitted them from generation to generation. And don't neglect the contemporary retellers who set them down in print. How can the reader discern who the writer is? What responsibility does the reader have to interpret and reconstruct the tales according to social and ethical precepts? What values are being conveyed implicitly and explicitly?

The process of creating traditional literature is ongoing. While it is interesting to trace the history of different tales, it must be understood that there is little evidence of the very beginnings of most of the folk tales. Even literary tales, invented by a writer such as Hans Christian Andersen, probably came from other older folk tales. What matters is not so much the history, but the development of the tale as well as the contemporary retellings and reconstructions. As we will demonstrate in our analysis of Cinderella tales in the next chapter, even the narrowly defined discourse of Cinderella varies widely, according to the intentions of its retellers.

Traditional literature may be among the last of the literary types that retain some "purity" of genre. Although publishers have produced lavish picture books of the European fairy and folk tales, and although there are contemporary retellings, fractured versions, and restructurings of the "classic" tales, nevertheless, the structures of the tales largely prevail. There is the youngest brother, the kind and innocent simpleton, who wins the hand of the princess. There is the beautiful young woman who is rescued by and marries the prince, and there is the wicked stepmother/witch who symbolizes evil incarnate. These tales, even now, take the opportunity to reinforce the values of the society, which is providing the tale, not only to children, but to all of the members of the community.

In *Don't Bet on the Prince*, Jack Zipes (1986) urges us to design a socio-psychological theory that will help us grasp how fairy tales function within a socialization process. He says that to talk about fairy tales today is "to talk about power, violence, alienation, social conditions, child-rearing, and sex roles" (Zipes, 1986: 2). We would add sociopolitical understanding to that list.

The point here is that fantasy can convey and inculcate values and ideologies, very often in a more captivating way than stark reality. To prove that point, think about what springs to mind immediately when you are asked, "What does a princess look like? How about a prince? Tell us about stepmothers." In our many years' experience of working with teachers, young students, and librarians, we have had consistent responses to these questions: Princesses usually are described as blonde and blue-eyed; princes are tall, dark and handsome; and stepmothers are wicked and ugly. When we ask, "Do you really believe this?" some nod, some shake their heads "no", but they do not appear shocked when we say, "yes, you do."

This activity has particular personal application to Masha. She explains:

My mother died when I was 17. She was my best friend and I was heart broken. When my father remarried almost 2 years later, it was to a woman who was loving and funny and bright and competent. She was sensitive to my feelings and my needs, and she lovingly cared for my two sisters and me. When I talk about her I refer to her as my second mother. I cannot force myself to say she is my "stepmother." I'm an adult and I know the difference between fantasy and reality. And to this day I cannot call her my stepmother. What is the source of this resistance?

Tzvetan Todorov (2000) links genre to human discourse, and reveals that old genres are imbedded in new ones. He maintains that genres are the product of infinite transformations, that is, utterances that go through significant modifications over time, shaping readers' expectations and serving as models for writers to emulate. Genres are intertextual (drawn from literary and nonliterary sources), heteroglot (many languages, many voices), polygeneric (multiple genres, hybrids, amalgamations, layers), discursive (have sociopolitical, historical values and assumptions imbedded in them), ideological (imbued with particular worldviews or preconceptions), and dynamic (everchanging). Genres exist in relation to other genres, as Todorov (2000) and Bakhtin (1986) remind us. They are social constructs, historical evidence, and "cultural archives" (Leitch, 1991).

Each genre requires awareness on the part of the reader, a scaffold that critical multicultural analysis offers the reader to go beyond the form dedicated by tradition. It is this lens that we will use in our consideration of Cinderella in the next chapter.

Classroom Applications

- Genres shape reading expectations. In small groups, invite children to generate lists of the expectations they hold for the genres they are familiar with. Experiment with ways of challenging these expectations.
- Analyze the photographs and illustrations represented in books. How do the images, along with the text, offer positions of power to view the story from?

Recommendations for Classroom Research

- Which genres are present and absent from your curriculum and classroom library? Why?
- What factors contribute to the formation and longevity of a genre?

Suggestions for Further Reading

Bang, Molly. (2000). *Picture this: How pictures work.* New York: SeaStar Books.
Hunt, Peter. (Ed.). (1992). *Literature for children: Contemporary criticism.* New York: Routledge.
Nikolajeva, Maria & Scott, Carole. (2001). *How picture books work.* New York: Garland Publishing.
Nodelman, Perry & Reimer, Mavis. (2003). *The pleasures of children's literature* (3rd ed.). Boston: Allyn and Bacon.
Stephens, John. (1992). *Language and ideology in children's fiction.* New York: Longman.
Zipes, Jack. (2006). *Why fairy tales stick: The evolution and relevance of a genre.* New York: Routledge.

References

Children's Literature

Adoff, Arnold. (1973/2002). *Black is brown is tan.* Illustrated by Emily Arnold McCully. New York: HarperCollins Publishers.
Adoff, Arnold. (Ed.). (1973). *The poetry of Black America: Anthology of the 20th century.* New York: Harper & Row.

Alexander, Lloyd. (1999). *The book of three.* New York: Holt.

Alexie, Sherman. (2007) *The absolutely true diary of a part-time Indian.* Illustrated by Ellen Forney. New York: Little, Brown and Company.

Brisson, Pat. (1998). *The summer my father was ten.* Illustrated by Andrea Shine. Honesdale, PA: Boyds Mills Press.

Bruchac, Joseph. (2001) *Bowman's Store.* New York: Lee and Low Books

Bunting, Eve. (1989). *Terrible things: An allegory of the Holocaust.* Illustrated Stephen Gammell. Philadelphia: Jewish Publication Society.

Cole, Kenneth. (2001). *No bad news.* Photography by John Ruebartsch. Morton Grove, IL: Albert Whitman & Co.

Cooper, Susan. (1973). *The dark is rising.* Illustrated by Alan E. Cober. New York: Atheneum.

Emberley, Barbara. (1967). *Drummer Hoff.* Illustrated by Ed Emberley. Englewood Cliffs, NJ: Prentice-Hall.

Frank, Anne. (1952). *Diary of a young girl* (trans. By B. M. Mooyaart-Doubleday). Garden City, NY: Doubleday

Freedman, Russell. (1987). *Lincoln: A photobiography.* New York: Clarion Books.

Gilman, Phoebe. (1992/2007). *Something from nothing.* Toronto: Scholastic Canada.

Herrera, Juan Filipe. (1999). *CrashBoomLove: A novel in verse.* Albuquerque: University of New Mexico Press.

Hesse, Karen. (1997). *Out of the dust.* New York: Scholastic Press.

Hinton, S.E. (1967) *The outsiders.* New York: Viking Press.

Hopkins, Lee Bennett. (1994). *Hand in hand: An American history through poetry.* New York: Simon & Schuster.

Jiménez, Francisco. (1997). *The circuit: Stories from the life of a migrant child.* Boston: Houghton Mifflin Company.

Jiménez, Francisco. (2000). *The Christmas gift/El regalo de Navidad.* Illustrated by Claire B. Cotts. Boston: Houghton Mifflin Company.

Jiménez, Francisco. (2001). *Breaking through.* Boston: Houghton Mifflin Company.

Lawlor, Laurie. (2001) *Hellen Keller: Rebellious spirit.* New York: Holiday House.

Lowry, Lois. (1993) *The giver.* Boston: Houghton Mifflin

Moon, Brian. (1999). *Literary terms: A practical glossary.* Urbana, IL: NCTE.

Nye, Naomi Shihab. (2008), *Honeybee.* New York: Greenwillow.

Pullman, Philip. (1996). *The golden compass.* New York: Random House.

Robinet, Harriette Gillem. (2000). *Walking to the bus—rider blues.* New York: Atheneum Books for Young Readers.

Taback, Simms. (1999). *Joseph had a little overcoat.* New York: Viking.

Taylor, Mildred. (1976). *Roll of thunder, hear my cry.* New York: Dial Press.

Tillage, Leon. (1997) *Leon's story.* Sunburst Book: Farrar, Straus & Giroux.

Wiesner, David. (2001). *The three pigs.* New York: Clarion Books.

Woodson, Jacqueline. (2001). *The other side.* Illustrated by Earl B. Lewis. New York: Putnam's Sons.

Yolen, Jane. (1987). *Owl moon.* Illustrated by John Schoenherr. New York: Philomel Books.

Yolen, Jane. (1988). *The devil's arithmetic.* New York: Viking Kestrel.

Secondary Sources

Alexander, Joy. (2005). The verse-novel: A new genre. *Children's Literature in Education,* 36(3), 269–283.

Bader, Barbara. (1976). *American picturebooks from Noah's ark to the beast within.* New York: Macmillan.

Bakhtin, Michel M. (1986). The problem of speech genres. In C. Emerson & M. Holquist, *Speech genres and other late essays* (V. W. McGee, Trans., pp. 60–102). Austin: University of Texas Press.

Barthes, Roland. (1977). *The death of the author. Image-Music-Text* (S. Heath, Trans., pp. 142–148). New York: The Noonday Press.

Beebe, Thomas. (1994). "Introduction: Why genre?" In *The ideology of genre: A comparative study of generic instability* (pp. 1–29). University Park, PA: The Pennsylvania State University Press.

Eagleton, Terry. (1976). *Marxism and literary criticism.* Berkeley: University of California Press.

Eagleton, Terry. (1996). *Literary theory: An introduction* (2nd ed.). Minneapolis: The University of Minnesota Press.

Foucault, Michel. (1984). "What is an author?" P. Rabinow (Ed.), In *The Foucault reader* (pp. 101–120). New York: Pantheon Books.

Goldstone, Bette P. (2004). Postmodern picture books: A new subgenre. *Language Arts,* 81(3), 196–204.

Hodge, Robert. (1990). *Genre and domain. In Literature as discourse.* New York: Johns Hopkins University Press.

Hunt, Peter. (1992). *Poetry, response and education.* In Peter Hunt (Ed.), Literature for children: Contemporary criticism (pp. 126–139). New York: Routledge.

Kohl, Herbert. (1995). The story of Rosa Parks and the Montgomery Bus Boycott revisited. In *Should we burn Babar? Essays on children's literature and the power of stories* (pp. 30–56). New York: The New Press.

Kozol, Jonathan. (1975). Great men and women (Tailored for school use). *Learning Magazine,* December, 16–20.

Leitch, Vincent B. (1991). (De)Coding (generic) discourse. *Genre,* 24(1), 83–98.

Lewis, David. (2001). *Reading contemporary picture books: Picturing text.* New York: Routledge/Falmer.

Loewen, James. (1995) *Lies my teacher told me.* New York: The New Press

Lynn, Ruth Nadelman. (1983). *Fantasy literature for children: An annotated checklist and reference guide* (2nd ed.). New York: R. R. Bowker Co.

McCord, Phyllis Frus. (1986). The ideology of form: The nonfiction novel. *Genre,* 19(1), 59–79.

Mikkelsen, Nina. (2000). *Words and pictures: Lessons in children's literature and literacies.* Boston: McGraw Hill.

Moebius, William. (1986). Introduction to picturebook codes. *Word & Image,* 2(2), 141–158.

Muller, Lauren & the Poetry for the People Collective (Eds.). (1995). *June Jordan's poetry for the people: A revolutionary blueprint.* New York: Routledge.

Nikolajeva, Maria & Scott, Carole. (2001). *How picturebooks work.* New York: Garland Publishing.

Nilsen, Alleen Pace & Donelson, Kenneth L. (2001). *Literature for today's young adults* (6th ed.). New York: Longman.

Nodelman, Perry. (1988). *Words about pictures: The narrative art of children's picture books.* Athens, GA: The University of Georgia Press.

Stephens, John. (1992). *Language and ideology in children's fiction.* New York: Longman.

Stephens, John. (1999). Maintaining distinctions: Realism, voice, and subject position in Australian young adult fiction. In S. L. Beckett (Ed.), *Transcending boundaries: Writing for a dual audience of children and adults* (pp. 183–198). New York: Garland.

Swanger, David. (1999). Paradigm, poetry, and multiculturalism. *Multicultural Perspectives,* 1(2), 13–16.

Threadgold, Terry. (1989). Talking about genre: Ideologies and incompatible discourses. *Cultural Studies,* 3(1), 102–127.

Todorov, Tzvetan. (2000). The origins of genres. In David Duff (Ed.), *Modern Genre Theory* (pp. 193–209). New York: Longman.

Zarnoski, M. (1998). Coming out from under the spell of stories: Critiquing historical narratives, *The New Advocate* 8(3): 345–356.

Zipes, Jack. (Ed.). (1986). *Don't bet on the Prince.* New York: Routledge.

CHAPTER **9**

Cinderella: The Social Construction of Gender

Like race and class, gender is not simply a biological phenomenon; it is a socially and ideologically bound identity. Despite the fact that in the United States in the last century women have gained in social status and power, there are many areas where women still occupy a lower position. Indeed, as late as 2004 a woman was generally earning 78 cents to every dollar earned by a man. In March 2005, the president of Harvard University, thinking he had a "scientific" evidence to support his assertion, publicly commented that women are not constructed to be scientists. His faculty voted "no confidence" as a result, and he was forced to leave his post. A new president, a woman, was selected to replace him.

Gender is not just about women. Men also are entangled by gendered expectations. Men in nursing, teaching, and other occupations mostly associated with women are not given the same respect as women who are in positions traditionally assigned or attributed to men. To move into a man's occupation is moving up. To work at a job conventionally reserved for or associated with women's work, is to move down, and be assigned lower social status.

It is important to acknowledge that not only gender, class, and race, but also ability, sexual orientation, age, and language contribute to social manifestations of privilege and prejudice. A woman of color experiences gender differently from a White woman of similar class standing. A poor White woman is perceived differently from her more affluent White sisters.

This chapter contains an analysis of the social construction of gender in children's literature, notably fantasy, and specifically Cinderella, making visible how gender is socially created. It guides the reader to unpack such issues as gender, class, and race, across cultures and across centuries, and to develop a critical eye and ear by introducing variants of the same folk or fairy tale, hopefully sparking discussions about culture, values, power, and social norms.

Traditional literature originated with the folk of all of the populated continents, and formed a communications system among and within peoples over time and long before the advent of print. The tales reflected values, mores, acceptable behavior, consequences of behavior, battles between good and evil, and the assumptions of responsible citizenry. Depending on when the folkloric collectors captured them and set them down in print, the tales reflected society at the time of the telling. They were originally intended for all of the members of a community, no matter the age of the audience.

Cinderella as a Genre

Cinderella is the tale that we examine extensively. The traditional *Cinderella* is a genre in and of itself, containing certain key ingredients of plot and character and shaping the reader's expectations. The story generally depicts an obedient and innocent girl, born into a family of privilege, forced to become a menial servant to a nasty stepmother, and finally regaining affluent status, usually through the aid of a magical being. In some of the tales this being is a fish, in some an ox, bull, or cow, and in some, an old woman or an old man. For the most part, the Cinderella character marries royalty, after successfully identifying herself (or himself) as the rightful owner of an artifact (usually a shoe) that has been left behind at an event such as a fancy ball or a series of celebrations.

We have selected *Cinderella* primarily because more versions of this tale exist than any other. It is probably the most familiar story for children and adults alike. It represents a number of values and attitudes that are commonly viewed as "social." There are enough differences among the versions to make it interesting for readers to compare and contrast the way the elements of the story as well as the ingredients of the culture are handled. There are even a number of male Cinderellas both in the oral tradition and contemporary retellings. By selecting *Cinderella* we invite children to exercise critical literacies practices, that is, detect ideologies and go beyond their own lived experience of what is beautiful and virtuous. We want them to understand and acquire multiple perspectives as well as develop critical thinking habits. Old traditions, historical constructs, the ability to identify allies and enemies, and a consideration of punishment and rewards are all embedded in the retellings of the folk and fairy tales.

As Michael Levy (2000) reminds us in his provocative and scholarly article, "What if Your Fairy Godmother Were an Ox? The Many Cinderellas of Southesast Asia":

> *Cinderella*, for all of its apparent distance from our world, does deal with important issues. It's about children's fear of losing a parent and of losing their place in the family. It's about having an appropriate relationship with the natural and for that matter the supernatutral world. It's about the importance of doing what's right despite the difficulties that might ensue. And, finally, it's also about acceptable female behavior and what girls can and should do to take control of their own lives.
>
> (Levy, 2000: 185)

Many of the European-based Cinderella tales teach that good girls should be meek, obedient, heterosexual, able bodied, White, and grateful. Beauty is defined as being blonde, blue-eyed, petite, and slender. Happiness is found by marrying a rich man. If a poor orphan is unhappy with her situation, she can wish for a fairy godmother or some other form of magic to solve her problems.

This passive Cinderella certainly does not show readers how to voice their concerns or organize for social change. Rather, she is often the model of the inactive and beautiful victim who does not dare to dream of freedom. She is aided by a magical being and eventually marries a handsome prince, whose inner qualities are seldom revealed to the reader.

Although Cinderella is frequently depicted as the victim of her stepmother's and stepsisters' domination, she also participates in the oppression by colluding with her oppressors via her unquestioning obedience to their commands. On the other hand, in the chapter, "Once Upon a Time," in her book, *Touch Magic*, Jane Yolen (1981/2000) challenges us to consider, particularly in some of the Asian versions, the pre-Disney tales, and in the contemporary recastings of the story, that a number of Cinderellas are spirited and resistant to domination.

Sometimes Cinderella participates in her own rescue and exhibits active, resourceful qualities, no matter how downtrodden she has become. For the most part, however, she is totally dependent on magical intervention and is content to wait until she can be identified and rescued. Assumptions vary, however, depending on the source of the tale, the author and illustrator, the intent, and the context. In contemporary times, just as in times past, the different versions of the tales depend on the politics, the audience, and the purpose of the telling.

In any study of the tales, there is inevitably a comparison with others of the same type. Sometimes the features to be compared are structural (e.g., setting, characters, motif, and magical artifact) and sometimes the discourse is the focus of comparison. Often, the intent of the comparison is simply to compare plot similarities in order to examine their effect on the telling. There is an inherent pleasure to be gleaned from detecting similarities and differences, and readers of all ages enjoy pointing them out, almost like uncovering clues and solving a detective story.

In our view, the critical and cross-cultural analysis of fairy tale variants is worthy of pursuit, examining which cultural statements and questions these stories are responding to. The issue at hand, we believe, is not just what we read, but also how we read, and what we do with what we read. Point of view shapes the telling of the story. It affects both the story and the reader.

In this chapter we use critical multicultural analysis to examine Cinderella stories from many countries and sources produced especially for children. The versions of the stories we analyze were published, for the most part, in the past 30 years. They are in circulation and are the ones most likely to be in the hands of contemporary children.

The different Cinderellas share common elements but the ideologies vary. The narratives are shaped by their historical, cultural, and sociopolitical contexts. For most of the male Cinderellas, bulls and cows serve as sources of magic. Female Asian Cinderellas tend to have fish as magical aides, although oxen figure prominently in several of the Southeast Asian tales. It is interesting to note that versions derived from the French writer Perrault contain fairy godmothers, while those from the German Grimm Brothers do not (see Zipes, 1986). Some of the godmothers actively enlist Cinderella's collaboration. Others require her total obedience. In some of the stories, the prince sends emissaries to fetch his bride. In others, he participates in person. In some tales (again those descending from Perrault) Cinderella forgives her stepfamily. In others (found in the Grimm variants) she tacitly condones violent punishment to be wrought against her oppressors. Even though the storyline is basically the same, the details, especially in contemporary reconstructions, create widely divergent products.

In the play of power, the stepmother and stepsisters dominate and collude. The father colludes or is a victim disposed of in one way or another. Cinderella often is deliberately and doggedly patient and kind, as if these qualities function as resistance along the path for acquiring agency rather than collusion with her enemies in her own oppression. The women she lives with prey on her. The domestic sphere affords the stepmother, in particular, inordinate power. All the unmarried women, including Cinderella, are dependent upon the patriarch's ability to confer economic stability, which translates into social power. The whole family appears to be vying for societal position, except for Cinderella, who seems to be without social ambition.

The father is usually a shadowy figure who simply goes along with the stepmother's injustice. In some versions, the father is well intentioned. The implication, when he marries after the death of Cinderella's mother, is that he wants his daughter to have a mother. In some stories he is the unwitting fool. In others he is very weak and submits to whatever his wife dictates. In a few he is a villain who abuses his wife and uses her for his own advancement. In most of the versions, however, especially the European and American, he is a nonentity: he either disappears or dies.

In almost all of the versions the prince is not only one-dimensional, he is almost invisible. He is a function, not a person. In some of the stories the Prince himself searches for Cinderella with the slipper in hand. In others he is so removed from the process that he sends courtiers on his behalf, trusting that they will do his bidding and relieving himself of the unnecessary effort. Who is this Prince with whom Cinderella must now spend the rest of her life? What does she know about her husband? What does he know about her? What sort of married life will they have together? The Cinderella promise in all of the stories is not only fortune and contentment, but also the adoption of her husband's lifestyle. Will she live in isolation from other women? Will she have other female allies? The reader has no idea of what the Prince enjoys, what he thinks, and/or how he will govern. The Cinderella genre avoids the expectations of the conventional fairy tale pattern in which the Prince actively fights dragons, overcomes social adversity, and even cleverly outwits villains in order to capture the hand of the fair princess. In Cinderella tales he is the door prize rather than the centerpiece of the action.

Men hold the power and wealth and provide the rewards. The Cinderella stories are a window into how women relate to each other and perpetuate gendered subject positions in the text and, by extension, in society. Most Cinderellas begin in high estate as daughters of well-to-do fathers. They lose their positions when their mother dies, their father remarries and either dies or relinquishes control, and Cinderella is forced into servitude. The happy ending is that Cinderella regains her status, but not in her own right. Rather, she receives her upper class status as a function of her husband's position. Rarely does the story follow Cinderella past her triumphant marriage to the Prince.

Diane Stanley (2006) has constructed a markedly unusual and engaging Cinderella tale. *Bella at Midnight* is set in the middle ages and features a brave and beautiful protagonist whose father, a knight, rejects her because her mother died as a result of giving birth to her. Bella is left in the care of a peasant family until her father remarries and sends for her. Each of the characters in this novel has the opportunity to make his or her voice heard, in turn, as a narrator. The wicked stepmother is not wicked. She is not attractive, but the reader understands her motivation and her unhappiness, especially because her story is included along with her daughters'. It is easier for us as readers to empathize, even with the "villain", because we know the reasons for their attitudes and behavior.

The prince, Julian, was also nurtured as an infant by Bella's caretakers. He was a fourth child and not considered very important. He and Bella played happily together, and even when he was sent back to the castle, he would visit frequently with "Princess Bella."

Although the expected features of the genre, such as the glass slippers, are interwoven throughout the novel, it is the changes that make an important difference. The venomous and grieving father, the nurturing peasant family, the sympathetic stepsister, and the heroic character of Bella lift this tale beyond its familiar unfolding. When Bella is forced to return to her father's mansion she feels decidedly out of place and prefers to stay in the kitchen near the hearth. Here Bella forges a relationship with the cook, who teaches her how to read. Bella is a hero of mythic proportions when she singlehandedly prevents a bloody war and saves Julian's life.

Perhaps the most telling difference is that there is a context for the behavior of each of the characters. Stanley investigates class and gender as they existed in medieval times. She also weaves a complex web that goes far beyond the familiar Cinderella.

Historical and Cross-cultural Analyses of Cinderella

Contrary to popular belief, neither Perrault nor Disney created the Cinderella story. There is, however, some controversy about who the first Cinderella was. Somewhere between the sixth and first centuries B.C.E. the Roman historian, Strabo, chronicled a story about a Greek slave girl named Rhodopis who married the pharaoh, Amasis. By all accounts, she was a very beautiful woman with golden hair and rosy cheeks. She may have been a prostitute or a courtesan. Before her sojourn with the pharaoh she resided, probably as a slave, in the household of Charaxos, a wealthy Greek merchant, brother to the famed poet, Sappho.

Shirley Climo adapted her story to fit the Cinderella genre more closely, bringing her to life in *The Egyptian Cinderella*, inserting as an element of the plot her mistreatment by the women of the Egyptian court. The story line includes an eagle that seizes Rhodopis's golden sandal and deposits it in the lap of the pharaoh, who then orders a search for the woman to whom the sandal belongs. Lo and behold, Rhodopis is identified. One might argue that although Rhodopis may have been the owner of the slipper, she was decidedly not Egyptian. In any case this story contains few of the ingredients of the Cinderella genre.

Most experts agree that the first Cinderella was Chinese, and her name was Yeh-Shen. According to the cover blurb of *Yeh-Shen*[1] by Ai-Ling Louie, Chinese manuscripts dating from the T'ang Dynasty (618 to 906 C.E.), supposedly depicting the story as having been introduced orally "before the time of Chin (222–206 B.C.E.)," are acknowledged to contain the first written literary depiction of Cinderella. This story describes a beautiful young girl persecuted by a wicked stepmother and her nasty stepsister. Also included in the cast of characters are a wondrous fish, and then, later, a mystical sage. A golden shoe functions as the artifact used to locate the prince's bride. The prince is the king of an island people and Yeh-Shen's father had been a cave chief of Southern China, so this version affirms Cinderella's upper class origins.

A number of scholars such as Ramond De Loy Jameson (1932) affirm this origin, but for some there is a question of the authenticity of the T'ang manuscript of *Yeh-Shen*. Folklorists provide many arguments that are worthy of further research. We could spend hours speculating on and tracking down the possible influences the Asian Cinderellas had on the European tales and vice versa. Although the scholarly exploration is fascinating and endless, it is sufficient to acknowledge the possibilities of the Chinese and other Asian Cinderellas far predating the European versions.

One of the reasons for looking at numerous adaptations and retellings of Cinderella is that children can analyze and discuss how beauty is communicated. Since there are Cinderellas all over the world, with some estimates saying that there are over 1,000 versions, the criteria for beauty vary, and the blonde, blue-eyed "ideal" takes its place alongside the Cinderellas who have very different physical features. It may well be, because ancient Chinese people admired tiny feet, that the small shoe became the means of locating the true princess. Western readers may not be aware of the fact that until not too many years ago the practice of binding the feet of Chinese women, particularly those from the aristocracy, from an early age deformed the feet so badly that the women could not walk, and had to be carried from place to place. Beauty and wealth were generally equated; there was no need for the wealthy woman to walk. Women's refusal to have their feet bound became a sign of independence and resisting of authority in modern times. But foot binding is still within the memory of some Chinese women today.

Many of the stories set in Asia include references to magical fish, the killing of the fish, and the continuation of the magic via the fish bones. In a number of these tales the happy ending does not translate to a marriage.

In some versions, the Cinderella character is killed, comes back to life, and finally vanquishes the evil stepmother or stepsister. Life and death are fluid in several Asian versions of the tale: in some retellings the mother offers herself as a living sacrifice so that the family may have food or survive economically. In most of these tales she is betrayed by her husband, who takes a second wife, and goes back on his word to return his first wife to life. In several of the stories the characters are reincarnated before they are actually restored to their original form.

In most of the Asian retellings, the Cinderella character perseveres even though she is abused, and violence and trickery are used against her. The quality of the perseverance shows much more resistance than many of the European Cinderellas. In contrast to the meekly obedient protagonist who passively endures the life of a drudge, her Asian counterpart tends to the care and feeding of a fish, conspires with elder advisors, and even returns to life several times. She has identifying strengths that the Prince recognizes. The socioeconomic status of the father (and therefore, Cinderella) varies among the retellings. Sometimes it is a regained status (i.e., riches-to-rags-to-riches) and sometimes it is an acquired status (i.e., rags-to-riches).

In *The Enchanted Anklet*, an Indo-Canadian version, translated and adapted by the Indian-born author, Lila Mehta, the protagonist, Cinduri, begins in middle-class standing. The artifact left behind is a jeweled anklet (hence the title of the tale). Hindu ritual figures throughout the story as a backdrop. The snake, who performs the function of the magical advisor as well as the dead mother, is a traditional Hindu symbol of strength and might. Of all the Asian Cinderellas, this story is most reminiscent of the European versions because Cinduri marries the Prince and lives happily ever after. Her wicked stepmother and stepsister fail to tend their farm successfully and are forced to become beggars. A tree that is uprooted by lightning kills them. No redemption here.

In *Wishbones: A Folk Tale from China*, retold by Barbara Ker Wilson, Yeh Hsien is the daughter of a cave chieftain. In this version, her father loves her dearly, but does not figure much in the plot. His second wife and her daughter persecute Yeh Hsien. Yeh Hsien catches a fish that becomes her pet, and through trickery, the stepmother captures, kills, and cooks the fish. When Yeh Hsien discovers the disappearance of the fish, an old man appears to her and informs her that the bones of the dead fish are magic. He advises her to hide the bones and her every wish will be granted.

Up to this point, this story is identical to the other version by Ai-Ling Louie, but in this retelling, Yeh Hsien systematically acquires treasures, including embroidered silk robes, which she hides in her corner of the cave. Yeh Hsien attends the cave festival by means of the treasures she has accumulated. She enjoys the festival, runs home because she fears her stepmother and stepsister have recognized her, and drops one of her violet slippers. The cave people find her slipper and sell it to the ruler of a neighboring kingdom. His messengers locate Yeh Hsien who becomes queen of the land. The most startling detail that is different from the other retellings is that Yeh Hsien's husband abuses the power of the fish bones until at last they refuse to grant any more wishes. The king is appropriately ashamed and buries the fish bones which are ultimately washed away by the tide and never again seen.

The Brocaded Slipper, told by Lynette Dyer Vuong, conveys a Vietnamese version of the story. Tam is the Cinderella character and Cam is her wicked stepsister. Tam's father dies and she is pressed into servitude as a result of Cam's trickery. There is a magic fish, which gets killed and cooked, but whose bones produce, among other treasure, a pair of slippers. The crowned prince gets hold of one of the slippers and vows to marry the owner. Tam is given impossible tasks to perform, and does so with the aid of some pigeons. She dresses in the other treasured items the fish bones provide and is selected by the Prince to be his bride. The story continues beyond Tam's marriage. She is visiting at home for her father's memorial ceremony and she is killed by her stepmother, but her soul transforms into an oriole, a peach tree, a loom, a persimmon tree, and a peasant's daughter. Meanwhile, the Prince is persuaded to marry Cam, although his heart still pines for Tam. Finally, the Prince visits an old woman's cottage and recognizes the culinary artistry of the meal the old woman provides him. Tam appears and they have a joyful reunion. Cam falls off a wall in her attempt to escape and is killed. Finally, Tam lives happily ever after with her Prince.

Lê Thi Thanh (1998), in her commentary on Vietnamese Cinderella versions, informs us that "Vietnamese farmers not only produce agricultural products but also make friends with them. They often name their children after the crops to appreciate their nourishing values" (Thanh, 1998: 3). Thanh goes on to point out that "from the traditional viewpoint of Vietnamese morality, happiness is neither magic from the fairy nor a gift from the stepmother; it is gained by conquest with patience and hard work" (Thanh, 1998: 9). The transformations that Tam undergoes are reflective of her perseverance, kind-heartedness, and endurance. In the Southeast Asian varieties of Cinderella, Michael Levy (2000) notes that "death simply doesn't end things" (Levy, 2000: 181). The presence of the dead and reincarnation are central to these stories, influenced by Buddhism and Hinduism.

Kongi and Potgi: A Cinderella Story from Korea, adapted (with Stephanie Haboush Plunkett) and illustrated by Oki S. Han, provides similarities to the other Asian Cinderellas, and also contains some significant differences. Notably, the Cinderella character's community actively intervenes on her behalf, as do stray animals and creatures on the nearby hillside. Kongi's father has remarried, really for Kongi's sake. Kongi is glad for her father's sake, because he has been lonely. Kongi and her father are mutually loving and supportive until the marriage. Kongi's father, although well meaning, is weak and cannot prevent his wife and stepdaughter from abusing his beloved daughter. Neither Kongi nor her father protests, ostensibly for fear of making things worse. The stepmother sets difficult tasks for Kongi, but Kongi succeeds because she is aided by an ox, a toad, a flock of sparrows, and ultimately, a rainbow and angels. Kongi attends a bride selection party at the palace, but runs away because she is so flustered by the prince's attention. She leaves behind her a jewel-like slipper, which is the artifact proving that she is the rightful partner to the prince.

At her wedding reception, Kongi forgives her stepmother and stepsister, which makes her father very proud of her. The story ends by reaffirming the values of the culture: "Over the years Kongi had learned to be patient, humble, and kind—qualities that helped her to serve her people well" (n.p.). Her stepmother and stepsister reform and become good people who do good deeds. Unlike several of the European Cinderellas, especially in the Grimms' collection in which the wicked stepsisters and stepmothers are bloodily and painfully executed, in some of the Asian stories there is the opportunity for redemption as part of the possibility for continuing to live a just life. To be fair, this is also an option in some of the European versions of *Cinderella*, notably, those patterned on Perrault's creation.

According to Alan Dundes (1982/1988), the first European *Cinderella* was published in 1558 by Bonaaventure des Periers, followed closely by the posthumous publication in 1634 of Giambattista Basile's *Il Pentamerone*, a collection of European folktales, which included "The Cat Cinderella." Charles Perrault wrote *Cinderella* in the late seventeenth century for the French court. The Grimm brothers set their version into print in the early nineteenth century. The French and German versions seem to have found the widest audiences. In the late nineteenth century, Andrew Lang produced the English version, which was identical to Perrault's in every detail. Differences exist between these two European retellings. The French tale has a godmother who is a fairy, and Cinderella forgives her stepsisters, invites them to the court, and matches them with husbands. In contrast in the German tale, the deceased mother's spirit is the aide to Cinderella and the stepsisters' toes and heels are cut off to fit into the slipper. They also get their eyes plucked out at the end of the story.

In his *Don't Bet on the Prince*, Jack Zipes argues that "It is no longer possible to ignore the connections between the aesthetic components of the fairy tales, whether they be old or new, and their historical function within a socialization process which forms taste, mores, values, and habits" (Zipes, 1986: 2).

How are the plot variants shaped by the historical and sociopolitical status of women in the particular culture? How are class and race part of this status? What are the cultural implications of the magical intervention? In the Grimm version, the help comes from a hazel twig, a tree, and some birds, all part of nature. For his courtly audience Perrault creates a fairy godmother. Any of these differences could provide sources for inquiry and conversation.

Charles Perrault and the Grimm Brothers have hegemony over the production of fairy tales for child audiences. Modern retellings, for the most part, start with the base of either Perrault or Grimm, and, therefore, a northern European construct. There are, however, many picture books as well as novels that are twists or inventions of the Cinderella theme that enjoy great popularity among young readers. Shen's Books catalogue alone offers more than sixty titles, and there are hundreds of adaptations and reconstructions available in libraries and bookstores. All of these benefit from critical multicultural analysis, perhaps the more so, because they appear to be more contemporary and savvy in the ways of the postmodern world.

Many adults are resistant to analyzing fairy tales because "it breaks their magic." Whose magic? What does the magic signify? The status quo? Does the magic embody the act of collusion or go along with the power structure? We believe that when we examine these fairy tales we add an important layer of meaning, making visible the social circumstances they reflect, thus deepening the reading experience.

In John Steptoe's book, *Mufaro's Beautiful Daughters*, set in Zimbabwe, Africa, the strikingly attractive sisters provide a view of beauty that is different from Northern European, Southern European, Asian, Caribbean, or contemporary Canadian and American images. Moreover, the fact that these two sisters are identical twins leads young readers to the conclusion that, indeed, beauty is only skin deep.

Some facets of the Cinderella story that appear in this book include a nasty sister, a Prince's quest for a bride, and some magical intervention. On the other hand, Nyasha, the unfailingly sweet tempered, kind sister, is not forced into menial servitude; she enjoys the chores of tending a garden. Further, her father does not play favorites. Both sisters are invited to the ball, and they sustain their high status throughout the story. Nyasha embraces menial work, while Manyara is determined that she will place her sister in servitude when she (Manyara) becomes queen of the castle. It is doubtful that Nyasha would see serving as a punishment. On the other hand, one wonders if she will have the opportunity to maintain her cherished habits when she is the Prince's wife.

We must remember that this rendition, purportedly of an African tale, is a retold piece. It is noteworthy that John Steptoe's *Mufaro's Beautiful Daughters* is loosely based on a folktale. The source is a nineteenth-century collection called *Kaffir Folk-lore* by George McCall Theal. The stories were collected and set in writing by native people under the direction of and with copious notes added by Theal, who held numerous positions in South Africa, including that of a mission teacher as well as a border magistrate. Theal's opinions of native traits and customs are often demeaning, for example, "Kaffir ideas of some kinds of morality are very low" (Theal, 1985: 209). He speaks of the people as uncivilized, and his use of the term "Kaffir" is, in and of itself, derogatory.

The landscape of Zimbabwe may have inspired John Steptoe's work, but his Western messages and values are imbedded in his story of these two beautiful sisters, for example, the ironic ending of Manyara becoming a servant in her sister's household. It is precisely because Steptoe's illustrations of these two young women leave no doubt as to their beauty that this book is valuable for a classroom, no matter what the setting or derivation. But it would be a mistake to pretend that the study of the story would provide insight into the culture of Zimbabwe.

Children need to see many forms of beauty so that they dispel the stereotypic automatic notion that to be beautiful a woman must be White, fair haired, blue-eyed, and dainty. Different cultures maintain different notions of what is beautiful, and it is to the advantage of the reader to be able to widen his or her concept of the array of characteristics that are deemed beautiful, even beyond personal physical attraction.

Reconstructed Cinderellas

In the classic tales male dominance requires that Cinderella be sweet and passive. The stepsisters are nasty, usually physically unattractive, and they are punished, but the degree of punishment depends on the author's perspective. In her focus on modern day girls and women in literature, *Waking Sleeping Beauty: Feminist Voices in Children's Novels*, Roberta Seelinger Trites (1997) points out that some reconstructed stories are designed to free the female protagonists from "inevitably growing into passivity" (Trites, 1997: 11). For the most part, however, these stories continue to represent heterosexuality as the norm. The assumption is that marriage is the happy ending. Indeed, the female protagonist has been transformed into a self-possessed willful, non-stereotypic person in her own right.

Trites maintains that "In rewriting folktales to advance feminist ideologies and to identify female subjectivity, feminist writers are both protesting the powerlessness of women inherent in our culture's old folkways and giving voice to a new set of values: a set that allows for the princess to have power, a set that allows Sleeping Beauty to wake up not to a destiny that immerses her in her husband's life but to a destiny that is self-defined" (Trites, 1997: 45).

Even though these stories are reconstructed, stereotypes often circulate through them: They are not immune to biased attitudes and behaviors. For example, in *Cinder Edna*, by Ellen Jackson, Edna is portrayed as independent, direct, and active. She is attracted to Rupert, the prince's younger brother, who is a perfect match for Edna, especially because they both "knew some good jokes." Unfortunately, the beginnings of a few jokes that they share sound like stems of ethnic humor, for example, the "anteater from Afghanistan" and the "banana from Barbados". In some ways, these beginnings may set up the reader to expect and excuse this kind of humor. Nevertheless, many of the retold tales do counteract the seriously gendered and classed messages of the classic tales even though the expected happy ending is usually that the Cinderella figure and the prince get married.

In *Bubba The Cowboy Prince*, by Helen Ketteman, the classic storyline unfolds in language that deviates from its usually delicate, enchanting style. In this story it takes on the pattern of the Texas ranching community. One would hardly find in a classic fairy tale the admonition to ". . . watch out for them cow patties . . . you know how Daddy hates for you to track up the house" (n.p.). The protagonists in this case are male, and Bubba experiences the same lowly status as any female Cinderella. One major difference is that Bubba enjoys ranching (like Nyasha from *Mufaro's Beautiful Daughters*, who enjoys tending her garden). The potential royal partner, Ms. Lurleen, is "the prettiest and richest gal in the county." (She looks remarkably like Dolly Parton.) Despite her success, she is lonely, so she fulfills the classic practice of hosting a fancy dance in order to attract potential suitors. Appropriate for a Cinderella reconstruction, set in Texas, the magical intervention comes from a "fairy godcow." The cow outfits Bubba with dazzling new clothes and a beautiful white stallion. One last departure from the classic tale has Ms. Lurleen identifying Bubba as the owner of a dirty, old boot. But what really affirms that she has found her true love, is how odiferous he is from working with the cows. Lurleen recognizes his smell, asks him to marry her, and the two live happily ever after.

This story is a romp and a turning of the tale on its head. The pattern is recognizable with enough regional, colloquial vocabulary that attributes it to a particular context. There is no mistaking that it is a Cinderella story, broadly played, and we know from the beginning how the story will end. The biggest change in the story line is, even when Bubba is forced to labor, he has agency; he loves the work that he is doing.

Yet another reconstructed Cinderella is *Raisel's Riddle* by Erica Silverman. In this book the setting is a Jewish community in a village in Poland, over one hundred years ago. The father figure is Raisel's kind grandfather, who dies, and Raisel is left on her own. Rather than become dependent on her community, Raisel travels to another location and seeks work in the home of the Rabbi (as close to a king as a poor Jewish girl can get). The wicked stepmother figure is the Rabbi's cook who resents any interference in her kitchen. There are no artifacts that Raisel loses; it is her knowledge of a riddle that the Prince (the Rabbi's son) seeks in order to find his mate. In this story knowledge is valued, as is kindness and ingenuity. Raisel does receive help from a fairy godmother (in the guise of a hungry old woman whom Raisel befriends) but it is clearly her own ability and active intervention that bring Raisel her prize.

This retelling has some of the elements of the classical story but the artifacts have changed. The significant differences include a clear philosophical stance, so that it is not a shallow message. The Cinderella character has agency; nobody can conquer her. Even though the evil cook tries to thwart her, Raisel manages to overcome the oppression. When locked in the kitchen she pounds on the door to be set free. The prince is not looking for a woman with certain physical characteristics, but an intellectual partner. Although there are still traditional elements such as the Purim ball and marriage as the happy ending after minimal interaction between the bride and groom, in *Raisel's Riddle*, the implication is that Raisel and the Rabbi's son will be life partners.

Fanny's Dream, by Caralyn Buehner, illustrated by her husband Mark, provides an antidote to the usual romantic fantasy of most of the Cinderella retellings. The story is set in rural Wyoming. Fanny, a sturdy, stocky daughter of a farmer, dreams of marrying a tall, rich, and handsome prince. She wants this prince to take her away from her life of toil, wait and dote on her. She knows this can only be accomplished with the aid of a fairy godmother but it does not work out that way for her. Instead, while she is waiting for her fairy godmother to appear, she encounters and consents to marry Heber Jensen, a short, stout, and hardworking farmer. The two are committed to each other, and make a life together that is neither easy nor romantic, but is mutually satisfying. They are productively interdependent, and their relationship is loving, as well as one that contains some humor and fun. It is clear that they care deeply about each other and their growing family. When, at last, a fairy godmother does appear, Fanny easily decides to refuse her services and returns gladly to her family.

The Cinderella elements of romantic love between two gorgeous characters, arranged for by a supernatural being, are examined in the light of reality in this picture book. The fantasy of love without the necessity for commitment and devotion is overturned and replaced by the satisfaction of a hard-won good life, bolstered by the ability to laugh and build together. This is no fairy tale. The author/illustrator team invites young readers to consider what love consists of and how it grows. The message is clear, but it is embedded in the story, and is not tract. Fanny, and by implication, all young people, have choices as to how they will live their lives. The fairy godmother who appears (albeit tardily) represents Fanny's dream come true, but Fanny realizes that her true dream has been the life she actively has chosen and works to maintain. It is noteworthy that Fanny and her family are reading *Cinderella* in the last panel of the book.

Classroom Applications

Units of study comparing Cinderellas abound in classrooms where teachers are eager to invite their students to engage in critical multicultural awareness and analysis. Nowhere is this more sensitive and difficult an undertaking than in the arena of Native American collections of Cinderella tales. Fortunately, scholars are readily available to assist in the processes of deconstructing and contextualizing these stories. One such expert, Debbie A. Reese (Nambé Pueblo), is an Assistant Professor of American Indian Studies at the University of Illinois at Urbana-Champaign. Her blog critiques literature, offers recommendations for teaching, and keeps the reader up to date on events and issues in Native American education. Cynthia Leitich Smith is a gifted and award-winning author of books containing Native American themes and characters. She is a tribal member of the Muscogee (Creek) Nation. She also maintains an active and informative blog, particularly focusing on books with Native American content. Joseph Bruchac, of Abenaki heritage, is probably the best known expert on Native American life and culture. He is also a prolific writer of children's books. Beverly Slapin and Doris Seale, who is a Santee, Dakota, and Cree librarian and educator, are well-respected directors of Oyate, a non-profit group that provides information and materials about Native Peoples for use in the curriculum. In a quest to uncover the ideologies and implicit values represented in the texts of so-called Cinderellas it would be enlightening to consult these resources to guide the discussion.

In a particularly informative article in the January 2007 issue of *Language Arts*, Dr. Reese demonstrates the differences between portraying culture and conforming to the Cinderella genre. She unpacks three versions of Turkey Girl, a "Zuni Cinderella" to convey her message. In looking at the elements of these stories Reese provides specific examples of how the florid language used in one story may capture the reader's attention, but it does not represent the accurate language of the people. The intent of the story is acknowledged to explain something about the land and the tracks the turkeys have left on it, whereas the Cinderella variant focuses on the Cinderella character.

As previously stated, presenting Cinderella stories in Native American settings is problematic and likely to convey false messages to young readers. One may wonder if this is the case with all cultures. Perhaps it would be wise to issue a warning to all teachers and children not to confuse the Cinderella story with the culture of a people. For example, *The Irish Cinderlad*, retold by Shirley Climo, clearly contains ingredients of the Cinderella genre, albeit tailored for a change in gender: Becan's feet are enormous and he is located by means of a gigantic boot; there is no ball, but there is the opportunity to rescue the princess from the clutches of a dragon. There is a nasty stepmother and her daughters and there is a magical bull who aids Becan in his survival. The tale is similar in pattern to other Cinderlads, but there is no evidence of particular Irish or any other culture. In her "Author's Note" Climo lists other Cinderlads from Scandinavia to Africa, India, and Japan, who have similar plots. In all cases the stories are set in a magical or fictitious land and reflect no specific people.

Comparing the different versions can be an engaging and thought-provoking classroom activity, especially if the examination of the tales involves more than simple story grammar (e.g., a comparison of the characters, plot, setting, and ending). A look at the socioeconomic status of Cinderella and the other characters in the story, and how this status affects their behavior and assumptions might be one avenue of exploration. Standards of beauty and how important they are to the action might be another.

Inviting children to make a multimedia collage of representations of gender across texts (e.g., newspapers, advertisements, literature, TV commercials, music videos, etc.) will help them see the prevalence of gender in our everyday lives. They can locate patterns across these texts as well as analyze the gender roles available for boys and men.

Recommendations for Classroom Research

Every work of literature is a product of culture, whether it is intentional on the part of the author or not. The adaptor reflects his or her perspective on life, assumptions about good and evil, and transmission of values. Even in a purportedly Chinese story, the adaptation reflects twentieth- or twenty-first-century United States or some aspect thereof. The audience is children who live in a globalized world, and not an isolated culturally specific group that was the audience for the oral folktale. Culture is a negotiated, commonly constructed set of knowledge, beliefs, ways of thinking, norms, morals, history, laws, language, customs, and habits that hold a group together. Culture evolves, shifts, and reacts depending on the sociopolitical and economic context, geography, and composition of the community.

A critical multicultural analysis encompasses questions about how society is organized, how power is distributed, how texts construct race, gender, and class, and how the aesthetic of a story, which includes discourse, positions the characters as well as the reader. It is worth looking at the power structure within the family, a microcosm of society, as well as how power is exercised. Cinderella exercises power in her compliance and collusion with characters outside the family. The absence of the father is a literary device in a number of cases, rendering him invisible or, at the least, ineffective. He is a bystander more often than not.

These stories bring us up close to the social processes among women. In many cases, the fairy godmother is a woman. In just about all of the Cinderellas there are gradations in how the Cinderella character responds to abuse. The abuse consists mainly of extrusion and lack of affection, with Cinderella ostensibly longing for acceptance, and willing to do almost anything to achieve it. She is clearly more socially responsive than her stepmother and stepsisters. They long for acceptance into the upper class, and it is only in the end, in the Perrault derivatives that they achieve their goal. Ironically, it is done totally through the largesse of Cinderella.

In retracing the development of the contemporary Cinderella, including Asian, early European, and U.S. Cinderellas, our focus is on her social construction over time and bringing her up to date. There are many perspectives on who we think Cinderella is today. Young readers have a wealth of models to look at critically in terms of power and status. The staying power or persistence of Cinderella is palpable despite the fact that Cinderella changes over time, across cultures, and within cultures. However, in most of the contemporary portraits, she is still disturbingly White. She is also, for the most part, isolated from any visible community and, except for some animal helpers, essentially without friends. Further, there are changes in the setting, the appearance, and the power of the Fairy Godmother, but the power relations remain.

In no place does the realm function as a factor. The Prince, and eventually Cinderella rule the people. The monarchy is left intact. It is difficult to imagine that a lively Cinderella would be attracted to the sterile life of the court. Who is this Prince with whom Cinderella must now spend the rest of her life? What does she know about her husband? What does he know about her? What sort of married life will they have together? The Cinderella promise in all of the stories is wealth and happiness, but also the adoption of the husband's life. Will she live in isolation from other women? Will she have other female allies? What will happen to her family? Cinderella's is rewarded in the end because of virtue and playing along with the status quo (position of women). In what ways is virtue tied to complacency? Collusion? Depending on the version, her stepmother and stepsisters are horribly maimed and killed or are invited to court where Cinderella finds "suitable" husbands for them.

In looking at Cinderella or any literature for children derived from the oral tradition, the reader needs to be open to a variety of cultural implications as well as social divisions across gender, race, and class lines. Analysis might bring up in what ways do religious ideologies (e.g., Judeo-Christian, Muslim) shape this story line, especially how Cinderella is constructed across these tales.

How is work depicted? How is leisure portrayed? What are the messages about class distinctions and expectations? What does Cinderella want? She wants agency. She does not want to be bossed around by her stepmother and stepsisters. She also wants romantic love. Within the Asian stories, although marriage is the outcome, she is not really looking for romantic love, which does not seem a social practice of these societies. In terms of the way the stories are represented to children, what she wants is to be herself.

Suggestions for Further Reading

Dundes, Alan. (Ed.). (1982/1988). *Cinderella: A Casebook*. Madison, WI: The University of Wisconsin Press.

Kelley, J. E. (2004). Timeless and timely fairy tales, ideologies, and the modern classroom. In Terrell A. Young (Ed.), *Happily ever after: Sharing folk literature with elementary and middle school students* (pp. 316–329). Newark, DE: International Reading Association.

Kelley, Jane E. (2008). Power relationships in Rumpelstiltskin: A textual comparison of a traditional and a reconstructed fairy tale. *Children's Literature in Education*, 39, 31–41.

Levy, Michael. (2000). What if your fairy godmother were an ox? The many Cinderellas of Southeast Asia. *The Lion and the Unicorn*, 24(2), 173–187.

Stephens, John. (1996). Gender, genre and children's literature. *Signal*, 79, 17–30.

Stephens, John. (Ed.). (2002). *Ways of being male: Representing masculinities in children's literature and film*. New York: Routledge.

Stephens, John & McCallum, Robyn. (1998). *Retelling stories, framing culture: Traditional story and metanarratives in children's literature*. New York: Garland Publishers.

Trites, Roberta Seelinger. (1997). *Waking sleeping beauty: Feminist voices in children's novels*. Iowa City: University of Iowa Press.

Zipes, Jack David. (2006). *Fairy tales and the art of subversion: The classical genre for children and the process of civilization*. New York: Routledge.

Zipes, Jack David. (2006). *Why fairy tales stick: The evolution and relevance of a genre*. New York: Routledge.

References

Children's Literature

Buehner, Caralyn. (1996). *Fanny's dream*. Illustrated by Mark Buehner. New York: Dial Books for Young Readers.

Climo, Shirley. (1989). *The Egyptian Cinderella*. Illustrated by Ruth Heller. New York: Crowell.

Climo, Shirley. (1996). *The Irish Cinderlad*. Illustrated by Loretta Krupinski. New York: HarperCollins Publishers.

Han, Oki S. & Plunkett, Stephanie Haboush. (1994). *Kongi and Potgi: a Cinderella story from Korea*. Illustrated by Oki S. Han. New York: Dial Books.

Jackson, Ellen B. (1994). *Cinder Edna*. Illustrated by Kevin O'Malley. New York: Lothrop, Lee & Shepard.

Ketteman, Helen. (1997). *Bubba the Cowboy Prince: A fractured Texas tale*. Illustrated by James Warhola. New York: Scholastic Press.

Louie, Ai-Ling. (1982). *Yeh-Shen: a Cinderella story from China*. Illustrated by Ed Young. New York: Philomel Books.

Mehta, Lila. (1985). *The enchanted anklet: A Cinderella story from India*. Illustrated by Neela Chhaniara. Toronto: Lilmur.

Perrault, Charles, Anthea Bell & Loek Koopmans. (1999). *Cinderella: A fairy tale* (trans. by Anthea Bell). Illustrated by Loek Koopmans. New York: North-South Books.

Silverman, Erica. (1999). *Raisel's riddle*. Illustrated by Susan Gaber. New York: Farrar, Straus & Giroux.

Stanley, Diane. (2006). *Bella at midnight*. Illustrated by Bagram Ibatoulline. New Work: HarperCollins.

Steptoe, John. (1987). *Mufaro's beautiful daughters: An African tale*. Illustrated by John Steptoe. New York: Lothrop, Lee & Shepard Books.

Vuong, Lynette Dyer. (1982). *The brocaded slipper and other Vietnamese tales*. Illustrated by Vo-Dinh Mai. Reading, MA: Addison-Wesley.

Wilson, Barbara Ker. (1999). *Wishbones: a folk tale from China*. Illustrated by Meilo So. London: Frances Lincoln.

Secondary Sources

Dundes, Alan. (Ed). (1982/1988). *Cinderella: A casebook*. Madison: University of Wisconsin Press.

Jameson, Ramond De Loy (1932). *Three lectures on Chinese folklore*. North China Union Language School, 12–164.

Levy, Michael. (2000). What if your fairy godmother were an ox? The many Cinderellas of Southeast Asia. *The Lion and the Unicorn*, 24(2), 173–187.

Reese, Debbie. (2007). Proceed with caution: Using Native American folktales in the classroom. *Language Arts*, 84(3), 245–256.

Thanh, Lê Thi. (1998). Vietnamese Cinderella: Tam and Cam: Substance and shadow. Final paper for EDUC 784: *Issues in Children's Literature*, University of Massachusetts, Amherst.

Theal, George McCall. (1985). Kaffir Folk-lore: a selection from the traditional tales current among the people living on the eastern border of the cape colony: with copious explanatory notes (2nd ed.). Retrieved on September 23, 2007, from http://2020ok.com/books/5/kaffir-folk-lore-a-selection-from-the-traditional-tales-current-among-the-people-living-on-the-eastern-border-of-the-cape-colony-with-copious-explanatory-notes-9205.htm.

Trites, Roberta Seelinger. (1997). *Waking Sleeping Beauty: Feminist voices in children's novels*. Iowa City: University of Iowa Press.

Yolen, Jane. (1981/2000). *Touch magic: Fantasy, faerie & folklore in the literature of childhood.* Little Rock, AR: August House Publishers.

Zipes, Jack. (1986). *Don't bet on the Prince.* New York: Methuen, Inc.

Endnote

1. There exist multiple spellings of "Yen-Shen" (e.g., Yeh Hsien and Sheh Hsien).

CHAPTER 10

Shock of Hair: The Endurance of Hair as a Cultural Theme in Children's Literature

A well-intentioned European American teacher presented *Nappy Hair*, by Carolivia Herron, to her third grade class of African American and Latino children. The children enjoyed this story so much that the teacher, Ruth Sherman, made black-and-white copies of the book for the children to bring home. The dissemination of this book beyond the classroom enraged some of the parent community (only one of whom had a child in the class). This group perceived the book illustrations as racist practices on the part of the teacher, the illustrator, and the author. A group of parents came to school en masse to protest. Most of the protesters had not read the book. The teacher, intimidated by what appeared to be the potentially violent anger of the crowd, left the building and did not return, not even to say "good-bye" to the children.

Ms. Sherman did know her children, in terms of their pleasure in the book, but she did not consider that these children had lives and cultural experiences outside the classroom. Children bring multiple identities and contexts with them to the classroom. The controversy surrounding this book demonstrates that with social issues, it is not only what we read, but also how we read and what we do with what we read. Reading is a sociopolitical activity, and the response to how this book was presented to a group of children clearly bears this out. The book separated from this incident, merits analysis and critique. But it is likely that the controversy surrounding its presentation by this one teacher will be always associated with this text.

The format of the book, a "call-and-response," is familiar to those readers who participate in church services or storytelling sessions that include these language practices in their gatherings. In African American churches, the preacher calls (says a line in a prayer or sermon), and one or more people in the congregation respond spontaneously by repeating a line or a word, or say "Amen," or an improvisational contribution.

Call-and-response relates to West African conventions that express a strong sense of community and spontaneity. It became a means of unifying slaves who were not allowed to meet in large groups, except in church. The call-and-response, as well as other musical forms, was a way of challenging the suppression of communication among the slaves. Sometimes there were subtle messages interwoven into the music conveying news of runaways and potential uprisings as well as information about everyday life. Some Native American groups use this technique in their storytelling. It is a popular strategy with many contemporary storytellers to engage the audience.

Not every African American child will be familiar with this ritual of call-and-response, and it may be distancing or confusing for some young readers to be plunged into this format without some explanation, preparation, or demonstration on the part of the adult. According to Adaeze Eneaweci and Opal Moore (1999–2000), Herron herself is the young protagonist in the story. Her uncle engaged in this type of narrative at a family picnic when Herron was a young child. The incident was captured on tape, and Herron wrote the story for inclusion as a chapter in a book for adults. An editor recommended that it be published as a children's book, and so it was.

The text describes a family gathering at which Uncle Mordecai waxes eloquent in his teasing Brenda about her nappy hair. But in the process he also conveys a sense of history and oppression, which forms a subtext to the celebration of Brenda's decidedly thick and unruly hair. Throughout, the call-and-response format makes demands on the reader. Perhaps a group could participate in the reading of the text, thus making the book a libretto of sorts, and the readers a choral ensemble. The book is a departure from the conventional, and takes some sophistication and knowledge to handle well. It might be an excellent text for a class of future teachers to discuss. It is challenging for any group of adults to grapple with; it merits contemplation.

There is certainly no doubt about the authenticity of the book: Few people question the sincerity of the author's wish to impart a sense of African American culture. It is difficult to predict how an audience will respond to this attempt. One reader sent a critique to Amazon.com protesting:

My 10-year-old daughter hated the book on sight. She . . . announced that the book did not make her feel better about her own hair. It made her feel terrible. As an adult, I loved the simple story and the historical context for discussing, yes, nappy hair . . . . To an adult who has finally come to terms with the immutable facts of her slave heritage, this book is beautiful in its language, its illustrations and its story. To a child, it is an embarrassing, deeply personal, and sometimes overwhelming topic. While the intended purpose of the book is to raise self-esteem, it is unsuccessful because it does not communicate to our youth in a way that he or she is able to accept the message. As a mother and a teacher, I am saddened that my daughter is not ready to read this book. Maybe she will be when she reaches an adult acceptance of herself. This book is to be appreciated more by its adult readers than by its young readers.

(www.amazon.com/Nappy-Dragonfly-Books-Carolivia-Herron/
dp/0679894454)

This, of course, is one person's point of view. Another reader offered another perspective:

This book gave me one of the best memories with my niece and nephew. It is very hard to find a book that reaches an eleven-year-old and a five-year-old. As they were having a picnic style dinner I was reading them this book. They enjoyed themselves so much. Laughter was all over the place. There were even shouts of LORD give me nappy hair! It let my little people know that nappy hair is perfect in God's eyes.

(www.amazon.com/review/product/0679894454/
ref=cm_cr_pr_link_2?%5Fencoding=UTF8&pageNumber=
2&sortBy=bySubmissionDateDescending)

The power base in this story resides in the male god: "this is my world, and this chile . . . is going to have the nappiest hair in the world." Nappy hair is a God given feature of Black people, and it is here to stay, not without its problems. Brenda appears content with her hair; it is the angels and family who are troubled by it. The family demonstrates that her hair will not respond to processing and straightening, which are impositions of the White world. Brenda's hair represents independence, nonconformity, and endurance of her African roots.

This book represents the tension in the African American community. The child represents those who have not succumbed to the White standard of beauty. The community has groomed their hair so that it is "tamed." Brenda is free from such definitions of beauty.

For many African Americans, picture books depicting distinctively Afrocentric hairstyles demonstrate a resistance to conform to White standards of beauty. On the other hand, some books reflect the stereotype of African Americans who want to conform to White standards of beauty and endure chemical treatments, extensions and other tortures to make their hair less "nappy," considering their African hair to be "bad" or "inferior." Consideration of these factors makes the book something that will be approached differently by caring adults. The controversy also centers around how the messages conveyed by the words and images are interpreted by the audience.

The lines are clearly drawn: for some people the book is affirming and helpful; for others it is a reminder of the pain that our society inflicts on children who are different from the established standard. Cornell West (1990) addresses the dilemma of "double consciousness" as being caught "between a quest for White approval and acceptance and an endeavor to overcome the internalized association of Blackness with inferiority" (West, 1990: 28). This book, seemingly aimed at children, brings out this dilemma. Hair is an enduring cultural theme in children's literature.

The Cross-cultural Politics of Hair

For Samson in the Old Testament, hair was the entire source of his strength. Ask a Canadian and American audience what a princess looks like, and they will almost unanimously and immediately respond, "She has blonde hair." Rapunzel's hair was her asset and her attraction for the Prince, as well as a means of access to the Wicked Witch. When African slaves were transported from Africa, the slave traders shaved their heads. According to Ayana D. Byrd and Lori L. Tharps (2001)

> [T]he shaved head was the first step the Europeans took to erase the slave's culture and alter the relationship between the African and his or her hair . . . arriving without their signature hairstyles, Mandigos, Fulanis, Ibos, and Ashantis entered the New World, just as the Europeans intended, like anonymous chattel.
>
> (Byrd & Tharps, 2001: 10–11)

When Native Americans were placed in boarding schools, in order to deculturalize and assimilate them, in addition to their clothes being removed and changed, their hair was cut. When people join a religious group, or the army, there is often a ritual haircutting that symbolizes a giving-up of one's identity and secular involvement. Loss of hair can be an emotional hardship for aging adults, as is graying hair to some adults. An elaborate coiffure is, for some people, a sign of affluence and high social status. Certainly adolescents demonstrate their rebellion when they color and style their hair in what adults perceive to be an affront to social norms.

While the scholarly book, *Hair: Its Power and Meaning in Asian Cultures*, edited by Alf Hiltebeitel and Barbara D. Miller (1998), explores many aspects of hair in Asian cultures, it also highlights the political, social, religious, gender, and sexual implications of hair. The ubiquitous cultural theme of hair in children's books illuminates how these social meanings are imbedded in the text and illustrations, emerging from particular historical and sociopolitical conditions.

Hair There and Everywhere by Karin Luisa Badt is a nonfiction children's book that includes and informs a wide audience. It uses the theme of hair as a unifier and catalogs hair diversity across cultures and time, without establishing a hierarchy of value. The table of contents includes "Combing Through Cultures," which displays hairstyles specific to girls in the Black Forest region of Germany, Aymara Indian women of Bolivia, Hmong women in Guizhou Province of China, Yoruban women from Lagos, Nigeria, and discusses other groups' historic styles and contemporary fashion. The photos are respectful, beautiful, and show great variety.

Another section of this informative, aesthetically pleasing, and sometimes astounding book is titled "Your Part in Society." The text explains that hair can "say something about your social status" (n.p.). Examples are given for historic Sumeria (Iraq), France, Japan, and Rome. Although the book contains no contemporary illustrations of this function of hair, a lively discussion could certainly ensue if young readers were invited to add to this page with today's examples. It must be noted that the book does address similar issues in the section on "Political Hair." Historical examples are included, such as the Manchus in the Qing Dynasty in China forcefully imposing a specific queue hairstyle on the male Han Chinese as a symbol of Han Chinese submission to Manchu rule, and the hairstyle called *ogun pari* that Nigerian women wore in 1970 to commemorate the end of a civil war. Two pages portray youthful protest in the United States and England in the 1960s and 1970s. Again, readers might be invited to collect and comment on photographs from newspapers and magazines reflecting today's political hairstyles. The book is successful in its cross-cultural examination: more than 50 different groups are highlighted in pictures and text. In no instance is a group singled out as "quaint" or "exotic." The author's research seems thorough and scholarly. The ending of the book considers how cultures influence each other and how some styles become international. Hair becomes a symbol of unity as well as difference.

Another book that includes a worldview of hair is *Hats off to Hair* by Virginia Kroll. This is a gallery of hairstyles for young boys and girls with no qualitative or judgmental comments. At the end of the book, the author places the styles in their historical as well as cultural contexts. The children are racially and culturally diverse, and the hairstyles are realistic rather than fanciful. The book reminds us that hair differences also exist within cultures. While this book has no plot or specific characters to whom to relate, it is useful as a catalog and affirmation of difference.

Sandra Cisneros also features different hair types in *Hairs/Pelitos: A story in English and Spanish* from *The House on Mango Street*. (A picture book version of this short story exists.) The characters are within a close Mexican-American family that is described in affectionate and affirming terms. Hair in this short piece is endearing and special to each of the family members. At no point does the author imply either stereotyping or valuing one kind of hair over another, although it demonstrates that hair can also be a commodity or asset. The acceptance of each family member and the strength of the loving family permeates both the text and the illustrations.

Erandi's Braids, by Antonio Hernández Madrigal, is about a Mexican child in the 1940s who endures her braids being cut off so that she can earn money for her family to buy a new fishing net. Hair in those days was bought by merchants for use in the production of wigs, eyelashes, and fine embroidery. In this story hair is a vehicle, a commodity for helping the family through rough economic times, and the child, though fearful of the experience, and wanting her mother to protect her, is, in the end, glad she made the sacrifice.

The story is reminiscent of the O. Henry short story, *The Gift of the Magi*, in which the young newlyweds sacrifice their most valued possessions in order to please the other. For the young bride, it is her hair, which she has cut and sold in order to afford to buy her beloved husband a chain for his treasured gold watch. He, in the meantime, has pawned his watch in order to purchase ornamental clips for her long, luxuriant hair. Jo, in *Little Women*, is another character who sells her hair (her only claim to beauty) in order to have the money to buy a ticket for her mother to visit the father of the family who lies ill in a military hospital. In these stories, readers appreciate the extreme sacrifice it takes to have one's hair cut, even though the characters acknowledge that it will grow back. The psychological ramifications are strongly conveyed here.

Hair is not always an ornament or an asset. Anne, in the series of stories by L.M. Montgomery set in Canada's Prince Edward Island, has flaming red hair that is the scourge of her existence. She is automatically assumed to be bad tempered and impatient because of her red hair. In *Anne of Green Gables*, she internalizes this bias, and tries to dye her hair so that she will no longer be viewed negatively. Unfortunately the dye she uses turns her hair green and she is forced to suffer even more reprimands and character assassinations.

For many African Americans, picture books depicting distinctively Afro-centric hairstyles demonstrate a resistance to White standards of beauty. As Michelle H. Martin points out in her *The Horn Book Magazine* article of May 1999, "Regardless of what was taken from African Americans, this vestige of Africa, this hair . . . endures (287)."

Books reflect and are a product of culture. Culture is a complex social construct. It is not static, isolated, permanent, inflexible, or bounded by hard perimeters. It is relentlessly changing in response to historical, social, economic, political, geographical, intra- and intercultural factors. Power relations play key roles in this dynamism. Critical (analyzing how power works) and multicultural (considering specific historical and sociopolitical factors) analysis captures how culture is constructed, thus investigating how cultural themes emerge and circulate from particular circumstances. Young readers need to learn to analyze what they read in the light of historical and sociopolitical considerations.

In this chapter, we explore the cultural meanings and ideologies (i.e., worldviews) associated with African-American hair by analyzing a number of children's books written and/or illustrated by "insiders" as well as "outsiders" and published from 1978 to 2002. We particularly explore how language use (i.e., text) and illustrations shape how the story gets told. We examine issues of cultural affirmation and reclamation, and cultural misrepresentation.

Why We Chose Hair

We chose the theme of hair because there are so many social and political meanings surrounding this theme; and, because it is not just an African American issue, it is a historical issue across race and class lines. Certainly, the controversy around Carolivia Herron's *Nappy Hair* greatly contributed to our awareness of this cultural theme. But it must nevertheless be acknowledged as a deeply significant issue in African American culture. It also turns out that this theme appears frequently in literature for children. We thought it was important to examine this cultural theme, even though we are not "insiders" in the African American community. In response to critics who doubt that people outside a particular culture can represent that culture through art and print because it is not their blood heritage, "I suggest that blood be bigger than what we're born with, that blood keep growing and growing as we live; otherwise how will we become true citizens of the world?" says Naomi Shihab Nye (1995: 7).

We consider ourselves to be allies, and we want to tackle the daunting task of writing about a sociopolitical theme with respect and with a critical multicultural lens. Our analyses challenge discourses surrounding this issue and uncover how the power relations of race, class and gender construct this cultural theme. We also believe that, as allies and outsiders, we can provide a distance that helps to clarify the issues, adding our voices to the mix of insiders with many disparate views. Since there are always more differences within a group than there are among groups, it is our conviction that by examining the issue with a critical multicultural lens, we will illuminate the process that enables readers to take control over the texts.

Difficult as it may be, it is necessary to face history, current society, and ourselves if we wish to change the future. It is also important for allies to speak out and to express solidarity over historical and/or sociopolitical issues. As Toni Morrison (1992) maintains in *Playing in the Dark: Whiteness and the Literary Imagination,* "The contemplation of this black presence is central to any understanding of our national literature and should not be permitted to hover at the margins of the literary imagination" (Morrison, 1992: 5).

All too often, artful language and illustrations mask underlying messages that may be hurtful to a significant population of children. Unwitting readers internalize stereotyping, discrimination, and racism. Even more often, the preponderance of literature provides access and visibility to an already privileged majority, and affirms biased messages about and to children both outside and inside the circle of privilege.

Critical multicultural reading is a sociopolitical activity. The dialogue is shaped by each context involving particular relations and structures of power, values, beliefs, goals, and economic and political conditions. A child raised in circumstances of extreme rural poverty will use different lenses to make sense of a text than will a child from a suburban middle-class environment. Stories are imbedded with ideologies. The more astute we as readers can be and the greater our repertoires of understandings, the better we can be at uncovering the social and political implications of each work of literature.

Methodology

We located 18 books published over a span of more than twenty years (1978 to 2002), reflecting the cultural theme of hair, either directly in the text, through the illustrations, or a combination of both. The characters in these books, for the most part, are African American. Although we will deal with books about hair in other populations, our focus will be particularly on the books conveying the theme of hair connected to the African-American experience in order to provide a comprehensive model for examining cultural themes in children's books.

We organized the text collection in chronological order, keeping in mind Mitzi Myers' (1988) question: What cultural statement is this text responding to? Books are responses to historical and sociopolitical circumstances as well as other texts. We read and reread these texts against each other and secondary sources about children's literature and this cultural theme. We were careful to gather multiple perspectives from within and outside the African American culture, in order to deconstruct and reconstruct our understanding of this cultural theme. We believe that multiple viewpoints and texts are necessary for constructing an understanding of the past and present conditions of any cultural theme.

We engaged in dialogue with children, other adults, and people from varying backgrounds and expertise. We looked at this theme over time, recognizing, as McGillis (1996) points out, that all reading is political, and that critical analysis helps to name the ideological positions of the text and reader. He further states that literary texts are mirrors of historical and sociopolitical ideologies. Several current books, most written by contemporary African-American authors, especially affirm and support the special and beautiful qualities of hair in the African heritage, while some reflect dominant ideologies about hair beauty.

Hair as a Cultural Theme in Children's Literature

Honey I Love and Other Love Poems, by Eloise Greenfield, illustrated by Leo and Diane Dillon, is a collection of sixteen poems told from the point of view of a young child as she engages in and comments on her everyday life. The illustrations depict the young protagonist in a natural Afro as well as elaborate and ornamental hairstyles. The Dillons' illustrations are black, white, and gray pencil-on-paper drawings of the main character and her hair. Hair dominates each page, as if it is another character in the story, a subtext, almost a dream, beyond the activity featured in the illustrations. Hair is an adornment, a fantasy. The softness contributes to the fantasy and the aesthetic. The illustrations are imbued with emotion.

Interestingly, there is a separate volume of the title poem alone, made into a picture book with illustrations by Jan Spivey Gilchrist. This version targets the preschool reader. The images show the main character, a young girl, engaged in everyday activities with different family members and friends. Her hair is significantly beautiful, and is consistently realistic. Her hairstyle is less imaginative than in the earlier text, but it is clearly a statement about her self-worth and attractiveness. The illustrations in this volume are in vibrant color. The young protagonist's joy in herself emanates from the combination of text and image. Although hair is noticeable in almost every frame, it complements the text rather than forming a separate entity.

The Dillon edition is contemplative and reflective and the Gilchrist illustrations are bouncy and lively. It is noteworthy that unlike the other books we are critiquing here, in neither of the two versions of *Honey I Love* is there a statement in the text about the beauty of African American hair. The pictures portray hair so aesthetically as to provide this undeniable conclusion.

Cornrows, written by Camille Yarbrough and illustrated by Carole Byard, provides a context for the cornrow hairstyle by linking it to African societies. Cornrows entail sectioning of hair and braiding it tightly against the scalp, similar to the planting of rows of corn. The book provides information about such cultural artifacts as royal stools, sculpture, and ritual masquerade. It tells not only of hair design as symbols, but also includes the fact that the people across Africa, from Egypt to Swaziland, Senegal, and Somalia wore braids. The number and pattern of braids indicated information about the clan, their village, societal position, and even, in some cases, their religion.

In the process of braiding her great-grandchildren's hair, the great grandmother, assisted by the children's mother, communicates African American history from pre-slavery times to contemporary times. The illustrations demonstrate several varieties of "cornrowed" hairstyles. The rhythm of the text combined with the images in many shades of black, gray and white provides a strong foundation, affirming African American identity. This is a proactive book focusing on historical fact. People and customs are respected. This is a family that demonstrates affection and mutual admiration for each of its members. Hair is a vehicle for acquiring knowledge and affirming identity.

In Nancy Cote's *Palm Trees*, the story of a mother and the way she cares for her child is beautifully rendered. Millie, a pre-adolescent girl, is anxious because her mother just secured a job and needs to leave early in the morning, so that Millie must now comb her own hair. She must also get herself dressed and occupied. The setting of this book is a city. The story is about more than hair: Friendship figures very strongly as well as a sense of being cared for. The protagonist is an appealing young girl whose behavior is very reasonable.

Millie is challenged by the daunting task of fixing her hair herself for the first time. Millie wishes she had not inherited her father's "tight curls," but rather had her mother's "soft brown waves." She finally does manage to arrange her hair in an unusual, but comfortable style. It looks like she has two palm trees growing at the top of her head. She is now ready to meet with her friend, Renee, for a play date.

When the two girls get together, Renee seems to be teasing her and laughing at her hairdo. Millie is devastated and runs home. She almost cuts off her hair, but is prevented from doing this by Renee's arrival. Renee has taken the time and trouble to arrange her own hair with three palm trees on top of her head. The two girls then spend the rest of the day arranging and rearranging their hair, deciding, in the end, that they like the palm tree hairdo best. Mother returns home from work and is greeted by two happy girls.

The illustrations of this supportive and nurturing book match the storyline. Readers can peruse the pages and note details that reinforce the plot as well as provide clues to upcoming events. The characters are respectfully and realistically drawn. The setting is neither idealized nor demonized. It is decidedly a crowded city neighborhood, but there is no sense of oppression or poverty. People are portrayed at work, shopping, and going about their lives in an everyday manner. The message is not hammered home, but develops with the plot and characters. Readers might speculate about the whereabouts of the father; they might also wonder that Millie has reached such an advanced age without ever having done her own hair. It might also be worthwhile for readers to suggest ways adults might have intervened in response to Renee's reaction, or they might recommend other responses on Millie's part. This is a book worth owning; it can be approached at many levels.

My Hair is Beautiful . . . Because It's Mine!, by Paula deJoie, communicates the same message of pride and affirmation. On every page is an image of a beautiful Black child with a distinctive hairdo. It ends with the declaration, "My hair is beautiful because it's MINE!" The illustrations depict accurately and positively the great range of hair possibilities for African American children. It even mentions one child's hair as a style like an African Queen's thus linking the child to her roots. This is a lovely board book for young children, especially in reflecting the individual's understanding of self. (This book is part of the Black Butterfly Board Books, an affirming series.) The book makes no attempt to be overtly political; certainly this is an age-appropriate decision on the part of the author and illustrator.

The book, *Wild, Wild Hair* by the renowned poet, Nikki Grimes, tells the story of a young girl's Monday morning experience of having her mother comb her "wild hair" into twenty braids. The child dreads the process of "raking" through her curly, thick hair and tries to hide. It is an easy-to-read book, part of the Hello Readers Series, at an accessible level for young children: The story is told in rhyming verse and captures the universal experience of a parent helping groom a lively, rambunctious, and not too cooperative young child. The book's illustrations place the child in an affluent home, an important contribution to show the class diversity that exists within the African American community. The ending demonstrates that the struggle was worth it; the child's hair is beautifully and elaborately braided and the child and mother are both content.

Even when there are so many attractive features included in the illustrations and story, we can invite children to engage with ideas being communicated and ask questions such as: Why Monday morning? It is hard to believe that the mother would permit her daughter to go to sleep without preparing her hair on the eve of a school week for the combing they both know will occur in the morning. Why is it only the mother who can locate the child, especially since she always hides in the same place? If the children put themselves in the parents' shoes, what would they say or do differently? One difficulty readers have with this otherwise charming story is that it might be perceived as making some negative associations with "natural" Black hair: It is "wild, wild hair" and "a mess."

A number of books attempt to convey the message of cultural affirmation through the image of hair. *I Love My Hair!* by Natasha Anastasia Tarpley succeeds in this intent. From the text it seems that this child is the only one in her class with African hair because the children tease her when she wears her hair in an Afro. Then the illustrations show the teacher and a male companion, both in African garb, wearing their hair in Afros, lovingly and supportively affirming the child and her heritage. The teacher introduces the political aspect of particular hairstyles. She explains that wearing the Afro is a way "to stand up for what they believed, to let the world know that they were proud of who they were and where they came from." In this story the mother is shown as loving, caring, and admiring of her daughter's beautiful hair. The child is heartened by the combination of affection and pride, and feels liberated to the point where one day she thinks she will fly.

The illustrations are designed to contest stereotypes: They situate the child within an African American family who are not poor and who reside in a suburban community clearly populated by many African Americans. Notice the bookcase in the child's room, filled with books. This is a book that can invite discussion among the students: Why was the young girl teased? How is wearing one's hair in a certain style a political statement?

What are some other ways we can stand up for ourselves and help our friends to withstand teasing?

In all of the books we have read and analyzed, *Haircuts at Sleepy Sam's* by Michael Strickland, and *Bippity Bop Barbershop*, by Natasha Anastasia Tarpley, are the only ones with male protagonists. The settings are two barbershops. Julia J. Thompson (1998) reminds us that the beauty salon brings a variety of women together to explore cultural norms. She claims that "the beauty salon can, by extension, be seen as an important site of cultural production . . ." (Thompson, 1998: 239). The same is true of the barbershop. It is a space for negotiating one's cultural identity. In *Haircuts at Sleepy Sam's*, it is clear that the mother knows exactly what hairstyle she wants her three sons to have and they know what haircuts they want, but it is Sam, the barber, who makes the final decisions for all of them. The barbershop is a meeting place for a number of men in the Black community, and it is this ambience that communicates well the sense of self-pride and joviality that pervades the entire story. The mother gracefully accepts her sons' new styles even though they are very different from what she explicitly requested.

The illustrations in this amiable book are realistic. The characters are attractive and have a definite presence. No mention is made of "good hair" or "bad hair" although Sam does say "You're no longer nappy" as he finishes the youngest boy's haircut. But the statement is made as a comment on fact, not as a value judgment.

There is a clear indication in this story that the "bald fade" cut is the preferred style of the day for young people but this is a comment on styles and fashion, not on class or aesthetics. Readers might ask why the mother bothers to write out instructions when she knows that Sam will do as he pleases anyway. It might also be worthwhile for readers to discuss the derivation of hairstyles and their designation as "in style" or out. How do the trends evolve? It might be an interesting project to visit a hair salon or barbershop and see what's on the walls, and what the customers as well as the hairstylists prefer in terms of hairstyles. How does the hairstyle relate to current culture?

In *Bippity Bop Barbershop* by Natasha Anastasia Tarpley, the author teams up again with illustrator E.B. Lewis (this is the same pair that gave us *I Love My Hair*) to focus this time on the hair experience of a young boy and his father. In this story Miles' dad is taking him to the barbershop for his first professional haircut. Although he is not frightened at first, the combination of the well-intentioned men congregating in the barbershop telling him to be brave, together with the unexpectedly ferocious sound of the electric clippers, causes Miles to hide beneath the protective cape. Miles' dad lovingly reassures him, and the haircut is completed successfully. Mr. Seymour, the barber, has been Miles' dad's barber since childhood. This rite of passage is completed when Miles' dad requests and receives a haircut just like his son's, and the two joyfully walk home together.

Hair is only one of the factors binding the father and son. Miles makes it clear from the beginning that he identifies strongly with his dad. They even dress "in matching blue jeans and gym shoes" (n.p.). Since Miles is the narrator, it is his perspective that the reader is treated to. The barbershop is depicted as a place to gather. The illustrations picture a wide variety of Black men, with different features, ages, and hairstyles. Mr. Seymour is never portrayed.

Another book aimed at young children is *Happy to be Nappy*, by bell hooks. The intent of this book is to overturn the negative connotations of "nappy." The language is a fun romp. The illustrations are not wedded to the text; they have a life of their own and provide a fantasy world of blocks of color, swirls, dots of ink, splotches, and fuzzy outlines. The book communicates a sense of joy. As Hazel Rochman (1999: 2064) comments in her review in *Booklist*, "It's a greeting card." It would be unreasonable to expect anything deep or substantive in a greeting card. If this book is on the shelf among others that reinforce the positive features of natural African hair, it will provide a light and playful companion piece. There is no one character whom we follow. The cartoon-like faces sport a wide array of colors, facial features and shapes of hair. The hair itself prances and dances on the page and rarely lies close to the scalp of its owner. There is no context, plot, setting, or characterization. The hair is everywhere. The overall tone is affirming. An interesting activity might be to read the book aloud to children and have them draw their own pictures, and then compare and contrast them with the original illustrations.

Crowning Glory by Joyce Carol Thomas is a collection of illustrated poems, providing a context of a particular extended family with cousins, aunts, grandmother, and great-grandmother celebrating African-American hair and educating the reader about the variety of hairstyles and methods of hairdressing. This positive attitude toward hair is summed up in the final poem, "Crowning Glory." The author notes that she has written this collection as "a tribute to my beautician mother and all her hairdressing foremothers" (n.p.).

The illustrations are particularly tender because they are portraits of the author's daughter and seven granddaughters. The collection is a joy-filled peon of praise for the glorious natural (comb picked), wound with thread, "braided, pressed, dreadlocked, hot-curled, crowned with ribbons, and beaded with jewels" hair.

Classroom Applications

In highlighting the cultural theme of hair in children's books, we examine issues of cultural affirmation and reclamation, and cultural misrepresentation. We maintain that an uncontested reading puts the reader in the power of the author, illustrator, and society's biases. Roderick McGillis (1996: 113) informs us that "texts reproduce the dominant values of a culture at a particular time." A non-resistant reading helps engrain dominant worldviews and gets in the way of readers imagining new possibilities for being in the world. As teachers and children acquire and use language to analyze power relations, they practice social critique and change.

Teachers must serve as role models, and must be willing to engage with all types of literature. Mary Dilg (1999) emphasizes that teachers and children should "search together for comfortable [critical and respectful] language with which to speak to each other and to take some of their first steps in engaging in honest dialogue with each other, across cultural lines, about each other's identities, fears, and uncertainties" (Dilg, 1999: 38). This kind of dialogue will help children discern racialized, classed, and gendered texts and images, and take responsibility for maintaining, challenging, and constructing culture.

Tony Watkins (1992) reminds us that

> . . . the stories we tell our children, the narratives we give them to make sense of cultural experience, constitute a kind of mapping, maps of meaning that enable our children to make sense of the world. They contribute to children's sense of identity, an identity that is simultaneously personal and social: narratives, we might say, shape the way children find a "home" in the world.
>
> (Watkins, 1992: 183)

All books are culturally coded. A passive stance, that is, one that accepts the authors' words and illustrators' images unquestioningly, is not neutral. It maintains the status quo and the explicit message of the author and/or illustrator, and robs power from the individual reader.

Recommendations for Classroom Research

There are many cultural themes that are possible to explore through literature. Young readers need to be taught to recognize and acknowledge the universalities and differences in cultural thematic explorations, locating the historical and sociopolitical factors that have contributed to these social patterns. Time, setting, class depiction, and cultural difference are but a few of the conditions affecting the perception and attitude of the reader. The same theme can be portrayed in many different ways. Readers need to expand their understanding of their own social identities, as well as the social identities of others. It is useful for teachers and children to look at the representation of culturally specific themes (like the theme of hair) over time to determine by critical multicultural analysis what different social and political meanings adhere to the texts above and beyond their language and illustrations.

As two White women concerned with looking at how culture works and is represented in children's literature, we have attempted to examine carefully the points of view of people from within as well as from outside the culture. We have explored conflicting views, different interpretations of the issues, and delved into the complexities. We strongly recommend that this type of analysis be undertaken in order to read critically and multiculturally and to re/contextualize cultural themes.

Suggestions for Further Reading

Banks, Ingrid. (2000). *Hair matters: Beauty, power, and Black women's consciousness.* New York: New York University Press.

Byrd, Ayana & Tharps, Lori L. (2002). *Hair story: Untangling the roots of Black hair in America.* New York: St. Martin's Griffin.

Ilyin, Natalia. (2000). *Blonde like me: The roots of the blonde myth in our culture.* New York: Touchstone.

Jacobs-Huey, Lanita. (2006). *From the kitchen to the parlor: Language and becoming African American women's hair care.* New York: Oxford University Press.

Kreamer, Anne. (2007). *Going gray: What I learned about beauty, sex, work, motherhood, authenticity, and everything else that really matters.* Boston: Little, Brown and Co.

Lester, Neal A. (2000). Nappy edges and goldy locks: African-American daughters and the politics of hair. *The Lion and the Unicorn,* 24(2), 201–224.

Weitz, Rose. (2004). *Rapunzel's daughters: What women's hair tells us about women's lives.* New York: Farrar, Strauss & Giroux.

References

Children's Literature

Alcott, Louisa May. (1867/1994). *Little women.* Illustrated by Valerie Alderson. New York: Oxford University Press. (Original work published 1867.)

Badt, Karin Luisa. (1994). *Hair there and everywhere.* Chicago: Children's Press.

Cisneros, Sandra. (1994). *Hairs/pelitos.* Illustrated by Terry Ybanez. New York: Knopf: Distributed by Random House.

Cote, Nancy. (1993). *Palm trees.* Illustrated by Nancy Cote. New York: Four Winds Press.

DeJoie, Paula. (1996). *My hair is beautiful . . . Because it's mine.* Illustrated by Paula deJoie. New York: Writers and Readers Publishing: Distributed by Black Butterfly Children's Books.

Greenfield, Eloise. (2003). *Honey, I love.* Illustrated by Jan Spivey Gilchrist. New York: HarperCollins.

Greenfield, Eloise. (1978). *Honey, I love, and other love poems.* Illustrated by Leo and Diane Dillon. New York: Crowell.

Grimes, Nikki. (1996). *Wild, wild hair.* Illustrated by George Cephas Ford. New York: Scholastic.

Henry, O. (1980). *The gift of the Magi.* Illustrated by Byron Glaser. Mankato, MN: Creative Education. (Original published 1906).

Herron, Carolivia. (1997). *Nappy hair.* Illustrated by Joe Cepeda. New York: Knopf : Distributed by Random House.

Hiltebeitel, Alf, and Barbara D. Miller. (1998). *Hair: Its power and meaning in Asian cultures.* State University of New York Press.

hooks, bell. (1999). *Happy to be nappy.* Illustrated by Christopher Raschka. New York: Hyperion Books for Children.

Kroll, Virginia L. (1995). *Hats off to hair!* Illustrated by Kay Life. Watertown, MA: Charlesbridge.

Madrigal, Antonio Hernández. (1999). *Erandi's braids.* Illustrated by Tomie De Paola. New York: Putnam.

Montgomery, L. M. (1994). *Anne of Green Gables.* Illustrated by Inga Moore. New York: Holt. (Original work published 1908).

Strickland, Michael R. (1998). *Haircuts at Sleepy Sam's.* Illustrated by Keaf Holliday. Honesdale, PA: Boyds Mills Press Inc.

Tarpley, Natasha. (1997). *I love my hair!* Illustrated by Earl B. Lewis. Boston: Little Brown.

Tarpley, Natasha. (2002). *Bippity Bop Barbershop.* Illustrated by E. B. Lewis. Boston: Little, Brown.

Thomas, Joyce Carol. (2002). *Crowning glory.* Illustrated by Brenda Joysmith. New York: HarperCollins.

Yarbrough, Camille. (1979). *Cornrows.* Illustrated by Carole, M. Byard. New York: Coward McCann & Geoghegan.

Zelinsky, Paul O. (1997). *Rapunzel.* Illustrated by author. New York: Dutton Children's Books.

Secondary Sources

Byrd, Ayana D. & Lori L. Tharps. (2001). *Hair story: Untangling the roots of Black hair in America.* New York: St. Martin's Press.

Dilg, Mary. (1999). The opening of the American mind: Challenges in the cross-cultural teaching of literature. *Race and culture in the classroom: Teaching and learning through multicultural education.* New York: Teachers' College Press.

Enekwechi, Adaeza & Opal Moore. (1999). Children's literature and the politics of hair in books for African American children. *Children's Literature Quarterly* 24(4), 195–200.

Martin, Michelle. (1999). Never too nappy. *The Horn Book Magazine,* 75(3), 283–289.

McGillis, Roderick. (1996). Class action: Politics and critical practices. *The nimble reader: Literary theory and children's literature.* New York: Twayne Publishers.

Morrison, Toni. (1992). *Playing in the dark: Whiteness and the literary imagination.* Cambridge, MA: Harvard University Press.

Myers, Mitzi. (1988). Missed opportunities and critical malpractice: New historicism and children's literature. *Children's Literature Association Quarterly,* 13(1), 41–43.

Nye, Naomi Shihab. (1995). Introduction. In *The tree is older than you are: A bilingual gathering of poems and stories from Mexico.* Paintings by Mexican Artists. New York: Aladdin.

Rochman, Hazel. (1999). Review of *Happy to be Nappy. Booklist,* 95(22).

Thompson, Julia J. (1998). Cuts and culture in Kathmandu. In Alf Hiltebeitel and Barbara D. Miller (Ed.), *Hair: Its power and meaning in Asian cultures.* New York: State University of New York Press.

Watkins, Tony. (1992). Cultural studies, new historicism and children's literature. In Peter Hunt (Ed.), *Literature for children: Contemporary criticism.* New York: Routledge.

West, Cornell. (1990). The new cultural politics of difference. In Russell Ferguson (Ed.), *Out there : Marginalization and contemporary cultures: Documentary sources in contemporary art.* New York: New Museum of Contemporary Art & Cambridge, MA: MIT Press.

CHAPTER 11

Teaching Critical Multicultural Analysis

We wrote this book to disturb the scholarly and pedagogical silence around how class, race, and gender work together in children's literature. We have great respect for the authors and scholars whose work has embraced what has been called multicultural children's literature. At this point we are especially interested in moving beyond the limited definition of multicultural children's literature as literature by and/or about people of color. We acknowledge and support a focus on literature with people who have historically, ideologically, and politically been underserved and rendered nearly invisible. We argue that we should analyze how dominant ideologies function in text and images. To accomplish this kind of examination we theorize a critical multicultural analysis of children's literature, grounded in critical multicultural education, feminist poststructuralism, cultural studies, critical literary theory, critical pedagogy, critical literacies, and critical discourse analysis. This historical, sociopolitical, and narrative lens creates a space for us to problematize the literary category of multicultural children's literature, taking up the power relation of class alongside race and gender. Our intent is to show how reading power exposes the interlocking systems of classism, sexism, and racism. Critical multicultural analysis leads to reading cultural diversity against these power relations.

Critical multicultural analysis can contribute to the construction, deconstruction, and reconstruction of ourselves and U.S. society. It alerts us to how text and images in children's books can position readers in the interests of coercive power relations. Resistant reading practices can also lead us to collective ways of being in the world. In the process of critical multicultural reading, power is located and a site is created for social transformation. Critical multicultural analysis challenges fixed and bounded notions of culture, identity, class, race, gender, and power, and makes visible the social construction of culture, power, genre, focalization, and story closure.

The cultural themes emerge recursively (back and forth) and reflexively (analyzing the analysis) as we read the text collections alongside secondary sources. The characters exercise power within the contexts of family, school, community, and society, showing how they re/organize in response to specific historical and sociopolitical circumstances. The microinteractions between and among characters reveal how they create and recreate culture. The analyses demonstrate that culture is complex and socially constructed; race, class, and gender re/organize family lives and communities; and genres, characters, and story closures are socially made.

The Social Construction of Culture

The text collections permitted us entry into many cultural experiences. Our analyses of the text collections illustrate the complexities of culture by connecting them to the power relations of class, gender, and race. Reading power expands our understanding of the core dimensions of culture (Dirks, Eley & Ortner, 1994) in the following ways:

- from culture as a shared experience to one that is conflictual and shaped by the power relations of gender, race, and class;
- from culture as a timeless entity to a historically constituted [dynamic] experience; and
- from culture possessing "relative coherence and internal consistency" to "culture as multiple discourses, occasionally coming together in large systemic configuration [e.g., Gee's Discourse with a Big 'D'], but more often coexisting within dynamic fields of interaction and conflict."

(Dirks, Eley & Ortner, 1994: 3–6)

Culture is historically a complex web of power relations enacted at the individual, group, and institutional levels. Critical multicultural analysis of the text collections demonstrates how culture is socially made through genres, story closures, the social processes (responses and re-organizations) among the characters, and books' focalization. Bronwyn Davies (1993/2003) states:

> Poststructuralist theory argues that people are not *socialised* into the social world, but that they go through a process of *subjectification*.

In socialization theory, the focus is on the process of shaping the individual that is undertaken by others. In poststructuralist theory the focus is on the way each person actively takes up the discourses through which they and others speak/write the world into existence *as if they were their own*. Through those discourses they are made speaking subjects at the same time as they are subjected to the constitutive force of those discourses.

(Davies, 1993/2003: 13–14)

People are defined in relation to other people: discourses are always defined in relation to other discourses. Critical multicultural analysis is an examination of the process of "doing" society, and in this doing or participation, everyone is an active partner in the "process of subjectification." The text collections show that adults, young adults, and children are social and political beings, capable of resisting and taking collective action for social change, as well as dominating and colluding with dominant ideologies and practices. The microinteractions among story characters demonstrate them acting and reacting to each other, constructing and reconstructing the worlds in which they live. They are complex actors, utilizing their cultural, linguistic, sociopolitical, and economic capital to create new social relationships and possibilities, and to recreate culture. A complex view of culture and identity shows how these processes are inextricably linked and socially constructed.

The Social Construction of Class, Race, and Gender

The text collections function as genealogies of multiculturalism and power. The power relations of class, race, and gender are implicated in the construction of cultural experiences. In the text collections, class relations are everywhere and expressed in gendered and raced ways. Class describes multiple social relations and experiences, re/organizing family and community structures and responses. In many cases, race and class discourses are inseparable and interdiscursive, that is, they draw on each other. Racism and classism form intergroup and intragroup power relations. There are numerous manifestations of racism, many driven by economic oppression. Reading class shows the deeper dimensions of racism and sexism.

The Social Construction of Genres, Characters, and Story Closures

Genres exist in relation to other genres (Bakhtin, 1986; Todorov, 2000). Many of the children's books that we analyzed are hybrid genres. Genres are social constructs that can become historical evidence and "cultural archives" (Leitch, 1991). They are phenomena of culture and history.

The social identities of the focalizer shape the perspective of the story because perception is relational; it is bound up in the social processes of race, class, and gender and shapes how the reader "sees" the story. For example, in the Mexican American migrant farmworker collection, the Chicana perspective brings the reader up close to the gender roles of women in the stories and interrogates them.

The story closure shapes the meaning of the story. Open story closures invite questioning, where fixed endings confirm the ideology reflected in the text. Historical and sociopolitical conditions are the sources for the plot. Critical multicultural analysis has sociopolitical and pedagogical implications.

The Sociopolitical Implications of Critical Multicultural Analysis

In the old days, coal miners often carried a canary with them into the mine to alert them of danger ahead. If the canary collapsed along the way, this would warn the miners of the presence of poisonous gases. Race is the miner's canary (Guinier & Torres, 2002) and class is the noxious gas. Lani Guinier and Gerald Torres (2002: 12) maintain that the canary is "diagnostic, signaling the need for more systemic critique." Reading children's literature through a critical multicultural lens provides a space to analyze how culture and power are inextricably tied. Race, class, and gender are social arrangements that work together and form hierarchical arrangements of social power.

Critical multicultural analysis shows how power is exercised by examining the microinteractions among characters. As readers we can locate power and envision "local democracies" through these analyses. Children's literature is ethnography (Greene, 1988; Ortner, 1991): It offers the reader great cultural/power detail through the social processes experienced by the characters, providing windows into society. Dominant ideologies are imbued in their construction through discourse.

Children's literature puts a human face on sociopolitical circumstances and invites readers to consider in which ways they are implicated in coercive power relations. Readers can consider in what ways they can resist classist/racist ideologies and participate in collaborative power. Children's literature can play a role in informing readers about specific cultural experiences, as well as show how race, class, and gender function together. The texts provide a vantage point to understand social and cultural conditions, and to read beyond the texts. Critical multicultural analysis demonstrates that readers are active in creating our society, and readers are active in creating who they are.

Reading class and its raced and gendered manifestations can lead readers to understanding classism across culture and consider re/organizing across these social lines (Collins, 2000; hooks, 2000). As readers, we can also learn to read along the continuum of how power is exercised. People exercise power according to their perceived place in the world. We can deconstruct reading subject positions offered by the text by reconstructing how power is exercised.

Authors and illustrators have the power to use the transformative nature of art. In other words, although authors are shaped by discourses, they are also in a position to shape discourses. Davies (1993: 197) asserts that "Until we have invented new storylines, new discourses, we are still enmeshed in the old. And even when we invent the new, the old can still claim us, draw us in with their familiarity and the hooks of our old and current unsatisfied desires." If authors and illustrators embrace the power of art and think about the choices they make as they construct a story, the construction of the literary text can invite the reader to see a deeper view of reality that is often masked by prevailing ideologies and the text's aesthetic appeal. Eagleton (1976: 18) maintains: "Authentic art always transcends the ideological limits of its time, yielding us insight into the realities which ideology hides from view." According to John Steinbeck, a writer's responsibility is to "expos[e] our many grievous faults and failures, with dredging up to the light our dark and dangerous dreams, for the purpose of improvement" as well as "to declare and to celebrate [humans'] proven capacity for greatness of heart and spirit" (Reef, 1996: 136). Storylines can offer alternative ways of being in the world.

Authors can explore the narrative strategies available in constructing their stories and think about which narrative structures and focalizers (character perspectives) invite social critique and offer other possibilities for re/organizing how we live as a society. Sociopolitical imagination takes into account the instability of identity, both individual and cultural, and the power structures in which we reside. This kind of writing situates texts within the discursive fields that create us as much as we can them; these narrative strategies, including open story closures, create spaces for deconstruction and reconstruction.

Illustrators can experiment with different ways of rendering the cultural experience described in the text. As our analyses demonstrate, color, line, and the spatial position of the characters shape the reader's view of the events depicted. Illustrators can create images that challenge the text and create a dialogic, unsettling dominant ideologies.

We agree with James Gee (1999: 1) that it is imperative that we study "how the details of language get recruited, 'on site,' to 'pull off' specific social activities and social identities ('memberships' in various social groups, cultures, and institutions). In the process, we will see that language-in-use is everywhere and always 'political'." He defines politics as "anything and anyplace where human social interactions and relationships have implications for how 'social goods' are or ought to be distributed ... 'social' [he] means anything that a group of people believes to be a source of power, status, or worth" (Gee, 1999: 2). The distribution of social goods is raced, classed, and gendered. These power relations are naturalized and normalized, making them invisible and commonsensical.

Critical multicultural analysis can help people re/organize across social lines and link up with people and groups who share a commitment to social justice. Like Gee (1999), we believe that one of the goals of education should be to help children map out the dominant ideologies that have been instrumental in perpetuating social inequities and distributing power in the United States. Critical multicultural analysis helps us map out dominant discourses, the power matrix, and make informed decisions about whether we want to interrupt these social processes or perpetuate them with how we exercise power in our daily lives. It deepens our understanding of these power relations and helps us to become conscious that everything we do is political because it involves and affects other people.

People are forever changed when they become aware or make connections with new understandings. Paulo Freire (1991) maintains:

> Reading the world always precedes reading the word, and reading the word implies continually reading the world. As I suggested earlier, this movement from the world to the word and from the word to the world is always present; even the spoken word flows from our reading of the world. In a way, however, we can go further, and say that reading the word is not preceded merely by reading the world, but by a certain form of *writing* it or *re-writing* it, that is, of transforming it by means of conscious practical work. For me, this dynamic movement is central to the literacy process.
>
> (Freire, 1991: 144)

Children learn to question the status quo and not to merely master particular discourse practices, but to analyze and resist unequal power relations. Critical pedagogies across the grades can play a key part in this work.

The Pedagogical Implications of Critical Multicultural Analysis

The pedagogical implications have sociopolitical consequence. Language is inherently ideological and all literature is a historical and cultural product. Keeping the history of underrepresentation in children's literature at the center of literacies teaching is imperative. Teachers should strive to have a culturally diverse collection of books in their classroom libraries. Multiple books about a cultural experience offer a more complex picture of the cultural group, that is, children's literature as ethnography provides detailed descriptions and diverse perspectives of a situation or condition. Critical multicultural teachers constantly reconsider how they teach speaking, listening, writing, reading, representing, and viewing, and apply literary study as a tool for social change and justice.

What to Read

The research literature on what is currently known as multicultural children's literature outlines the benefits of literature that validates the lived experiences of children, recognizes social difference, and contributes to the development of empathy in children and respect and understanding between and among cultures (Duren, 2000; Hinton-Johnson, 2002; Kauffman & Short, 2001; MacPhee, 1997; Norton, 1990; Singer & Smith, 2003). The present corpus of children's literature must be transformed into a literature that represents the cultural diversity of the United States; otherwise, it will empower only a few children.

First and foremost, readers need to see themselves mirrored in books since, "from reading stories about their own culture, children have opportunities to see how others go through experiences similar to theirs, develop strategies to [name and negotiate] issues in their [lives], and identify themselves with their inherited culture" (Lu, 1998: 2). However, it is identification through representation, the connecting with similar experience, that children can find spaces to name the manifestations of power in their own lives (Cai, 2008). Representation leads to the negotiation of identity. As teachers, we cannot assume that there is a complete alignment between the reader and the cultural representation (Dudley-Marling, 2003). A variety of texts representing the same cultural experience allows children choices for "reading who they are." In addition, readers need to go beyond themselves to images, ideas, and cultures that are outside their daily realities and vicariously experience another culture. These texts expand children's understanding of the world, opening the window to a panoramic view of society.

The door represents the reader's critical engagement with the ideologies of class, race, and gender imbedded in the literature. Mirrors reflect our language use and windows afford expanses to new understandings, whereas doors invite action. We reclaim these metaphors because of their prolific use in the field, and because metaphors are useful for deconstructing old understandings and assumptions and constructing new knowledge (Lakoff & Johnson, 1980).

Texts are sites for negotiation. The more we know, the more we are able to interrogate texts. The more we are exposed to multiple experiences, the more are able to juxtapose what we have lived and read against those experiences. One text and one author cannot do it all; it is the reading of multiple texts and the juxtaposition of these texts against lived experience and secondary sources that is central. Children's literature can redress injustice as much as reflect it. It can inspire readers to reflect on their lived experience, re-imagine socially just worlds, provide new ways of exercising power, and offer tools for building cultural and historical understanding.

Examining class, race, and gender cross-culturally can be transformative because it helps to demonstrate how class and race connect cultural experience across different historical and sociopolitical circumstances. Cross-cultural perspectives show how cultures are not bounded but are porous and dynamic. All literature can lead to critical multicultural investigations. However, we need to consider the classroom diet of children's literature. Variety is paramount.

While books that showcase similar cross-cultural experiences ("we are all the same" stories), what we have come to call cultural catalogs (e.g., Ann Morris's *Houses and Homes* or Lori Mitchell's *Different Just Like Me*), demonstrate similarities across cultures, portraying universality as a human condition and reducing diversity to simplistic terms. The cultural catalogs speak to common human experience, connections that are worthy of consideration, but it is dangerous to begin and end there. The treatment of universal themes tends to oversimplify diversity and reduce it to sameness, obfuscating the social construction of difference, privilege, and power.

Books with social justice as a theme focus on the explicitly rendered sociopolitical issues among individuals, communities, and society. Proponents of this approach select books that have overtly political messages and stimulate conversations with readers about their implications (Harste, Leland, Lewison, Ociepka, & Vasque, 2000). These texts have storylines that reflect the explicit exercise of coercive power and invite critiquing of the microinteractions among characters, reconstructing them toward collaborative power.

Herb Kohl (1995) calls for radical literature. Literature with democratic plots, while instructive, also needs to be problematized. These books are not free of dominant ideologies. While the text may focus on democratic reading subject positions (exercise of collaborative power), readers must examine the multiple ways characters exercise power throughout the story. Radical literature, among other attributes, offers representations of how groups of people organize for social action. However, few of these storylines are available. *A Chair for My Mother*, by Vera B. Williams, and *Magical*

Hands, by Marjorie Barker, are examples of such books; however, regrettably, few of these stories are available.

More recently, the metafictive devices of postmodern texts (i.e., texts that are self-conscious about their construction) purport to lead children to critical reading (Goldstone, 2004). The teaching of postmodern texts is grounded by genre studies. The textual features are not immune to the nexus of language and power. The metafictive devices shape how the story gets told. For example, while *Voices in the Park*, by Anthony Browne, offers multiple class perspectives on the same event, its images echo racialized stereotypes. All texts, including postmodern picture books, cultural catalogs, social justice theme books, and radical literature, need to be problematized. They do not guarantee critical responses on the part of readers. These texts do not necessarily foster critical reading: Teachers need to be active in demonstrating how to read all books critically and multiculturally.

Many of these texts are considered controversial and cannot be found in the canon of the basal reader. Controversial storylines recognize diversity, invoke critique, and invite dialogue. All children's books are cultural products and require critical analysis. Traditionally, adults and children have been socialized to read in particular ways within school settings. These controversial texts might disrupt conventional school literacies practices (i.e., how reading is taught and which texts are used in schools), and replace them with analytical conversations that will enhance the children's abilities to be independent and discerning readers.

How to Read

A number of researchers concur that teachers avoid "multicultural children's literature" because they are unprepared and lack the background and knowledge to feel comfortable engaging in teaching these texts (Cooper & Floyd, 2002; Davis, Brown, Liedel-Rice, & Soeder, 2005; Harris & Willis, 2003; Hinton-Johnson, 2002; Jenkins, 1999). The majority of the teaching force is White, middle-class women who are inexperienced with addressing the complexities of power imbued in these texts. But it is key to awaken a sense of inquiry in teachers who are willing to critically engage with this analytical approach.

Examining and reconsidering the teaching practices of reading is an entry point into critical multicultural analysis. Teaching is a text that can be analyzed. What assumptions about reading, writing, literature, and culture do we hold? All books are culturally coded. A passive stance, that is, one that accepts the authors' words and illustrators' images unquestioningly, is not neutral. It maintains the status quo and the explicit messages of the author and/or illustrator, and usurps power from the individual reader as well as the community of readers. Critical multicultural investigations of children's literature focus on the analysis of power relations as factors in the trends of what gets written and illustrated and what gets published.

Critical multicultural analysis comes from the same family as critical literacies. The "critical" in critical multicultural analysis means keeping the power relations of class, race, and gender at the center of our investigations of children's literature, thus connecting our reading to sociopolitical and economic justice. "Multicultural" signals the diverse historical and cultural experiences within these power relations. Critical multicultural analysis requires several shifts in the conventional thinking about reading:

- from reader-response reading practices connecting reading to the reader and beyond to sociopolitical structures, recursively;
- from viewing meaning as reflected or locked in the text to recognizing reading comprehension as intertextual processes, with meaning emerging and changing; and,
- from genre studies to examining how genres are historically, socially, and discursively constructed and shape how stories get told.

How texts are constructed (e.g., generic conventions, focalization, and story closure) positions readers to produce particular meanings. Reading children's books alongside each other and with secondary sources helps readers resist the reading subject positions constructed by the text and create alternative or resistant readings that support collective worldviews. Critical multicultural analysis offers possibilities for taking up different reading subject positions.

The reading subject positions offered by a critical multicultural analysis are constructed intertextually, by reading the narrative against particular literary and nonliterary texts, and generic considerations. Through these dialogic strategies, the reader challenges class, gender, and race ideologies imbedded in the text, thus exposing the processes whereby these worldviews are constructed and rendered natural in texts. Thus, the meaning of texts lies within the space among texts (Bakhtin, 1981), contexts, and the reader(s). Stephens (1992) argues that ". . . in most modes of narration the representations of interaction between characters and society, whereby a character 'discovers' its [sic] own subjectivity, is reproduced on another level in the audience engagement with the text, which is largely on terms determined *by* the text" (Stephens, 1992: 63–64).

The teaching of literature should begin with social justice. If we are committed to socially just teaching, what kind of literacy practices will take us there? We concur with Nathalie Wooldridge (2001) that critical literacies practices lead to "critically reading our teaching." She offers a set of

questions that help name the sociopolitical implications of our pedagogical decisions:

- What view of knowledge do we present (e.g., who has it? where is it
found? what counts as knowledge? what/whose knowledge is seen as
valuable?)?
- How else might the lesson have been taught/the aims achieved?
- How do we construct ourselves as teacher in the lesson (e.g., as source
of knowledge, as person who controls?)? How are the students constructed (e.g., as passive recipients, as having something done to
them?)? What/whose views do we present, and therefore, whose views
are not represented or being seen?
- What are the students learning besides particular content? (e.g.,
about learning, the uses of literacy, what it is to be a student, [what it
is to be a teacher], what it is to be poor/[girl/boy/person of color]?)

(Wooldridge, 1991: 267)

We would add: What texts and reading practices do we privilege in our
classrooms? What kind of citizens are our literacy practices constructing?
How teachers choose to teach children how to read children's literature
will shape the reading subject positions available to them as well as their
identity formation.

Critical multicultural analysis of children's literature creates a site to
consider subject positions of dehumanization, collusion, resistance, and
agency as they are enacted among characters. Critical multicultural analysis as collaborative practice through dialogue within text circles allows
histories and discourses to bump against each other and scaffold children's understanding of the power relations. While analyzing multiculturalism through children's literature will not solve social injustice, teachers as
facilitators of these critical and collaborative processes help children to
engage with texts at a deeper level, contributing to their overall literacy
learning (Dietrich & Ralph, 1995; Harris & Willis, 2003; Singer & Smith,
2003) and understanding of themselves and the world (Moller, 2002;
Moller & Allen, 2000).

Many teachers are inexperienced with the multiculturalism rendered in
children's literature as well as the power relations of class, race, and gender.
Because many teachers lack the background knowledge to feel comfortable
in engaging with power, they resist teaching literature that takes them
outside their cultural experience (Wollman-Bonilla, 1998). Book clubs
(Kooy, 2007; Smith & Strickland, 2001) can create spaces for teachers to
experience children's literature that might be unfamiliar, and to develop
background knowledge and language to read and teach literature critically
and multiculturally.

Text Circles – Harvey Daniels (2006) challenges teachers to problematize the literature circle structure in the language arts curriculum. He recommends that teachers reconsider the circle roles, consider the explicit teaching of reading strategies and guide the children's social skills, as well as diversify the texts by bringing in nonfiction. We propose practicing the reading of multiple texts (including everyday texts) alongside each other. Critical multicultural analysis of children's literature creates spaces for teachers and students, for children to be teachers and for teachers to be learners. Children teach about issues that are relevant to them, providing that they volunteer to do so. Certainly, their contributions to dialogues around literature will expand.

Multiple Texts and Multimodalities – Everyday texts, like children's literature, are socially constructed and are imbued with dominant worldviews. Using these texts alongside children's literature will guide children's critical analysis. Because juxtaposing texts helps amplify ideologies in texts and images responding to children's books through multimodalities of writing, drama, visual arts, and digital technologies creates opportunities for children to reconstruct texts (Lotherington, 2006; Peterson, Booth & Jupiter, 2009).

Cultural Themes – It is useful for teachers and children to look at the representation of culturally specific themes (e.g., literacy and particular cultural group experience) over time to determine by critical analysis what different meanings and social connotations adhere to the texts above and beyond their language and illustrations. Consider Mitzi Myers' (1988: 42) provocative question: "What kinds of cultural statements and questions is the work responding to?" For example, the perceptions and realities of working people are rarely explored in children's literature, and if so, these depictions of labor are "downplayed, camouflaged, obscured, and its significance distorted" (Nikolajeva, 2002: 307). Children can examine work as a cultural theme and take notice of the working conditions of the families as well as how characters exercise power in microinteractions related to their work.

Author Study – The literacy practice of author study can serve as a laboratory. It can refute the notion that the author is the only source of meaning. A critical multicultural analysis of an author's collection of books locates the discursive threads that are contained in the author's writings. The multiple texts afford the opportunity to examine themes, endings, characters, and ideologies. Foucault (1984) maintains that the "author-function" points to our society's fixation with and fear of the "proliferation of meaning," that is, we associate single meanings with single texts.

If we consider the author as an "ideological figure," as Foucault recommends, the reader can delve deeper into the text and investigate how discourses circulate in the texts. Multiple discourses become apparent and reading subject positions are located.

Text Production – Children can write their own stories as ways of talking back to publishers. These stories can be sites for further deconstruction of the discourses that are responsible for constituting who they are as people. In doing so, these stories become evidence of the dominant discourses circulating in their writing. Bronwyn Davies (2000: 144) proposes: "The texts of [children's] own speaking and writing [and representing] can then become the material that they use to acquire the skills of deconstruction." Text production can make visible the discursive practices that are responsible for constituting us. Inviting children to write stories and publish books is a way to "catch language in the act of shaping subjectivities" (Davies, 2000: 142). At the same time, children possess the authority to reflect on these shapings of self, and implore them to respeak, rewrite, and reread themselves and their world.

Subjectivity is a process of becoming. Social transformation can only occur when people develop a critical consciousness of power relations and possibilities for changing or undoing hierarchical social arrangements. Critical multicultural analysis provides a site for deconstruction and reconstruction. This site offers readers cognitive and social flexibility in how readers perceive the world, by questioning and theorizing, and taking up collectively minded worldviews. It is reading literature as a process, with a historical and sociopolitical imagination. It is catching language in the process of reproducing power relations, summoning readers who can be and not be in the world. Our language needs respeaking and rewriting, which will offer new possibilities for selfhood and new ways of being in the world. Critical multicultural analysis can contribute to this process.

We advocate for reading that awakens children to the sociopolitical context of the world. This kind of reading connects books to lived experience and invites readers to develop empathy for others. The practice of locating cultural themes becomes an entry point for considering the social construction of cultural practice and experience. Envisioning how power affects the reader and others and incorporating democratic participation leads to the consistent pattern of reading as if it mattered.

Social transformation is not an armchair activity. Antonia Darder and Gerald Torres (1999: 188) are quick to add that a shift in "theoretical language will not necessarily alter power relations in any given society" but it can give us tools for analyzing "how power is practiced and maintained."

Reading with a critical multicultural lens creates a space for resocializing for social justice. Apprenticing through language and literacies practices are ways we can re-imagine ourselves, our society. Real structural change also needs to take place and as citizens of a democracy we must examine how we help maintain and perpetuate dominant ideologies that are realized in institutional policies and everyday practice. Democracy only exists through citizen participation. Democracy, by definition, cannot mean merely that schools prepare children for the workforce (Gramsci, 2000). It must mean that every "citizen" learns to participate locally, nationally, and globally. Schools can offer the conditions for children to learn democratic participation. Literacy practices, like critical multicultural analysis of children's literature, can contribute to this process.

Classroom Applications

- Replicate with your students Shannon's (1986) study of "Children's Choices" published every October in *The Reading Teacher* by conducting a critical multicultural analysis of the ways the protagonists of select texts exercise coercive and/or collaborative power. What ideologies are imbedded in these texts that are children's favorites?
- Invite children to write their own stories as ways of talking back at the publishing world as well as a way of becoming more conscious of how they use language. Children's stories can be sites for deconstruction and reconstruction. Consider multiple genres for this work.

Recommendations for Classroom Research

- Take stock of your own literacy experiences. In what ways were you invited to read children's literature when you were an elementary school and high school, and college student? What kind of texts were used within these contexts? What are the prevalent practices that you notice across your literacy history?
- In what ways do book awards recognize texts produced by writers and artists from different cultural communities? In what ways do these awards as well as national and international book awards shape your book selection?
- Reconsider critical multicultural analysis and use your classroom research to focus and refocus our multi-layered lens.
- What happens when children are invited to conduct critical multicultural analysis of class, race, and gender ideologies as rendered in texts independently and collaboratively? Analyze children's reading

response journals against classroom dialogue (e.g., large and small group). Examine your participation on paper and in class. What roles does your participation construct for you?

Suggestions for Further Reading

Ada, Alma Flor & Campoy, F. Isabel. (2004). *Authors in the classroom: A transformative education process.* Boston: Pearson/Allyn and Bacon.

Bomer, Randy & Bomer, Katherine. (2001). *For a better world: Reading and writing for social action.* Portsmouth, NH: Heinemann.

Botelho, Maria José, Turner, Vionette & Wright, Mary. (2006). We have stories to tell: Gathering and publishing stories in a Puerto Rican community. *School Talk,* 11(4), 2–3.

Christensen, Linda. (2000). *Reading, writing, and rising up: Teaching about social justice and the power of the written word.* Rethinking Schools Ltd.

Comber, Barbara. (2006). Critical literacy educators at work: Examining dispositions, discursive resources and repertoires of practice. In Karyn Cooper & Robert White (Eds.), *The practical critical educator: Critical inquiry and educational practice* (pp. 51–65). Dordrecht, The Netherlands: Springer.

Comber, Barbara & Nixon, Helen. (2005). Children reread and rewrite their local neighborhoods: Critical literacies and identity work. In Janet Evans (Ed.), *Literacy moves on: Popular culture, new technologies, and critical literacy in the elementary classroom.* Portsmouth, NH: Heinemann.

Comber, Barbara & Simpson, Anne. (Eds.). (2001). *Negotiating critical literacies in classrooms.* Mahwah, NJ: Lawrence Erlbaum Associates.

Compton-Lilly, Catherine. (2004). *Confronting racism, poverty, and power: Classroom strategies to change the world.* Portsmouth, NH: Heinemann.

Cummins, J. (2004). Multiliteracies pedagogy and the role of identity texts. In K. Leithwood, P. McAdie, N. Bascia, & A. Rodigue (Eds.). *Teaching for deep understanding: Towards the Ontario curriculum that we need.* Toronto: OISE/UT and the Elementary Federation of Teachers of Ontario.

Cummins, Jim, Brown, Kristin & Sayers, Dennis. (2007). *Literacy, technology, and diversity: Teaching for success in changing times.* Pearson/Allyn and Bacon.

Dudley-Marling, Curt. (2003). "I'm not from Pakistan": Multicultural literature and the problem of representation. In D. L. Fox & K. G. Short (Eds.), *Stories matter: The complexity of cultural authenticity in children's literature.* Urbana, IL: NCTE.

Grobman, Laurie. (2007). *Multicultural hybridity: Transforming American literary scholarship & pedagogy.* Urbana, IL: National Council of Teachers of English.

Heffernan, Lee. (2004). *Critical literacy and writer's workshop: Bringing purpose and passion to student writing.* Newark, DE: International Reading Association.

Kamler, Barbara. (2001). Relocating voice and transformation. In *Relocating the personal: A critical writing pedagogy.* New York: State University of New York Press.

Kist, William. (2005). *New literacies in action: Teaching and learning in multiple media.* New York: Teachers College Press.

Knobel, Michele & Healy, Annah. (Eds.). (1998). *Critical literacies in the primary classroom.* Australia: Primary English Teaching Association.

McLaughlin, Maureen & Glenn L. DeVoogd. (2004). Critical literacy as comprehension: Expanding reader response. *Journal of Adolescent & Adult Literacy,* 48(1), 52–62.

McLaughlin, Maureen & Glenn L. DeVoogd. (2004). *Critical literacy: Enhancing students' comprehension of text.* New York: Scholastic.

Mellor, Bronwyn & Patterson, Annette. (2001). *Investigating texts: Analyzing fiction and nonfiction in high school.* Urbana, IL: National Council of Teachers of English.

Mellor, Bronwyn, Patterson, Annette & O'Neill, Marnie. (2000). *Reading fiction: Applying literary theory to short stories.* Urbana, IL: National Council of Teachers of English.

Mellor, Bronwyn, Patterson, Annette & O'Neill, Marnie. (2000). *Reading stories: Activities and texts for critical readings*. Urbana, IL: National Council of Teachers of English.

Moon, Brian. (2000). *Studying literature: New approaches to poetry and fiction*. Urbana, IL: National Council of Teachers of English.

Nieto, Sonia & Bode, Patty. (2008). *Affirming diversity: The sociopolitical context of multicultural education* (5th edition). Boston: Pearson/Allyn and Bacon.

Pahl, Kate & Jennifer Rowsell. (2005). *Literacy and education: Understanding the New Literacy Studies in the classroom*. Paul Chapman Publishers.

Peterson, Shelley Stagg, Booth, David & Jupiter, Carol. (2009). *Plugged-in literature: Technology and children's literature in classrooms*. Winnipeg: Portage & Main Press.

Schecter, Sandra R. & Cummins, Jim. (Eds.). *Multilingual education in practice: Using diversity as a resource*. Portsmouth, NH: Heinemann.

Serafini, Frank. (2003). Informing our practices: Modernist, transactional, and critical perspectives on children's literature and reading instruction. Retrieved on June 12, 2004, from www.readingonline.org.

Vasquez, Vivian. (2004). *Negotiating critical literacies with young children*. Mahwah, NJ: Lawrence Erlbaum Associates.

Vasquez, Vivian et al. (2003). *Getting beyond "I like the book": Creating space for critical literacy in K-6 classrooms*. Newark, DE: International Reading Association.

Wilson, Lorraine. (2002). *Reading to live: How to teach reading for today's world*. Portsmouth, NH: Heinemann.

Wilson, Lorraine. (2006). *Writing to live: How to teach writing for today's world*. Portsmouth, NH: Heinemann.

References

Children's Literature

Barker, Marjorie. (1989). *Magical hands*. Illustrated by Yoshi. Saxonville, MA: Picture Book Studio.

Browne, Anthony. (1998). *Voices in the park*. Illustrated by author. New York: DK Publishers.

Mitchell, Lori. (2001). *Different just like me*. Cambridge, MA: Charlesbridge Publishing.

Morris, Ann. (1992). *Houses and homes*. Photography by author. New York: Lothrop & Shepard Books.

Williams, Vera B. (1992). *A chair for my mother*. Illustrated by author. New York: Greenwillow.

Secondary Sources

Bakhtin, Michel M. (1981). Discourse in the novel. In M. Holquist (Ed., Trans.), *The dialogic imagination: Four essays* (C. Emerson, Trans., pp. 259–422). Austin: University of Texas Press.

Bakhtin, Michel M. (1986). The problem of speech genres. In C. Emerson & M. Holquist (Eds.), *Speech genres and other late essays* (V. W. McGee, Trans., pp. 60–102). Austin: University of Texas Press.

Cai, Mingshui. (2008). Transactional theory and the study of multicultural literature. *Language Arts*, 85(3), 212–220.

Collins, Patricia Hill. (2000). Toward a new vision: Race, class, and gender as categories of analysis and connection. In M. Adams, W. J. Blumenfeld, R. Castañeda, H. W. Hackman, M. L. Peters, & X. Zúñiga (Eds.), *Readings for diversity and social justice* (pp. 457–462). New York: Routledge.

Cooper, Patricia M. & Floyd, Connie. (2002). White teachers and multicultural children's literature: Contradictions and inhibitions. *NCTE 2002 Midwinter Research Conference*. (pp. 1–9).

Daniels, Harvey. (2006). What's the next big thing with literature circles? *Voices in the Middle,* 13(4), 10–15.

Darder, Antonia. (2002). *Reinventing Paulo Freire: A pedagogy of love.* Boulder, CO: Westview.

Darder, Antonia & Torres, Rodolfo D. (1999). Shattering the "race" lens: Toward a critical theory of racism. In R. H. Tai & M. L. Kenyatta, (Eds.), *Critical ethnicity: Countering the waves of identity politics* (pp. 173–192). New York: Rowman & Littlefield.

Davies, Bronwyn. (1993). *Shards of glass: Children reading and writing beyond gendered identities.* Cresskill, NJ: Hampton.

Davies, Brownyn. (1993/2003). *Shards of glass: Children reading and writing beyond gendered identities* (revised edition). Cresskill, NJ: Hampton.

Davies, Bronwyn. (2000). *A body of writing: 1990–1999.* Walnut Creek, CA: AltaMira Press.

Davis, Kathryn, L., Brown, Bernice, G., Liedel-Rice, Anne, & Soeder, Pamela. (2005). Experiencing diversity through children's multicultural literature. *Kappa Delta Phi Record.* 41(4), 176–179.

Dietrich, Deborah & Ralph, Kathleen S. (1995). Crossing borders: multicultural literature in the classroom. *The Journal of Educational Issues of Language Minority Students.* 15, 1–7.

Dirks, Nicholas B., Eley, Geoff & Ortner, Sherry B. (1994). Introduction. In N. B. Dirks, G. Eley, & S. B. Ortner (Eds.), *Culture/power/history: A reader in contemporary social theory* (pp. 3–45). Princeton, NJ: Princeton University Press.

Dudley-Marling, Curt. (2003). "I'm not from Pakistan": Multicultural Literature and the problem of representation. In D. L. Fox & K. G. Short (Eds.), *Stories matter: The complexity of cultural authenticity in children's literature.* Urbana, IL: National Council of Teacher of English.

Duren, Emma Buffington. (2000). Critical multiculturalism and racism in children's literature. *Multicultural Education.* 7(3), 16–20.

Eagleton, Terry. (1976). *Marxism and literary criticism.* Berkeley: University of California Press.

Foucault, Michel. (1984). What is an author? In P. Rabinow (Ed.), *The Foucault reader* (pp. 101–120). New York: Pantheon Books.

Freire, P. (1991). The importance of the act of reading. In C. Mitchell & K. Weiler, *Rewriting literacy: Culture and the discourse of the Other.* Westport, CT: Bergin & Garvey.

Gee, James Paul. (1999). *An introduction to discourse analysis: Theory and method.* New York: Routledge.

Goldstone, Bette P. (2004). Postmodern picture books: A new subgenre. *Language Arts,* 81(3), 196–204.

Gramsci, Antonio. (2000). *The Antonio Gramsci reader: Selected writings 1916–1935* (D. Forgacs, Ed.). New York: New York University Press.

Greene, Maxine. (1988). Qualitative research and the uses of literature. In R. R. Sherman & R. B. Webb (Eds.), *Qualitative research in education: Focus and methods* (pp. 175–189). London: The Falmer Press.

Guinier, Lani & Torres, Gerald. (2002). *The miner's canary: Enlisting race, resisting power, transforming democracy.* Cambridge, MA: Harvard University Press.

Harris, Violet J. & Willis, Arlette I. (2003). Multiculturalism, literature, and curriculum issues. In J. Flood, D. Lapp, J. R. Squire, & J. M. Jensen (Eds.), *Handbook of research on teaching the English language arts.* (2nd ed., pp. 825–834). Mahwah, NJ: Erlbaum Associates.

Harste, J.C., Leland, C., Lewison, M., Ociepka, A., & Vasquez, V. (2000). Supporting critical conversations in classrooms. In K. M. Pierce (Ed.), *Adventuring with books* (pp. 507–512). Urbana, IL: National Council of Teachers of English.

Hinton-Johnson, Kaa Vonia. (2002). In the process of becoming multicultural: reflections of a first year teacher. *The New Advocate.* 15, (4), 309–313.

hooks, bell. (2000). *Where we stand: Class matters.* New York: Routledge.

Jenkins, Esther. (1999). Multi-ethnic literature: promise and problems. *Elementary English*, 50(5), 693–699.

Kauffman, Gloria & Short, Kathy. (2001). Talking about books: critical conversations about identity. *Language Arts*, 78(3), 279–286.

Kohl, Herbert. (1995). A plea for radical children's literature. In *Should we burn Babar? Essays on children's literature and the power of stories* (pp. 57–93). New York: The New Press.

Kooy, Mary. (2007). *Telling stories in book clubs: Women teachers and professional development*. Dordrecht, The Netherlands: Springer.

Lakoff, George & Johnson, Mark. (1980). *Metaphors we live by*. Chicago: University of Chicago Press.

Leitch, Vincent B. (1991). (De)Coding (generic) discourse. *Genre*, 24(1), 83–98.

Lotherington, Heather & Chow, S. (2006). Rewriting "Goldilocks" in the urban, multicultural elementary school. *The Reading Teacher*, 60(3).

Lu, Mei-Yu. (1998). Multicultural children's literature in the elementary classroom. ERIC Clearinghouse on Reading, English, and Communication Skills ED 423552 (p. 1–5).

MacPhee, Joyce S. (1997). That's not fair! A white teacher reports on white first graders' responses to multicultural literature. *Language Arts*, 74(1), 33–40.

Moller, Karla, (2002). Providing support for dialogue in literature discussions about social justice. *Language Arts*, 79(6), 467–477.

Moller, Karla, J., & Allen, JoBeth. (2000). Connecting, resisting, and searching for safer places: Students respond to Mildred Taylor's *The Friendship*. *Journal of Literacy Research*, 32(2), 145–186.

Myers, Mitzi. (1988). Missed opportunities and critical malpractice: New historicism and children's literature. *Children's Literature Association Quarterly*, 13(1), 41–43.

Nikolajeva, Maria. (2002). "A dream of complete idleness": Depiction of labor in children's fiction. *The Lion and the Unicorn*, 26(3), 305–321.

Norton, Donna. (1990). Teaching multicultural literature in the reading curriculum. *The Reading Teacher*, 44(1), 28–40.

Ortner, Sherry. (1991). Reading America: Preliminary notes on class and culture. In *Recapturing Anthropology*. Santa Fe, NM: School of American Research Press.

Peterson, Shelley Stagg, Booth, David & Jupiter, Carol. (2009). *Plugged-in literature: Technology and children's literature in classrooms*. Winnipeg: Portage & Main Press.

Reef, (1996). Reef, Catherine. (1996). *John Steinbeck*. New York: Clarion Books.

Singer, Judith & Smith, Sally. (2003). The potential of multicultural literature: changing understanding of self and others. *Multicultural Perspectives*, 5(2), 17–23.

Smith, Michael, W., & Stickland, Dorothy, S. (2001). Complements or conflicts: conceptions of discussions and multicultural literature in a teachers-as-readers discussion group. *Journal of Literacy Research*, 33(1), 137–167.

Stephens, John. (1992). Language and ideology in children's fiction. Longman.

Todorov, Tzvetan. (2000). The origins of genres. In D. Duff (Ed.), *Modern genre theory* (pp. 193–209). New York: Longman.

Wollman-Bonilla, Julie E. (1998). Outrageous viewpoints: teachers' criteria for rejecting works of children's literature. *Language Arts*, 75(4), 287–295.

Wooldridge, Nathalie. (2001). Tensions and ambiguities in critical literacy. In B. Comber & A. Simpson, *Negotiating critical literacies in classrooms* (pp. 259–270). Mahwah, NJ: Lawrence Erlbaum Associates.

Further Dialogue with Mingshui Cai, Patrick Shannon, and Junko Yokota

We are bringing together years and years of personal, professional, and academic experience with issues connected to multicultural children's literature and literacies teaching. Over the years, we have grappled with theories and practices that are aligned with socially just teaching and research. This book brings together two lived experiences in dialogue with many texts. From the first pages of this book, we invited you, the reader, to critically read our work. Because we are committed to contributing to the dialogue on the critical teaching of children's literature, we wanted to initiate a conversation with colleagues who have been engaged with these issues for many years. Mingshui Cai, Patrick Shannon, and Junko Yokota graciously accepted our invitation to participate in an e-mail dialogue over a period of two weeks, in response to Chapters 4 and 5, and to our proposal of critical multicultural analysis of children's literature. We posted our responses and reacted to each other's contributions. What follows is a negotiated version of our dialogue.

Patrick

Fourteen years ago in "I Am the Canon" (Shannon, 1994), I attempted to articulate what Maria José and Masha define as a critical multicultural lens for children's literature. My prose was clumsy, but my intent was sincere— to discuss multiple discourses and issues of power. In my work with pre-service and inservice teachers, I chose to discuss the social construction of conditions of normality in which the Other is identified. My hopes were that these teachers would see themselves as implicated in the labels of "normal" and "other" on many dimensions and recognize that the use of these labels was more a statement of power than of biological, historical or moral fact. Together, we worked (and still work) to expose privilege in its many forms, to name our shifting roles in forms of oppression, and to fight the canon (in all the texts that surround us). I hope Maria José and Masha would agree that such work could be a form of multicultural analysis.

In the United States, times are hard. The ninth ward in New Orleans is still razed—three years after Katrina. The U.S. PATRIOT Act leaves the U.S. Constitution in tatters with habeas corpus and privacy rights eviscerated. Torture is condoned. The federal government has sub-contracted for a wall to be built along the Mexican border. The occupation of Iraq is in its sixth year. The Supreme Court uses technicalities to prevent women from suing for equal pay and threaten women's right to choose. Millions of families have had their mortgages foreclosed.

Often, hard times draw hard lines between and among groups. Currently, few seem willing or able to step over these lines in order to use a critical multicultural lens to perform multicultural analysis on any texts. Perhaps it's fear or greed that keeps many from acknowledging the human connections among us all. In John Edgar Wideman's words, "We's all one person, all the same body" despite all apparent difference. Yet, we act as if neglect, surveillance, torture, exclusion, occupation, discrimination, and exploitation "by design would never happen to their [our] people." But they do happen. We are diminished as human beings regardless of whether we suffer, inflict, or stand by silently in the face of particular circumstances of hard times. We will be complicit unless we act in order to reconcile theories of recognition with theories of redistribution.

Maria José and Masha recommend critical multicultural analysis as such an act in these hard times. They present classroom practices that bring recognition of differences within investigations of power during literature studies, theorizing their work with post-structural and critical discourses. Since 1994, however, the teaching of reading has fallen on hard times as well. Government policies and reports tout the discourse of science as the answer to all questions about literacy and text, positioning all other discourses as useless at best, and harmful at worst. Science is the modern enforcer of normality as well—Hernstein and Murray's Bell Curve is also called the "normal curve". To get to critical multicultural analysis, we must address the power of science in the teaching of reading.

Mingshui

I agree that critical multicultural analysis of any literature, including multicultural literature, challenges dominant ideologies and discourses which are held as the "norm." This approach should be used in the classroom practice of teaching literature, especially what is considered the canon, the "norm" of literature, so to speak. Daniel Hade (1997) argued along the same line when he proposed that we "read multiculturally," that is, adopt a critical stance toward a text and read the signs of race, class, gender in it. My question is: If we can read any text multiculturally or do a critical multicultural analysis of it, do we still need a literary category called multicultural literature? The concept of multicultural literature seems to have been expanded and diluted to the point that it has lost its meaning. Let's put it to rest for the moment and use the term "multiethnic literature" instead. Do we still need a category of multiethnic literature? Historically, multiethnic literature has claimed a space in children's literature for the marginalized ethnic groups, especially people of color. It has been a vehicle to fight the hegemony of the dominant culture in the publication of children's literature. It embodies the dream of equity for oppressed groups. Once it came into being, however, some writers from the mainstream culture took it over and wittingly or unwittingly, smuggled their dominant discourses into it. The drawn-out insider vs. outsider debate is in essence a power struggle over the control of this niche in children's literature.

This is a battle between the dominant and dominated groups. Yes, power is a complex matrix. Many forces are playing against each other even within the same cultural group. When reflected in literature, race, class, gender, and other social political issues may play out in the same text. However, distinguishing between dominant and dominated groups does not necessarily render power relations to dualisms or mask power relations, just as distinguishing between "dominant ideologies" and "dominated ideologies," "dominant discourses" and "dominated discourses" does not lead to dualism or the cover up of complicated power relations. Within a text we may find binary oppositions between white and black, male and female, upper class and lower class. One group holds power over the other. For example, in *Esperanza Rising*, white people discriminate against Mexican immigrants, Mexican males (e.g., Esperanza's uncles) control the fate of females (e.g., Esperanza and her mother), upper class (e.g., Esperanza and her father) holds a superior position over lower class (e.g., Miguel). The issues of race, class, and gender are interlocked into a complex matrix of power relations. When we classify this book as multiethnic literature that represents the dominated racial group, we highlight the power relation between oppressing and oppressed racial groups. Anyone who reads the book will see the main conflict in the story is racial conflict. To focus on the conflict between dominant and dominated racial groups in this book, however, does not mean we will certainly ignore intra group power relations and reduce the text to racial essentialism. We just foreground the power struggle between racial groups to address an important issue in a racialized society.

Another concern with the use of "multiethnic literature" is that the term is divisive, signifying "that White is the normative term against which all other groups are defined as 'Other.'" For the oppressed groups to be recognized as "Other" is better than oblivion. Historically, oppressed groups' cultures were not recognized and almost wiped out. The stories by and through which they live (Gates, Jr.) were not heard. They have been marginalized and alienated, forced to accept the norm and assimilate into the mainstream culture. The emerging of multiethnic literature as "Other" is actually a challenge to the norm. By comparing and contrasting this literature about the Other and the literature of the dominant culture, readers may learn how ideological hegemony is challenged in the former while maintained in the latter. The term "multiethnic literature" seems divisive. But multiethnic literature does not create borders that separate; it only reveals borders that have already existed. To expose the divide is the first step to fight for recognition, understanding, acceptance, and eventually canonical status. Multiethnic literature does not just provide information about the Other (by the way, the discourse of Otherness does not necessarily imply that its cultural identity is fixed and unified; if it did, the discourse of dominant culture would also imply its identity is fixed and unified) but more importantly it also exposes "White privilege" and institutionalized racial oppression. It fosters not only "children's cultural imagination" but also "a historical and sociopolitical imagination." To interrogate literature of the dominant culture is one way to challenge its ideological hegemony; to read multiethnic literature like *Esperanza Rising* is another. The critical multicultural approach should not exclude multiethnic literature.

Again, do we need the literary category of multiethnic literature? If it is eliminated, will there be more or less books about ethnic minorities, or parallel cultures as Virginia Hamilton put it? Will the power relation in the world of children's literature be more balanced or lopsided?

Masha

I think that the key question is the one Mingshui raised: do we need the term, multicultural children's literature (or multi-ethnic children's literature)? I think we need the practice of critical multicultural analysis, partly because I think it does not require bending the language (many cultures in one book? restricted to people of color? owning a particular ideology?) but mostly because I think it's important to teach children and ourselves to look at what we read constantly with a critical eye, looking at how the text handles culture in general and specifically. I like what Rudine [Sims Bishop] has been doing with her writing: focusing specifically on literature by and about African Americans and not labeling it "multicultural." There is no ambiguity about the population, and I think that it fosters good conversation about authenticity and scholarship.

Mingshui

If we eliminate multicultural literature and multiethnic literature, should we also eliminate multicultural education and multicultural analysis? And replace them with, say, democratic or diversity education and specific critical approach to literary analysis such as post-structuralist, postcolonial, neo- Marxist, or feminist?

Masha

I think that Sonia Nieto makes a good case for preserving "multicultural education" but she recognizes that perhaps in the future, we will all be talking about critical anti-bias education and we will assume and indeed practice it without the necessity for a label. So far all of the other labels are narrow and open to even more challenges and "yah-but's."

Mingshui

What does "multicultural" really mean in all those terms? To me, terms with the epithet "multicultural" were generated to decentralize the dominant culture. Once the binary opposition of dominant culture and dominated cultures are eliminated, all those terms cease to be meaningful. But when will that be? Multiculturalism is not only about diversity but also about equality and equity. In either the implementation of multicultural education or the reading of multicultural literature, we may focus on diversity only and do not talk about power structures and struggles. The problem lies in our practice, not in the labels.

Maria José

When Masha and I first began developing our lens of critical multicultural analysis we stepped away from the pedagogical/literary category of multicultural children's literature, because it was getting in the way of us problematizing multicultural children's literature and the teaching of children's literature in general, as well as considering the complexities of power. But as we moved away from this category, it felt dangerous. The diversity of histories and cultures in our midst became obscured. We found ourselves gravitating back to the issues that multicultural children's literature represents. As you know, we argue that the history of underrepresentation in the United States needs to be at the center of this work; otherwise, critical multicultural analysis is not truly grounded within U.S. history and present sociopolitical circumstances. We agree with Stuart Hall that it is through representation that we negotiate our identities. We argue that it is through critical multicultural analysis of cultural representations that we negotiate spaces for resistance of dominant worldviews and taking action in the world.

The children's literature that finally brought me to this work was when I took stock of what was happening to Francisco Jiménez's work. His children's books were being recognized by regional and national awards. Folks were deeming them as pure representations of the Mexican American culture. As I read them, I found these practices of recognition to be problematic. He was bringing us up close to the classism and racism that Mexican American migrant farmworkers live on a daily basis. I don't deny that his work is an important contribution to the field of children's literature, and to Mexican American children's literature because he places this community on the landscape. But that's not all that Francisco is doing. He also is exposing intrafamily, intragroup, and intergroup exercise of power, complexities that were getting diluted by the prevailing definition of culture that anchors multicultural children's lilterature. Culture and power are inseparable.

Many children are underrepresented. White privilege oftentimes is conflated with class. White children (this is a gross lumping of people, just like all the other cultural labels are) who are poor also experience discrimination because they don't possess the cultural capital of the middle and upper classes. Race cannot be addressed in isolation from class. We were careful to consult with scholars of color, since we are two White women of working-class background. They argue for the examination of class and gender alongside race, showing the complex dimensions of power.

As I read Patrick's contribution, especially the third paragraph, I was reminded of Nelson Mandela's words that he shared with a crowd of thousands and thousands of people in Boston, Massachusetts during the mid-1980s. He reminded us: "If South Africa is not free, you are not free." Those words rang through my being as he uttered them. You see, I've been trying to understand power all my life. As a peasant child in the Azores, I saw how my father, even though he was an elder (someone highly regarded in our village), was discriminated by the aristocracy that resided in the cities north and south of us. Within my own family, trying to understand my older siblings' frustration with our family's economic situation, which was a disconnect with their middle-class college experiences. Within my own cultural community, interactions between my family and priests, supervisors, teachers, affluent people, and the list continues. This book springs out of my lived experience as a Portuguese American of peasant, working- and middle-class background. I see and hear the world differently.

As we became aware of the cultural construction of children's literature, we had the enormous task of naming the particular reading lenses that were unfolding before us. We knew that the word "critical" had to be part of the name. Critical, for us, signifies that an imbalance of power exists in the United States as well as the role that language can play in its maintainence. We decided to use "multicultural," even though it has been co-opted and misunderstood, because it signifies the multiple histories among us. We try to address the science of reading in Chapter 2 where we historicize literacy (Western) and school literacies. We have read across many texts and located several themes related to literacy practices that we examine. We connect these themes to sociopolitical factors: These themes are not endemic to the children, families and/or communities represented. The texts help us to show how social institutions like schools are implicated in these themes. For example, we invite the reader to rethink the label of "struggling reader" and invite how critical literacies practices are rarely reflected in texts for children. A lot of the books represent code breaking and text using practices. Rare moments exist among characters using their prior knowledge to make sense of texts and literacies as social tools for social change. Why aren't these practices represented in children's literature?

Patrick's recommendation to reconcile theories of recognition with theories of redistribution is important. I'm wondering if one can exist without the other. Can these theories reside side by side? Is redistribution enough? Certainly recognition alone is not enough. What are we redistributing? In what ways does redistribution create spaces for us to negotiate our identities? Reconstruct power? I agree with Masha: Perhaps the direction we might want to go in is speaking to the specificity of particular cultural experiences, much like the work of Rudine Sims Bishop on African Americans, Sonia Nieto on Puerto Ricans, and Debbie Reese on Native Americans. The cautionary word for culturally specific work is not to isolate the cultural experience from the power structure in which it resides, but to re/contextualize it in its history(ies) and the broader sociopolitical context, keeping in mind that the book's construction and the social processes among the characters are not immune to these social factors.

Going back to Mingshui's questions, what should we do? Do we eliminate multiethnic children's literature and multicultural education? What comes to mind is what the social scientist Immanuel Wallerstein (core-periphery studies) once said: If we lived in a socially just world, the social sciences would fail to exist. (This statement is instructive when we consider the role of multicultural children's literature in schools and communities.) I wonder if that would be the case. I also wonder if the teaching and research practices of the social sciences help reproduce, maintain, and perpetuate social inequities. Nevertheless, we need the social sciences, that is, we need to consider the texts that we use. I agree with Mingshui: We need to examine our practice which includes considering what we read, as well as how we read and what we do with what we read.

Mingshui

I got a question about the definition of "critical multicultural analysis." How do you define "multicultural" in the term? How is the term different from, say, "social political criticism"? Maybe you have already defined it somewhere in your book but I missed it.

Maria José

Because words get meaning from the words around them, "multicultural" signals to us the diversity of histories and cultural experiences among us, keeping our definition of culture in mind. "Critical" reminds us that there's an imbalance of power. When I first designed the heuristics [see Appendices C and D] to represent the power continuum and critical multicultural analysis, I was careful to ground both processes within the power relations of race, class, and gender. The spiral on the continuum and the swirl on the critical multicultural analysis diagram signify the dynamism, fluidity, and recursivity of these processes. These dynamic representations demonstrate the role of reflexivity (thinking about thinking and practice) in this work. These words are imperfect. They are ones that we have at hand at the present time.

Mingshui

I'd like to make a few final comments: First, I still believe that to decenterize the dominant culture in the four phases of Stuart Hall's model of communication: production, circulation, consumption, and reproduction of message, in our case, literature, the term multicultural literature serves as a slogan that sends out a clearer and more powerful message than such specialized terms as African American literature, Mexican American literature, and Chinese American literature.

Second, culture is not fixed; it is constantly changing. Culture is not monolithic; it is complex. Cultures do not have clearly defined borders: they permeate each other. While we emphasize the intracultural fluidity and complexity and intercultural influence, however, we should not deny the existence of culture as an entity, which in Nieto's words, is bound by "a combination of factors that include a common history, geographic location, language, social class, and religion." Some cultures are more unified, stable, and have more clearly defined boundaries than others. For example, Amish culture is more so than, say, Jewish culture. The more factors a group of people share, the more closely bound they are. "European American" is a very loosely bound group. So are males or females. However, when we analyze the gender power relations, we have to treat males and females as separate cultural groups. The labels of "the grossly lumped" groups may give a false impression of intracultural unity and we should be aware of their limitations, but they are indispensable for analyzing intercultural power relations.

Third, I agree that race cannot be addressed in isolation from class or gender, but I have a different understanding of how white privilege is conflated with class. Yes, poor white people experience discrimination because they do not possess the cultural capital of the middle and upper classes. But that discrimination is class discrimination, not racial discrimination. Historically, white people, rich or poor, possessed privilege over and discriminate against black people and other ethnic minorities, rich or poor. That is white (racial) privilege and racial discrimination. Again, take *Esperanza Rising*, for example. The poor Okies were discriminated against but they still have "white privilege" over Mexicans. Rich white people may enjoy more white privilege than poor white people. A rich plantation owner, for example, could have many black slaves while a poor white farmer might not be able to own one even if he was granted the right to slave ownership. Although poor white people have racial privilege, they experience the same class oppression and discrimination as poor black people. This common ground may unite them in a joint fight against the ruling classes. Racial issues are, in the final analysis, class issues. Racist ideologies and discourses are created by white ruling classes to serve their own interests.

I appreciate this opportunity to share my thoughts on multicultural issues in children's literature and benefit from the insights of other participants in this dialogue.

Patrick

I own two sweatshirts. One from the University of Wisconsin, a university our daughter attends, and one from Penn State, where our son studies. Both are grey with the university name stitched across the front in school colors. It's cold here, and I've worn both this week. I work at Penn State and students and faculty commented on my attire the day I wore my Wisconsin one. They read my shirt text as disloyal to our campus and cause, teasing me that I have gone to the dark side. "We are Penn State," they cry when I wear the one with the blue lettering. If I explain that the shirt is a gift from our daughter who tries to trace the genetic evolution of corn in John Doebley's lab, they smile at my proud reading of the Wisconsin text.

Last month 32 students were arrested during a sit-in after our Old Main administration building closed. The police took the students away in handcuffs. They were there to protest a reading of my Penn State sweatshirt that is different than the loyalty declaration my students and colleagues make. These protesters don't read the Penn State text as a statement of solidarity with the Penn State mission. Rather, they read the text as hiding the social relations with which the sweatshirt is produced. They are not proud to wear Penn State college apparel because Penn State administrators have not signed the Designated Suppliers Program (DSP), which would ensure sweatshop free labor in the college apparel production process. They attach more meaning to my sweatshirt—We are Penn State, and We Support Sweatshop Labor.

These protesters and many behind them (our son is the branch president of Student Labor Action Project) are engaged in critical multicultural analysis and literacy lessons that bridge theories of recognition and redistribution. They read a multicultural, multiethnic, or transnational text that crosses many borders in its production, while attempting to demystify the power relations, in order to improve the literacy on campus and improve the jobs (lives?) of the workers who produce the college apparel text.

Race, ethnicity, gender, and class mix, perhaps inseparably, within these texts and readings. These (protester, student) literacy teachers believe that if they can help college students, faculty members, alumni, administrators, and the Board of Trustees to read Penn State apparel with a critical multi-cultural lens, then together these "new" readers can force the Penn State administrators to sign the DSP. They seek to establish connections between the real producers and customers (readers) and to provoke action on these new connections—this new knowledge. Every step of the way, these teachers confront power.

The science of the matter is not settled. Many economists consider sweat-shops to be an essential step in the development of an economy, providing employment for the displaced agricultural worker (perhaps with the belief that none of their people will ever work in one).

The business of the matter is not settled. After Kathy Lee Gifford's line of clothing was connected with sweatshop production in the 1990s, the college apparel industry (Nike, Adidas, etc.) formed a corporate sponsored group to monitor labor conditions. Penn State uses this corporate service.

The law enforcement is not settled. Although outlawed in the United States, sweatshops still run in many major cities on immigrant labor.

The emotions are not settled on the matter. The customers for Penn State apparel are proud of their association with the university, and despite the facts, are reluctant to believe that their university could be involved in unethical economic practices.

The politics of the matter are settled. The Board of Trustees and the University President must sign this agreement. While pressures can be applied, very few people control this situation on the Penn State campus. While other university boards and presidents have signed the DSP (Wisconsin, Cornell and 30 others), ours remain reluctant to read with a critical multicultural lens.

I indulge in this long metaphor in order to suggest that we have many allies working to help people engage in multicultural analyses of the texts in their lives. These allies assault readers' comfort with the status quo, the barriers that keep others in discomfort, and literacy practices that support both. In a global economy, every text is multinational, multicultural, multiethnic and complicated by the nexus of power that surrounds it. We are all caught in this web, unless we realize our agency to identify, name, and act. How do we work together to recognize and redistribute? I think this book points us in a useful direction.

Junko

How "lived experiences" shape my thinking

Reading the chapters of this book and Mingshui Cai's and Patrick Shannon's responses, I feel enriched by the deep thinking, eloquent expressions, and engaging challenges that were presented. It is a privilege to have this opportunity to explore "where I am" at this moment in my understanding of multicultural literature and think about it with others. Maria José and Masha recognized that my own operating definitions of multicultural literature changed from publications in 1993 to 2001. And over the 15 years that I have written and taught on this topic, I'm glad that I've learned and adapted my view of the world as I engage in critical discussions with others. But most of all, I realize that, for me, it's the personally "lived experiences" that have deeply affected and challenged my own beliefs and have shaped the continuous development of my understandings.

In reading Maria José and Masha's chapters, I was reminded of my own responses to various terms that have been used over time. I remember when the "people of color" became popular, and Mingshui and I worked together as colleagues at University of Northern Iowa. We looked at each other and asked, "How yellow do you feel today?" The recognition of color as the identifier of diversity felt strange. My perception of the concept of color was heightened when my daughter's principal said to me, "I don't know how many children of color attend my elementary school because I'm color blind." I found this statement incredibly naïve, and responded, "I do. There are three. My daughter, her classmate, and his cousin." But this was in the early 1990s, and there has been considerable progress in our understanding and recognition of such concepts since then. We've recognized the need for listening to the book creators and the researchers who offer "insider perspectives." In the 1990s, I presented many talks and papers about the need for being more inclusive in the literature offered to our students. I focused on "cultural authenticity" as the criteria for selecting and evaluating the literature and I called for recognition and inclusion of multiple perspectives. Yet I knew that simply having multiple cultures represented did not solve the multicultural questions. I recognized that well-intentioned images of children around the world, wearing "native costumes" and happily holding hands were a huge problem in reinforcing stereotypes.

Once, after I presented a keynote talk at a conference, Jack Zipes commented that my points were interesting but "not enough." He felt that if the goal was for true cultural understanding, merely adding culturally authentic books to the repertoire of what children read was not enough. I wrote a chapter on "Diverse Perspectives" in a textbook for college students. Co-author Charlie Temple said to me that I needed to be stronger in my advocacy for multicultural literature. At that time, I was only beginning to understand the role of power and politics as related to the reading of literature. Why was this? Perhaps it's because, as one colleague said to me, "Even among those of us identified as 'minority,' it's not all the same because you're from a privileged minority so you get the benefit of doubt." She was implying that I had not suffered from the oppression that others may have. On one job interview for a university faculty position, I was told by one committee member, "You're from the wrong minority. In fact, it's people like you who are taking up space we need for other minorities to be represented." Was it that I hadn't had the experience of being among the oppressed that allowed me to focus on "authentic portrayal" and "inclusiveness" in an idealistic way? I realize this is not true for many—and in fact, sometimes it's people from outside an oppressed group who are able to be more analytically perceptive because of their deep study and committed beliefs about issues of equity. For me, it took specific incidences in the past few months for me to understand how it feels to have others impose their power on me in oppressive ways.

Jane Addams Award & Outstanding International Book Award Committees

My participation in these two book award committees during the past year gave me much to be thankful for: being part of a group that carefully considered the important issues related to culture and portrayal as well as the implications of how these stories might be perceived by readers, based on how they were told. All books that were considered for these awards were either books relating to social justice or international books. Although many were excellent, others had problems that were recognized through perceptive discussion. I came to believe that targeting the lens through which we evaluate books is very important; when asked to consider books for different reasons, each lens requires a new way of considering the book. The most dangerous was the presentation of issues that addressed problems of our world yet resolved them through unrealistic or even condescending ways. It doesn't help readers when the solution offered only leaves readers feeling hopeless that such solutions could occur. These kinds of books sometimes perpetuate the recognition that there are stories that need to be heard but seek ways of resolving issues through stereotypical means. In other words, such books fulfill what Maria José and Masha cite in Chapter 3, In 1976, the Council on Interracial Books for Children questioned the source of values imbedded in children's books. They argued that they were not from an individual, but from society as a whole: "Children's books generally reflect the needs of those who dominate that society . . . the prevailing values are supportive of the existing [power] structure."

As the multicultural publishing increased throughout the 1990s, Marc Aronson questioned the need for a "separate set of ethnically-based awards" (i.e., Coretta Scott King and Pura Belpré Awards) since all such books qualify for general awards as well, and they had begun to get widespread recognition in high profile awards such as the Newbery and the Sibert. However, it's not about multicultural books being qualified for major awards that are based on literary quality of which cultural depiction is not the major criteria or the lens through which we critique the book. My participation in the two committees (Jane Addams and Outstanding International Books) endorses my belief that having awards that clearly hold specific criteria is as important as general awards for quality literature. Although there are more authors and illustrators representing diverse voices, the publishing industry has not diversified as much. It may take another generation before the more diverse field of newer editors become established in the publishing field. In this era of corporate culture making decisions based on the bottom line of each book rather than balancing the publishing agenda based on editorial vision, this represents a big problem. The question today must go far beyond that of representation, but to that of gate-keeping. Who is reviewing, reading and buying? Who's talking and who's listening? Is it the scholars? Or is it also people who work directly with children? What about editors, publishers, reviewers and others who directly impact what is made available and accessible to young readers? Like policymakers that impact what is happening in education, the publishing industry directly impacts what is available to be read. Reviewers play an important role in featuring aspects of books that should be noted. They can gloss over cultural issues that they do not notice, or they can help make readers aware of cultural issues if they choose to write about them in their reviews. Frankly, I find it troubling that in 2007, two books that go against my beliefs about depicting cultural experiences caught my attention as books that received high levels of attention, earning starred reviews and spots on recommended booklists.

Problematic terminology and concepts

Tolerance – I'm currently living in Munich, spending five months doing research at the International Youth Library (IYL). I submitted my research proposal on the topic, "international books that provide fodder for understanding issues related to peace and social justice" but it ended up being translated into German and back into English as "Peace and Tolerance." While this is a phrase I often hear used, "tolerance" has a negative tinge in nuance as opposed to adopting a more positive stance towards understanding and taking action to contribute to a more equitable world. Tolerance simply implies putting up with differences rather than understanding them.

Other – I've been reading research and engaged in discussions with people from around the world. I read such key concepts as "otherness," "cultural alterity" and "post colonialism." With the best intention while giving much attention to the plight of those who have not been represented in previous times, for me, the terminology gives off negative connotations of inferiority. Sometimes, it allows a reinforcement of the concept of "the poor others" who are to be pitied so their stories can be told; at worst, there cam be condescending attention.

Parallel Cultures – After reading Maria José and Masha's book, there can be no doubt that power plays such an inevitable role that there can be no such thing as truly parallel cultures. This is another idealistic yet not realistically achievable concept.

Back to my experiences in Munich . . .

The most powerful book I read last year is *The Book Thief* by Marcus Zusak. It takes place during the Holocaust, and the Jewish people are walked from Pasing train station (where I am now living), along the Würm River (the path I take to get to the International Youth Library every day), to Dachau Concentration Camp. Visiting Dachau on a cold, gray day of snow blowing around was a sobering experience. After the Venezuelan journalist who is also studying at the IYL spent four hours at Dachau, he noted that the Holocaust is not over—there is still Guantanamo. And that's only one of the multitude of things going on in our world today that shows that merely reading about the past and giving voice to those experiences is not enough. As an educator, I feel the need to consider the ways in which those who work with children can scaffold children's understanding and probing of these tough issues through the questions they ask, the responses they give, and the guidance they can provide.

Continuing the work . . .

I've just returned from attending my daughter's graduation from Grinnell College. In my daughter's graduation packet was a pledge card for graduates to sign, saying that they will consider the societal and environmental impact of career choices and employment decisions they make. I had the good fortune of riding to the airport with Judith Butler, commencement speaker and highly regarded feminist philosopher whose advocacy to become an activist has been inspirational to many, especially as Grinnell students responded to hate mail and crimes to call for a "hate-free" school. As a parent, I was glad to hear a "call for action" as the graduates step on into the world beyond their school.

I'm told that my views are "too pedagogical" by those who are outside the field of education. There are those who believe that any way in which we as adults try to influence the thinking of children takes away from their ability to think for themselves or to recognize their ability to do so. Yet I believe we have responsibilities; I hold on to the hope that by going beyond that of making quality multicultural literature available, we can and will provide opportunities for fostering the kind of thinking and discussion that will likely lead to eventual action . . . that which makes a real difference in our world.

Children's Book Awards

The following chronologically organized list is not exhaustive or politically neutral. We have made particular decisions to arrange this list so the reader can examine how the inception of particular awards are responses to other awards and/or lack of representation and recognition of particular cultural groups in the publishing of children's literature. While we gathered this information from book award homepages, additional information is available from these websites as well as from affiliated organizations.

International

- *Jane Addams Children's Book Award*

www.janeaddamspeace.org/index.asp

The Women's International League for Peace and Freedom (WILPF) and the Jane Addams Peace Association established the Jane Addams Children's Book Awards in 1953. The awards annually honor authors and illustrators of children's books for their success in promoting peace, social justice, world community, and race and gender equality. The picture book genre was added in 1993. Along with award winning books, honor books are recognized in each category.

- *Hans Christian Andersen Award*

www.ibby.org/index.php?id=273

It is awarded biennially in recognition of authors, since 1956, and illustrators, since 1966, for their lasting contributions to children's literature. The award, also known as the "Little Nobel Prize," is patronized by her Majesty Queen Margrethe II of Denmark and presented by the International Board on Books for Young People (IBBY). The national sections of IBBY and an internationally renowned jury of children's literature specialists are in charge of nomination and award desicions.

Canadian

- *Governor General's Literary Award*

www.gg.ca/honours/awards/gga/index_e.asp
www.canadacouncil.ca/prizes/ggla

Having evolved into one of Canada's most prestigious awards since its inception in 1937 by the Governor General Lord Tweedsmuir (John Buchan, author of *The Thirty-Nine Steps*) and initiated by the Canadian Authors Association, the Governor General's *Literary* Award honors publications in both French and English for adults. The Canada Council for the Arts continued with the sponsorship and added prizes for works written in French in 1959, and extended its recognition to children's literature in the categories of text, illustration and translation in 1987. Since 1988, the BMO Financial Group has joined the sponsorship of the award.

- *Canadian Library Association Book of the Year for Children Award*

www.cla.ca/AM/Template.cfm?Section=Book_of_the_Year_for_
Children_Award

Sponsored by National Book Service, this award was launched by the Canadian Association of Children's Librarians in 1947. It recognizes books written by Canadian citizens or permanent residents, in any format of creative writing that are suitable for children up to age 12. The recipients are selected by a committee of the Association, with input from its membership.

- Canadian Library Association Young Adult Canadian Book Award

www.cla.ca/AM/
Template.cfm?Section=Young_Adult_Canadian_Book_Award

The award was founded in 1980 by the Young Adult Caucus of the Saskatchewan Library Association, and is administered by the Young Adult Services Interest Group of the Canadian Library Association. This award acknowledges English language books published in Canada by Canadian citizens or permanent residents for young adult readers between the ages of 13 and 18.

- *Norma Fleck Award for Canadian Children's Non-Fiction*

www.bookcentre.ca/awards/norma_fleck/index.shtml

Initiated in May 1999 by Dr. Jim Fleck to honor his mother, Norma Marie Byrnes, the Norma Fleck Award for Canadian Children's nonfiction is sponsored by the Fleck Family Foundation and administered by the Canadian Children's Book Centre. This award acknowledges Canada's outstanding nonfiction books for young people. Appraised by a jury of children literature professionals, criteria for this award include: exceptionality of the text, presentation of subject matter, and complementary illustrations.

National

- *John Newbery Medal*

www.ala.org/ala/alsc/awardsscholarships/literaryawds/newberymedal/
newberymedal.htm

Established in 1922 in honor of John Newbery, an 18th-century publisher of children's books, the John Newbery Medal is presented by the Association for Library Service to Children of the American Library Association (ALA) to the most distinguished American children's book published the previous year. As the first children's book award in the world, it is regarded as one of the most prestigious awards for children's literature in the United States. The purpose of the award is to encourage the writing and reading of original creative work in the field of children's literature. The selection criteria of the award book and honor books are generally based on the following elements: interpretation of the theme or concept; presentation of information including accuracy, clarity, and organization; development of plot; delineation of characters and setting; appropriateness of style; excellence of presentation for a child audience; the text and illustrations; and, overall design of the book.

- *Caldecott Medal*

www.ala.org/ala/alsc/awardsscholarships/literaryawds/caldecottmedal/
caldecottmedal.htm

Established in 1937 and named in recognition of 19th-century English illustrator, Randolph Caldecott, the award is presented annually by the Association for Library Service to Children, part of the American Library Association. This award honors exceptional illustrators of American children's picture books that are published in English by citizens or residents of the United States. Criteria for the award include: originality, artistic technique, distinctive visual interpretation, appropriateness of style of illustration, excellence of presentation for a child audience, the written text, and overall design of the book.

- *Laura Ingalls Wilder Medal*

www.ala.org/ala/alsc/awardsscholarships/literaryawds/wildermedal/
wildermedal.htm

Inaugurated in 1954 and named for Laura Ingalls Wilder, an elementary school teacher who published her first book at the age of 65, this medal is presented by the Association for Library Service to Children, a division of the American Library Association. The award honors authors or illustrators whose books published in the United States have contributed significantly to children's literature during a period of at least ten years. From 1960 to 1980 this award was conferred every five years, between 1980 and 2001 every three years, and beginning in 2001 every other year. Other evaluation criteria include whether the nominated works have demonstrated leading examples for the genre to which they belong, and contributed to new trends in publication of children's books.

- *The Mildred L. Batchelder Award*

www.ala.org/ala/alsc/awardsscholarships/literaryawds/batchelderaward/
batchelderaward.htm

This annual award was established in honor of Mildred L. Batchelder, a former executive director of the Association for Library Service to Children, who encouraged the translation of quality children's literature, striving to promote better understanding and communication between people across various cultures. First presented in 1966, this award is given to American publishers for translating and publishing in the United States children's books that are originally published in other languages and countries. The award criteria focuses on the text, the authentic relationship between the original and the translation, and the quality of the U.S. book, which include: interpretation of the theme; presentation of information; development of plot; delineation of characters; appropriateness of style; the potential appeal to a child audience; and, the overall design and/or illustration.

- *Carter G. Woodson Book Award*

www.socialstudies.org/awards/woodson/

Intended to encourage the writing and reading of exemplary social studies books for young readers that aptly contend with ethnic minorities and relations in the United States, the award was established in 1974 by the National Council for Social Studies. One book from the elementary (K-6), middle (5–8), and secondary (7–12) divisions receive awards. Each year outstanding runner-up books are recognized as Carter G. Woodson Honor Books. Five key traits comprise the overall evaluation criteria of text and illustrations: respect for diversity; insight provided into the experiences of racial/ethnic groups; depiction of interactions among racial/ethnic groups; balanced representation of particular racial/ethnic groups; and, exemption from patronizing, distorting, and stereotyping.

- *IRA Children's and Young Adult's Book Awards*

www.reading.org/association/awards/childrens_ira.html

Initiated in 1974, this award acknowledges an author's first or second published book written for children or young adults (ages birth to 17 years). Awards recognize fiction and nonfiction in three categories: primary, intermediate, and young adult. All books, in any language or from any country, are considered.

- *NCTE Award for Excellence in Poetry for Children*

www.ncte.org/about/awards/sect/elem/106857.htm

Initiating its award in 1977, the National Council of Teachers of English acknowledges a living American poet every three years for his or her enduring contribution to children's literature. Essential considerations for the selection include: imagination; authenticity of voice; evidence of a strong persona; universality/timelessness; potential for growth and evolution in terms of craft and artistic stamina; excellence in technical and artistic presentation, evidence of different styles and modes of expression, evidence of risk and innovation; potential for stirring fresh insights and feelings; and, the appeal to children.

- *Scott O'Dell Award for Historical Fiction*

www.scottodell.com/odellaward.html

This award was initiated in 1982 by Scott O'Dell to promote the writing of historical fiction and to increase young readers' interest in history, in the hope to help shape their country and their world. The award honors distinguished books of historical fiction, which are written in English by a U.S. citizen and produced by a U.S. publisher for children or young adults in the "New World" (Canada, the United States, Mexico, Central or South America).

- *NCTE Orbis Pictus Award for Outstanding Nonfiction for Children*

www.ncte.org/elem/awards/orbispictus/106877.htm

First presented in 1990, this annual literary award was created by the National Council of Teachers of English to recognize exceptional works of nonfiction for children, which are published in the United States. This award is named for the work of Johannes Amos Comenius, *Orbis Pictus— The World in Pictures* (1657), which is considered to be the first book published for children. The award acknowledges one book and up to five honor books every year, based on the following literary criteria: accuracy of facts, organization, design, style, and writing.

- *Michael L. Printz Award*

www.ala.org/ala/yalsa/booklistsawards/printzaward/Printz.cfm

First granted in 2002, the Michael L. Printz Award is named in honor of a former school teacher librarian of the Topeka West High School in Kansas. Printz was a long-time active member of the Young Adult Library Services Association (YALSA), a division of the American Library Association. Sponsored by *Booklist*, a publication of the American Library Association, and administered by YALSA, the award recognizes exceptional books of young adult literature, written for readers aged from 12 to 18. The Printz and four honor book award winners are acknowledged annually by a committee of nine YALSA members. Criteria for the award include: diversity; presentation as a self-contained entity (not dependent on other media for its meaning or pleasure); and, book components such as story, voice, style, setting, characters, theme, illustration and, overall design.

- *Theodore Seuss Geisel Book Award*

www.ala.org/ala/alsc/awardsscholarships/literaryawds/geiselaward/
GeiselAward.htm

Initiated in 2004 and named in honor of the world-distinguished author of children's literature, Theodor Geisel, this annual award recognizes American authors and illustrators of outstanding beginning reader books published in English in the United States. The winning and honor books, written by citizens or residents of the United States, are selected for their literary and artistic achievements that demonstrate creativity and imagination to encourage and enrich children's reading engagement.

Regional

- *Boston Globe-Horn Book Award*

www.hbook.com/bghb/default.asp

Among the most prestigious prizes in the United States and first presented by *The Boston Globe* and *The Horn Book Magazine* in 1967, this award honors books for children and young adults in three categories: picture book, fiction and poetry, and nonfiction. The awarded books, with two honor books selected in each category, must be published in the United States but the authors and illustrators may be citizens of any country.

- *Ezra Jack Keats New Writer and New Illustrator Award*

www.ezra-jack-keats.org/bookawards/index.html

Established in 1985 and named for Ezra Jack Keats, a famous author and illustrator of children's literature, this award is sponsored by The New York Public Library and the Ezra Jack Keats Foundation. It annually honors novice writers and illustrators of children's picture books, who each have fewer than five books published. The selection criteria, as reflected in Ezra Jack Keats' focus on traditionally underrepresented populations include: the universal qualities of childhood, a strong belief in family and community, creativity, and love of learning.

Culturally Specific

African-American
- *Coretta Scott King Book Award*

www.ala.org/ala/emiert/corettascottkingbookaward/corettascott.cfm

Established in 1970, this award is conferred annually by the Coretta Scott King Committee under the Ethnic Multicultural Information Exchange Round Table (EMIERT) of the American Library Association (ALA), honoring the contribution of Dr. Martin Luther King Jr. and the commitment of Mrs. Coretta Scott King to the work for peace and world fellowship. This award is presented in recognition of African American authors and illustrators for their exceptional contributions to the promotion of understanding and appreciation of the African American experience and to the realization of the American Dream, as defined by Dr. Martin Luther King Jr. The winning works must be published in the United States. The intention is for these works of literature to foster in young readers attitudes and behaviors necessary for participation in a culturally diverse democratic society. The award promotes the representation of the African American experience in the form of literature and the graphic arts, including biographical, historical and social history treatments. Selection criteria include: accuracy of information presented, originality, suitability for the intended young readers (preschool-grade 4, grades 5–8 and grades 9–12), clear plot, and well developed characters.

Asian-American
- *Asian/Pacific American Award for Literature*

www.apalaweb.org/awards/awards.htm

This annual award was developed by the Asian/Pacific American Librarians Association, with the goal to honor and encourage original writings and illustrations that depict Asian/Pacific American heritage. The first award was presented in 2006. Award winners and honor books, based on literary and artistic presentations, are recognized in three categories: adult fiction, illustration in children's literature and youth literature. The titles must be published in English by U.S. citizens or permanent residents, but not necessarily by Asian/Pacific Americans.

Jewish
- *National Jewish Book Awards*

www.jewishbookcouncil.org/page.php?7

This award is the longest running awards program in the field of Jewish literature in the United States and Canada since its inception in 1948. The Jewish Book Council presents this award to authors or illustrators of children's books of Jewish content. The purpose of the award is to encourage the reading, writing and publishing of distinctive English language books that deal with Jewish themes. Beginning in 2002, one nonfiction book has been selected annually as the winner of the Everett Family Foundation Jewish Book of the Year Award.

- *Sydney Taylor Book Award*

www.jewishlibraries.org/ajlweb/awards/st_books.htm

This annual award, established in 1968 by the Association of Jewish Libraries, recognizes two children's books, one for younger and one for older readers, that authentically depicts the Jewish experience. This award honors Sydney Taylor, author of the All-of-a-kind family series.

Latino
- *Tomás Rivera Mexican American Children's Book Award*

www.education.txstate.edu/departments/Tomas-Rivera-Book-Award-Project-Link.html

This book award was established in 1995 by Texas State University College of Education, honoring its distinguished alumnus, Dr. Tomás Rivera. Rivera was one of the first authors to represent the Mexican American migrant farmworker experience in literature. This annual award recognizes exceptional authors and illustrators of Mexican American literature, fiction or nonfiction, created for children and young adults (from birth to age 16). The selection criteria include: accurate depictions of Mexican American experience, exemption from stereotypes, and rich characterization.

- *Pura Belpré Award*

http://www.ala.org/ala/alsc/awardsscholarships/literaryawds/belpremedal/belprmedal.htm

With its inception in 1996, this award acknowledges a Latino/Latina writer and illustrator for representing the Latino cultural experience in literature for children and young adults. The award is jointly sponsored by two of the American Library Association affiliates: the Association for Library Service to Children and the National Association to Promote Library and Information Services to Latinos and the Spanish-Speaking. The award is named in honor of Pura Belpré, an author, storyteller and the first Latina librarian of the New York Public Library. (Puerto Rican children have enjoyed her retellings of Puerto Rican folklore in the United States.) Two medals (one to a Latino author and one to a Latino illustrator) are awarded biennially, but beginning with the 2009 award, it is presented annually, at the Annual Conference of the American Library Association. The award-winning and honor books must be published in the United States or Puerto Rico and created by residents or citizens of the United States or Puerto Rico. All genres are eligible for consideration. General criteria for selection include: suitability for intended young readers' understandings and appreciations; originality; and, excellence in quality.

- *Américas Book Award for Children's and Young Adult Literature*

www.uwm.edu/Dept/CLACS/outreach/americas.html

Initiated in 1993, this award is presented to outstanding U.S. books published in English or Spanish that authentically engage children or young adults in reading about Latin America, the Caribbean, or Latinos/as in the United States. Sponsored by the national Consortium of Latin American Studies Programs (CLASP), the award honors works of fiction, poetry, folklore, or selected nonfiction. The award endeavors to affirm cultural heritages and surpass political borders. Selection criteria for the award winners and commended titles include: distinctive literary quality; cultural contextualization; exceptional integration of text; illustration and design; and, potential for classroom use.

Native American
  • *American Indian Youth Services Literature Award*
www.aila.library.sd.gov/activities/youthlitaward.htm

Created in 2006 by the American Indian Library Association, this award honors distinguished writing and illustrations by and about American Indians in three categories: picture book, middle school, and young adult. Meritorious books are selected generally based on appropriateness for intended readers, artistic elements of book design, and accurate and real-istic portrayals of Native American cultures during different periods of time. The Native cultural traits include: significance of community, extended family structures, harmony between material and non-material aspects of life, and the respect for the relationship among all aspects of Mother Earth.

Children's Book Publishers

The following list of independent presses shows the collaborative work emanating from cultural communities as they struggle for representation in the publishing of children's books and school curricula. Please note that these culturally specific texts are not immune to dominant ideologies. The large publishing houses are organized by conglomerate to foreground how their decision-making power is concentrated in few hands. These amalgamations are shifting ground because holdings and ventures change all the time. It is important to take notice of the holdings of each conglomerate because its overall activities influence children's book publishing. We have organized the independent presses according to cultural specialization as well as compiled a list of presses that are committed to publishing representations of multiculturalism. The conglomerates are organized alphabetically. We have collected this information from publishers' websites.

Independent Presses
African-American
- **Africa World Press & The Red Sea Press**

www.africaworldpressbooks.com

These "sister presses" specialize in the publication and distribution of books about the African world, including new editions of out-of-print books or U.S. editions of books originally published in other countries.

They also publish books on African, African-American, Caribbean and Latin American issues, and those from other parts of the developing world.

- **Just Us Books**

www.justusbooks.com

Just Us Books, established by parents Wade and Cheryl Hudson, produces Afro-centric books for children. The press is the result of the Hudsons' desperate search for books for their own children about Black history, heritage, and experience.

- **New Day Press**

www.newdaypress.com

The New Day Press publishes books on African-American history and biography for children and young adults. It conducts its marketing through direct mail.

- **Third World Press**

www.thirdworldpressinc.com

The Third World Press is one of the largest independent Black-owned presses in the United States, publishing books by and about people of the African diaspora focussing on themes about race, culture, politics, and social health.

Asian-American

- **Asia for Kids**

www.asiaforkids.com

Asia for Kids distributes selected Asian and Asian-American print materials and related products, which are presented in English and Asian languages, with an emphasis on specific Asian cultural heritages and language learning. The countries/cultures represented include: China, Japan, Korea, Vietnam, the Philippines, Laos, Cambodia, Taiwan, Thailand, Hmong, India, Bangladesh, Pakistan, the Middle East, Bali, Indonesia, Nepal, Burma/Myanmar, and Tibet.

- **Asian American Curriculum Project (formerly Japanese American Curriculum Project)**

www.asianamericanbooks.com

As a non-profit voluntary educational organization, the Asian American Curriculum Project (AACP) distributes print and video/audio materials that represent the diversity of Asian and Asian American experiences for readers of all ages.

- **Barnaby Books**

www.barnabybooks.com

This publisher produces children's books based in Honolulu, Hawaii, featuring fairy tales involving a Hawaiian twist and Hawaiian legends, and providing suggestions about classroom reading activities for school children.

- **Bess Press**

www.besspress.com

As an independent book publishing company located in Honolulu, Hawaii, the Bess Press publishes trade titles, including children's literature and curriculum titles on Hawaiian and Pacific island histories, languages, language arts, reading, literatures, culture and science, and reference books.

- **China Books**

www.chinabooks.com

As the United States' oldest distributor of books on Chinese language and culture, China Books is expanding its business to Chinese cultural products, including video/audio materials, software, and arts, and has become part of the Sino United Publishing Ltd.

- **Heian International**

www.heian.com

Heian International distributes books and materials on themes including Asian fairy tales, origami crafts, philosophy, and dictionaries, hoping to promote peace through a better understanding among cultures.

- **Many Cultures Publishing**

www.studycenter.org/test/mcp_04.html

This press distributes curriculum materials with multicultural contexts, most of which are bilingual publications with teacher guides, including storybooks of folktales from Asian cultures such as India, Cambodia, and the Philippines.

- **Polychrome Publishing Co.**

www.polychromebooks.com

This is an independent press publishing children's stories from the Asian American community for a multicultural society, with emphasis on character and identity development and diverse cultural heritages and experiences in order to promote racial, ethnic, cultural, and religious tolerance and understanding.

Latino

- **BOPO Bilingual Books**

www.bopobooks.com

Books Offering Profound Opportunities (BOPO) publishes family-oriented children's picture books in both English and Spanish.

- **Latin American Literary Review Press**

www.lalrp.org

This press publishes books dealing with the cultural heritages of Latin America and Spain, with an emphasis on translations of creative writing and literary criticism. Its publications of young adult titles were first offered in 1989.

- **Piñata Books/Arte Público**

www.arte.uh.edu

As Arte Público Press' imprints, based at the University of Houston, for children and young adults, Piñata Books and Recovering divisions publish books by U.S. Latino/a authors, which deal with the themes of languages, characters, and customs of Latino cultures in the United States.

Native American

- **Daybreak Star**

www.unitedindians.com/daybreak.html

Daybreak Star is the publishing division of the United Indians of All Tribes Foundation. It publishes mostly nonfiction and some fiction, portraying diverse Native cultures and histories, with a focus on the lives of contemporary Native American children.

- **Oyate**

www.oyate.org

Oyate is a non-profit organization working to help all children understand and acknowledge the "historical truths" of all nations through activities including the distribution of selected children's, young adult, and educators' books and materials from Native-owned presses, with an emphasis on work by Native writers and artists.

- **Pemmican Publications**

www.pemmican.mb.ca

Pemmican Publications Inc., founded as a non-profit organization by the Manitoba Métis Federation, publishes picture books for young readers and novels for older children, with an emphasis on work by Canadian Métis writers and illustrators who present stories about Métis experience.

- **Theytus Books**

www.theytusbooks.ca

"Theytus" is a Salishan word meaning "preserving for the sake of handing down." As a division of the En'owkin Centre, this press aims to present Native cultures and worldviews to young readers by producing and promoting appropriate reading materials and information generated by Native authors, illustrators, and artists of all nations.

Canadian

- **Annick Press**

(See entry under Independent Presses Committed to Representing Multiculturalism.)

- **Fifth House**

http://www.fitzhenry.ca/fifthhouse.aspx

As a Fitzhenry & Whiteside company, this Western-Canadian press specializes in nonfiction and books about Western Canadian (and Canadian) history, culture, and environment.

- **Kids Can Press**

www.KidsCanPress.com

Located in midtown Toronto, Kids Can Press produces Canadian books for children between the ages 1 and 14, including nonfiction, novels, picture books, early readers, educational workbooks, and craft books.

- **Libros Tigrillo/Groundwood Books**

(See entry under Independent Presses Committed to Representing Multiculturalism.)

- **Orca Book Publishers**

www.orcabook.com

Orca publishes books by Canadian authors for children, teens, and "reluctant readers" of all ages. Its publications encompass a wide range from picture books through juvenile fiction, novels to teachers' guides, featuring the educational, social, cultural, and economic life of the Province of British Columbia and the country.

- **Pemmican Publications**

(See entry under Native American presses.)

- **Ronsdale Press**

www.ronsdalepress.com

As a Vancouver-based literary publisher, Ronsdale publishes books by multicultural writers from across Canada, demonstrating a special interest in dual language books. Its publications include fiction, poetry, regional history, biography and autobiography, books of ideas about Canada, as well as children's books aiming to provide Canadian readers with new insights into themselves and their country.

- **Second Story Press**

www.secondstorypress.on.ca

As a member of the Association of Canadian Publishers, the Organization of Book Publishers of Ontario, and the Canadian Children's Book Centre and receiving funding from the Canada Council for the Arts and the Ontario Arts Council, the publication list of Second Story Press includes children's fiction, nonfiction and picture books, and young adult fiction and nonfiction.

- **Theytus Books**

(See entry under Native American presses.)

- **Tundra Books**

www.tundrabooks.com

Tundra is a Canadian publisher, aiming to create opportunities for people to tell their own stories and to introduce complex stories for young readers by integrating art forms such as drama, painting, and dance into children's books.

- **Women's Press**

(See entry under Independent Presses Committed to Representing Multiculturalism.)

Independent Presses Committed to Representing Multiculturalism

- **Annick Press**

www.annickpress.com

This Canada-based press publishes children's literature which explores both the contemporary and historic world in the form of nonfiction and picture books for young readers, and fiction titles for middle and young adult readers.

- **A.R.T.S. Inc.**

www.arts-inc.org

Featuring multicultural heritages of immigrant communities and initiated by the Chinese and Latino neighborhoods of the Lower East Side of New York City, A.R.T.S. Inc. publishes for youth and adults, artists, and educators in four program areas: school program, community arts, folklore and language, and publications.

- **August House Books**

www.augusthouse.com

As a multimedia publisher of children's stories, multicultural folktale anthologies and resource books, August House develops collections of stories from around the world, which contribute to good character and crosscultural understanding of young readers.

- **Barefoot Books**

www.barefoot-books.com

This children's publisher specializes in picture books from traditional cultures all over the world, with a specific focus on introducing cultures to children in the form of language, art, music, and dance through books and other multimedia materials.

- **Candlewick Press**

www.candlewick.com

This press is an employee-owned publishing house which produces picture

310 • Appendix B

books, fiction, nonfiction, poetry collections, and activity books for young readers of all ages.

- **Children's Book Press**

www.childrensbookpress.org

This press is a nonprofit publisher of multicultural and bilingual children's picture books, with an emphasis on the roles of culture and history in the world of children.

- **Groundwood Books**

www.groundwoodbooks.com

Groundwood Books publishes fiction, picture books, and nonfiction for children of all ages in Canada, the United States and Latin America (through its Libros Tigrillo), with its primary focus on the works by Canadian writers and illustrators, and stories of people whose voices are underrepresented in print published by media conglomerates.

- **Lee & Low**

www.leeandlow.com

By working with artists of color and authors and illustrators new to children's book publishing, this independent publisher specializes in realistic children's stories set in contemporary and historic settings which explore multicultural contexts about African, Asian, Latino, Middle Eastern, and Native American cultures. Some publications are available in Spanish.

- **Lerner Publishing Group**

www.lernerbooks.com

This is the United State's largest independently-owned children's book publisher, producing nonfiction and fiction books for grades K-12 on a variety of subjects.

- **Carolina Wren Press**

www.carolinawrenpress.org

Carolina Wren Press is a nonprofit organization publishing and distributing books of fiction, poetry, nonfiction, and children's literature, particularly by writers of underrepresented groups (e.g., new authors, authors of color, female authors, and gay/lesbian authors).

- **Open Hand Publishing**

www.openhand.com

Aiming to both inform and cultivate a humanistic spirit, this publishing house produces adult and children's books that reflect the diverse cultures within the United States.

- **Silver Moon Press**

www.silvermoonpress.com

This is a new and growing children's book publisher with publications in such areas as science, multiculturalism, biographies, and historical fiction. The Silver Moon Press has also made its history books into television series for children.

- **Sleeping Bear Press**

www.sleepingbearpress.com

The Sleeping Bear Press specializes in illustrated picture books, particularly through regional stories and legends with both entertaining and educational content.

- **Women's Press**

www.womenspress.ca

This press is Canada's oldest English language feminist publisher since 1972 and an imprint of Canadian Scholars' Press since 2000. It publishes children's texts that represent the cultural and social diversity of Canada.

Conglomerates

Bertelsmann AG

This German-based conglomerate consists of six corporate divisions: RTL Group, the broadcaster in Europe; Gruner + Jahr, the European magazine publisher; BMG, Bertelsmann Music Group; Random House, the trade book publisher; Direct Group, the book and music club group; and arvato, an international media and communications service provider. Its English and bilingual children's books fall under the umbrella of Random House Children's Books, whose imprints include: Alfred A. Knopf, Bantam, Beginner Books, Crown, David Fickling Books, Delacorte Press, Disney Books for Young Readers, Doubleday, Dragonfly, First Time Books, Golden Books, Landmark Books, Laurel-Leaf, Picturebacks, Random House Books for Young Readers, Robin Corey Books, Schwartz & Wade Books, Sesame Workshop, Step into Reading, Stepping Stone Books, Wendy Lamb Books, and Yearling. More information on Bertelsmann's holdings as a mega-corporation can be found at:

www.bertelsmann.com
www.ketupa.net/bertelsmann.htm

- **Alfred A. Knopf Books for Young Readers**

This imprint publishes of board books, picture books, novels and non-fiction for children of all ages. Knopf Trade Paperbacks publishes paperback novels for middle and young adult readers, particularly those originally published by Alfred A. Knopf Books for Young Readers in hardcover.

www.randomhouse.com/kids/about/imprints.html

- **Bantam Books**

Bantam publishes commercial paperbacks in both rack and digest-size formats, with a focus on movie and television tie-ins and original paperback series.

www.randomhouse.com/kids/about/imprints.html

- **David Fickling Books**

As the first bi-continental children's book publisher, David Fickling Books brings UK children's literature to young readers in the United States.

www.randomhouse.com/kids/about/imprints.html

- **Disney Books for Young Readers**

This publisher produces books based on Disney productions, in such formats as coloring and activity books, storybooks, novelty books, and early readers.

www.randomhouse.com/kids/about/imprints.html

- **Delacorte Press Books for Young Readers**

Delacorte publishes literary and commercial novels originally released in hardcover for middle-grade and young adult readers. In addition, Delacorte produces original paperback young adult fiction and nonfiction for educational purposes and general interest.

www.randomhouse.com/kids/about/imprints.html

- **Doubleday Books for Young Readers**

Doubleday specializes in picture books along with illustrated gift books for audiences of all ages.

www.randomhouse.com/kids/about/imprints.html

- **Dragonfly**

Dragonfly specializes in paperback picture books for newly independent readers.

www.randomhouse.com/kids/about/imprints.html

- **Golden Books**

Golden Books publishes picture books and reprints classic titles for children.

www.randomhouse.com/kids/about/imprints.html

- **Laurel-Leaf**

Laurel-Leaf publishes of paperback books for teenagers, including reprints of contemporary and classic fiction, mystery, fantasy, romance, suspense, and nonfiction.

www.randomhouse.com/kids/about/imprints.html

- **Random House Books for Young Readers**

This imprint publishes books for beginners to young adult readers.

www.randomhouse.com/kids/about/imprints.html

- **Random House Children's Books**

This press publishes books in all formats from board books to activity books to picture books and novels for preschoolers through young adults.

www.randomhouse.com/kids/index.pperl

- **Schwartz and Wade Books**

The newest imprint of Random House Children's Books, Schwartz and Wade publishes picture books in addition to its hardcover line.

www.randomhouse.com/kids/about/imprints.html

- **Wendy Lamb Books**

This imprint specializes in fiction for middle-grade and young adult readers.

www.randomhouse.com/kids/about/imprints.html

- **Yearling Books**

This paperback imprint publishes books for parents, teachers, and children ages 8 through 12, including categories such as contemporary and historical fiction, fantasy, mystery, and adventure.

www.randomhouse.com/kids/about/imprints.html

The News Corporation

One of the three largest international media groups, operating in numerous sectors on most continents, The News Corporation's ventures include: film production and distribution, television production and broadcasting, advertising, newspaper and magazine publishing, book publishing, football teams and other sports ownership, multimedia, information technology and music publishing. Its associate publishing houses produce English language and bilingual children's books. They are primarily under the umbrella of HarperCollins Children's Books, including Amistad Press, The Julie Andrews Collection, Avon Books, Collins, Joanna Cotler Books, Eos, Laura Geringer Books, Greenwillow Books, HarperCollins e-books, HarperEntertainment, HarperFestival, HarperTeen, HarperTrophy, Rayo, Katherine Tegen Books, and TOKYOPOP. For more information on the holdings of the News Corporation megacorporation visit:

www.newscorp.com
www.ketupa.net/murdoch.htm

- **Amistad Press**

This press publishes works by and about people of African descent on subjects and themes that have significant influence on the intellectual, cultural, and historical perspectives of a world audience.

www.harpercollins.com/imprints/index.aspx?imprintid=518006

- **Avon Books**

Avon Books publishes series and popular fiction for young readers and includes romance, mystery, adventure, and fantasy.

www.harpercollinschildrens.com/HarperChildrens/Home/
ImprintBooks.aspx?TCId=100&SIId=9439&ST=7

- **Eos**

Eos specializes in science fiction and fantasy.

www.harpercollinschildrens.com/HarperChildrens/Home/
ImprintBooks.aspx?TCId=100&SIId=9455&ST=7

- **Greenwillow Books**

As a producer of books for children of every age. This publishing house claims that its titles meet a standard of "honesty, emotion and depth— conveyed by an author or an artist who has something that is worth saying to children and who says it in a way that is worth reading."

www.harpercollinschildrens.com/HarperChildrens/Home/
ImprintBooks.aspx?TCId=100&SIId=9438&ST=7

- **HarperChildren's Audio**

This imprint offers children's and young adult books in CD and audio cassette formats.

www.harpercollinschildrens.com/HarperChildrens/Home/
ImprintBooks.aspx?TCId=100&SIId=9445&ST=7

- **HarperCollins Children's Books**

A division of HarperCollins Publishers, this imprint is one of the world's leading English-language publishers.

www.harpercollinschildrens.com/harperchildrens
www.harpercollinschildrens.com/HarperChildrens/Home/
ImprintBooks.aspx?TCId=100&SIId=150215&ST=7

- **Joanna Cotler Books**

This imprint publishes literary and commercial picture books and fiction for all ages.

www.harpercollinschildrens.com/HarperChildrens/Home/
ImprintBooks.aspx?TCId=100&SIId=9456&ST=7

- **HarperEntertainment**

HarperEntertainment is home to current movie and TV tie-in titles, from preschool through young adult.

www.harpercollinschildrens.com/HarperChildrens/Home/
ImprintBooks.aspx?TCId=100&SIId=226118&ST=7

- **HarperFestival**

HarperFestival releases books, novelties, and merchandise for children from birth to age 6, and includes holiday titles as well as character-based programs.

www.harpercollinschildrens.com/HarperChildrens/Home/
ImprintBooks.aspx?TCId=100&SIId=9446&ST=7

- **HarperTeen**

HarperTeen publishes books for teenagers, including contemporary novels, series, literary tales, and leisure reading.

www.harpercollinschildrens.com/HarperChildrens/Home/
ImprintBooks.aspx?TCId=100&SIId=346439&ST=7

- **HarperTrophy**

HarperTrophy is a paperback imprint and publishes picture books and novels.

www.harpercollinschildrens.com/HarperChildrens/Home/
ImprintBooks.aspx?TCId=100&SIId=9453&ST=7

- **Katherine Tegen Books**

This imprint is a specialist in the narrative style.

www.harpercollinschildrens.com/HarperChildrens/Home/
ImprintBooks.aspx?TCId=100&SIId=9452&ST=7

- **Laura Geringer Books**

Laura Geringer Books promises to provide children with award-winning, best-selling, and innovative authors and artists who "push the envelope" and set new standards of excellence.

www.harpercollinschildrens.com/HarperChildrens/Home/
ImprintBooks.aspx?TCId=100&SIId=9447&ST=7

- **Rayo**

Ravo publishes Spanish, English, and bilingual titles.

www.harpercollinschildrens.com/HarperChildrens/Home/
ImprintBooks.aspx?TCId=100&SIId=9440&ST=7

- **The Julie Andrews Collection**

This collection reflects "themes of integrity, creativity, and the gifts of nature" in its books for young readers of all ages.

www.julieandrewscollection.com

- **TOKYOPOP**

This imprint is a youth-oriented entertainment brand publishing Manga titles based on existing HarperCollins works, as well as original Manga titles. (Manga are serialized graphic novels based on Japanese characters.)

www.harpercollinschildrens.com/HarperChildrens/Home/
ImprintBooks.aspx?TCId=100&SIId=331665&ST=7

Pearson, Limited

The UK-based Pearson conglomerate encompasses general and financial publishers, merchant banking, and Madame Tussauds and Royal Doulton china. Its publishing conglomerate is a book, newspaper, magazine, and television production and information services group. Its associate English language and bilingual publishing interests are housed under the Penguin

Young Readers Group, and include the imprints presented in the next section. More information on Pearson's holdings as a megacorporation can be found at:

www.pearson.com/index.cfm
www.ketupa.net/pearson.htm

• BBC Children's Books

BBC Children's Books complement children's entertainment and information shows on the BBC, CBBC and CBeebies. Each series draws on the underlying themes of programs and attempts to enrich children's reading abilities. In addition, this publisher claims that "every book also stands alone as entertaining and educational in its own right."

www.penguin.co.uk/static/cs/uk/0/bbc/index.html

• Dial Books for Young Readers

Dial is a hardcover, trade, children's book division, publishing picture books and novels for children, from preschool through young adult.

www.us.penguingroup.com/static/html/aboutus/youngreaders/dial.html

• Dutton Children's Books

Dutton Children's Books publishes hardcover titles, fiction, and nonfiction, for babies through young adults.

www.us.penguingroup.com/static/html/aboutus/youngreaders/
duttonyr.html

• Firebird

Firebird is a science fiction and fantasy imprint, designed to appeal to teenagers and adults alike.

www.firebirdbooks.com

• Frederick Warne

Frederick Warne develops classic book-based children's character brands by publishing illustrated books, and commissioning video and television programming for both Peter Rabbit and Spot.

www.us.penguingroup.com/static/html/aboutus/youngreaders/
warne.html

www.books.funwithspot.com
www.books.peterrabbit.com

- **G.P. Putnam's Sons Books for Young Readers**

G.P. Putnam's Sons publishes trade hardcover books for children, including picture books and fiction.

www.us.penguingroup.com/static/html/aboutus/youngreaders/
putnamyr.html

- **Grosset & Dunlap**

A mass-market publisher of picture books and popular novels for children, and produces a series of leveled paperback readers, paperback storybooks, sticker storybooks, and movie tie-in titles.

www.us.penguingroup.com/static/html/aboutus/youngreaders/
grosset.html

- **Penguin Young Readers Group**

The Group publishes a full range of fiction and nonfiction, from classics to bestsellers.

www.us.penguingroup.com/static/html/yr/index.html

- **Philomel Books**

Philomel publishes books for young readers and parents, including illustrated books and novels.

www.us.penguingroup.com/static/html/aboutus/youngreaders/
philomel.html

- **Speak**

Launched by Puffin, Speak is an imprint that publishes fiction and nonfiction for young adults.

www.us.penguingroup.com/static/html/aboutus/youngreaders/speak.html

- **Viking Children's Books**

The publications of Viking Children's Books range from books for young children to fiction and nonfiction for teenagers.

www.us.penguingroup.com/static/html/aboutus/youngreaders/
vikingyr.html

Reed Elsevier

Reed Elsevier is a transnational publisher with activities in online information services, consumer magazines, business and scientific journals, and consumer and specialist book publishing. Its publishing of children's English or bilingual books is merged under Harcourt Children's Books, including Gulliver Books, Silver Whistle, Red Wagon Books, Harcourt Young Classics, Green Light Readers, Voyager Books/Libros Viajeros, Harcourt Paperbacks, Odyssey Classics, and Magic Carpet Books. For more information about Reed Elsevier's ventures as a megacorporation visit:

www.reed-elsevier.com
www.ketupa.net/elsevier.htm

- **Harcourt Children's Books**
Harcourt Children's Books publishes books for children of all ages, including interactive books for toddlers, picture books for young children, science fiction and fantasy novels for preteen and teens, and historical fiction.

www.harcourtbooks.com/ childrensbooks/default.asp?source=topnav

- **Harcourt Education**
This imprint is a global education company publishing material for students and teachers in pre-K through grade 12, adult learners, and for readers of all ages.

www.harcourt.com

- **Harcourt International**
Harcourt is an international provider of professional classroom materials for pre-K through adult education.

www.harcourtschool.com/ieg

- **Harcourt Religion Publishers**
This imprint publishes for children and adults pursuing a Catholic education.

www.your.harcourtreligion.com/home/index.html

- **Holt, Rinehart and Winston**
Holt, Rinehart and Winston markets classroom instructional materials for grades 6 to 12, including curriculum-based textbooks, eLearning sites, and CD-ROMs.

ww.hrw.com

- **Harcourt School Publishers**
Harcourt School publishes for grades pre-K to 6 school textbooks and related instructional materials, including eLearning components, in a wide range of subject areas.

www.harcourtschool.com

- **Harcourt Trade Publishers**

This publisher produces books and related products for readers of all ages.

www.harcourtbooks.com

- **Rigby**

Rigby produces literacy materials for children and teachers.

www.rigby.harcourtachieve.com/en-US/rigby.htm

- **Saxon Publishers**

Saxon publishes materials for teachers and young, adolescent, and adult learners.

www.saxonpublishers.harcourtachieve.com/en-US/saxonpublishers.htm

- **Steck-Vaugh**

This imprint publishes materials used in preschools, K–12 classrooms, homes, libraries, workplace learning centers, GED classes, adult literacy programs, basic adult education courses, and ESL programs.

www.steckvaughn.harcourtachieve.com/en-US/steckvaughn.htm

Scholastic

As the world's largest publisher and distributor of children's books and related products for home and school, the Scholastic Corporation is a U.S. company publishing educational materials for schools, teachers, and parents. It has the exclusive U.S. publishing rights to the Harry Potter book series. Its business consists of trade books, school-based book clubs and book fairs, and Scholastic at Home continuity programs. Scholastic acquired other media companies, including Klutz Press, the animated television production company Soup2Nuts, the K-12 educational software publisher Tom Snyder Productions, and the reference publisher Grolier.

www.scholastic.com/kids

Here are some of Scholastic's ventures:

- **Scholastic at Home**

A direct-to-home parent resource for products and services that educate and entertain children.

- **Scholastic Book Clubs**

Scholastic Book Clubs purport to reach more than one million teachers and a million plus children and parents through school-based and grade-specific clubs, promoting children's books and reading materials from publishers around the world.

- **Scholastic Book Fairs**

Scholastic Book Fairs claim to hosts more than 120,000 book-sale events each year for newly released works, award-winning titles, classics, best-sellers, and interactive software from more than 150 publishers, and reach in excess of two million teachers and 35 million children and their families with these products that are aimed at readers in preschool through 9th grade.

- **Scholastic Trade Books**

Scholastic publishes hardcover, paperback, and novelty books for children of all ages.

Viacom

Viacom (Video & Audio Communications) is a U.S. media and entertainment conglomerate that absorbed and then spun off the CBS broadcasting group. It is involved in the areas of television, motion pictures and a wide range of digital media, including MTV Networks, BET Networks, Paramount Pictures, Paramount Home Entertainment, and DreamWorks. Its associate publishing houses of children's English books primarily are amalgamated under Simon & Schuster Children's Publishing, whose imprints includes Aladdin Paperbacks, Atheneum Books for Young Readers, Little Simon, Margaret K. McElderry Books, Simon & Schuster Books for Young Readers, Simon Pulse, Simon Spotlight, Nickelodeon Books, Anne Schwartz Books, Archway Paperbacks and Minstrel Books, and Lisa Drew Books. For more information about Viacom's holdings as a megacorporation visit:

www.viacom.com/aboutviacom/Pages/default.aspx
www.ketupa.net/viacom.htm

- **Aladdin Paperbacks**

In addition to publishing reprints from imprints of hardcover releases, Aladdin Paperbacks targets readers aged 4 to 12 years old. Its catalogue includes the Ready-to-Read series, a line for beginning readers, and the Ready-for-Chapters books designed for newly independent readers.

www.simonsays.com

- **Atheneum Books for Young Readers**

This is a hardcover imprint with a focus on literary fiction and picture books for preschoolers through young adults.

www.simonsays.com

- **Simon & Schuster Books for Young Readers**

Simon & Schuster publishes fiction and nonfiction for a variety of age groups, from infant to young adult.

www.simonsays.com

- **Simon Spotlight**

This imprint publishes media tie-in titles from for children in preschool through middle grades.

www.simonsays.com

Vivendi SA

Vivendi SA, formerly known as Vivendi Universal, is a French media conglomerate with activities in music, television and film, publishing, telecommunications, the Internet, sports, theme parks, and interactive games. The section of its publishing business in English or bilingual children's books is merged under the Houghton Mifflin Children's Book Group, including Houghton Mifflin Books for Children, Clarion Books, Kingfisher Publications, Graphia, Walter Lorraine Books, and American Heritage Reference. These links provide more information on Vivendi SA's ventures as a megacorporation:

www.vivendiuniversal.com
www.ketupa.net/vivendi.htm

- **American Heritage Reference**

This imprint specializes in dictionaries and reference material for children learning English and Spanish.

www.houghtonmifflinbooks.com/ahd/spanish.shtml#children

- **Clarion Books**

Clarion publishes nonfiction as well as fiction and picture books.

www.houghtonmifflinbooks.com/clarion

- **Graphia**

Graphia publishes paperbacks for young adults including fiction, nonfiction, poetry and graphic novels.

www.houghtonmifflinbooks.com/graphia

- **Houghton Mifflin Children's Books**

The publications of Houghton Mifflin Children's Books include nonfiction as well as fiction and picture books.

www.houghtonmifflinbooks.com/hmcochild

- **Kingfisher Publications**

Kingfisher publishes nonfiction and fiction for children of all ages, including reference books, activity books, early learning books, classic anthologies, and picture books.

www.houghtonmifflinbooks.com/kingfisher

Von Holtzbrinck

The German von Holtzbrinck group is a family-owned company, active in more than 80 countries and publishing works in both print and electronic media. The section of its publishing business in English and bilingual children's books is mostly merged under Macmillan Children's Books, and includes Farrar, Straus and Giroux Books for Young Readers, Feiwel and Friends, Henry Holt Books for Young Readers, Priddy Books, Roaring Brook Press, Square Fish, Starscape, and Tor Teen Books. A list of Von Holtzbrinck holdings can be found at:

www.holtzbrinck.com
www.ketupa.net/holtzbrinck.htm

- **Farrar, Straus and Giroux Books for Young Readers**

This imprint publishes picture books, fiction, and nonfiction for toddlers through young adults, with paperbacks published under the name of Sunburst Paperback and selected Spanish works under the Mirasol/Libros Juveniles imprint.

www.fsgkidsbooks.com

- **Feiwel and Friends**

This press publishes children's fiction and nonfiction literature for young and young-adult readers, including hardcover, paperback series, and individual titles.

www.feiwelandfriends.com

- **Henry Holt Books for Young Readers**

Henry Holt is a publisher of picture books, chapter books, and novels for preschoolers through young adults.

www.henryholtchildrensbooks.com

- **Macmillan US**

Macmillan comprises of the U.S. publishing activities of Holtzbrinck, which includes literature, textbooks and academic publishing.

www.us.macmillan.com/splash

- **Priddy Books**

Priddy Books publishes photographic books for children from birth onwards and provides translations in languages other than English.

www.priddybooks.com

- **Roaring Brook Press**

This press publishes picture books, fiction, and nonfiction for young readers, from toddler to teen.

www.us.macmillan.com/splash/publishers/roaring-brook-press.html

Square Fish

This publisher reprints for children and adolescent readers the works of Farrar, Straus and Giroux; Henry Holt; and Roaring Brook backlists.

www.squarefishbooks.com

Starscape

Starscape publishes science fiction and fantasy novels for middle grade readers ages 10 and up (grades 5 and up), in both hardcover and paperback.

www.tor-forge.com/Starscape.aspx

Tor Teen Books

This imprint publishes hardcover and paperback science fiction and fantasy novels for young adult readers ages 13 and up (grades 8 and up).

www.tor-forge.com/TorTeen.aspx

Power Continuum

How Power is Exercised

Janet Tonell, Lakeside Graphics of Toronto, Ontario, Canada

Critical Multicultural Analysis

Critical Multicultural Analysis

Janet Tonell, Lakeside Graphics of Toronto, Ontario, Canada

The Mexican American Migrant Farmworker
Text Collection: Publishing Practices

DATE	TITLE	AUTHOR	ILLUSTRATOR	PUBLISHER	GENRE	LANGUAGE USE	AWARDS	COMMENTS
1992	*A Migrant Family.*	Brimner, Larry Dane.	Photography by author.	Lerner Publications Co.	Nonfiction—photo-essay.	English with some Spanish text.		The author's note expresses thanks to those who made this book possible. His gratitude is stated in Spanish. At the end, the text includes further readings.
1993	*Amelia's Road.*	Altman, Linda Jacobs.	Sanchez, Enrique O.	Lee & Low Books.	Realistic fiction—picture book.	English with *los caminos* as only words in Spanish.		Available in Spanish from the publisher. The author's note provides some background information on migrant farmwork.

DATE	TITLE	AUTHOR	ILLUSTRATOR	PUBLISHER	GENRE	LANGUAGE USE	AWARDS	COMMENTS
1993	Radio Man/Don Radio: A Story in English and Spanish.	Dorros, Arthur. Translated by Sandra Dorros.	Illustrated by author.	HarperCollins	Realistic fiction—picture book.	Bilingual text. English text includes Spanish vocabulary. Glossary for Spanish phrases.	Américas Award for Children's and Young Adult Literature.	
1993/2001	Voices from the Fields: Children of Migrant Farmworkers Tell Their Stories.	Atkins, S. Beth.	Photography by author.	Little, Brown and Company/Scholastic.	Nonfiction—photo-essay with poetry included.	English with some Spanish vocabulary.	Américas Award for Children's and Young Adult Literature.	Reprinted in 2001. Foreword in new edition written by Francisco Jiménez.
1994	Jesse.	Soto, Gary.		Harcourt Brace.	Realistic fiction—young adult novel.		Society of School Librarians International Book Awards Honor.	Scholastic paperback published in 1996.
1995	Calling the Doves: El Canto de las Palomas.	Herrera, Juan Felipe.	Simmons, Elly.	Children's Book Press.	Realistic fiction—picture book.	Bilingual text, English/Spanish.	Américas Award for Children's and Young Adult Literature; Ezra Keats New Writer Award, 1997; Friends of Children and Literature (FOCAL) Award, 1997.	In two sections, the Spanish text is first.

1995	—y no se lo trago la tierra/ . . . And the Earth Did Not Devour Him.	Rivera, Tomás.		Arte Público Press (Third Edition).	Realistic Fiction/semi-autobiographical—young adult novel.	Bilingual edition.	Won first national award for Chicano literature.	First published in 1970.
1996	Going Home.	Bunting, Eve.	Diaz, David.	Harper-Collins.	Realistic fiction—picture book.	English text with a few Spanish words.	Américas Award for Children's and Young Adult Literature; Tomás Rivera Mexican American Children's Book Award Nominee.	
1996	Migrant Worker: A Boy from the Rio Grande Valley.	Hoyt-Goldsmith, Diane.	Photography by Lawrence Migdale.	Holiday House.	Nonfiction—Picture book.	English with Spanish vocabulary Glossary included.	Tomás Rivera Mexican American Children's Book Award Nominee.	
1996	Under the Feet of Jesus.	Viramontes, Helena Maria		Plume/Penguin Books.	Realistic fiction—young adult novel.			
1997	Gathering the Sun: An Alphabet in Spanish and English.	Ada, Alma Flor.	Silva, Simón.	Harper-Collins.	Realistic fiction—picture book.	The Spanish alphabet with Spanish text first, then English translation.	Américas Award for Children's and Young Adult Literature; Tomás Rivera Mexican American Children's Book Award Nominee.	

DATE	TITLE	AUTHOR	ILLUSTRATOR	PUBLISHER	GENRE	LANGUAGE USE	AWARDS	COMMENTS
1997	*The Circuit: Stories from the Life of a Migrant Child.*	Jiménez, Francisco.		Houghton Mifflin Co.	Semi-autobiographical/ Realistic fiction—young adult novel.	English with a sprinkling of Spanish.	Américas Award for Children's and Young Adult Literature; Boston Globe-Horn Book Award, 1998; Friends of Children and Literature (FOCAL) Award, 2000; Jane Addams Children's Book Award Honor Book, 1998; John and Patricia Beatty Award, 1998.	A Spanish version, *Cajas de Cartón*, published in 2000, is available from Houghton Mifflin Co.
1997	*Tomás and the Library Lady.*	Mora, Pat.	Colón, Raul.	Alfred A. Knopf.	Realistic fiction— picture book.	English with a small sprinkling of Spanish.	Tomás Rivera Mexican American Children's Book Award.	This book is available in Spanish from Knopf. *Tomás y la Senora de la Biblioteca* was published in 1997. The author's note provides a biographical sketch of Tomás Rivera.

Year	Title	Author	Publisher	Genre	Language	Awards	Notes
1998	*Joyride.*	Olson, Gretchen.	Caroline House/Boyds Mills Press.	Realistic fiction—young adult novel.		Society of School Librarians International Book Awards Honor.	
1998	*La Mariposa.*	Jiménez, Francisco.	Houghton Mifflin Co.	Realistic fiction—picture book.	English with some Spanish vocabulary. Glossary included.	Américas Award for Children's and Young Adult Literature; Tomás Rivera Mexican American Children's Book Award Nominee.	*La Mariposa* is also available in Spanish. This story is based on one of the short stories from *The Circuit,* also published by the same publisher.
1999	*Barefoot Heart: Stories of a Migrant Child.*	Hart, Elva Treviño.	Bilingual Press/Editorial Bilingüe.	Realistic fiction—nonfiction—autobiography.	English with some Spanish.	American Book Award; Alex Awards, 2000.	All royalties from the sales of this book will be donated to scholarship funds.
1999	*CrashBoom-Love: A Novel in Verse.*	Herrera, Juan Felipe.	University of New Mexico Press.	Realistic fiction—young adult novel in free verse.	In verse, sprinkled with Spanish. Translations footnoted.	Américas Award for Children's and Young Adult Literature.	
2000	*The Upside Down Boy: El Niño de Cabeza.*	Herrera, Juan Felipe.	Children's Book Press.	Realistic fiction—picture book.	Bilingual text, English/Spanish.		In two sections, the Spanish text is first. The author's note is in Spanish first.

DATE	TITLE	AUTHOR	ILLUSTRATOR	PUBLISHER	GENRE	LANGUAGE USE	AWARDS	COMMENTS
2000	*The Christmas Gift: El Regalo de Navidad.*	Jiménez, Francisco.	Cotts, Claire B.	Houghton Mifflin Co.	Realistic fiction—picture book.	Bilingual text, English/Spanish.	Américas Award for Children's and Young Adult Literature.	This story is based on one of the short stories from *The Circuit,* also published by the same publisher. The author's note connects this story to his personal life.
2000	*Esperanza Rising.*	Ryan, Pam Muñoz.		Scholastic Press.	Semi-biographical realistic fiction—young adult novel.	English with a sprinkling of Spanish.	Américas Award for Children's and Young Adult Literature Honor Book; Jane Addams Children's Book Award, 2001; Pura Belpré Award, 2002.	The author's grandmother is the inspiration for this story. *Esperanza Rising* is loosely based on her life story.
2001	*Harvest.*	Ancona, George.	Photography by author.	Marshall Cavendish.	Non-fiction—photo-essay.	English with some words in Spanish. Glossary included.	Américas Award for Children's and Young Adult Literature.	

Year	Title	Author	Illustrator	Publisher	Genre	Language	Awards	Notes
2001	*Breaking Through.*	Jiménez, Francisco		Houghton Mifflin Co.	Semi-autobiographical-realist fiction—young adult novel.	English with a sprinkling of Spanish.	Américas Award for Children's and Young Adult Literature; Pura Belpré Award Honor Book; Tomás Rivera Mexican American Children's Book Award.	The sequel to *The Circuit. Breaking Through* is available in Spanish as *Senderos Fronterizos*, published by Houghton Mifflin in 2002.
2002	*First Day in Grapes.*	Pérez, L. King.	Casilla, Robert.	Lee & Low Books.	Semi-biographical—realistic fiction—picture book.	English with some Spanish vocabulary.	Pura Belpré Award Honor Book.	The author based this story on her husband's experiences as a migrant child.
2003	*Under the Same Sky.*	DeFelice, Cynthia.		Farrar, Straus and Giroux.	Realistic fiction—young adult novel.			
2005	*Downtown Boy.*	Herrera, Juan Felipe		Scholastic Press	Realistic fiction—young adult novel in free verse.	In verse, sprinkled with Spanish.	Tomás Rivera Mexican American Children's Book Award in 2007.	

Children's Literature Journals

Best Books for Kids & Teens
This annual publication is produced by the Canadian Children's Book Centre for teachers, librarians, parents, and booksellers, selecting the best titles from newly published Canadian children's books, magazines, and audio and video materials.

www.bookcentre.ca/programs/ourchoice.shtml

Bookbird: A Journal of International Children's Literature
Open to any topic in the field of international children's literature as well as to children's literature studies, *Bookbird* is a refereed journal published quarterly by the International Board on Books for Young People (IBBY).

www.ibby.org/index.php?id=254

Book Links
Published by the American Library Association, *Book Links* provides information for using books in the classroom, with a focus on core curriculum areas, including science, social studies, language arts, history, the arts, geography, and multicultural literature.

www.ala.org/booklinks/

Booklist
Published by the American Library Association, *Booklist* is a book and media review journal, with coverage on themes such as biography,

young adult, multicultural literature, graphic novels, romance, and sports.

www.ala.org/booklist/

Bulletin of the Center for Children's Books

As a children's book review journal for school and public librarians, the *Bulletin* is published monthly, except for August, by The Johns Hopkins University Press for the Graduate School of Library and Information Science at the University of Illinois at Urbana-Champaign.

www.bccb.lis.uiuc.edu

Canadian Children's Literature / Littérature canadienne pour la jeunesse (CCL/LCJ)

Housed at the Centre for Research in Young People's Texts and Cultures under the sponsorship of the Vice President (Research) and the Dean of Arts at the University of Winnipeg, *CCL/LCJ* is a bilingual refereed academic journal with a specific focus on texts for and about children in Canada of all ethnic and cultural backgrounds, in a range of media in English, French and other languages.

www.ccl.uwinnipeg.ca/

Canadian Children's Book News

Published by the Canadian Children's Book Centre, *Canadian Children's Book News* provides parents, teachers, librarians, and booksellers with news, book reviews, author and illustrator interviews, profiles of publishers and bookstores, and information about the world of children's books in Canada.

www.bookcentre.ca/programs/booknews.shtml

CCBC Choices

Published by the Cooperative Children's Book Center (CCBC) of the School of Education at the University of Wisconsin-Madison, *CCBC Choices* provides annotated entries and recommended lists for books of children and young adults as well as documents trends in U.S. publishing practices.

www.education.wisc.edu/ccbc/books/choices.asp

Children's Literature

With a specific focus on theoretically based articles of key issues and criticism in children's literature, *Children's Literature* is the annual publication of the Children's Literature Association, published by the Johns Hopkins University Press.

www.chla.wikispaces.com/Childrens+Literature

Children's Literature Association Quarterly

With coverage on all aspects of research and scholarship in children's literature, the *Children's Literature Association Quarterly*, the journal of the Children's Literature Association, is housed in the Department of Literature and Philosophy at Georgia Southern University and published by the Johns Hopkins University Press.

www.chla.wikispaces.com/ChLAQ

Children's Literature in Education: An International Quarterly

This quarterly journal, published by Springer, features articles based on literary and pedagogical theory, critiques of classic and contemporary writing for children, and reviews on reading-related topics for teachers, teachers-in-training, librarians, writers, and parents.

www.springer.com/linguistics/languages+%26+literature/journal/10583

The Dragon Lode

Providing a forum for exchange of ideas regarding curriculum and pedagogy of children's literature in the development of literacy, this juried journal is housed at Central Missouri State University in Warrensburg, supported by the College of Education and Human Services as well as the Department of Curriculum and Instruction, and published bi-annually by the International Reading Association Children's Literature and the Children's Literature and Reading Special Interest Group.

www.reading.ccsu.edu/TheDragonLode/default.html

The Horn Book Magazine

This bi-monthly journal has published articles, editorials on, and reviews of children's and young adult literature since 1924.

www.hbook.com/magazine/default.asp

Journal of African American Children's Literature

With a focus on African American children's literature that is written and/or illustrated by African Americans, this journal aims to provide educators of African American students with positive insights into their history, culture, and traditions.

www.web.coehs.siu.edu/public/jaacl/homepage.asp

Journal of Children's Literature

Published twice annually by the Children's Literature Assembly of the National Council of Teachers of English, the *Journal of Children's Literature* is a refereed journal committed to the teaching and scholarship of children's literature.

www.childrensliteratureassembly.org/journal3.htm

Journal of Youth Services in Libraries

Serving as a vehicle for continuing education among librarians working with children and young adults, the *Journal of Youth Services in Libraries* is the official publication of two divisions of the American Library Association: the Association for Library Service to Children and the Young Adult Library Services Association.

www.scholar.lib.vt.edu/ejournals/JYSL/

The Lion and the Unicorn

The Lion and the Unicorn, published by the John Hopkins Press, is a theme- and genre-centered scholarly journal of international scope of literature for children, with its coverage including the state of the publishing industry, regional authors, comparative studies of significant books and genres, new developments in theory, the art of illustration, the mass media, and popular culture.

www.lionunicornbooks.co.uk

Magpies: Talking about Books for Children

Magpies includes reviews of new children's and young adult books published in Australia and across the world, articles on children's literature, author or illustrator interviews, information on awards, and children's literature in Australia.

www.magpies.net.au

The New Advocate

This journal focuses on children's experiences of literature in the classroom, as well as the pedagogical issues of the teaching of children's literature and multiculturalism. While this journal is no longer published, back issues are worthy of consideration.

Papers: Explorations into Children's Literature

Published three times a year by the School of Literary and Communication Studies of Deakin University, *Papers* is a refereed scholarly journal committed to critical essays on children's literature.

School Library Journal
This journal provides librarians who work with young people in schools and public libraries with information needed to integrate libraries into the school curriculum, and help them become leaders in the areas of technology, reading, and information literacy, and create high-quality collections for children and young adults.

www.schoollibraryjournal.com

The Looking Glass: New Perspectives on Children's Literature
Featuring scholarly as well as more practical articles about children's books, *The Looking Glass* is an electronic journal aiming to promote critical analysis and creation of literature for children.

www.the-looking-glass.net

Relevant Journals

Language Arts
Published bi-monthly on both theory and classroom practice, this journal provides a forum for discussions on all aspects of language arts learning and teaching among elementary and middle school teachers and teacher educators of children primarily in pre-K through grade 8.

www.ncte.org/pubs/journals/la

Multicultural Perspectives
As a quarterly journal published by the National Association for Multicultural Education, *Multicultural Perspectives* features articles, reviews, program descriptions, and other pieces by and for multicultural educators and activists around the world. See the "Guide to Resources" section for book reviews.

www.nameorg.org/publications.html

MultiCultural Review
As the official publication of the Ethnic and MultiCultural Information Exchange Round Table of the American Library Association, *MultiCultural Review* is committed to reviews about diversity by offering classroom resources which focus on differences in ethnicity, race, spirituality, religion, disability, and language.

www.mcreview.com/

The Reading Teacher
This journal provides information and solutions based on research and

practice to transform children's reading and enable them to become proficient readers.

www.reading.org/publications/journals/rt/

Rethinking Schools

As an activist publication, with articles written by and for teachers, parents and students, *Rethinking Schools* aims to balance classroom practice and educational theory while addressing problems such as basal readers, standardized testing, textbook-dominated curriculum, key policy issues, and those facing urban schools, particularly issues of race and class.

www.rethinkingschools.org/

Teaching Tolerance

Teaching Tolerance, a free journal published by the Southern Poverty Law Center, provides learning engagements and reviews of educational materials that promote respect for diversity in the classroom and beyond.

www.tolerance.org/teach/index.jsp

Online Resources

American Library Association: Association of Library Services to Children
www.ala.org/alsc/

American Library Association: Young Adult Library Services Association
www.ala.org/yalsa/

Canadian Children's Book Centre (CCBC)
www.bookcentre.ca

Center for the Study of Books in Spanish for Children and Adolescents
www.csusm.edu/csb/english/

ChildLit
www.childlit.org

Children's Literature Comprehensive Database
www.childrenslit.com

Children's Literature Web Guide
www.ucalgary.ca/~dKbrown/

The Cooperative Children's Book Center, University of Wisconsin-Madison
www.education.wisc.edu/ccbc/

Cynthia Leitch Smith
www.cynthialeitichsmith.com

Debbie Reese
www.nah.uiuc.edu/faculty-Reese.htm

Fairrosa Cyber Library of Children's Literature
www.fairrosa.info

International Reading Association
www.reading.org

Kay Vandergrift of Rutgers University's Social History of Children's Literature
www.scils.rutgers.edu/~kvander/HistoryofChildLit/index.html

Kay E. Vandergrift's Special Interest Page
www.scils.rutgers.edu/~kvander/

National Association for Multicultural Education (NAME)
www.nameorg.org

National Council for Teachers of English
www.ncte.org

Tucson Teachers Applying Whole Language (TAWL)
www.tucsontawl.org

United States Board on Books for Young People
www.usbby.org

Index